D1714692

Wittgenstein
and Legal Theory

New Perspectives on Law, Culture, and Society
Robert W. Gordon and Margaret Jane Radin, Series Editors

Wittgenstein and Legal Theory,
edited by Dennis M. Patterson

Pragmatism in Law and Society,
edited by Michael Brint and William Weaver

Feminist Legal Theory: Readings in Law and Gender,
edited by Katharine T. Bartlett and Rosanne Kennedy

FORTHCOMING

Fighting Words: Racist Speech and the First Amendment,
Charles R. Lawrence, Mari J. Matsuda,
Kimberle Crenshaw, and Richard Delgado

*In Whose Name? Feminist Legal Theory and
the Experience of Women,* Christine A. Littleton

Constitutional Interpretation,
edited by Susan J. Brison and Walter Sinnott-Armstrong

*The Philosophy of International Law:
A Human Rights Approach,* Fernando R. Teson

Wittgenstein
and Legal Theory

EDITED BY
Dennis M. Patterson

K.
230
.W592
W57
1992

Westview Press
BOULDER • SAN FRANCISCO • OXFORD

New Perspectives on Law, Culture, and Society

Copyright © 1992 by Westview Press, Inc., except for Chapters 2, 3, 4, 8, and 10, which are © the authors, and Chapter 5, which is © Boston University Law Review.

Published in 1992 in the United States of America by Westview Press, Inc., 5500 Central Avenue, Boulder, Colorado 80301-2847, and in the United Kingdom by Westview Press, 36 Lonsdale Road, Summertown, Oxford OX2 7EW

Library of Congress Cataloging-in-Publication Data
Wittgenstein and legal theory / edited by Dennis M. Patterson.
    p.   cm. — (New Perspectives on law, culture, and society)
    ISBN 0-8133-0107-6
    1. Wittgenstein, Ludwig, 1889–1951. 2. Law—Philosophy.
3. Jurisprudence. I. Patterson, Dennis M. (Dennis Michael), 1955–
II. Series.
K230.W592W57   1992
340′.1—dc20   91-39759
                                                                                        CIP

Printed and bound in the United States of America

The paper used in this publication meets the requirements
of the American National Standard for Permanence of Paper
for Printed Library Materials Z39.48-1984.

10   9   8   7   6   5   4   3   2   1

Contents

About the Contributors   ix
Introduction, Dennis M. Patterson   xi

PART ONE: Practices

1   The Epistemology of Judging: Wittgenstein and
    Deliberative Practices, *Thomas Morawetz*   3

2   "Our Real Need": Not Explanation, But Education,
    Thomas D. Eisele   29

3   The Acceptance of a Legal System, *Roger A. Shiner*   59

4   Law's Pragmatism: Law as Practice and Narrative,
    Dennis M. Patterson   85

PART TWO: Rules

5   Reconsidering the Rule of Law, *Margaret Jane Radin*   125

6   Wittgenstein and the Sceptical Fallacy,
    Gene Anne Smith   157

7   No Easy Cases? *Andrei Marmor*   189

8   The Application (and Mis-Application) of Wittgenstein's
    Rule-Following Considerations to Legal Theory,
    Brian Bix   209

9 Rules and the Rule-Following Argument,
Frederick Schauer 225

PART THREE: Politics

10 Political World, *Brian Langille* 233

11 Are Judges Liars? A Wittgensteinian Critique of
Law's Empire, Charles Yablon 249

About the Book and Editor 265

About the Contributors

Brian Bix is a graduate of Harvard Law School. He is currently attending Balliol College, Oxford.

Thomas D. Eisele is Associate Professor of Law at the University of Tennessee, where he teaches courses in jurisprudence and property law. He holds a J.D. from Harvard University and a Ph.D. (Philosophy) from the University of Michigan.

Brian Langille is Professor of Law at the Faculty of Law, University of Toronto. He is Director of the Legal Theory Workshop there and his main interests are contracts, labour law, and legal theory.

Andrei Marmor is a lecturer in law and jurisprudence at the Faculty of Law in Tel-Aviv University. His book *Interpretation and Legal Theory* is forthcoming.

Thomas Morawetz is Professor of Law at the University of Connecticut School of Law. His books include *Wittgenstein and Knowledge* and *The Philosophy of Law*. He is currently at work on a series of articles on methodology in legal philosophy, with special attention to the use and abuse of the metaphor of games.

Dennis M. Patterson is Professor of Law at Rutgers University, School of Law–Camden. He is the author of three books in commercial law and many articles in legal and philosophical journals.

Margaret Jane Radin is Professor of Law, Stanford University Law School. She has published numerous articles in legal and philosophical journals.

Frederick Schauer is Frank Stanton Professor of the First Amendment at Harvard. He is author of *Free Speech: A Philosophical Enquiry* (1982). Forthcoming is *Playing By the Rules: A Philosophical Examination of Rule-Based Decisionmaking in Law and in Life*.

Roger Shiner is Professor of Philosophy at the University of Alberta. He has published widely: He is an editor of *Canadian Philosophical Reviews* and Executive Editor of *APEIRON: a journal for ancient philosophy and science.*

Gene Anne Smith is Associate Professor of Law at the University of Saskatchewan. Her research interests are in the areas of jurisprudence and administrative law.

Charles Yablon teaches at the Cardozo School of Law of Yeshiva University in New York City.

Introduction

Dennis M. Patterson

Never before in its history has the law been the subject of so many—and so varied—non-legal perspectives. In the modern era there have always been sociological and philosophical approaches to law. But with the growth of the "Law and" movement, the analysis of law has become far more diverse than the traditional methodologies and perspectives just mentioned. Just one perspective, that of law and literature, has brought to bear all manner of literary theory on legal discourse. Professors of English now teach in law schools, and interdisciplinary symposia fill the pages of law reviews. In fact, the cross-talk between law and allied disciplines has become so intense that some have seen fit to question the continuing autonomy of law as an independent discourse.

It is against this background that this volume of essays takes its place. Indeed, it is curious that despite the obvious influence of his thought in many fields outside of philosophy, precious little has been written about what role Wittgenstein's thought might play in the analysis of law. This is especially puzzling because many of the themes in Wittgenstein's thought after 1929 bear so directly on legal issues. In addition to his well known remarks on meaning, understanding, and certainty, Wittgenstein has written a great deal on problems of the language of the mental, the relationship between theory and explanation, and the place of ethics in the world.

If there is anything that can be regarded as "central" to Wittgenstein's "later" philosophy, it is his rejection of the traditional methods of philosophy. Right from the start of *Philosophical Investigations,* Wittgenstein again and again propounds the message that the only way one can avoid error in thought is through a careful investigation of the grammar of language. The central shift from the earlier (Tractarian) to the later (post-1929) period is the rejection of a philosophy that seeks disclosure of the formal structure of language in favor of one that achieves a clear surview of grammar.

Of particular interest in this connection, especially in the light of the ever-increasing importance of "theory" in academic law, is Wittgenstein's claim that "philosophy leaves everything as it is." In an era when academic lawyers seek solutions to problems of interpretation and meaning by resorting to elaborate hypothetical models of rational behavior, the "therapeutic" aspects of Wittgenstein's thought become all the more important. From the Wittgensteinian perspective, the problem with approaches to law as diverse as Public Choice Theory and Originalism is not that they are "wrong" as much as they are fundamentally misguided. The speaking of language—the fact that communication takes place—is not to be "explained" by a theory that asks the question "what would economic actors with complete information agree to?" Rather, problems of meaning and understanding are solved by clarifying the role of grammar of our concepts in our practices. Perspicuity not reductionism is the goal of Wittgenstein's *Denkweise.*

Most of the essays in this book first appeared in a special issue of *The Canadian Journal of Law and Jurisprudence*. The original essays have been joined by two previously published articles on Wittgenstein and legal theory. Taken together, the essays in this volume demonstrate the influence and significance of Wittgenstein's thought for law. It is hoped that this book will provide an incentive for legal scholars to consider anew the importance of Wittgenstein's thought to law and the extent to which much of the confusion in contemporary legal theory can be seen for what it is.

I wish to thank Joseph Raz for pointing several of the authors in my direction and for his support of this project. I am immensely grateful to Dick Bronaugh for making my maiden voyage as an editor a relatively painless affair. To Spencer Carr, I owe a debt of thanks for his enthusiastic support of this project. To the authors, I express my appreciation for their diligence in bringing this volume to fruition.

PART ONE

Practices

1

The Epistemology of Judging:
Wittgenstein and Deliberative Practices

Thomas Morawetz

1. Introduction

Wittgenstein seeks to inoculate us against the lure of metaphors.[1] The conundrums of philosophy are, he implies, often the misbegotten offspring of abused metaphors. How many rooms are needed to house the "furniture of our mind"? With what key do others gain access to my "private" thoughts and feelings?[2]

Jurisprudence has its own syllabus of philosophical puzzles. One of the hardiest is the issue of judicial license and judicial standards. This issue has special fascination for American legal theorists because of the pivotal role played by the Supreme Court in exercising the power of judicial review by interpreting the Constitution.[3] American theorists have taken for granted,[4] and other theorists have seemed to acquiesce in this assumption,[5] that to understand the nature of law is to understand how appellate judges find and/or make law.[6]

An early version of this paper was prepared for the Seminar in Legal Philosophy, held at the University of Western Ontario in August 1989. I wish to thank the participants, and especially Jules Coleman, Dennis Patterson, and Donald Regan, for their helpful comments.

1. L. Wittgenstein, *Philosophical Investigations*, G. Anscombe, trans., (New York: Macmillan, 1968), 3d ed., cf. Part I, section 115: "A *picture* held us captive. And we could not get outside it, for it lay in our language and language seemed to repeat it to us inexorably." and Part I, section 193: "The machine as symbolizing its action: the action of a machine—I might say at first—seems to be there in it from the start. What does that mean?—If we know the machine, everything else, that is its movement, seems to be already completely determined."

2. Wittgenstein's own examples of abused metaphors are much richer and more layered. Consider his observation about the metaphor of expression: "Misleading parallel: the expression of pain is a cry—the expression of thought, a proposition."
   As if the purpose of the proposition were to convey to one person how it is with another; only, so to speak, in his thinking part and not in his stomach." (*Philosophical Investigations, supra* n. 1, Part I, section 317.)
   Consider also the following: "One might also say: Surely the owner of the visual room would have to be the same kind of thing as it is; but he is not to be found in it, and there is no outside." (*Philosophical Investigations, supra* n. 1, Part I, section 399.)

3. H.L.A. Hart remarks on this preoccupation and seeks to explain it in "American Jurisprudence through English Eyes" in *Essays in Jurisprudence and Philosophy* (Oxford: Clarendon Press, 1983).

4. The work of Ronald Dworkin best illustrates this central preoccupation with the question of how judges find law as the key to the understanding of the concept of law. This position was first sketched in "The Model of Rules I and II" in *Taking Rights Seriously* (Cambridge: Harvard Univ. Press, 1978), and remains the methodological basis of Dworkin's work in *Law's Empire* (Cambridge: Harvard Univ. Press, 1986).

5. In recent jurisprudence, the task of analyzing law is treated as the task of analyzing legal reasoning, and the main "official" reservoir of legal reasoning is judicial opinions. This was not the case for such earlier jurisprudential theorists as John Austin and Hans Kelsen, for whom the analysis of law was more or less the analysis of statutes. Thus, such British theorists as Neil MacCormick give as much centrality to judicial reasoning as does any American theorist. On the other hand, Joseph Raz continues in the older tradition that does not give precedence to judicial opinions over statutes as the main resource for speculation about the nature of law. See N. MacCormick, *Legal Reasoning and Legal Theory* (Oxford: Clarendon Press, 1978), and J. Raz, *The Concept of a Legal System* (Oxford: Clarendon Press, 1970).

6. Throughout this article, my references to judicial reasoning are intended to characterize appellate decisions. Even more restrictively, I am concerned largely with constitutional interpretation at the appellate level. I am prepared to generalize my description of "deliberate practices" to judicial decision-making on a broader scale, but do not do so in this article.

Judicial review and the power of judges receive scrutiny periodically. The last fifteen years have been one such period, distinguished by a splendid outpouring of articles and books.[7] Nonetheless, the issue remains largely unclarified notwithstanding the best efforts of inventive writers. Indeed, the most recent writings represent a scaling back of ambitions, in effect a tacit admission of failure.[8]

One Wittgensteinian explanation of such cycles in philosophy is that they involve the dogged pursuit of a metaphor. I shall argue that in the recent debates over constitutional interpretation the metaphor at issue has been the metaphor of a game, with its implications that judging is a rule-governed activity and judges are like the players of games.

In one respect this metaphor is special because it is the Wittgensteinian metaphor par excellence, the metaphor Wittgenstein himself is taken to have perpetrated.[9] Many writers take as one of Wittgenstein's signal contributions to philosophy the suggestion that discourse is to be understood on the model of "language games".[10] This suggestion is, as I shall argue, doubly misleading because Wittgenstein is not merely concerned with language and because his concern with discourse is not bounded by the metaphor of games.[11] In examining the metaphor of games, therefore, I shall be considering its merits as a general metaphor for discourse, as a representation of what concerns Wittgenstein himself, *and* as a metaphor for legal discourse, specifically judicial interpretation.

The trajectory of the debates over constitutional interpretation in the last fifteen years is relatively clear. The concern in this round of the perennial

---

7. Any attempt to list the main contributors to this movement risks offending by omission—and any adequate list would be formidably long. Even a partial and inadequate list would have to include Paul Brest, Ronald Dworkin, John Hart Ely, Owen Fiss, Stanley Fish, Thomas Grey, Richard Kay, Sanford Levinson, Michael Perry, Jefferson Powell, Lawrence Tribe, and Mark Tushnet.

8. The main argument of Mark Tushnet's recent *Red White and Blue* (Cambridge, Mass: Harvard Univ. Press, 1988) is that all attempts to formulate a standard for constitutional interpretation on the basis of "grand theory" have self-destructed and they have done so because they are grounded on the untenable assumptions of liberalism. The recent work of Michael Perry (*Morality Politics and Law* (New York: Oxford Univ. Press, 1988)) and Sanford Levinson (*Constitutional Faith* (Princeton, N.J.: Princeton Univ. Press, 1988)) is not so much a frontal attempt to develop criteria for constitutional interpretation as an oblique investigation of the nuances and implications of the idea of constitutionalism.

9. The term "game" does double duty in Wittgenstein's *Philosophical Investigations* and in his other works. The use of the word "game" (*Spiel*) is itself an example of a "language-game" (*Sprachspiel*). Wittgenstein uses it to demonstrate that using language (participating in the "language-game") is not a matter of following rules, in particular not a matter of following rules that specify the necessary or sufficient conditions for using particular words correctly, not in other words a matter of understanding the "essence" of, e.g., a game. Compare *Philosophical Investigations, supra* n. 1, part I, section 65: "For someone might object against me: 'You take the easy way out! You talk about all sorts of language-games, but have nowhere said what the essence of a language-game, and hence of language, is: what is common to all these activities, and what makes them into language or parts of language. . . .'
     And this is true.—Instead of producing something common to all that we call language, I am saying that these phenomena have no one thing in common which makes us use the same word for all,—but that they are *related* to one another in many different ways."

10. Wittgenstein himself uses the term (*Sprachspiel*) frequently in *Philosophical Investigations* and elsewhere but, as I argue below (text at n. 48), his own examples and questions (a) invite generalization to non-linguistic practices and (b) reject unequivocally the paradigmatic use of any particular conception of a game.

11. It cannot be emphasized too strongly that I am not referring to Wittgenstein's own use of the word "game" (*Spiel*) but to its use by those who see the essence of a game as a matter of acting in conformity with shared and mutually identifiable rules and sharing a conception of the point or goal to be achieved through participation. Wittgenstein argues persuasively against such essentialism; *supra* n. 9 and n. 48 below. Much post-Wittgensteinian philosophy, including contemporary jurisprudence, rests heavily on such essentialist assumptions.

debate, as in previous rounds,[12] is fear of judicial power and license. The first step in framing the issue is to note the failure of any purely formalistic account of decision-making.[13] To say that judges apply law cannot mean that they do so deductively or by appeal to a straightforward algorithm. Hard cases arise, and hard cases are by definition ones in which both outcomes and methods of resolution are endlessly controversial. If this is so, what is the boundary of judicial power? If judges may choose among methods of resolution that are their own invention, is their power to remake law without limit?[14]

The second step is to meet the challenge of describing standards and techniques of judicial interpretation. The task is simultaneously descriptive and normative. A theorist claims to make explicit the techniques that are generally implicit in the process of judicial interpretation.[15] But the theorist also claims thereby to be positing an ideal that is implicit in the role, an ideal that judges may or may not realize. The task is both hortatory and critical. The theorist speaks to judges in the hope of illuminating what they do and to critics of the judicial process in the hope of sharpening the critics' tools.

Implicit in the theorist's understanding of her task is the assumption that only one technique of interpretation is the correct way of proceeding, that only one set of rules characterizes judicial interpretation. To think otherwise, to concede that several acceptable techniques may coincide, is to readmit indeterminacy and license. If judges have the capacity to choose among several acceptable ways of proceeding, then the fear of license is well grounded and the critic is disarmed. The fear is not so much that *anything goes* in judicial interpretation, not that judges may appropriately consult astrological charts or their bias in favor of diminutive plaintiffs in making decisions.[16] The fear is rather that within the range of defensible strategies, judges may effect and justify almost any outcome.

The third step, then, is to defend a particular strategy as the unique strategy that informs and constrains judicial interpretation. The theorist must argue first that the strategy is practicable, that it can in fact be carried out, and that it determines solutions to problems.[17] The theorist must also argue that the

---

12. The trajectory of this phenomenon seems to have a twenty-five year or so cycle. Legal realism in the late 1920's and early 1930's revolutionized thinking about judicial decision-making. See L. Kalman, *Legal Realism at Yale, 1927-1960* (Chapel Hill: Univ. of North Carolina Press, 1986). In the late 1950's, the writings of Alexander Bickel and Herbert Wechsler, among others, marked another significant revival of interest.

13. The most influential critique of formalism in recent jurisprudence has been that of H. L. A. Hart, *The Concept of Law* (Oxford: Clarendon Press, 1961), chapter vii. An interesting recent example of the revival of formalism is E. Weinrib, "Legal Formality: On the Immanent Rationality of Law" (1988), 97 *Yale L. J.* 949.

14. The first half, chapters 1 through 5, of Tushnet, *Red White and Blue, supra,* n. 8, is a critique of formalist and anti-formalist theories of judicial decision-making. (Tushnet uses the term "formalism" more broadly than I do here or than Weinrib does, see n. 13. Formalism, for Hart and Weinrib, characterizes decision-making by recourse to the "internal logic" of legal propositions. Formalism, for Tushnet, refers to any theoretical attempt to prescribe standards for decision-making.)

15. For a discussion of the claim that this is, as a general matter, the task of philosophy, see A. Danto, *What Philosophy Is: A Guide to the Elements* (London: Cambridge Univ. Press, 1968); R. Rorty, *The Linguistic Turn* (Chicago: Univ. of Chicago Press, 1967), introduction.

16. There is an important distinction here between the factors that affect judicial decisions and the reasons that are used by judges to justify opinions. Legal realism was concerned as much with the former as with the latter. The contemporary debate is primarily about the latter, about what counts as justification in "official" judicial reasoning. The term "reasoning" is, of course, ambiguous, referring both to the process of discovery (or of arriving at an opinion) and the process of justification.

17. To say that a standard *determines* a result is not to say that a particular result follows deductively from

strategy yields correct, or at least sound, answers.

This is not to say that all theorists share optimism about defining and defending a strategy of judicial interpretation. Counterpoised against such optimists are theorists who argue that the quest for a unique constraining strategy of judicial interpretation is doomed, and that the project itself is mired in contradiction.[18]

A diagnosis of the debate must begin with two observations. First, the very conception of the theoretical project is grounded on the metaphor of games. If we are to understand judges as constrained, we must understand the rules by which they must be playing. Such rules are both descriptive and normative.[19] In the absence of such rules, judges must be seen as unconstrained.

By the same token, judges' attempts to justify favored outcomes by writing opinions makes sense if they are playing by the same rules. In other words, they must recognize reasons as relevant or irrelevant to decisions in the same way, must have the same methods for assigning weight to relevant reasons, and so forth. Unless this is so, unless they are playing the same game by the same rules, the process of justification in opinion writing is empty rhetoric. The task of the theorist, then, is to identify the rules of the game whereby judicial interpretation, and its explication in opinion writing, takes place—so that the true constraints of the process can be made explicit, so that correct decisions and techniques can be identified, and so that deviants can be chastised and corrected.

The second preliminary observation is that this account of the theoretical task seems wildly at odds with judicial practice, now and in any foreseeable future. The untheoretical observer's view is that judges do and will continue to decide cases in different ways. They will continue to write justificatory opinions in which they genuinely speak to each other but with different commitments about what is relevant and with little hope that, over time, diversity will turn into consensus.

From the point of view of the theorist, the situation is paradoxical. A player of chess plays with a player of Chinese checkers, and they in turn play with

the standard or that application of the standard dictates one particular result in a particular case. Analogously, the rules of a game like chess determine the course of play but allow for many possible different moves. They constrain and order the results but allow for a range of alternatives.

With regard to judicial reasoning, the adoption of a standard has two consequences. First, it mandates the kinds of reasons that can be given in justification of particular results. Second, in doing the former, it limits the range of results that may be reached.

18. As indicated above, this is largely the argument of the first part of Tushnet, *Red White and Blue*. See also other writers in the Critical Legal Studies movement, especially R. Unger, *The Critical Legal Studies Movement* (Cambridge, Mass.: Harvard Univ. Press, 1986), and D. Kennedy, "The Structure of Blackstone's Commentaries" (1979), 28 *Buffalo L. R.* 205. Owen Fiss labels the practitioners of critical legal studies "nihilists" and defends the label in "The Death of Law?" (1986), 72 *Cornell L. R.* 1.

19. The rules of many activities are both descriptive and normative. The rules of driving or swimming characterize the activity and are implicated in any description. At the same time, they also characterize a standard of performance. One can carry out the rules in a marginal or an exemplary way, without or with skill and expertise.

Two qualifications. (a) To say there are rules for driving or swimming is not to prejudge whether there is a *single* way to carry out the activity or many alternative ways. Indeed the meaningfulness of that question may depend on the level of generality at which the rules are posed.

(b) The rules of games such as chess and baseball are in part purely descriptive. The rule that a team in baseball retires after three players are "out" is hard to construe as normative, i.e. as a basis for evaluating better or worse games.

a third who is playing bridge. Each justifies her moves by appealing to her particular game. And they persist. And yet they understand each other. How can this be so?

In Part 2 of this paper I shall examine the metaphor of games as a general philosophical strategy for analyzing discourse and human understanding. I shall look at some misapplications of the idea that the Wittgenstinian [author's preferred spelling, eds.] notion of a practice can best be understood as a "language game". I shall describe what I call "deliberative practices" to clarify the ways in which practices are not illuminated by the theoretical paradigm of a game.

Part 3 describes ways in which the metaphor of games gives a distorted view of judicial interpretation and it concludes that judicial interpretation is a paradigmatic case of a deliberative practice. Part 4 is a critique of the aims of recent theory about judicial, and particularly constitutional, interpretation insofar as the agenda of such theorists rests implicitly on the metaphor of games. My conclusion draws more general lessons for philosophical method in legal theory.

2. Games and Practices

a. Wittgenstein and Practices

The concept of a practice is at once among the most useful and most disputed tools of twentieth-century philosophy.[20] Many philosophers trace their use of it to Wittgenstein, and the Wittgenstinian concept, as a philosophical tool, is often assimilated to that of a "language game". After explaining the concept in Wittgenstein, I shall argue that, used in a certain way, the notion of a language game is doubly misleading.

An intuitive look at practices may begin with such nonlinguistic activities as driving or swimming. In each case, persons acquire skills or ways of proceeding that become habitual and unreflective. When we call such skills "second nature", we mean that, though they are socially and culturally acquired, such ways of proceeding become as much a part of us as our genetic endowment.

A habitual repertoire has distinctive features. Each technique involves ways of perceiving, feeling, and acting. A good driver makes judgments about road conditions and the disposition of other drivers, apprehends dangers, and acts accordingly. What she does unreflectively can, however, be made conscious. Ordinarily the need to do so will not arise.[21]

---

20. Philosophers who have discussed Wittgenstein's use of the concept most illuminatingly are P. Hacker, *Insight and Illusion* (Oxford: Clarendon Press, 1972), S. Kripke, *Wittgenstein on Rules and Private Language* (Oxford: Basil Blackwell, 1982), S. Hilmy, *The Later Wittgenstein* (Oxford: Basil Blackwell, 1987), and R. Rorty, *Philosophy and the Mirror of Nature* (Princeton, N.J.: Princeton Univ. Press, 1979). The implications of the notion of a practice, and of the concomitant distinction between being inside and outside a practice, go far beyond the realm of Wittgenstein studies and are explored in contemporary philosophical movements from hermeneutics to neo-Kantianism and neo-Hegelianism. See, for example, H-G. Gadamer, *Truth and Method,* G. Baden and J. Cumming trans., (New York: Continuum, 1975) and *Hegel's Dialectic* (New Haven: Yale Univ. Press, 1976), Hoy, *The Critical Circle* (Berkeley: Univ. of California Press, 1978), G. Shapiro and A. Sica, *Hermeneutics: Questions and Prospects* (Amherst: Univ. of Mass Press, 1984), and R. Geuss, *The Idea of a Critical Theory* (Cambridge: Cambridge Univ. Press, 1981).

21. The need to do so will arise if one is instructing someone else or if one has to relearn the activity after, for example, an injury.

A characterization of what is involved in having such a skill, in being a good driver, will be at once descriptive and normative. The characteristics of a driver (in general) are distinguished only in degree from the characteristics of a good driver. To be able to identify driving is also to be able to detect good driving. Both thresholds are inherently vague. No clear and simple criterion distinguishes those who cannot drive from those who do so very badly. Similarly, not everyone will agree on the marks of very good driving. But the range of understandable disagreement is small.[22]

Some of our practices are primarily communicative (as driving obviously is not). And some of our communicative practices, by far the most important ones, are linguistic.[23] Wittgenstein attends to such aspects of language as color-descriptions and expressions of pain. Just as driving is a skill that individuals acquire because a public practice, a shared activity, already exists, so too perceptions of color and distinctions among kinds of pain manifest the acquired skills of those who have been initiated into certain practices. Persons identify colors and pains to the extent that a place exists for the recognition of color and the expression of pain in the relevant practices of a culture.[24]

Some philosophers have seen this suggestion as revolutionary and counter-intuitive. The philosophical assumption of most empiricists has been that the domain of private experience is fully configured and that the public arena of language is merely a set of conventions and labels attached to the distinct elements of private experience.[25] But Wittgenstein challenges this. He asks us to reflect on what it could be like to experience a color for which a place was not already prepared in the experiential realm shared with others.[26]

b. Deliberative Practices

These considerations about practices in general and about simple linguistic practices have implications for more complex practices that involve deliberation. I shall explain the ways in which deliberation about, say, judicial

22. This means merely that one can anticipate the range of variation in criteria for driving—and one can anticipate the kinds of criteria that simply make no sense (unless an exceptional context is created). One person may tend to favor careful drivers who obey speed limits, while another may favor accident avoidance even at excessive speed. But it would be hard to understand "crashing into as many red cars as possible" as a standard for good driving (unless the act is part of a contest, etc.).
23. Non-linguistic ones are waving and pointing. See Wittgenstein, *Philosophical Investigations, supra*, n. 1, part I, section 454.
24. In *Philosophical Investigations, supra* n. 1, Wittgenstein discusses color in Part I, sections 273 through 278. Consider, for example, section 275:
    Look at the blue of the sky and say to yourself "How blue the sky is!"—When you do it spontaneously—without philosophical intentions—the idea never crosses your mind that this impression of colour belongs only to you. . . .
    See also Wittgenstein, *Remarks on Colour*, L.L. McAlister trans. (Oxford: Basil Blackwell, 1977). Wittgenstein's extensive discussion of pain in *Philosophical Investigations* is to be found in Part I at sections 283 to 304, 310 to 317, 350 to 351, 384, and 391 through 398. Consider section 384: "You learned the *concept* 'pain' when you learned language."
25. In the history of British empiricism, John Locke held a distinctive theory along these lines. See *An Essay on Human Understanding* (Oxford: Clarendon Press,1894). In the twentieth century, Bertrand Russell and A. J. Ayer clung to many of the traditional tenets of British empiricism.
26. *Philosophical Investigations, supra* n. 1, Part I, section 381: How do I know that this colour is red?— It would be an answer to say, "I have learnt English."
    Two qualifications are relevant. (a) An individual may experience colors that have no *simple* name. One may say that one wants "a slightly pinkish shade of pale ochre" on one's wall. But the color one envisions is a color that one imagines others capable of envisioning. (b) The communal color language may change over time. Words like "indigo" and "cerise" may fall in and out of ordinary use.

decisions is more complex than deliberation about color or pain.

All practices allow the possibility, indeed the inevitability, of idiosyncracy within shared ways of proceeding. Even if it is true that persons have a shared conception of the nature of driving, each driver also has a personal style. Even good drivers differ in style. Each of us has a distinctive way of using color language. I may tend not to discriminate among various shades of red; a friend may tend to distinguish sharply between scarlet and crimson; another friend may use these two terms in a distinctively different way from the first friend.[27]

In deliberative activities this possibility of diversity within shared, and mutually understood, ways of proceeding is especially significant. A deliberative practice involves discourse with the shared purpose of forming and defending judgments. Examples of deliberative practices are esthetic debate, moral reasoning, historical discourse, and judicial decision-making. The subject may be the beauty of an object, or whether an action is right, or whether an event is a turning point in history, or whether a plaintiff has a right to a favorable judgment. All such debates have certain features in common. All refer to widely shared activities and/or institutions in civilized societies. All are realms of discourse that seem almost indispensable in the transactions of civilized persons. In all these domains, the main debates extend over the history of civilization and seem intractable.[28]

It is equally important to see what draws participants together as to see what separates them.[29] Even when they disagree, they recognize the argumentative strategies of others. They share a sense of what reasons are relevant to the common discourse. Discussing beauty, they may consider symmetry and asymmetry, balance and imbalance, representational aspects of the object, context, purpose. They will not consider relevant whether the artist had long or short life, whether her name began with a vowel or consonant, or whether the object or performance is privately or publicly financed. These observations may sccm trivial, but only bccausc thcy arc so familiar, so much a part of what we do. They are "second nature". Each participant can anticipate[30] the moves that others will make. The practice consists in the recognition of a family of reasoning strategies that admit a spectrum of judgments.

But it is not the case that anything counts. To say that any move is permissible is to say that no move is permissible. Just as in driving or in identifying colors, the publicly shared understanding of what moves are

---

27. It is important that the question which of the three of us is *correct* in his use of color terms may be a meaningless question. All three ways of speaking may be appropriate in different contexts and there may be no general criteria, relevant to all contexts, for distinguishing scarlet from crimson. When and where they are needed, new conventions will be invented.

28. This point is true whether one is speaking of individuals, and saying that these subjects have concerned persons in all cultures and been richly debated over the course of history, or speaking of so-called schools of thought, and saying that distinctive points of view about these issues (objectivism vs. subjectivism, realism vs. idealism, relativism vs. absolutism) have recurred insistently over the history of human speculation.

29. For an extended discussion of this point see T. Morawetz, *Wittgenstein and Knowledge: The Importance of On Certainty* (Amherst: Univ. of Mass. Press, 1978).

30. That is to say, one can anticipate a range of intelligible moves and responses. If a response is wholly unexpected and seems unintelligible or nonsensical, one can construct the kinds of conversational bridges that would make it intelligible. Of course, conversations sometimes take surprising turns within the bounds of these constraints.

comprehensible ways of proceeding is what makes the practice possible.

If participants are able to discuss beauty, justice, and historical influence because they have learned what is relevant to such discourse, how is it that they do not all act the same, all reaching the same conclusions in the same way? In simpler practices, color identification for example, differences among individuals are usually treated as *de minimis*. In general, it is neither of philosophical nor practical interest to argue at length over whether a color sample is really midnight blue or indigo. This is another way of saying that color language is not really a deliberative practice.

Deliberative practices are characterized both by what binds participants together and what distinguishes them. No two persons have had the same history or the same characteristics. Some are more credulous than others, more perceptive, more doubtful, more hesitant. Much more importantly, each will have a characteristic way of reasoning that cuts across the several deliberative practices in which she participates and represents an interpretive orientation to the world, a way of sorting out the phenomena of experience and making sense of them.

This needs explanation. I shall first look at examples drawn from deliberative practices other than legal reasoning. In section 3, I shall look at judicial interpretation directly.

Consider first debates about beauty. How diverse may be the reasons given to justify and explain esthetic judgments? What kinds of different strategies may participants in the practice expect to meet? One person may offer psychological grounds for attributing beauty. Another may refer to inherent properties of the object itself. Yet another may look to the ways in which the object expresses the intentions of the artist, and/or the quality of those intentions. A fourth may appeal to the social and political role of the object as a basis for esthetic merit.[31]

A debate among such participants is complicated even further by the fact that these several strategies of reasoning are not independent of each other. Each participant will to some extent take account of the reasons offered by others by finding a place for them within her own favored strategy.[32] One may explain psychological response as a manifestation of inherent features of the object, while another may say that accounts of inherent features are reducible to psychological factors. Thus, a part of each participant's way of proceeding will be a strategy for incorporating or dismissing the favored strategies of others. And each in turn will recognize and anticipate such moves as part of the ongoing practice.[33]

Two observations. The diverse strategies that make up a deliberative practice compete insofar as there is no natural order of precedence among cate-

31. An anthology of historical approaches is A. Hofstadter and R. Kuhns, *Philosophies of Art and Beauty* (New York: Modern Library, 1964). A collection of recent diverse writings is C. Harrison and F. Orton, *Modernism, Criticism, Realism* (San Francisco: Harper and Row, 1984).
32. By using the word "strategy" for what others may call (and for what I call elsewhere) a "way of proceeding" and "way of reasoning", I do not imply that these strategies serve ulterior aims or that they involve strategic planning.
33. Compare *Philosophical Investigations, supra,* n. 1, Part I, section 241: "'So you are saying that human agreement decides what is true and what is false?'—It is what human beings *say* that is true and false; and they agree in the *language* they use. That is not agreement in opinions but in form of life."

gories of facts, among categories of reasons and justifications. For example, psychological explanations are not inherently more basic than political and economic explanations, nor is the reverse true. Appeals to the inherent features of a work of art are neither more nor less basic a mode of justification (in esthetic reasoning) than appeals to the creator's intentions.[34] In defending one's own judgment in a particular case, one is also defending one's *style* of judgment, one's way of ordering the data of experience to give some kinds precedence. The attempt to convince others is not only an attempt to make them agree with one's own conclusions but also to bring them around to deploying reasons in the same way.[35]

The second observation is that the persuasive attempts of each participant are not, as one might think, doomed.[36] To say that each participant has a particular way of proceeding in reasoning is not to say that he is condemned to repeat the same moves forever. Individual participants differ not only in judgments and in ways of reaching those judgments, but also in their susceptibility to persuasion, to considering and adopting other points of view and other strategies. Similarly, the practice itself, as a collection of strategies mutually recognized by participants, evolves. In retrospect[37] a theorist finds that some strategies gain currency while others go into temporary or permanent eclipse.[38]

Other deliberative practices can be analyzed similarly. One historian will use the influence of ideas as the *explanans* that unlocks historical change, another will look to economic motives and events, while still another will stress the charismatic influence of leaders.[39] In moral discourse, some theorists will see altruistic utilitarianism as offering the most coherent account of reasons relevant to moral judgment, another will see psychologistic or hedonistic utilitarianism as basic, while another will say that moral reasoning is essentially deontological.[40]

34. Reductionism was more widely discussed in the philosophy of science and of social science a generation ago that it is today. Compare E. Nagel, *The Structure of Science* (New York. Harcourt and Bruce, 1961) with H. Brown, *Perception, Theory and Commitment* (New York: Columbia Univ. Press, 1979).

35. This fact, I would argue, is what fuels debate within deliberative practices. Participants manifest and seek to validate their ways of thinking through participation. (This is a truism rather than a claim for empirical psychology.)

36. Wittgenstein is sometimes falsely charged with conservatism. The suggestion is that innovation and change are ruled out by a practice-based account of experience because individuals can only learn and do what others have done before them. This shows a misunderstanding of Wittgenstein and of practices. Part of what one learns in acquiring a practice is the constraints within which creativity and innovation are possible. See relevant discussion in D. Pole, *The Later Philosophy of Wittgenstein* (London: Athlone Press, 1958) and D. Bloor, *Wittgenstein: A Social Theory of Knowledge* (New York: Columbia Univ. Press, 1983), at pp. 160-173.

37. Hegel's familiar reference to the owl of Minerva implies that shifts in collective ways of thinking can only be appreciated and understood retrospectively. See G. Hegel, *The Philosophy of Right,* Knox trans. (Oxford: Clarendon Press, 1942), preface: "The owl of Minerva spreads its wings only with the falling of the Dusk." Thomas Kuhn's innovative work on scientific revolutions has the same implication. The nature and significance of a scientific revolution can only be appreciated after it has occurred and after a new way of thinking has came to inhabit "normal science". See below at n. 67.
Arguably, certain political and esthetic manifestoes are self-conscious attempts to alter prevailing practices. They are Janus-faced. Their contemporaneous intelligibility depends on their relationship to existing practices but they are prospective attempts to transform those very practices. Consider for example the esthetic manifestoes of Kandinsky, Apollinaire, Mondrian, and the futurists.

38. Examples in politics are the hierarchic presuppositions of feudalism and of Renaissance statecraft.

39. These ways of looking at history are attributable, respectively, to Max Weber, Friedrich Engels, and Thomas Carlisle (and their followers).

40. The philosophers most closely identified with these positions are, respectively, John Stuart Mill,

c. On Language Games

Wittgenstein does not give an account of deliberative practices. His examples of practices are simpler: discourse about color, communicative expressions of pain, and so on.[41] Nonetheless, certain themes of his account of knowledge, certainty and judgment seem fundamental to any general account of discourse. An individual's ways of reasoning and understanding, and arguing and judging, are spontaneous ways of organizing experience that reflect a shared practice. Reasoning and understanding are parts of a learned repertoire as much as are swimming and driving. Every practice is as simple and as complicated as it needs to be to serve as a tool for organizing experience and proceeding through it. If we have not invented a sharp distinction between crimson and scarlet, the reason is that we do not ordinarily need it. If we operate with different but related strategies in reaching legal decisions as judges, then an account of the practice must recognize and respect the diversity and relatedness of those strategies. Philosophy, Wittgenstein tells us, leaves everything as it is.[42]

The term "language game" is doubly misleading. The analogy of driving and swimming demonstrates that some practices are non-linguistic. Practices that *do* involve language are not exclusively linguistic. Necessarily, the experiences and expectations of color identification presuppose that there are linguistic conventions through which we have been taught and by which we communicate. But the skill of color recognition is no more reducible to skill in using words like "yellow" than the skills of driving are reducible to the skill of using terms like "stop" and "accelerate".

The same goes for deliberative practices. The patterns of reasoning involved in forming and justifying judgments are patterns expressed in language and described through language. But the intellectual strategy that leads someone to explain social and economic phenomena by reducing them to patterns of individual psychology is not adequately described by rules that instruct one in the use of words.[43] By focusing on the idea that practices are made up of shared linguistic rules, some followers of Wittgenstein imply that on-going practices are more homogeneous than they really are.[44] It is important to remember how diverse are the variant strategies of historians, or moralists, or judges that are expressed in the same shared lexicon.

Just as deliberative practices are not, or not merely or primarily, activities of language, so too they are not very much like games. Some similarities are obvious and explain the seductiveness of the metaphor. One must be initiated

Thomas Hobbes, and Immanuel Kant. Each has influenced ethical theorists through subsequent generations. In my references to ethical theory I am assuming that the positions of various theories bridge questions of metaethics and questions of normative ethics. In other words, theorists reach what John Rawls calls "reflective equilibrium" with regard to reconciling metaethical commitments and substantive ethical judgments. See Rawls, *A Theory of Justice* (Cambridge: Harvard Univ. Press, 1971), at 20.

41. *Supra,* nn. 26 and 27.
42. *Philosophical Investigations,supra* n. 1, Part I, section 124. "Philosophy may in no way interfere with the actual use of language; it can in the end only describe it.
    For it cannot give it any foundation either.
    It leaves everything as it is."
43. See I. Hacking, *Why Does Language Matter to Philosophy?* (Cambridge: Cambridge Univ. Press, 1975), chapters 11-13.
44. See articles in S. Holtzman and C. Leich, *Wittgenstein: To Follow a Rule* (London: Routledge and Kegan Paul, 1981).

through a period of learning. Once one has become a participant, one can make appropriate or correct moves and one can make mistakes.[45] As in games,[46] some rules are constitutive rather than regulative. This means that a participant gains a new way of looking at a domain of experience that is constituted by the concepts and conceptual relationships she has learned. For example, thinking and talking about strikes and runs is meaningless outside the domain of baseball. To learn the rules of baseball is to enter a new domain of experience. Similarly, to learn the concept of a tort or a privacy right is not merely to acquire a new way of thinking about the world; the experienced world itself acquires new characteristics. The idea of a tort only belongs in a world governed by law.[47]

Practices are not games. Games have beginnings and ends. Usually they proceed by discrete moves, rounds, or turns. Games[48] are at bottom reducible to rules and all players must play by the same rules. Moreover, some of the rules must specify the point of playing, the goal that gives purpose to the players' moves. Players may differ in strategy and technique but there is ordinarily a clear distinction between the rules, on which they must agree, and the strategies of play, on which they may well differ.[49]

In characterizing a relatively simple linguistic practice, such as color language or pain language, the game analogy is compelling. It makes sense to say that in identifying shades of blue or describing aches, a condition of the recognition of and communication about such experiences is that participants follow the same rules.[50] Either they follow the same rules and are participants in a shared practice, or they do not and the scope of their color and pain experience remains inaccessible and uncertain.[51] But even in these prac-

---

45. See Wittgenstein, *On Certainty* (Oxford: Basil Blackwell, 1969), section 614.
46. J. Rawls, "Two Concepts of Rules", (1955) 64 *Philosophical Review* 3.
47. The distinction between constitutive and regulative rules (and between constitutive and descriptive concepts) has unclear borders. Consider, for example, the economist's use of the term "preference satisfaction." The term has technical significance in economic theory but also refers to a phenomenon that lives outside the domain of economic theory. The same can be said of the sociologist's use of the term "charisma." The same, however, cannot be said of "run" or "strike" in baseball.
48. Wittgenstein, as noted above at n. 9, admonishes us to remember that if we "look and see whether there is anything common to all" games, we "will not see something that is common to all, but similarities, relationships, and a whole series of them at that." He goes on, "I can think of no better expression to characterize these similarities than 'family resemblances'; for the various resemblances between members of a family: build, features, colour of eyes, gait, temperament, etc. etc. overlap and criss-cross in the same way.—And I shall say: 'games' form a family." *Philosophical Investigations, supra* n. 1, Part I, sections 66 and 67.
    My critique is of the use of a paradigm of games whereby all participants follow the same rules and have in mind the same point or purpose for engaging in the joint activity. Rawls and Kuhn use the paradigm to illuminate political and scientific activity.
49. In actual games and in the game-paradigm, the distinction is maintained between rules, by which all players must abide, and strategies, which players may devise on their own and which are likely to differ from player to player. It is relatively easy to sort out the activities of baseball players or chess players along these lines.
    The use of the game-paradigm for judges presupposes that in judging as well one can distinguish the rules from strategies. One of my main criticisms of the use of the metaphor of games for deliberative practices is that this distinction cannot be made in the case of judging. In other words, the quest for shared rules of relevance for justificatory reasons must yield to the recognition of a plurality of competing strategies of justification.
50. This is not to say that Robinson Crusoe, alone on a desert island, cannot notice a particular color of fruit and then reidentify the color elsewhere on the island. But terms that he invents and uses are in principle terms that he can share with any subsequent visitors to the island; in principle his language can be a public language. The "private language" question is much debated in writings on Wittgenstein. See, for example, Kripke, *supra* n. 20.
51. Compare *Philosophical Investigations, supra* n. 1, Part I, section 250: "Why can't a dog simulate

tices, the game analogy breaks down. For one thing, the rules of the practice are not constitutive of pain experience *in the same way* that the rules of chess are constitutive of the experience of castling and checkmating. For another, color and pain recognition does not proceed in goal-directed moves.

The game metaphor breaks down altogether in accounting for deliberative practices. A basic constraint of the metaphor is that justificatory arguments make sense only among participants who are playing by the same rules, who have the same standards of relevance for reasons. Among persons playing by different rules, justificatory moves are mere illusions and discourse proceeds at cross-purposes. Understanding this, participants must abandon their attempts or coerce (rather than persuade) others into playing by their rules.[52]

But in deliberative practices justificatory moves proceed in the face of differing strategies of reasoning. The practice consists in the recognition that these differing strategies exist and compete. From the standpoint of games, this characteristic of deliberative practices can only be a paradox. On discovering that others are playing by different rules, one will either bring them around to playing by the same rules or stop playing. Making further moves loses its point when others are playing a different game. The game itself loses its point.

And yet, the very point of deliberative practices seems to be to justify both a particular result and a particular *way* of reaching the result against those who reason differently. Participants have a stake not in a particular set of arbitrary rules but in a particular way of making sense of experience. A deliberative practice is a domain within which such different strategies compete. To give up or alter one's method of justification is not simply to decide to play by different rules but to decide to see the world differently.

Rather than saying that we can understand deliberative practices by seeing them as a kind of game, we might say rather that we can understand games as simplified, externalized, and therefore degenerate kinds of practices.[53] A justificatory response within a game ("Why did you move as you did?") may be a reminder of the shared rule or a reference to the player's strategy for winning.[54] The rules are fixed, arbitrary, and assumed to be known to all. But only the least important aspects of experience have this kind of simplicity. Only the least important aspects of life leave participants the option whether or not to play. In the more immediate and important practices—moral practices, psychological transactions, economic and professional judgments—we have

---

pain? Is he too honest? Could one teach a dog to simulate pain? Perhaps it is possible to teach him to howl on particular occasions as if he were in pain, even when he is not. But the surroundings which are necessary for this behaviour to be real simulation are missing."

52. In *On Certainty,* Wittgenstein says, in confronting those who reason differently, "we use our language-game to *combat* theirs," section 609. According to this assumption, reasoning and persuasion and justification are possible only among those who reason in the same way; otherwise, there is only competition and combat.

53. True games can be seen as mimicking the ordered or practice-like character of all conduct but in a form in which the goal is arbitrarily posited (and therefore bears no inherent relationship to human needs and desires) and in which moves and rules are simplified into relatively simple and rigid patterns.

54. See *supra* n. 49, for discussion of the distinction between rules and strategy in the context of a game—and for an argument that the distinction evaporates in a deliberative practice.

a stake unavoidably and the shared rules-and-strategies are endlessly controversial.

This conclusion about deliberative practices has implications for the role of
theorists. Games afford a clear distinction between players and observers,
insiders and outsiders.[55] Insiders play by the rules and justify their actions by
resort to the rules. Outsiders are not bound by the rules. As observers, their
questions about justification involve the justification of one set of rules in
comparison with other variants of the game.

In considering deliberative practices, we lose the sharpness of this distinction. In part, the distinction remains in place. Practitioners inhabit a particular strategy of moral argument, historical interpretation, and so on, while
theorists are occupied in noting and describing variant strategies. But part of
one's understanding of deliberative practices *as a theorist* involves an interpretation, necessarily controversial, of the point of the exercise—of the point
of esthetic activity, moral criticism, historical investigation. A theorist as
well as a practitioner will therefore have a stake in a particular strategy and an
attitude toward the point of the practice. This will color her account of the
practice. A justification of the practice from a theoretical standpoint will
look much like a justification given by a practitioner with a particular strategy within the practice.[56]

3. Legal Interpretation as a Deliberative Practice

a. Judges and Games

In this section I shall consider why the metaphor of games is a seductive
tool for understanding constitutional interpretation,[57] why this metaphor can
be said to confuse the analysis, and how the suggestion that judging is a
deliberative practice, rather than a game, satisfactorily explains what judges
do.

Three decades ago, political and legal philosophy in England and America
were reborn.[58] A crucial ingredient of this renaissance was the idea that political and legal reasoning constitute practices and that the job of theorists is to

---

55. One of the most widely discussed aspects of Hart's jurisprudential writings is his distinction between
an internal and an external point of view. This distinction has also occupied moral philosophy over the
last forty years. See Hart, n. 13 *supra*, at 55-60; P. Soper, *A Theory of Law* (Cambridge, Mass: Harvard
Univ. Press, 1984); K. Baier, *The Moral Point of View* (Ithaca: Cornell Univ. Press, 1958); B. Williams,
Ethics and the Limits of Philosophy (Cambridge Mass: Harvard Univ. Press, 1985); and T. Nagel,
The View from Nowhere (New York: Oxford Univ. Press, 1986).

56. Whether one is concerned with practitioners such as the justices of the U. S. Supreme Court or with
theorists such as Tushnet, Ely, Bork, Fiss, and Dworkin, each propounds a controversial account of the
point of the enterprise of judicial decision-making (and specifically constitutional interpretation).
Although the position of pure outsider can, in principle, be adopted, it leaves the theorist with little to
say. The reason philosophers are occupied with theories of law or morality or history but not with theories of baseball or chess is precisely because a theory of baseball would be uninteresting insofar as it
would not pose controversial alternatives with regard to the point of the practice. A theorist of baseball
would be a pure outsider, a pure describer, whereas a theorist of law or morality or history exists
self-consciously in tension between commitment to a controversial justification of the practice and
transcendence of that commitment.

57. *Supra* n. 6. The analysis need not be limited to constitutional decision-making or to appellate decision-
making, but I do not try to generalize the argument here.

58. During the reign of logical positivism in the 1930's through the 1950's, moral, political, and legal philosophy were in eclipse. Such then-popular theories as emotivism and prescriptivism implied that
moral and political discourse was not to be treated as a form of reasoning so much as a form of pure

uncover the constitutive rules[59] of these practices. This way of understanding the relevant methodology was common to self-described legal positivists and legal naturalists.[60] H. L. A. Hart described law as a complex game with two kinds of rules, those that instructed ordinary citizens on their obligations and rights and those that instructed officials in carrying forward institutional roles. To understand the task of judges is to understand the second-order rules that define their role.

The complexity of law as a practice becomes evident when we compare judges with the officials of real games. Ronald Dworkin reminds us that umpires in baseball exercise discretion in a different way from judges.[61] Umpires are entrusted with the task of making final judgments about particular actions and events[62] but the standards to be used are clearly and uncontroversially set for them. Even when umpires disagree about a result they do not and cannot disagree about the standards to be used in reaching the result.[63] Judges, on the other hand, disagree about method as well as result.

Judges and umpires differ in yet another respect. Umpires are not in any sense players in a second-order game since groups of umpires do not characteristically engage in deliberative moves and countermoves. They make spontaneous and final decisions and the game moves on. Panels of judges on the other hand engage in complex practices of interaction that are observed and analyzed. One level of analysis is the informal level of social and political maneuvering that is largely unrecorded and invisible, more guessed about than seen. Another level is the explicit dialogue whereby written opinions, including dissenting opinions, spell out both results and justificatory strategies. Although it is rare for a particular case to elicit written opinions (concurrences, dissents) from several members of the panel, judges quickly become identified with particular strategies and their dialogue persists over series of related cases. Thus, the implicit dialogue becomes explicit.

The second-order practice of judging is therefore unlike the activity of umpires because it involves moves and countermoves among participants who are responding to each other's strategies and are aware of doing so. The relevant moves are justificatory arguments. (With regard to judging, as with other deliberative practices, one may have the illusion that the interactive character of the activity is inessential. It seems as if one can make judicial decisions or write history or make moral judgments without taking into account and responding to the judgments—legal, historical, moral—of others.

---

expression or attempted coercion. See, for example, J. Urmson, *The Emotive Theory of Ethics* (London: Hutchinson Press, 1968) and T. Weldon, *The Vocabulary of Politics* (Baltimore: Penguin, 1953). Hart's *Concept of Law, supra* n. 13, and Rawls' *A Theory of Justice, supra* n. 40, are the most influential masterworks in the renaissance of political and legal philosophy under the rubric of linguistic analysis.

59. *Supra* n. 46.
60. The distinction sketched by Rawls in "Two Concepts of Rules" was elaborated and used both by Hart in *The Concept of Law* and by Dworkin in the essays in *Taking Rights Seriously, supra* n. 4, 13, and 46.
61. Dworkin, *Taking Rights Seriously,supra* n. 4, pp. 31-39. Here Dworkin distinguishes among several senses of discretion.
62. E.g. actions such as whether player x tagged up when he rounded second base, and events such as whether the ball was in the strike zone as it crossed home plate.
63. That is to say, they must abide by the rules of baseball as recorded and agreed-upon rules specifying what constitutes a strike, when a player must touch base, etc. The rules leave no effective room for ambiguity or interpretation.

This illusion parallels the illusion that it is inessential for the recognition of color or pain that there be a public practice of labeling and distinguishing among colors, or of identifying and diagnosing pains, into which persons are initiated. As with color and pain, one's awareness of what counts as a move in forming a legal and moral judgment or in defending an account of history presumes an established context in which there are justificatory moves and countermoves.)[64]

b. The Limits of a Kuhnian Account of Judging

Consider again the initial appeal of the metaphor of games as an idiom for the justificatory moves and countermoves of judging in general and constitutional interpretation in particular. The argument is straight-forward and exploits the comparison with color language. In describing color, we make sense and succeed in recognizing and communicating about color to the extent that we play by the same rules. What you call "red" is (more or less)[65] what I call "red". If we were to play by different rules we would have, at best, only the appearance of mutual understanding and communication. In that case, we would either bring others round to our way of speaking, adopt their rules, or decline to engage further with them.

The discovery that judges are playing by different rules seems to produce an impasse and a crisis. The considerable and imaginative efforts of recent theorists fall readily into place as attempts to address what they see as an impasse.[66] The impasse is explicable by noting two differences between the relatively simple game of color identification and the relatively complex one of judicial interpretation. The first difference is that discrepancies among players of the color game are immediately apparent. In the face of discrepancies, the game breaks down. Discrepant justificatory strategies among judges are less obvious. Decision making can proceed for some time under the public misconception that there are shared rules. The misconception may or may not be shared by the judges themselves.

The second difference explains the first. The practice of judging, unlike the practice of color identification, seems to call for a shared notion of the point of the activity which informs the rules governing reasoning and justification.[67] This shared notion is what Thomas Kuhn, in the context of analyzing scientific theory-building, calls a "paradigm". Judges, like historians and those engaged in moral reasoning, have a favored conception of the purpose served by their activity. In true games, the goal of play is easily and unambiguously

---

64. Just as one can imagine a single judge sitting in judgment, one can also imagine a person alone in the desert identifying colors. But in both cases, the event is imaginable because it is also imaginable as a collective enterprise, whereby several persons carry out judgments, argue among themselves, etc. Compare Wittgenstein's observations on this, *supra* n. 26 and accompanying text.
65. *Supra* n. 27.
66. Most of the theorists of the late 1970's and early 1980's speak eloquently about a sense of crisis and an impasse with regard to theorizing about judging. See, for example, J. Ely, *Democracy and Distrust* (Cambridge, Mass: Harvard Univ. Press, 1980), at 73-75; L. Tribe, *Constitutional Choices* (Cambridge, Mass: Harvard Univ. Press, 1985), at 3-21; and M. Perry, *The Constitution, The Courts, and Human Rights* (New Haven: Yale Univ. Press, 1982), at 9-36.
67. Kuhn's account of scientific discovery and change is explained in T. Kuhn, *The Structure of Scientific Revolutions* (Chicago: Univ. of Chicago Press, 1962). See also I. Lakatos and A. Musgrave, *Criticism and the Growth of Knowledge* (Cambridge: Cambridge University Press, 1970) and I. Hacking, *Scientific Revolutions* (Oxford: Oxford Univ. Press, 1981).

specified (checkmating the king, scoring the most runs). Kuhn argues that
in shared activities of research and reasoning there must be a similar consensus, a shared understanding of the kind of knowledge sought and of the methods appropriate to seeking it. But in such activities as judging, and writing
history, this shared understanding is problematic. Differing strategies of
justification may be evidence, in Kuhn's terms, of differing paradigmatic
understandings of the point of the activity.

This impasse yields a sense of crisis. Judges, unlike historians and individual
moral agents, have a political role and wield institutional power. Any political
actor becomes a threat to the security of the rule of law unless her power is constrained. Constraint for judges, in turn, seems to lie in the availability of a
widely shared and uncontroversial conception of the purpose to be served by
judges and of the rules for judging that flow from that conception. Some theorists prefer to say that such rules insure that judges will act objectively rather
than subjectively.[68] If, on the other hand, every conception is controversial
among both judges and theorists, then judges are in fact unconstrained, loose
and potentially destructive actors within the political structure.[69]

This analysis remains within the metaphor of games. Paradigm-driven
activities are sophisticated games in several senses. The success of the activity depends on a shared conception of the purposes of the activity and of the
rules to be followed. For Kuhn, of course, scientific research is the main
example. In the light of his account, the game metaphor must be relaxed only
slightly. It must be rethought to take account of the fact that the "game" of
scientific investigation and reasoning does not proceed by discrete moves,
does not begin and end at predetermined and rule-determined times, and is not
competitive in a zero-sum sense (whereby a win by one player entails an
equal loss by another).

The Kuhnian idea of an investigative paradigm—the idea of reasoning as a
modified game—is the missing link between the simple idea of a game and
the search for a theory of judicial interpretation. The effort of theorists is
directed not toward simple assimilation with games but toward eliciting a
shared idea of constitutional interpretation from which uncontroversial rules,
as constraints and as ideals, follow. The alternatives that have received the
most attention have long been familiar. Many writers favor adherence to the
structure and role of government as conceived by the founders of the constitution. Such "interpretivism" takes two forms, adherence to the intentions
of the founders insofar as it is discoverable through all kinds of historical
investigation and adherence to the text of the constitution and to its original
meaning.[70] By contrast, other writers (noninterpretivists) look to the evolution
of constitutional thought, in which the founders represent but one moment,
and stress the continual rethinking of the role and structure of government

68. This notion of judicial objectivity is put forward by Owen Fiss in "Objectivity and Interpretation" (1982), 34 *Stanford L. R.* 739.

69. See sources listed, *supra* n. 66.

70. Ely follows many other writers in adhering to the term "interpretivism." Tushnet and Brest, in their influential and persuasive critiques, prefer the term "originalism." See Tushnet, *supra* n. 8, and P. Brest, "The Misconceived Quest for the Original Understanding" (1980), 60 *Boston University L. R.* 204. See also R. Kay, "Adherence to the Original Intentions in Constitutional Adjudication: Three Objections and Responses" (1988), 82 *Northwestern University L. R.* 226.

represented in our constitutional history.[71] Such theorists tend to see judges as spokespersons for a consensus of received values and ideals that may be loosely connected to the thought of the founders, uninformed as it is by the events of the last 200 years.

Theorists debate both the practicability and merits of such theories. Defenders of interpretivism must wrestle with the question whether the intentions of the founders are in fact retrievable in a way that dictates a discrete strategy of decision in hard cases. Defenders of non-interpretivism must wrestle with the equally intractable question whether any current and continuing social consensus exists about the issues raised by contemporary constitutional questions. Critics of both positions argue, often compellingly, that reference to original intent and reference to a pervasive social consensus mask the indiscipline of judges and that neither form of rhetoric proceeds from genuinely constraining rules.[72]

In the rest of this section, I shall address the question at a higher level of abstraction. If we grant that judges proceed and think of themselves as proceeding in all of the ways described by theorists, are we required by the metaphor of games and the Kuhnian requirement of a shared paradigm to admit that there is no shared practice, only the facade of one? How well indeed does the metaphor of games, as modified through Kuhn's model, really fit our deliberative practices?

c. Judging as a Deliberative Practice

The behavior of judges does not fit the metaphor of games. The simple metaphor of a game—with its discrete moves and static, written rules, with its clearly distinguished beginning and end—is clearly irrelevant. The more complex notion, the Kuhnian paradigm, is overtly metaphorical and says that communicative practices are game-like in an essential way—constituted by shared rules that define what counts as a move, what the point of communication is, and what counts as a relevant reason or relevant justificatory argument in discourse. Kuhn suggests that scientific investigation, like color identification, proceeds because we agree about what counts as a justificatory move, because we agree about what kinds of evidence are relevant in the process of making and debating judgments, and because we have a shared commitment to the point of the deliberative enterprise.

That's not how judges work. I have already looked at debates among historians, at moral discourse, and at judging, to suggest that in describing deliberative practices, even this more complex use of the game metaphor is unhelpful. According to the metaphor, the possibility of genuine deliberation presupposes common strategies of deliberation. Judges must have in common a conception of the point of the practice and of the rules of relevance that govern justificatory moves. The absence of shared rules is a defect; the more diverse the rules by which different participants operate, the more defective the practice is. The practice cannot proceed unless the defect is

---

71. Dworkin and Fiss are examples. *Supra* nn. 4 and 68.
72. Tushnet, among others, offers a compelling argument of this kind. *Supra* n. 8.

cured. Judges who proceed in the face of such diversity re-enact the drama of Babel. By assumption, they cannot recognize each other's arguments as having justificatory force because they do not share the same assumptions about what counts as justification.

The actual practice of judges seems to fly in the face of this account. What this account describes as a defect is a definitive and inevitable feature of deliberation. Judges characteristically disagree not only about the results in particular cases but about the method through which results should be derived and defended. The distinction between interpretivists and non-interpretivists marks only the first layer of disagreement about method. Within the first (interpretivist) group, judges will differ about the level of generality with which the founders anticipated and set in motion a determinate structure and about the kinds of resources relevant to debates over their actions. Within the second (non-interpretivist) group, judges will differ in their conception of the kinds of goals and values appropriate to judicial (rather than, say, legislative) action and in their conception of the kinds of data—political, economic, sociological, psychological, historical—that are the "bottom line" of legal deliberation.

If such diversity seems ineradicable and if judicial deliberation (as constitutional interpretation) is characterized by such diversity, then the game metaphor is not a tool but an obstacle to understanding. The idea of a deliberative practice, as outlined in Section 2, is the alternative tool. A deliberative practice embraces participants with different commitments to different argumentative strategies and conceptions of goals. They are bound together not by shared rules but by mutual recognition of an array of relevant ways of proceeding. Deliberation proceeds as an activity in which each reaches and justifies judgments *and* deploys his justificatory strategy in part to persuade others to adopt it but also to vindicate his own way of making sense of experience.

This account explains an otherwise curious aspect of deliberative activity. A distinguishing feature of both games and Kuhnian game-like investigative paradigms is that implicit in each is a clear distinction between insiders and outsiders. In both games and game-like activities, the rules are settled during play. The role of an insider, a participant in the practice, is to make moves in accord with the rules and in the light of the mutually understood point of the practice. These moves may take the form of justificatory arguments in the case of scientific investigation for example.[73] The role of an outsider—an observer, commentator, or theorist—is to take note of the rules and illuminate them in the light of the implicit point of the practice. The outsider herself is not committed to the rules, is not in a position to make justificatory arguments, and must see the rules in some sense as an arbitrary posit. Thus the

---

73. This point illustrates the way in which the example of game-like activity, on the Kuhnian model, is midway between a real game and a deliberative practice. On the one hand is the requirement that participants must play by the same rules and must agree about the shared point or aim of their activity. In this sense, the model is a variant of a game. On the other hand the moves themselves are justificatory arguments, reasons for judgment. In this sense, the activity is like a deliberative practice. The distinction between insiders and outsiders (participants and theorists) is clearer in Kuhn's model than it is in a deliberative practice.

outsider may contemplate the possibility of chess played, hypothetically, by different rules and the historical reality of scientific investigation proceeding under different paradigms.[74]

Deliberative practices do not yield so clear a distinction between the roles of insiders and outsiders. The so-called rules of the practice and the point served by them are inherently disputable. Justification within the practice means not merely justifying particular conclusions but particular ways of reaching those conclusions.

It may be said that the insider/outsider distinction can be transposed to deliberative practices with little modification. The outsider as theorist would thus have the role of describing the practice as a family of strategies of justification rather than as a single rule-governed strategy. But this may be too simple. A neutral or impartial standpoint is available to the outsider of a game because the point of a game is given and uncontroversial. The same is true of game-like investigative paradigms. But with deliberative practices like judicial reasoning, moral reasoning, or explaining history, the point of the enterprise is itself controversial. Even the outsider must, in this sense, choose sides.

Explaining why this is so requires a more general discussion of being inside and outside a practice. This, in turn, requires us to attend briefly to such abstract and intractable issues as the nature and limits of philosophy, and the nature and limits of self-awareness. Consider three steps in the development of these issues.

(1) A spontaneous general attitude toward knowledge and belief, ingrained both in ordinary attitudes and in the history of philosophy, is commonly called foundationalism. A foundationalist believes that all sorts of questions—about history, about the physical world, about psychology—have answers. Any issue is such that there is some truth about the matter, and the task of investigation is to discover that truth, to bring one's beliefs into accord with what is the case. This may be easy or difficult—easy if we wish to discover whether we are wearing shoes, difficult if we wish to discover the origin of the universe or the biography of an ancient prophet—but the task is to do what needs to be done to grasp what is true.

An insight of philosophers from Kant onward is that what we say we know about events, objects, persons, etc., is not simply the result of getting immediately in touch with how things "really are". What we know is conditioned by how we know, not only our physical capacities but also our conceptual frameworks.[75] Wittgenstein and Kuhn in different ways draw conclusions from this insight. The ways in which we organize experience, ask questions about experience, and weigh evidence in drawing conclusions (forming beliefs, deciding what we know) are social practices, often widely shared

---

74. Critics of Kuhn question whether a theorist can indeed be an outsider in this sense or whether the reconstruction of scientific paradigms involves an implicit notion of rationality that transcends paradigms, a notion that allows us to speak meaningfully of progress in science. See, for related issues, I. Lakatos, "History of Science and Its Rational Reconstructions", and K. Popper, "The Rationality of Scientific Revolutions", in Hacking, *supra* n. 67.

75. See general discussion of conceptual frameworks in D. Davidson, "On the Very Idea of a Conceptual Scheme", in *Inquiries into Truth and Interpretation* (Oxford: Oxford Univ. Press, 1984); R. Rorty, *Contingency Irony and Solidarity* (Cambridge: Cambridge Univ. Press, 1989); and H. Putnam, *Realism and Reason, Philosophical Papers, volume 3* (Cambridge: Cambridge Univ. Press, 1983).

but nonetheless variable over time.

(2) If no thinker can, in principle, extricate herself from her ways of knowing, from the social practices by which she has grown accustomed to organizing experience, then she can never claim that a particular way of knowing is privileged over others. Nor can she claim that one variant practice (one way of looking into history or thinking about the universe) gets closer than others to what is true.

Foundationalists must therefore yield to nonfoundationalists. The role of epistemology is not to show how it is that we are getting ever closer to the truth, getting from mediated knowledge to immediate knowledge, but to show how knowledge is mediated.[76] The philosopher as epistemologist is the quintessential outsider with regard to the social practices of knowing. The insider is the inhabitant of the practice to whom the rules of the practice are second nature. Thus we come full circle to the metaphor of games in the sophisticated version suggested by Kuhn.

(3) It is necessary, in turn, to impeach this nonfoundationalist model and the metaphor on which it rests if we are to understand deliberative practices and specifically the practice of legal interpretation. The crucial point can be made in two interdependent ways. One is to say that deliberative practices do not involve (temporarily) settled ways of proceeding, within which reasoning and justification become possible, but competing ways of proceeding of which the various participants are aware. The other way of making the point is that the participants are simultaneously insiders and outsiders, insiders insofar as they are committed to a way of organizing experience that seems inescapable, outsiders insofar as they know that any justificatory move they can make is yet another move elaborating their own strategy within a deliberative practice.

In other words, deliberative practices do not permit theorists or practitioners to be outsiders in the nihilistic sense required by the metaphor of games. The foundationalist aspires to the possibility of being outside particular ways of thinking to apprehend reality in itself. The nonfoundationalist aspires to the possibility of being outside practices as games to achieve a point of indifference or neutrality toward all particular configurations of rules. Neither way of being outside is available *vis-a-vis* deliberative practices.

I am putting forward judicial interpretation—and whatever general understandings about law and legal systems follow from our understanding of judicial interpretation—as a clear example of a deliberative practice. I have been assuming that moral deliberation and debates about history yield other examples and that much of our reasoning activity has the character of a deliberative practice. But I shall leave aside any claims about just which kinds of reasoning fit the Kuhnian model and are in fact game-like and which, on the other hand, can be assimilated to judicial reasoning.[77]

---

76. One of the main ideas in Wittgenstein's *On Certainty, supra* n. 45, is that recognition that knowledge claims and claims about what is true can only occur within practices (or language-games) does not license skepticism or disenfranchise persons from using terms like "know" and "true." This recognition merely describes the conditions under which such terms *are* appropriately used. See Morawetz, *supra* n. 29, chapters 4 and 5.

77. No doubt some theorists would assimilate scientific investigation, Kuhn's main area of concern, with

These distinctions help explain the failure of the most representative recent theories of constitutional interpretation. I shall use my critique of the metaphor of games and of the consequent distinction between insiders and outsiders to show how and why theorists have failed to appreciate that judicial interpretation is a deliberative practice.

4. Theories of Constitutional Interpretation

No overview can do justice to the rich literature on constitutional interpretation of the last fifteen years. My concern is not with the details of the debates but with their shared aims and motivations. The fear and goals of these theorists are grounded in the metaphor of a game gone awry.[78] Their goal is to clarify and stabilize the rules of the game. This goal makes sense only as long as judicial interpretation is seen not as a deliberative practice but as a game. I shall suggest therefore that, at its most abstract level, the debate over constitutional interpretation is based on a misunderstanding of the kind of practice constitutional interpretation is and can be.

We have seen that we may simplify the matter by grouping theorists into three categories: interpretivists, noninterpretivists, and nihilists.[79] Interpretivists and noninterpretivists are committed to the constructive goal implicit in the game metaphor, the goal of finding and defending constraining standards for judicial interpretation that may be regarded as the rules of the game. By "constraining" I mean three things. First, the standards define a method of justifying deliberative judgments so that judges may not do "whatever they wish". Second, the standards define a correct or distinctly preferable method of justifying deliberative judgments. Third, the standards are rigorous enough to produce answers to hard questions of judicial interpretation. Each of these three aspects of constraint needs explanation.

The first sense of constraint poses the alternatives of license and rule-following; either there are discoverable rules that define decisionmaking or there are none. If there are discoverable rules, they are the rules of the game, the same for all judges. The second sense of constraint implies that in the actual practice of judges one can discover several alternative (rule-like) ways of proceeding. Unless one can show that one way of proceeding is correct (or superior to others), the collection of alternatives is tantamount to license. In other words, there is no middle ground between license and univocal rules. Specifically, to say that judges do not have license because they may choose among a limited set of alternative constraining rules is nonsense. The third sense of constraint is addressed to the relationship between rules (or methods or ways of proceeding) and decisions. It says that if judges may properly choose among alternative ways of proceeding, the results of deliberation are not constrained, but if there is only one correct or superior way of proceeding,

---

a deliberative practice and would contest the existence of shared paradigms. Perhaps the best account of the matter would suggest that the two models are not mutually exclusive, and that some areas of investigation and deliberation come closer to one model while others approximate the other.

78. *Supra* text at n. 49 and *passim*.
79. These categories are explained above at text accompanying nn. 12-14, 70-71, and 81-83.

then results are circumscribed.[80]

Nihilists agree that the goal of theory is to undercover a constraining theory, one that is constraining is all three senses. But they attempt to show that the goal cannot be achieved. After looking briefly at interpretive, noninterpretive, and nihilistic theory, I shall conclude by arguing that the underlying three-part notion of constraint is appropriate to an analysis of games but not to deliberative practices.

(1) Interpretivists are preoccupied with the first sense of constraint. They fear that judges will use the power of interpretation to effect political and social choices of their own. And they see the only adequate answer to that fear in the claim that concrete political and social choices have been taken out of the hands of judges *ab initio*, i.e., by the drafters of the Constitution. They argue that unless the constitution-making process can be seen as anticipating and answering such questions with some specificity, constraint is a mirage.[81]

The underlying scheme of analysis for interpretivists rests on three assumptions.

(a) Judges either are constrained by shared rules or are not constrained. In the latter case they have license, may make up or vary the rules at will. ("Rules" in this context means "criteria for justificatory reasons".)

(b) For judges to be constrained by shared rules, they must have recourse to a decisional method that does not essentially require judgments about contemporary values, social and political evolution, or social needs. A method that bases decision making on these latter considerations allows judges recourse to a panoply of subjective opinions and is tantamount to license.

(c) On the other hand, structural and substantive determinations made by the authors and ratifiers of the Constitution anticipate answers to constitutional hard questions and the shared rules of decision making require deference to those determinations. The very idea of constitutionalism also mandates such deference.

The interpretive theory is both descriptive and normative. It claims to unpack the idea of decision making and to describe the rules that underlie the practice, properly understood. But in doing so, it describes a standard and an ideal. Also, most interpretivists would argue that their theory is doubly a theory of constraint. It strongly constrains the sort of resources appropriate to decision making. It also constrains results, but less strongly.[82] Players playing

---

80. The relationship between rules and results is a complex one (not unlike the relationship between theories of metaethics and theories of substantive ethics). Practitioners who follow the same rules will not necessarily get the same results. The rules do not function as a decision procedure, nor do they put in place a deductive method. Rather, they are a criterion of relevance and importance for reasons. Historians who stress economic factors are more likely to attend to similar kinds of facts, but will not offer identical explanations. Judges who consult original intent will be disposed, one imagines, to entertain certain arguments about federalism but will not apply these arguments in the same way, nor will they necessarily come up with the same results in hard cases. The constraining effects of the rules of a game like baseball or of an experimental process in, say, biochemical research also allow for differing ways of carrying out the activity—but one must not draw the analogy too closely.

81. Such assumptions seem to underpin the work of writers as diverse as Robert Bork, Richard Kay, and John Hart Ely. See, for example, R. Bork, "Neutral Principles and Some First Amendment Problems", (1971) 47 *Indiana L. J.* 1, and "The Impossibility of Finding Welfare Rights in the Constitution", (1979) *Washington University L. Q.* 695; R. Kay, *supra* n. 70; and J. Ely, *supra* n. 66.

82. *Supra* n. 80.

by the same rules will, nonetheless, play differently. Judges who attend to original intent may disagree about what the constitution requires in particular cases.

Beyond this, interpretivists vary in the details. Some proffer interpretivism reluctantly, as a measure of the limits on judicial power to benefit society. Others put it forth enthusiastically, as one component of a framework in which government interferes minimally in persons' lives.[83] Some describe interpretivism as the only alternative to judicial license. Others claim only that it is a firmer constraint, a clearer rule, than others and defend it in the interest of institutional stability and predictability.[84]

(2) Non-interpretivists accept the same first premise. They reject, however, the second premise.

(b$_1$) Judges may be constrained by rules directing them to adhere to an evolved consensus about social value. Such rules may take various forms. According to various subtheories, judges may be required to reconstruct the abstract relationship between the individual and the state embodied in the Constitution, or they may be required to develop the best theory of constitutional rights that interprets concern and respect for individual autonomy, or they may be required to adhere to "disciplining rules" that insure fairness and conscientiousness in respecting shared values.[85]

(c$_1$) Adherence to such rules assures that judges will not decide in accord with whim, license, or personal preference. In other words they will decide objectively rather than subjectively. Such a procedure is in fact mandated by (or at least altogether consistent with) the Constitution, which anticipates that judicial interpretation will be shaped to the needs of the present rather than the dead hand of the past.

If the sticking point of interpretivism is that it may require judges to frustrate the best interests of the public in the interest of constitutionalism, the sticking point of noninterpretivism is that it presumes that the best interests will generally be transparent. The important point that I have emphasized throughout my analysis is that this expectation is unrealistic, *not* simply because judges have different "values" but because they have different ways of giving order to experience. What they share is mediated by language and the ways in which they differ are also reflected in language. The issue is not, as some political philosophers say, that some favor liberty and others equality.[86] The issue is rather that the ways in which persons fit psychological, economic, political, social experiences together, the ways in which they make sense of their own lives and the lives of others, differ significantly and that hard questions of decision making fall prey to that diversity. The fact that some are libertarian and others egalitarian is merely a symptom of this more

---

83. This contrast is reflected, respectively, in the work of Richard Kay on the one hand and Robert Bork (and Edwin Meese) on the other.
84. In this instance, the *former* view is held by Bork (and perhaps by Ely) while the latter is held by Kay.
85. Arguably these views are held respectively by Thomas Grey, Owen Fiss, and Ronald Dworkin. See, for example, T. Grey, "Do We Have an Unwritten Constitution?" (1975), 27 *Stanford L. R.* 703; O. Fiss, *supra* n. 68; and R. Dworkin, *supra* n. 4.
86. The tension between liberty and equality remains one of the principal conceptual ways in which alternative political theories are cast. It is possible to argue that this opposition is epiphenomenal and rests, in most cases, on deeper commitments to psychological, sociological, and methodological

encompassing and greater diversity.

(3) The distinction between interpretivists and non-interpretivists, apparently so clear, depends on a naive epistemology. It presupposes that one can, at will, assume either of two cognitive positions. The first is a value-neutral self-transposition into the attitudes and opinions of historical actors. The other is an appropriation of the values of one's culture and one's political tradition. Both are distinguishable from the identification and deploying of one's own personal values.[87]

A special contribution of hermeneutics is to show how fragile and dubious these distinctions are.[88] One's understanding of history is mediated through, and expressed within, the techniques of understanding—the categorical distinctions, the assumptions about value, etc.—that one employs as a particular participant in particular practices at a particular time in human history. Even if one can identify particular instances of tension between personal value preferences and a social consensus, or between a putative preference attributable to the founders and current attitudes, one cannot distinguish among these positions systematically. How one understands the past is colored by one's personal experiences. How one understands one's contemporaries affects one's decisions about values and goals.

The distinction between (b) and (b1) rests largely on a mistake about epistemology. The mistake is the following. Assume that one can distinguish (i) what the founders would have said about situation x, (ii) what a contemporary social consensus would maintain about situation x, and (iii) how Judge J would prefer to resolve situation x. To distinguish these conceptually is not the same as saying that judges either do or can follow one of the three methods of decision to the exclusion of the others. Indeed any judge's particular way of deciding will be affected by all three kinds of considerations. All three kinds affect each other in ways that only the foolhardy would claim to disentangle.

Equally foolhardy is the epistemological assumption that a judge can choose the perspective from which to decide a case. The particular way in which these three kinds of consideration color a judge's way of proceeding is neither volitional nor optional, no more volitional than the capacity to find a melody in a song or to notice a logical inconsistency or to avoid an on-coming truck in driving. All are aspects of participating in practices and all, while subject to reflection and conditioned by learning, are spontaneous responses to situations.[89]

The flaw, therefore, in much constitutional theory is represented by

assumptions made by the theorists who deploy various views about the relationship between liberty and equality. See, for example, A. Ryan, *The Idea of Freedom: Essays in Honour of Isaiah Berlin* (Oxford: Oxford University Press, 1979); A. Gutmann, *Liberal Equality* (Cambridge: Cambridge University Press, 1980); and S.M. McMurrin, *Liberty, Equality, and the Law: Selected Tanner Lectures on Moral Philosophy* (Salt Lake City: Univ. of Utah Press, 1987).

87. To be sure, the interpretivist rejects the distinction between the second and third of these stances, while the noninterpretivist defends it.
88. See D. Hoy, "Interpreting the Law: Hermeneutical and Poststructuralist Perspectives", (1985) 58 *Southern California L. R.* 135; T. Grey, "The Hermeneutics File" (1985), 58 *Southern California L. R.* 221; H-G. Gadamer, *supra* n. 20.
89. The last few paragraphs are to be taken as phenomenological and hermeneutical description. It is not clear to me how, other than through appeal to intuition, any theorist would "prove" these observations.

assumption (a). Judges are indeed constrained, but not by shared rules. They are constrained individually by a particular way of addressing and understanding interpretive questions and they are constrained collectively by the fact that the shared practice embraces a limited range of ways of proceeding. This limitation is mutually understood and recognized.

The idea that there must be a single set of shared rules, or license in the alternative, is dictated by the assumption that practices are like games. This paradigm, which *may*[90] work (as Kuhn suggests it does) for scientific investigation with its emphasis on progress and experimental manipulation of data to confirm or disconfirm hypotheses, works badly and distortingly when applied to deliberative practices, such as constitutional interpretation. But the assumption that license is the only alternative to shared rules runs deep in constitutional theory.

5. Conclusion

Wittgenstein says that philosophy describes our practices but does not change them.[91] Some have argued that the metaphor of games is well adapted to describing our practices, because it points us in the direction of eliciting and investigating the shared rules that characterize practices, rather than changing them. But the metaphor itself is coercive. Our more complex deliberative practices do not fit the simplicity of the metaphor and the attempt to find shared rules becomes, inevitably, a summons to change the practice, to harmonize the several ways of proceeding under a single paradigm. To heed this suggestion is to distort the phenomenon that one seeks to describe. Judges disagree, not only in results but in the ways in which they arrive at those results. It is not within the compass of jurisprudence to change this, nor is it within its power.

---

90. *Supra* n. 77.
91. *Supra* n. 42.

2

"Our Real Need": Not Explanation, But Education

Thomas D. Eisele

> The *preconceived idea* of crystalline purity can only be removed by turning our whole examination around. (One might say: the axis of reference of our examination must be rotated, but about the fixed point of our real need.)[1]

Wittgenstein wrote nothing on legal theory or law, so there is no obvious textual basis on which to draw possible connections between Wittgenstein and legal theory. And Wittgenstein abhorred theorizing in philosophy. So the odds are slim that Wittgenstein would have accommodated himself or his work to similar activity in the law. Where does this leave us?

At sea, which is where we normally are in life and, thus, where Wittgenstein wants us to recognize ourselves as being when doing philosophy too. But theory can disguise this fact from us, as it also can make us think that we have unrivalled powers of knowledge and understanding and explanation. Wittgenstein's criticism of theory, or the activity of theorizing, is meant to get us to see, and to acknowledge, our limits in this respect. But even though his terms and intent are mostly negative in tone and thrust, his criticism of theorizing has positive implications for how we should try to understand what we are doing and what we have done, including what we are doing and have done in the law. So, if understanding the law better is something that legal theory does or tries to do, and Wittgenstein's later work can help us understand the law better, then Wittgenstein's later philosophy is connected to the task set legal theory.

The truth of these claims for Wittgenstein's later philosophy and its relation to legal theory is, of course, a function of what one takes Wittgenstein's later philosophy to be, and of what one thinks legal theory can or should do. In this article, I offer an extended characterization of Wittgenstein's later philosophy in sections 1 and 2, and then I conclude with a brief example which may suggest ways in which we might relate Wittgenstein's later work to theorizing about the common law.

I appreciate Dennis Patterson's invitation to contribute to this symposium. This article surfaces more material from my unpublished doctoral dissertation, *Wittgenstein's Normative Naturalism: The Point of His Practice* (Department of Philosophy, University of Michigan, 1984), which I hope to publish in a substantially revised form. I continue to benefit from criticisms made by the members of my dissertation committee—Stephen L. White, Frithjof Bergmann, Ken Walton, and James Boyd White—and from research time and money granted me by the College of Law at Tennessee.

I dedicate this article to my daughter, Carolyn, who daily leads me to explore the necessities, and the rewards, of our shared lives.

1. L. Wittgenstein, *Philosophical Investigations*, G.E.M. Anscombe trans., (New York: Macmillan Co., 1968) 3d ed., §108a. All otherwise unidentified citations in the text are citations to this work. All emphases, oddities of punctuation, and British spellings in the quotations from Wittgenstein are in the original.

1. His Goal: Understanding What We Are Doing

A. The Mystery of the Ordinary

Wittgenstein's later philosophy is essentially concerned with understanding what we are doing when we act, speak, and think. These are topics for him because they are topics for philosophy, and he is interested in how and why philosophy has treated these matters. They are central to human life, and yet much about them remains a mystery to us, as inexplicable today as ever. I might put my first way of understanding Wittgenstein's later philosophy as follows: it attempts both to remove and to preserve the mystery that these matters hold for us. How does it do this?

Let us begin with a traditional philosophical problem, one that has become central to philosophy in the twentieth century, but also one that has been recognized and studied since the very inception of Western philosophy in Athens. John Searle asks, in the opening sentence of his book, *Speech Acts:* "How do words relate to the world?"[2] It is in the grip of such a question, be it asked for metaphysical or epistemological or ethical reasons, that a philosopher may start constructing various methods or ways of connecting words to the world. Typically, philosophers take one of two familiar routes. One is the causal or pseudo-scientific route, which attempts to account for the relations between words and world on a causal, scientific model, usually based upon some hypothetical explanation of how our minds work (e.g., brain states or processes). The second route is one that appeals to human conventions, attempting to explain the relations between words and the world in terms of conventions that we have posited or set up and that pre-determine, as it were, the agreement between words and world.

Wittgenstein chooses neither of these two traditional routes of explanation. Instead, his later philosophy can be understood as rejecting the desire to give, and the utility of giving, such reductionistic explanations of what we do. Their utility is nil in part because they reduce what we do and say and think to causal processes or to posited conventions, and this reduction falsifies the complicated reality of our lives. Reductionistic explanations based upon causes or conventions suggest that such matters are the foundations of our lives, but Wittgenstein does not think that we are so constituted. These misleading explanations work in effect by *substituting* the claimed causes or conventions for the surface phenomenon sought to be understood, reducing that phenomenon to these other things. This act of reduction assumes that we can best understand the studied phenomenon by learning what is beneath it, underlying it, either in terms of what caused it, or in terms of what conventions it might presuppose or imply, as though these matters were fundamental to the phenomenon, or foundational for it. But Wittgenstein suggests that this type of explanation changes not only the level at which we are considering the phenomenon in question; it in effect changes the phenomenon that we are investigating. However we try to understand these matters, whatever way

---

2. J. Searle, *Speech Acts* (Cambridge: Cambridge Univ. Press, 1969) at 3.

in which we try to bring ourselves to grips with them, it is with them—and not some reduced or skeletal construction of them—with which we must come to grips.

Even more important, however, than the disutility of reductionistic explanations (which defeat our real need, according to Wittgenstein), is our willingness to invent and entertain them as satisfying answers to our problems. This willingness on our part reveals to Wittgenstein another problem, and it is a problem with us. He asks: Why are we so inclined, so prepared, first to seek, then to fashion, and finally to accept these reductionistic explanations? Wittgenstein intends his later philosophy to fight this human proclivity for theoretical, reductionistic explanations (a proclivity neither stupid nor easy to extirpate), and his later philosophy does so not by denying their attractiveness to us, nor by denying the roles and functions they play in our lives. Rather, his philosophy fights this human proclivity for theory and explanation by making this same human tendency conscious to ourselves, so that we then can see that it is *this* that drives so much of our philosophical claims to know. Wittgenstein brings to consciousness not only the fact that it is we who desire these explanations—and hence that we are the ones for whom they are invented or constructed—but also the fact that we need not construct them. In other words, Wittgenstein brings to consciousness the fact that we desire something that we do not need (if we accept Wittgenstein's identification of that which is "our real need"). His therapy attempts to dissolve our desire.

Applying this general insight to a particular case, we might say, for example, that we do not need to construct theories of how words relate to the world, for the simple reason that we already have the data and phenomena that we need in order to understand how words relate to the world. Why construct a theory of this relationship (or series of relationships) when we already have the relationship or series present (in some sense) to ourselves? I do not say that this question has no respectable response on behalf of the theorist. Only, it is not obvious what a respectable response might be. So simply by raising this plain question, Wittgenstein begins to force us—if its revelatory power is what he takes it to be—to question responses and inclinations and proclivities we have never before doubted. Then we may begin to wonder, as Wittgenstein wants and encourages us to do, just what exactly our construction of theories and reductive explanations is in service of. As Stanley Cavell puts it, "If there is such a theory [to be had or gained,] it lies in the criteria themselves, or they are what any theory will have to explain."[3]

We already know—don't we?—that our words do normally, and naturally, connect with or relate to the world. If we admit or acknowledge this to ourselves, then we need to undertake two Wittgensteinian projects. First, we must activate our repressed or buried knowledge of *how* our words relate to the world, making it live again to ourselves, bringing it to consciousness again.[4] This becomes possible as a task or project only upon our recognition

---

3. S. Cavell, *The Claim of Reason* (Oxford: Clarendon Press, 1979) at 90.
4. I also study this buried or repressed knowledge in the law (and its relation to Wittgenstein's later philosophy) in my article, "The Activity of Being a Lawyer: The Imaginative Pursuit of Implications and Possibilities", (1987) 54 *Tenn. L. Rev.* 345, 350-351. And, in another article, I say more about how

that, up until now, our knowledge of such matters *has* been repressed. Once we reactivate this knowledge, or re-deploy it, then perhaps we shall learn to recognize how in fact words do manage to connect with or relate to the world. This activation entails our learning to see that—and how—*we* connect and relate our words with and to the world. So this knowledge is a kind of knowledge of human action and activity—practical knowledge of how we act—and, since it is ourselves who are acting and whom we are studying, it is simultaneously a kind of self-knowledge—a knowledge of who we are and what we are doing when we so act.

Second, we must gain some perspective on this plethora of phenomena, allowing our singular investigations to accrete or otherwise to settle and collect into some coherent capacity to respond to the problems bothering us. This capacity may develop out of our growing sense of the whole, the whole way we act and speak and think—from one perspective, we call this whole our "language", and from another our "culture" (but I do not take these two candidates to exhaust the possibilities).[5] Such a capacity or sense is not apt to be fully articulate or articulable, but it is something upon which we can call in our moments of doubt or panic—namely, exactly in those moments paradigmatic of philosophy and its questions or problems, which produce our quandaries and perplexities.

Gaining this perspective and cultivating this capacity or sense are what Wittgenstein calls our being able to gain a "perspicuous representation" of the ways in which we use words.

> A main source of our failure to understand is that we do not *command a clear view* of the use of our words.—Our grammar is lacking in this sort of perspicuity. A perspicuous representation produces just that understanding which consists in 'seeing connexions'. Hence the importance of finding and inventing *intermediate cases.*
>
> The concept of a perspicuous representation is of fundamental significance for us. It earmarks the form of account we give, the way we look at things. ...
> [§122]

We gain perspective on our use of words (and on our activities generally) not by extracting ourselves from our speech acts and activities, but rather exactly by re-immersing ourselves within them. Wittgenstein's suggestion

---

Wittgenstein, through his use of stories, tries to get us to reactivate such knowledge. *See* Eisele, "Wittgenstein's Instructive Narratives: Leaving the Lessons Latent", (March/June, 1990) 40 *J. Legal Educ.* 77.

5. Michael Oakeshott well-expresses the holistic sense I am after:
    [P]olitical education is not merely a matter of coming to understand a tradition, it is learning how to participate in a conversation: it is at once initiation into an inheritance in which we have a life interest, and the exploration of its intimations. There will always remain something of a mystery about how a tradition of political behaviour is learned, and perhaps the only certainty is that there is no point at which learning it can properly be said to begin. The politics of a community are not less individual (and not more so) than its language, and they are learned and practised in the same manner. We do not begin to learn our native language by learning the alphabet, or by learning its grammar; we do not begin by learning words, but words in use; we do not begin (as we begin in reading) with what is easy and go on to what is more difficult; we do not begin at school, but in the cradle; and what we say springs always from our manner of speaking. And this is true also of our political education; ... .
    M. Oakeshott, "Political Education", in *Rationalism in Politics and Other Essays* (New York: Basic Books, 1962), at 129.

here takes a metaphorical form, as though in gaining a perspective on language and thought we are learning our way around a web or maze. Language, he says, can be thought of as "an ancient city: a maze of little streets and squares" (§18) through which we find (or lose) our ways; and we also can conceive of it as "a labyrinth of paths" which we can "approach from *one* side and know [our] way about," but if we "approach the same place from another side ... [we may] no longer know [our] way about" (§203). Then gaining a perspicuous view of our uses of words can be thought of as mapping the ways and means of our *polis* of language, our community of speech and thought.

> [T]he very nature of the investigation ... compels us to travel over a wide field of thought criss-cross in every direction.—The philosophical remarks in this book are, as it were, a number of sketches of landscapes which were made in the course of these long and involved journeyings.
> [p. v b]

As we journey to and fro in working our way out of the particular philosophical quandaries in which we find ourselves at any specific point in space and time, our goal is not that of some passive view gained from on-high, but rather a heightened sense of our resources and capacities gained by renewing our acquaintance with them—things which as speakers and thinkers and actors we have always possessed in some sense but which require revivifying in our minds. The result of such journeyings is not a theory that explains our linguistic practice, but instead a renewed acquaintance with our linguistic ways, a heightened appreciation of their advantages and disadvantages, their benefits and costs, their values and prejudices, their powers and limitations and conditions. This amounts to a further education in our own practical mastery of words, the world, and ourselves, and it cannot be complete or therapeutic without an acknowledgment of the limits and conditions within which such mastery takes place, finds a home.

B. *Locating Our Limits and Conditions By Exploring Our Criteria and Grammar*

This may sound good in theory, but how does it work in practice? It is Wittgenstein's faith that our lives of practice and theory come together in the convening of what he calls our "criteria" and "grammar", the specific phenomena most often collected for study by his philosophical method (which I call his "normative naturalism"). Look at the following two sections from *Philosophical Investigations*, which pose questions similar to Searle's and also illustrate Wittgenstein's normative naturalism.

> What is the relation between name and thing named?—Well, what *is* it? Look at language-game (2) or at another one: there you can see the sort of thing this relation consists in. This relation may also consist, among many other things, in the fact that hearing the name calls before our mind the picture of what is named; and it also consists, among other things, in the name's being written on the thing named or being pronounced when that thing is pointed at.
> [§37]

How do words *refer* to sensations?—There doesn't seem to be any problem here; don't we talk about sensations every day, and give them names? But how is the connexion between the name and the thing named set up? This question is the same as: how does a human being learn the meaning of the names of sensations?—of the word "pain" for example. Here is one possibility: words are connected with the primitive, the natural, expressions of the sensation and used in their place. A child has hurt himself and he cries; and then adults talk to him and teach him exclamations and, later, sentences. They teach the child new pain-behaviour. [§244 a]

In both sections, the opening sentence voices a philosophical question akin to Searle's, a question which is meant by the philosopher who raises it to get to the bottom of things, or to the heart of things, for some particular aspect of our way of acting and speaking. Immediately, this philosophical question is responded to by a voice that, while taking seriously this philosophical question, is not captivated by philosophy. This responsive voice is independent of philosophy in the sense that it distances itself from the traditional philosophical mood of wonder; instead, this voice responds by entertaining the question posed by philosophy, but it does so by taking the question in a matter-of-fact mood of ordinary, down-to-earth, clearheaded thinking: "Well, what *is* it [the relation between name and thing named]? Look at language-game (2) or at another one: there you can see the sort of thing this relation consists in" (§37). And: "There doesn't seem to be any problem here; don't we talk about sensations every day, and give them names?" (§244 a) This voice says that naming something or referring to sensations is an ordinary activity that we do "every day" in our lives and language, so there ought to be no mystery about it. We engage in naming, we incorporate it into our everyday lives, making it a part of them and ourselves; we ought to know all about it.

Well, yes and no; we do and we don't. We do talk about sensations daily, refer to them daily, and in this sense they are an ordinary, everyday part of our experience. But, on the other hand, we don't fully understand what we do in our lives. Much of what we do every day is oblivious to itself, as though we sleep-walk through life, unconscious to our actions and activities. We simply do what we do and don't give it a second thought: it is—or has become—second nature to us. So, to *do* these actions daily, even to do them well on a daily basis, is not the same as knowing or understanding that which we do (even if it is done well); the mere doing does not guarantee knowledge or understanding of what is done or how it is accomplished. Knowledge or understanding of the kind desired requires something else, something like reflection on the activity done, giving it the second thought it deserves. We may do this if we realize that what has become second nature to us still is something what we have *acquired*, and hence is something that we might not otherwise have done, or might have done in a different way. So the challenge here is to bring all of this—what we have done and said, our actions and activities, and their imagined alternatives—to consciousness, to conscious inspection and reflection; then, perhaps we shall see what it is that we are doing and how we manage to do it.

Wittgenstein addresses this felt need in the following:

> If it is asked: "How do sentences manage to represent?" —the answer might be: "Don't you know? You certainly see it, when you use them." For nothing is concealed.
>
> How do sentences do it?—Don't you know? For nothing is hidden.
>
> But given this answer: "But you know how sentences do it, for nothing is concealed" one would like to retort "Yes, but it all goes by so quick, and I should like to see it as it were laid open to view."
> [§435]

It all goes by so quick ...; we should like to slow it down. Wittgenstein grants us our wish: he slows it down. Not by trying to slow down life, or life's activities—he knows that that would be impossible; as well, it might falsify the phenomenon under study. Rather, he slows it down by taking it apart piece by piece and examining it at our leisure. That is, he slows it down by slowing *us* down: making us stop and think and look and listen.

> Don't say: "There *must* be something common, or they would not be called 'games'"—but *look and see* whether there is anything common to all.—For if you look at them you will not see something that is common to *all*, but similarities, relationships, and a whole series of them at that. To repeat: don't think, but look! ...
> [§66 a]
>
> [W]e must learn to understand what it is that opposes such an examination of details in philosophy.
> [§52 b]
>
> One cannot guess how a word functions. One has to *look at* its use and learn from that.
>
> But the difficulty is to remove the prejudice which stands in the way of doing this. It is not a *stupid* prejudice.
> [§340]

We know "how sentences manage to represent" (§435 a), and we know "the relation between name and thing named" (§37), and we know "how words refer to sensations" (§244 a)—we know all of these things in the sense that we know *how to do* all of these things with words (i.e., we can do all of them in our language). But we may not know how they work, or what the conditions for their effectiveness may be, and the like, because we have not yet looked and seen what we are doing when and where and as we do these things with words. So Wittgenstein gets us, goads us, to look and see.

We have all of the information we need in front of us, or retrievable to us, in our ordinary experience and actions—"For nothing is concealed. ... For nothing is hidden" (§435 a,b). We all are members of the same community, we all speak the same language. This means that we all are practical masters (to greater or lesser extents) of the same institution or technique.

> To obey a rule, to make a report, to give an order, to play a game of chess, are *customs* (uses, institutions).
>
> To understand a sentence means to understand a language. To understand a language means to be master of a technique.
> [§199 b-c]

And we did not gain admittance to this institution, we did not become initiates of it, we did not master it, by learning anything in relation to the scientific causes or human conventions underlying it. Rather, our practical mastery of the institution and technique of language—of relating words to the world (and the world to words)—consists in knowing our ways around this enormously complicated and intricate form of life, being able to negotiate its terms and passages and conditions, knowing how to call upon and invoke (or how to withhold appropriately) words made available to us by our language in the contexts and circumstances presented us in this world. These anticipated and ensuing norms of our natural language (which Wittgenstein calls our "criteria" and "grammar") instantiate and inscribe our linguistic practice. They are that which we need to know better, that of which we need to get a more perspicuous view.

Look again at sections 37 and 244,[6] which deal with "the relation between name and thing named" (§37) and how "words refer to sensations" (§244 a). As an instance of the naming relation, Wittgenstein says: "Look at language-game (2) or at another one: there you can see the sort of thing this relation consists in" (§37). The "sort of thing" a naming relation "consists in"—its grammar or criteria—is now directly in view. The grammar of naming and names consists in the following facts, among other things: that, e.g., when someone is confused about what a particular thing is called, he or she asks its name; that when asked the name of a thing, we respond by giving it (rather than by giving a definition of it, or by drawing a picture of it); that when we want something brought to us, we call for it by name, which we accomplish by calling out its name; and so on and so forth. These are among the grammatical connections and criterial relations in which naming consists. "This relation may also consist, among many other things, in the fact that hearing the name calls before our mind the picture of what is named; and it also consists, among other things, in the name's being written on the thing named or being pronounced when that thing is pointed at" (§37). No *one* of these relations is necessary or sufficient just anywhere just anytime to *be*, to amount to, a naming relation; but naming consists of these connections and relations, at different times in different situations or circumstances.

The general moral that Wittgenstein draws from these specific instances is that, although their characteristic criteria and grammatical connections can and do vary, they still vary with the circumstances. So that an appreciation of the circumstances can help us to see which criteria may fit where, and what grammatical connections may become relevant when. And, despite this apparent indeterminacy, the control and guidance afforded us and our words

---

6. *See* text at 9-10, *supra.*

by these criterial and grammatical means suggest that not just anything can be said anywhere and still be meaningful or intelligible. There are limits. (They include our criteria and our grammar.)

For all their variety or variation, in the proper contexts or circumstances, our criteria provide us with our ordinary means of describing phenomena and objects and experiences and relations (etc.) as and where and when we find or have or possess them. In this respect, criteria relate us to these things, and they do so in virtue of their being "characteristic" of the things for which they are criteria. This is true in two senses. They are characteristic in that they are our normal or normative signs for identifying these things; and they are characteristic in that they serve to characterize—they function by describing—these things.[7]

For Wittgenstein, criteria provide the natural or normal or necessary means by which, and terms in which, we relate ourselves to the objects and phenomena and institutions and activities and experiences (etc.) of our world. We identify things as they are within certain contexts or specific circumstances on the basis of, or by means of, our criteria. The identity of a thing is what it "consists in," and what it consists in is a matter of the criterial relations and grammatical connections that it has with other things (including people). My understanding of this central aspect of Wittgenstein's later philosophy is that criteria are those means that we have of relating ourselves to things in the world, whereas grammar (as he calls it) or grammatical connections relate these things amongst themselves (constituting a grammatical system, something that we call a "language"). Or, perhaps a better way to put this distinction is as follows. Criteria illustrate that aspect of language that speaks to how *we* use language to relate it (and ourselves) to the world. Grammar, on the other hand, traces the internal connections between or among things (terms) within the language itself, or within the world itself (as a coherent system, or a system of coherencies), without making explicit reference to ourselves (although implicitly we—and our uses of language—are always there, embedded within the system, just as it is embedded within us, our community, and our world).

C. Grammar as the Network Our Lives Form

While our real need is to gain an understanding of what we do and say and think, such a need cannot be fulfilled by offering causal or conventional explanations. Here we must appreciate, among other things, the kind of problems posed in philosophy. These problems put into question matters that we rarely if ever otherwise doubt, things that we ordinarily take for granted. The subject-matter of philosophy is not in this respect esoteric or exotic; philosophy simply means to examine and explore, relentlessly but not uncharitably, the ordinary matters that our lives comprise, the mundane bases of our mundane lives. The surprise is that philosophy finds the results of its examination and exploration surprising, and we find them puzzling, even

---

7. *See also* Eisele, "The Activity of Being a Lawyer", *supra* n. 4, at 352.

unsettling. It is this ability of philosophy to find our ordinary lives interesting, exciting, and surprising, which Wittgenstein captures and cultivates in his later philosophy:

> Don't take it as a matter of course, but as a remarkable fact, that pictures and fictitious narratives give us pleasure, occupy our minds.
>
> ("Don't take it as a matter of course" means: find it surprising, as you do some things which disturb you. Then the puzzling aspect of the latter will disappear, by your accepting this fact as you do the other.)
> [§524 a-b]

It is Wittgenstein's ability to comprehend the paradoxical ordinariness and extraordinariness (or romance) of our lives—a capacity analogous to Keats' "negative capability"[8]—that makes me say that Wittgenstein's later philosophy attempts both to remove and to preserve the mystery that these matters hold for us.[9]

Wittgenstein recognizes that philosophy makes that which is ordinary, a matter of course, seem foreign to us, or suddenly distant from us. It dislocates or disorients us, making us feel as though our ordinary lives are strange, as though they were not ours but rather someone else's, about which we know little or nothing. (In a sense, this can be true.) And then, in the grip of such doubt, we are apt to feel the overwhelming need to know, which we interpret as the need to explain (to ourselves as well as anyone else).

He does not deny the reality of our confusion here; our confusion is genuine, not spurious. Unlike the Logical Positivists in this regard, Wittgenstein recognizes philosophical problems as real, not pseudo-problems. They evidence a real need, which is a need for clarity, or clarification. But we gain clarification not by constructing a scientific theory of causes or by offering an explanation based upon conventions, but rather by describing and imagining and otherwise investigating the facts and phenomena and categories and criteria that constitute our experience and practice, our way of living, seeing, speaking, thinking and acting. So we address our real need (as Wittgenstein puts it in the motto to my article) by turning our whole examination around, transforming it from one of theoretical explanation to one of descriptive and imaginative education. We rotate our work "about the fixed point of our real need" (§108 a)—which is clarification, leading to understanding.

Since a philosophical question arises in terms of (and is posed in) our everyday language, we ought to be able to answer or solve it in the same language, without having to appeal to some other discourse (e.g., a scientific one). Another way of putting this point is as follows: If the problem arises within the medium of ordinary language, then it is (in part at least) a problem of (or with) this same medium. We do not solve *this* problem if we change our method to that of another medium or language; instead, such a shift only serves to convert or transform the problem into something cognizable in the substituted medium.

---

8. J. Keats, *The Selected Letters of John Keats,* L. Trilling ed., (Garden City, N.Y.: Doubleday & Co., 1956), at 103. *See also* Eisele, "Review Essay/Dworkin's 'Full Political Theory of Law'", (Summer/Fall, 1988), 7 *Crim. Just. Ethics* 49, at 64-65.

9. *See* text at 6, *supra.*

When I talk about language (words, sentences, etc.) I must speak the language of every day. Is this language somehow too coarse and material for what we want to say? *Then how is another one to be constructed?*—And how strange that we should be able to do anything at all with the one we have!

In giving explanations I already have to use language full-blown (not some sort of preparatory, provisional one); this by itself shews that I can adduce only exterior facts about language.

Yes, but then how can these explanations satisfy us?—Well, your very questions were framed in this language; they had to be expressed in this language, if there was anything to ask!
[§120 a-c]

Our practical mastery of our language enables us to ask these questions; it also should enable us to answer them (if they are answerable). But then how are we to gain the perspective or purchase we need, on the things we do and say, in order to understand them?

For the phenomena and experiences and activities and media and institutions that bother us (at least, that bother us philosophically, or while we are doing philosophy), Wittgenstein indicates that "our real need" is to understand them as they are in life. Their living identity for him is bound up not with their underlying causal or conventional aspect (if such they have), but rather in their interrelatedness with all of the other phenomena and experiences and activities and media and institutions that constitute our lives and our world. Bishop Butler said, "Everything is what it is, and not another thing."[10] This rings true as well for Wittgenstein, but I think that he would wish to amplify it by saying that everything is what it is only in view of everything else with which it relates and to which it is connected. I take this to be the moral of his obscure remarks about grammar and essence and identity: *"Essence* is expressed by grammar" (§371); "Grammar tells what kind of object anything is. ..." (§373). Identity of this sort is based upon the criterial relations and grammatical connections each thing has or may have in our lives and language; the vision is frankly holistic.

In pursuing the linked notions of criterial relations and grammatical connections through his later philosophy, Wittgenstein enacts a reversal of philosophical direction. We must turn "our whole examination around," from one pitched on the false hope of transforming philosophy into either a natural or a social science, to one pitched on the true belief that philosophy transforms itself as it renews itself, in its continued faithfulness of response to the ever-present, ever-changing, gnawing questions put to humans in philosophy as it is, one of the humanities and no kind of science. This humanity studies humanity as and where and when it finds it in this world. Then where and how does Wittgenstein's later philosophy find humanity in this world? In the network or fabric of relations and connections (he sometimes calls it a "maze" or a "labyrinth" [see §18; §203]) formed by the lives and world we have woven and continue to weave through our activities, linguistic and otherwise.

---

10. Quoted in G. E. Moore, *Principia Ethica* (Cambridge: Cambridge Univ. Press, 1902), at ii.

D. The Allure of Theory

Looking for some underlying causal connection or some hidden human convention is not necessary in order to understand our linguistic activities. Rather, we need to look at, perhaps to rearrange or otherwise to organize, the materials and actions and experience and information we already have at hand. "The problems are solved, not by giving new information, but by arranging what we have always known" (§109). We need somehow to gain a synoptic view of what we do and say and think.

What is problematic for Wittgenstein—and that to which he tries in his later philosophy to make us sensitive as well—is the fact that usually we do not proceed in the way he suggests (which he sees as one natural way for us to behave). Much more often, we proceed in another way, which may be even more natural to us: we resort or retreat to theory, concocting theoretical explanations. Yet in these very situations, resorting to theory is not helpful, is not an aid to understanding; rather, it is the abnegation of understanding. We are substituting theory for understanding. Why?

Wittgenstein never says, to my knowledge, that all theories are wrong, or that all theorizing is a misleading activity. How could he (or anyone else) say such a thing? Saying such would only amount to more theoretical babbling— illustrating his true meaning, which is that theorizing allows us to speak in unserious or inauthentic ways, ignoring or forgetting the inconvenient facts of our linguistic practices and of our circumstances at large. This is one way of saying that theorizing can take place (and too often does take place) in the absence of any acquaintance with or recollection of the data and phenomena which the theorizing is intended to explain. This amounts to a kind of arrogance in our thought and speech, which vanity Wittgenstein is committed to opposing in all its forms.[11] Not in the false hope of ridding ourselves of the urge or temptation to theorize—that would be like hoping to rid ourselves of original sin. But, instead, in the sure and certain hope that we may inoculate ourselves against the allure of theory by acknowledging, again and again, its attraction for us, and yet bringing home to ourselves, our consciousness, the bitter knowledge that it often seduces and abandons our minds without advancing them to any insight. Theory can be empty. And theoretical speech can consist of pictures that we uncritically accept or follow. Then what Wittgenstein wants us to do is to subject these pictures, our theories, to criticism and scrutiny; he doesn't ask us to abandon them.

> The great difficulty here is not to represent the matter as if there were something one *couldn't* do. As if there really were an object, from which I derive its description, but I were unable to shew it to anyone.—And the best that I can propose is that we should yield to the temptation to use this picture, but then investigate how the *application* of the picture goes.
> [§374]

---

11. I say more about Wittgenstein's later philosophy and its negative application to legal theorizing, in my commentary, "Hegelian Vanity, Common Law Humility: On Legal Theory, Its Expression and Its Criticism", (1989) 10 *Cardozo L. Rev.* 915, 925-947. It is equally important to me, however, to indicate the positive work that can be done from a Wittgensteinian perspective in trying to gain some overview of the law and our activities within it. I intend my remarks in the second section of this article to begin to meet this need.

This is the only way to wean ourselves from this narcotic, and it requires some strong medicine (which Wittgenstein offers us as therapy), as well as some abstemiousness on our part. "And we may not advance any kind of theory. There must not be anything hypothetical in our considerations. We must do away with all *explanation*, and description alone must take its place. And this description gets its light, that is to say its purpose—from the philosophical problems" (§109).

This does not mean that theory and explanation have no place in our lives or our world, or in our philosophies. Instead, it means that we must ensure against theory and explanation being given or ceded more of a place in our lives or our philosophies than they rightfully (i.e., ordinarily, normally) have. The threat is that theory and explanation (as philosophical techniques or tools, as ways of understanding) may take over our lives and our minds, capturing our imaginations to the detriment of the rest of our capacities and techniques, our routes to understanding. It is in this sense that I take Wittgenstein's closing remark in section 109 to be expressing a cautionary tale for philosophy and philosophers: "Philosophy is a battle against the bewitchment of our intelligence by means of language"; in particular, I take it, by means of theoretical language, or language used in theorizing.

For Wittgenstein, the battle is joined at the level of description, and not that of explanation, because we do not yet understand where we are or what we do; these are matters to be investigated, not issues on which we can hold forth dispositively and definitively. And our offering of explanations *at this point* in our investigations is worthless. Worse than worthless, really, because the offer itself is misleading; it holds out false hope of clarity when in fact we live in confusion. To speak in terms of theories or explanations allows us to imagine that we know when in fact we do not know. It allows us to imagine, as Stanley Cavell puts it, that "we have explanations where in fact we lack them."[12] We do not know what we think we know. And yet, it also is true for Wittgenstein that, in a certain respect, we know more than we think we know.

Take, for example, causal reductionism and conventional reductionism. These explanations proceed on a theoretical level, one that presupposes a certain structural or underlying "crystalline purity" (§108 a) to our lives which those lives simply do not have. In the context of these two theoretical and reductionistic explanations, such a pure structure would be either a structure of causes or one of conventions. But what do we know of any such structure of causes or conventions? I believe that they are invented for the purpose of trying to explain the problems bothering us, trying to answer our need to know, to understand these matters. But they only have the form or structure of explanations because of the apparent vacuum in our ordinary lives, by which I mean our apparent ignorance or lack of any ordinary explanations for these matters that puzzle and perplex us. In our ordinary lives and world, while causes and conventions may certainly be a part of our experience, I doubt very much that their theoretical structure or explanatory nature is. Instead, the

---

12. S. Cavell, "Knowing and Acknowledging", in *Must We Mean What We Say?* (New York: Charles Scribner's Sons, 1969), at 258. *See also* Eisele, "Hegelian Vanity, Common Law Humility", *id,* at 928 & n. 47.

causes and conventions we experience are a part of our phenomenological lives only in the sense that anything is a part of those lives: they help to compose the fabric or weave of our experience, which Henry James calls "an immense sensibility". Our experience, he says, comprises "a kind of huge spider-web of the finest silken threads suspended in the chamber of consciousness, and catching every airborne particle in its tissue".[13]

Our lives and our world (by which I mean, the phenomena and experiences and activities and media and institutions that constitute them) *do* have a structure, *do* have a pattern—without a doubt. And Wittgenstein never denies this. In fact, he insists upon nothing less. But, if we want to understand the phenomena bothering us, then we need to look at and investigate *these* phenomena. For Wittgenstein, to see them in and for themselves is never to see them isolated or divorced from ordinary life; it is rather always to see the phenomena *in practice*, as thcy take place in our daily lives (i.e., as a part of our practices). In Wittgenstein's later philosophy, we continually proceed on the practical level of our ordinary language and everyday understanding; for him, it is quite sufficient (because ordinary language is the medium, the living system, within which our understanding takes its bearings and its terms of understanding).

The structure of our lives and language is not one of "crystalline purity"; rather, it is all the kind of tangled, complicated, intertwined affair meant to be illuminated and elicited by Wittgenstein's constant harping on and appealing to the "criteria" and "grammar" and "language-games" and "forms of life" that we have and possess and enact (and reject ...). The structure and coherence of our lives and language consist, *there*, in these interrelations and connections of phenomena. *There* is where and when and why and how our words relate to the world. And these emphatic demonstratives do not point to a structure of theory ("crystalline purity"); instead, they suggest that these are eminently practical matters, and hence that their structure (such as it is) is that of a practice, constituted by that which we in fact and in life do (and say and think ...). And despite its complexity, its terribly knotted and nested density, this practical structure of our lives and language is knowable and traceable by us. To make it known to us, and to trace it intelligibly (without falsifying or simplifying it), are the goal of Wittgenstein's later philosophy.

2. His Method: Philosophy as Educative Ethnography

A. *Is Wittgenstein an Anthropologist?*

Some commentators have said that Wittgenstein's later philosophy, in its concern for describing and assessing how we think and act and speak, is anthropological, even anthropocentric. One instance of this occurs in a very good introduction to Wittgenstein's work, David Pears' book in the Modern

---

13. H. James, "The Art of Fiction", in *Partial Portraits* (Ann Arbor: Univ. of Michigan Press, 1970), at 388. *See also* Eisele, "The Activity of Being a Lawyer", *supra* n. 4, at 358-359; and J. White, *The Legal Imagination* (Boston: Little, Brown & Co., 1973), at 48-49.

Masters series.[14] There Pears describes the transition in Western philosophical practice since Kant as a "shift toward anthropocentrism,"[15] and he claims that Wittgenstein's work, both early and late, contributes to this shift. Pears goes on to say that the later philosophy of Wittgenstein has a "positivistic" tenor, in that its method for understanding the world and our place within it "take[s] a psychological or anthropological form [often expressed by the proposition]: 'That is how people are.'"[16] Such philosophical anthropocentrism suggests, he claims, that "human nature provides a sufficiently firm basis"[17] for our philosophical needs.

This description usefully highlights a definite aspect of Wittgenstein's philosophical method worth emphasizing, but it also conflates this aspect with another aspect that needs to be kept distinct. The aspect of Wittgenstein's philosophical practice that I find to be truly anthropological is voiced in his frequent injunction to imagine strange people or "tribes" who do things quite differently from the way we do things. Here are several examples of this anthropological bent:

> Let us imagine a language for which the description given by Augustine is right. The language is meant to serve for communication between a builder A and an assistant B. A is building with building-stones: there are blocks, pillars, slabs and beams. B has to pass the stones, and in the order in which A needs them. For this purpose they use a language consisting of the words "block", "pillar", "slab", "beam". A calls them out;—B brings the stone which he has learnt to bring at such-and-such a call.—Conceive this as a complete primitive language.
> [§2 b]

> We could imagine that the language of §2 [above] was the *whole* language of A and B; even the whole language of a tribe. The children are brought up to perform *these* actions, to use *these* words as they do so, and to react in *this* way to the words of others.
> [§6 a]

> Suppose you came as an explorer into an unknown country with a language quite strange to you. In what circumstances would you say that the people there gave orders, understood them, obeyed them, rebelled against them, and so on?
> [§206 b]

> Let us imagine that the people in that country carried on the usual human activities and in the course of them employed, apparently, an articulate language. If we watch their behaviour we find it intelligible, it seems 'logical'. But when we try to learn their language we find it impossible to do so. For there is no regular connexion between what they say, the sounds they make, and their actions; but still these sounds are not superfluous, for if we gag one of the people, it has the same consequences as with us; without the sounds their actions fall into confusion—as I feel like putting it.

> Are we to say that these people have a language: orders, reports, and the rest?

---

14. D. Pears, *Ludwig Wittgenstein* (New York: Viking Press, 1970) (reissued with a new preface and identical pagination 1986). *See also* S. Cavell, *supra* n. 3, at 118-119.

15. *Id*. at 25.

16. *Id*. at 28.

17. *Id*.

There is not enough regularity for us to call it "language".
[§207 a-c]

Imagine people who could only think aloud. (As there are people who can only
read aloud.)
[§331]

All of these sections ask us to imagine other people, some quite different
from ourselves, who act in very different ways than we do. Then Wittgenstein
often (but not invariably) follows these descriptions by asking us to think
what we would say about such people, or such behavior, usually along some
particular dimension or criterion of assessment. Is it a language? Is it a rule?
Could we learn it or follow it? Do they calculate? Are they thinking?
    Here Wittgenstein is testing and prodding the limits of our understanding
of others, looking at the limits of our concepts and criteria in terms of how we
would apply them to others who differ from us in certain ways. What he
wants to know (and what he wants to get us to ask ourselves) is, How can we
relate ourselves to these others? *Can* we relate ourselves to them; or, instead,
do we not have that capacity? This becomes a question of how we are to
take these people—or what we are to take them to be (and to be doing). This
is not primarily a matter of our imaginative ability to empathize with them, to
project ourselves into another's shoes or skin and to see what it looks and
feels like from that position (although this capacity for empathetic
identification or projection seems to play a part in this conceptual investigation). More to the point, Wittgenstein wants to know whether we can subsume
these others under our concepts and criteria as they stand, or as they stand
stretched or complicated by his anthropological cases. Thus, he is asking us to
question what *our* position is with respect to these people. Can we understand
them *as* people, as significant others *to us*. Can we understand them from
this distance (our distance, our vantage point)? Can we feel at home with
them? How are they strange or foreign to us, how familiar or intelligible? He
asks us, in other words, to assess their position in terms of—and from the perspective of—our own, and to gauge the distance, or proximity, between the
two. This taking-the-measure-of-the-distance-between ourselves and others
(as a group or society or "tribe") seems to me to be a genuinely anthropological aspect of Wittgenstein's later philosophy.
    But in a number of other sections of the *Investigations*, Wittgenstein's
emphasis is importantly different from the one described above. He does not
ask us to imagine others at all, but rather *ourselves*, acting either as we normally do or else differently than we normally do. Here he is asking us to
investigate (from the inside) the actualities and possibilities of our own lives
and language *as applied to us*, either as we currently live our lives and speak
our language, or as we may wish or imagine ourselves living and speaking.
What he wants us to discover here are the possibilities and necessities of our
own concepts and criteria, which are revealed when we turn these concepts
and criteria on ourselves. Wittgenstein's idea is to see what capacity for projection and room for play, what flexibility and tension and rigidity, our con-

cepts and criteria have in characterizing ourselves at home, in familiar surroundings (if not always in the presence of familiar behavior).

As I read this second set of sections, there is no distance between *self and other* being anthropologically measured or tested. Rather, what is taking place is a measure or test of the actual distance that we travel, or the potential distance that we may travel, under our own gaze or gauge, in applying our concepts and criteria to actions and thoughts and words that, if not ours presently, are candidates for becoming ours. This investigation traces a trajectory *from a present self to a future self* (possibly a better self, certainly a different self). Here are some samples of this second kind of investigation:

> Suppose someone points to a vase and says "Look at that marvelous blue—the shape isn't the point."—Or: "Look at the marvelous shape—the colour doesn't matter." Without doubt you will do something *different* when you act upon these two invitations. But do you always do the *same* thing when you direct your attention to the colour? Imagine various different cases. To indicate a few: ...
> [§33 b]

> ... Imagine that you were supposed to paint a particular colour "C", which was the colour that appeared when the chemical substances X and Y combined.—Suppose that the colour struck you as brighter on one day than on another; would you not sometimes say: "I must be wrong, the colour is certainly the same as yesterday"? This shews that we do not always resort to what memory tells us as the verdict of the highest court of appeal.
> [§56]

> I say "There is a chair". What if I go up to it, meaning to fetch it, and it suddenly disappears from sight?—"So it wasn't a chair, but some kind of illusion".—But in a few moments we see it again and are able to touch it and so on.—"So the chair was there after all and its disappearance was some kind of illusion".—But suppose that after a time it disappears again—or seems to disappear. What are we to say now? Have you rules ready for such cases—rules saying whether one may use the word "chair" to include this kind of thing? But do we miss them when we use the word "chair"; and are we to say that we do not really attach any meaning to this word, because we are not equipped with rules for every possible application of it?
> [§80]

> Would it not be possible for us, however, to calculate as we actually do (all agreeing, and so on), and still at every step to have a feeling of being guided by the rules as by a spell, feeling astonishment at the fact that we agreed? (We might give thanks to the Deity for our agreement.)
> [§234]

> Look at a stone and imagine it having sensations.—One says to oneself: How could one so much as get the idea of ascribing a *sensation* to a *thing*? One might as well ascribe it to a number!—And now look at a wriggling fly and at once these difficulties vanish and pain seems able to get a foothold here, where before everything was, so to speak, too smooth for it.
> [§284 a]

These two sets of sections from the *Investigations* which illustrate what I am calling two "aspects" of Wittgenstein's later philosophical method—an anthropological and a self-scrutiny aspect—are importantly similar and also importantly different. Their similarities include these two: First, both aspects proceed by way of asking what we would say in these given (described) circumstances. Thus, both proceed by eliciting the criteria we have for calling things as we do (or would) call them. In this way, both seek to get us to elicit, and then to explore, what we are willing to say about things, including ourselves and others, and the bases or reasons we have (or may have, or may think of) for so speaking, for so wording the world.

Second, both the anthropological and the self-scrutiny aspects test not only our capacity for applying and analyzing our criteria, but also our capacity for accepting people as people. We are asked, that is, to consider *as people* either others or ourselves acting in certain ways, taking these actions or thoughts or expressions as exemplifying recognizably human attributes, exemplifying or instantiating at least a part of what it is to be a human being. So both aspects are lessons in how we take people, and what we take them to be. And in both instances, Wittgenstein is asking us to test the extent of our capacity for accepting or rejecting people as people, embracing or avoiding them, denying or recognizing their behavior and characteristics. In short, both aspects of Wittgenstein's philosophical practice test our ability to "read" people, ourselves as well as others.

Two human capacities are being examined in these anthropological and self-scrutiny phases of Wittgenstein's work, and they can be examined together because they are intertwined. The former capacity—our capacity for applying our concepts and criteria to people—is dependent upon the latter—our capacity for accepting or taking people as human beings. If we do not, or cannot, take others or ourselves as people, then our criteria cannot so much as come into use. Our criteria in this case have nothing to which to be applied, no host or subject to whom they apply, or whose existence or activity they characterize.

> ... What is disappointing about criteria?
>
> There is something they do not do; it can seem the essential. I have to know what they are for; I have to accept them, use them. This itself makes my use of them seem arbitrary, or private—as though they were never shared, or as if our sharing of them is either a fantastic accident or a kind of mass folly. ... To withhold, or hedge, our concepts of psychological states from a given creature, on the ground that our criteria cannot reach to the inner life of the creature, is specifically to withhold the source of my idea that living beings are things that feel; it is to withhold myself, to reject my response to anything as a living being; ... .[18]

There are important differences as well, however, between these two aspects of Wittgenstein's later philosophy, one of which is the following. The first set of sections asks us to imagine ourselves viewing someone else, different people; it invites us to try to imagine what sense these people might make to us. The second set of sections asks us to imagine ourselves here and now ("at home," I put it above[19]), acting or developing in a different way

---

18. S. Cavell, *supra* n. 3, at 83.
19. *See* text at 21, *supra*.

than we do act at the present time, or expect to act; it asks us to think about what sense we can make of ourselves if we were so to act. So the first set of sections asks us to conceive of other people as acting differently, and is concerned with whether we could understand them, or share their way of doing things, or recognize what they were doing as something that we also do (albeit somewhat differently). And the second set of sections asks us, What can we make of our present situation if it develops or evolves in a certain (imaginable, but unpredictable, or unlikely) way? In other words, What can we make from our present resources? What can we do from here (where we are, where we find ourselves) with these tools and materials and capacities?

I think that, by vacillating between an anthropological and a self-scrutiny perspective, Wittgenstein intends to surprise us: he demonstrates that what initially strikes us as being foreign to us (e.g., those tribes of strangers or primitive people) may suddenly seem not so strange, so foreign, to us. And, correspondingly, we also may be surprised to learn that what we have all along taken to be familiar or obvious is replete with unappreciated or neglected foreignness. (For example, look at section 524.[20]) It turns out that everything Wittgenstein cajoles us into investigating *can* be familiar or foreign to us—and that the alternation between these two possibilities is definitive for the kinds of subject he sets himself in his later studies.

Just such an alternation between foreign and familiar also is characteristic of self-knowledge; our knowledge of ourselves can alternate between appearing familiar or obvious—commonplace—and foreign or fantastic. And this alternation is something that we cannot control or predict. Then Wittgenstein's method can be thought of as trying to create situations in which the alternation or vacillation between foreignness and familiarity can be studied. (See, e.g., §§524-525, 595-596, 628.) If I am right about this strategy in Wittgenstein's later work, then the conception of Wittgenstein's later philosophy as ethnography, as anthropology, is misleading (unless we add an educative element to it).

Anthropology assumes a certain distance between ourselves and the world we are studying (and others in it), because the common model of anthropology is one of an observer observing and describing a foreign culture (the observed). This distance rests upon a notion that the perceiver is not a participant in the culture or activity being observed. It is foreign to him or her both because he or she is not an initiate, and because he or she cannot both participate in it while at the same time observing it. But in Wittgenstein's later philosophy we are studying ourselves and our own culture's resources. We are studying not only the distances between ourselves and others, but also those within ourselves, between our current self and any number of future selves.

An emphasis on the anthropological or anthropocentric aspect leaves out of account Wittgenstein's genius for simultaneously studying and including himself (and us) in the figures of his writing. It falsifies or slights his ability to find or place himself (and us) within the topics and subjects he discusses and investigates. Thus, the topic of self-knowledge is essential to the text of the

---

20. *See* text at 14, *supra.*

Philosophical Investigations, as it is central in his other late writings. But even this way of expressing the point puts it badly, because self-knowledge (as also the knowledge of others) is more than a topic for Wittgenstein in his later philosophy; it is his very method, the way he proceeds from topic to topic and subject to object. And proceeding by way of self-knowledge is not usually thought to be a defining characteristic of anthropological writing or procedure.

This leads me to think that Wittgenstein's later philosophy is centrally concerned with education, especially self-education, and that his vacillation between an anthropological and a self-scrutiny aspect is meant to cultivate this central concern. Wittgenstein wants us to learn from these studies of our criteria and grammar not only what we are and where we live, but also the possibilities of who we may become and how we may grow. What impresses him most, I think, is not how settled or unsettled our lives are, but rather how they habitually require *resettlement*, not only establishing but also re-establishing the terms and conditions upon which we can and do and should live. We and the lives we lead are open to change from birth, even including reversal or transformation. But once we have achieved our initial maturity, adulthood, with some significant formation of the self and the self's world, change and education entail not just growth but conversion, self-transformation.[21]

Our human capacities are such that they invite new experience which we assimilate with the old; and they function by way of our continuing ability to make suitable projections of old words into new contexts, new habitations, even if such habitations only afford us momentary stays against confusion.[22] So, while we live at sea, as I said in the opening paragraphs of this article, we yet have the tools and means of navigating, in particular because we have the capacity to learn, to educate ourselves.

Pears' comment, then, about the "positivistic" aspect of Wittgenstein's later work, ascribing to it a claim that "human nature provides a sufficiently firm basis" for our philosophical needs,[23] is misleading. It suggests a settled human nature, as though it were some solid, unchanging foundation, but this is not quite the way in which Wittgenstein appeals to human nature—the natural and normal—in his later writings. He does appeal to natural and normal human responses, ways of taking things, ways of seeing things, and so forth, but he appeals to them not in terms of their being fully realized or finally settled. These core capacities of human beings are never fully realized or settled in the sense that they might be achieved once for all or exercised in some exhaustive way, in full and final settlement of our nature. Rather, we share them, and hence share their potential, just as we can share the forms of

---

21. As Stanley Cavell says:
    > The anxiety in teaching, in serious communication, is that I myself require education. And for grownups this is not natural growth, but *change*. Conversion is a turning of our natural reactions; so it is symbolized as rebirth.

    S. Cavell, *supra* n. 3, at 125. *See also* Eisele, "The Legal Imagination and Language: A Philosophical Criticism", (1976) 47 *U. Colo. L. Rev.* 363, 412-413.
22. *See* R. Frost, "The Figure a Poem Makes", in *Selected Prose of Robert Frost*, H. Cox & E. Lathem eds., (New York: Holt, Rinehart and Winston, 1968), at 18.
23. *See* text at notes 16-17, *supra*.

life and the media within which these human capacities can be formed and exercised. In this respect, they do provide a basis of our lives (and a basis for philosophy, if it chooses to consider them) because they afford us fruitful, bountiful, regenerative ways of projecting ourselves and our concepts into new contexts and thereby making sense of them (and of us as we are there and then situated).

Wittgenstein appeals to these capacities and norms in terms of their nearly perpetual, inexhaustible capacity for feeding and supporting human learning and education. Yet they have this potential in part only because they (these capacities and norms) exist within the limits and conditions laid down by our inherited criteria, grammar, language-games, and forms of life. This Wittgensteinian view implies neither that "everything is settled" nor that "everything is possible". It simply encourages us not to give up hope, and not to forget what we have to work with. In particular, it urges us to test and measure and learn both the criterial and grammatical bases of ourselves and our lives as we and they are currently constituted, and to consider the possibilities of these matters as they may either foretell or forestall change (in terms of us or in terms of the world changing). Thus, as Cavell puts it, "the writer of the *Investigations* declares that philosophy does not speak first. Philosophy's virtue is[, rather, its] responsiveness."[24]

B. *Learning about the Common Law: Simpson v. Sugarman*

How does this view of Wittgenstein's later work relate to our study and understanding of law? I said earlier that for Wittgenstein the "practical structure of our lives and language is knowable and traceable by us," and that its true tracing in intelligible terms was the goal of his later work.[25] The practical structure of our legal lives and language largely consists in what we in the Anglo-American world call "the common law", and there is perhaps no better test of Wittgenstein's utility for legal theory than examining the extent to which Wittgenstein's insights might help us better to understand the common law. The need is great, if for no other reason than the fact that in this increasingly legislated legal world of ours, we are losing our natural affinity for common law habits of mind and styles of argument and analysis. And this need has not been addressed by contemporary legal theorists.

To my mind, the single best piece criticizing our impoverished theories of the common law is A.W.B. Simpson's article, "The Common Law and Legal Theory," first published in 1973 and now republished in revised form in a

---

24. Given in full, Cavell's words are these:
    ... [I]n beginning with the words of someone else—in choosing to stop there, in hearing philosophy called upon in these unstriking words—the writer of the *Investigations* declares that philosophy does not speak first. Philosophy's virtue is responsiveness. What makes it philosophy is not that its response will be total, but that it will be tireless, awake when others have all fallen asleep. Its commitment is to hear itself called on, and when called on—but only then, and only so far as it has an interest—to speak.
    S. Cavell, *This New Yet Unapproachable America: Lectures After Emerson After Wittgenstein* (Albuquerque, New Mexico: Living Batch Press, 1989), at 74.
25. *See* text at 18, *supra.*

recent collection edited by William Twining.[26] Simpson's essay begins with
the remark that "no very satisfactory analysis of the nature of the common
law has been provided by legal theory. Indeed the matter has received remark-
ably little sustained attention by theoretical writers."[27] Ironically, the very
next piece in the Twining collection (by David Sugarman) seems to confirm
Simpson's view. There we find the following characterization of the common law mind: "Stated baldly, it assumes that although law may appear to be
irrational, chaotic and particularistic, if one digs deep enough and knows
what one is looking for, then it will soon become evident that the law is an
internally coherent and unified body of rules."[28] With due respect for the
scholarship displayed in the remainder of Mr. Sugarman's article, and taking
account of his footnote disclaimer acknowledging that he is speaking here in
terms of an "ideal-type" or "model", I still do not see that this characterization
of the common law mind can be accepted.

Sugarman is claiming that this purported assumption of the common law
mind aptly describes the essence of the common law tradition and process.
But I do not find in the materials of the common law (most especially, not in
its judicial opinions) any such assumption or attitude. Can it truly be said that
the common law attitude is one of assurance in its internal coherence and
unity? I don't think so. It seems to me, instead, that the common law is only
too conscious of the fact that its development may be haphazard, that its
fecundity for problem-solving purposes may carry with it the vice of pro-
moting some incoherence and disunity among the rules and principles that it
engenders and invokes.[29] Indeed, Dworkin, among others, might say that
such a recognized tension within the common law is one of its positive
aspects, not a negative concern. However this may be, it seems to me that the
common law rests secure in the thought that, although its work may not yield
an internally coherent or unified body of rules, it still plays a valuable role in
our lives and culture. This sense of security stems not from some perversity
inhering in the common law, nor from any insensitivity to the desirability of
internal coherence and unity as virtues of a legal system. But the common law
seems to me to appreciate that the danger of its slighting these two values
(and others like them) is a risk that it must run if it is to respond to the facts
and equities of a particular party or specific case presented to it for decision.
This amounts to a refusal to sacrifice overriding needs and values for some
vaunted ideal of coherence or unity. The common law system is too empirical
and opportunistic to be attracted to such an ideal—yet it continues to be a

---

26. Simpson, "The Common Law and Legal Theory", in *Oxford Essays in Jurisprudence*, 2d Series,
A.W.B. Simpson ed., (Oxford: Clarendon Press, 1973), at 77; Simpson, "The Common Law and Legal
Theory" (rev.), in *Legal Theory and Common Law*, W. Twining ed., (New York: Basil Blackwell,
1986) at 8. Since Simpson has republished his claim, I take it that he believes (and I agree) that nothing in the theoretical writing of the past fifteen years has disproved him.
27. Simpson, *id.* at 77 (Twining republication, at 8).
28. Sugarman, "Legal Theory, the Common Law Mind and the Making of the Textbook Tradition", in
Legal Theory and Common Law,supra n. 26, at 26 (footnote omitted).
29. The following represents at least one attitude typical of the common law mind.
"The old fashioned English lawyer's idea of a satisfactory body of law was a chaos with a full index." T.
Holland, *Essays* 171 (1870). Holmes' review of Holland's book made this remark famous, or notorious. *See*
Holmes, "Book Review", (1870) 5 *Am. L. Rev.* 114. (I owe this quotation and the references to J. Dukeminier
& J. Krier, *Teacher's Manual for Property, Second Edition*, (Boston: Little, Brown & Co., 1988), at 299.)

principled system as well. But its pursuit of principles seems always to be undertaken in terms of what Oakeshott calls (in the context of politics) the pursuit of "intimations" of existing traditions of thought and action.

> [Our] activity, then, springs neither from instant desires, nor from general principles, but from the existing traditions of behaviour themselves. And the form it takes, because it can take no other, is the amendment of existing arrangements by exploring and pursuing what is intimated in them. The arrangements which constitute a society capable of political activity, whether they are customs or institutions or laws or diplomatic decisions, are at once coherent and incoherent; they compose a pattern and at the same time they intimate a sympathy for what does not fully appear. Political activity is the exploration of that sympathy; and consequently, relevant political reasoning will be the convincing exposure of a sympathy, present but not yet followed up, and the convincing demonstration that now is the appropriate moment for recognizing it.[30]

It cannot be said that the values and norms of the common law support the view that common law rules are either internally coherent or unified. This may be a goal for the common law (as it may be a goal for any legal system), but we should not confuse a hope or aspiration for an achievement. The rules we find or create within the common law tradition may or may not cohere with one another, just as they may or may not cohere with the form of life out of which they are generated and to which they are meant to apply. At various stages in its growth and development, the common law has generated and applied rules that were not coherent, either internally with one another or externally with the world to which they were being applied. The faith of the common law is, however, that such matters can be worked out to a satisfactory resolution, because we have the tools and the means with which to work with the law and to render it something good—but still only provisionally. Yet even this prudent possibility remains mostly a Fullerian aspiration,[31] not an accomplished fact.

In addition, it is not at all clear that the common law has existed or continues to exist as a body of rules. Simpson claims, to the contrary, that the common law exists in terms of its customs, or that its existence is based upon its source in our customs and customary ways of doing things.[32] And, in this sense, the common law can be said to be a way of approaching certain issues or problems, a congeries of attitudes and techniques applied to certain controversies and disputes in certain areas that are subject to the jurisdiction and competence of certain institutions and officials.[33] Although it is true that

---

30. M. Oakeshott, *supra* n. 5, at 123-124.
31. I am appealing here to Lon Fuller's notion that an internal morality of law exists for all legal systems, that this morality consists in several principles of legality, and that this morality states aspirations more so than duties. One such aspiration is that the rules within the system not contradict one another; yet another aspiration is that the announced rules be congruent with official actions in reading and applying those rules. *See* L. Fuller, *The Morality of Law* (New Haven: Yale Univ. Press, 1964), at 65-70, 81-91.
32. Simpson, *supra* n. 26, at 80, 91-94 (Twining republication, at 10, 18-21).
33. I use Simpson's article to emphasize the extent to which rules of law are generated by the common law process, and thus depend upon that process for their existence and intelligibility, in "The Activity of Being a Lawyer", *supra* n. 4, at 372-374, 377-385. I also discuss the common law as a way of acting, speaking, and thinking, in "Hegelian Vanity, Common Law Humility", *supra* n. 11, at 942-947. In this later article, I make use of Harry Jones' fine essay on the common law. *See* Jones, "Our Uncommon Common Law", (1975) 42 *Tenn. L. Rev.* 443.

a part of what we inherit from our forebearers and bequeath to our successors may be certain rules of law, we also inherit and bequeath ways of dealing with those rules—ways of reading, interpreting, understanding, applying, revising, revoking, and otherwise using them. And their uses are at least as important—although much more difficult to locate and express—as the rules themselves.

So it seems to me that Sugarman's description of the common law mind mistakes its normal attributes and condition. Also, Sugarman's description flies in the face of Simpson's contrary suggestion, namely, that the common law is nothing like a system of rules. In this regard, Sugarman's characterization implicitly accepts a positivistic portrait of the common law, which it is the purpose of Simpson's piece to reject:

> The predominant conception today is that the common law consists of a system of rules; in terms of this legal propositions (if correct) state what is contained in these rules. ... I wish to consider the utility of this conception, and to contrast it with an alternative idea—the idea that the common law is best understood as a system of customary law, that is, as a body of traditional ideas received within a caste of experts. ... Indeed in an important sense it is in general the case that one cannot say what the common law is, if its existence is conceived of as consisting of a set of rules, and if saying what the law is means reporting what rules are to be found in the catalogue. ... [I]t is a feature of the common law system that there is no way of settling the correct text or formulation of the rules, so that it is inherently impossible to state so much as a single rule in what Pollock called 'any authentic form of words'. How can it be said that the common law exists as a system of general rules, when it is impossible to say what they are? ... It is as if the system placed particular value upon dissension, obscurity, and the tentative character of judicial utterances. As a system of legal thought the common law then is inherently vague; it is a feature of the system that uniquely authentic statements of the rules which, so positivists tell us, comprise the common law, cannot be made.[34]

C. Milsom on the Multifarious Contexts of the Common Law

I agree with Simpson's complaint that traditional legal theories have failed to give us a satisfactory portrait or account of the common law.[35] In so far as the common law tradition and process are to be seen and understood as constituting not only a legal institution but also a legal technique, a kind of activity (one that essentially builds upon our linguistic capacities and sensibilities nurtured by our acquisition of a native language), then it is my sense that the need identified by Simpson has been filled not by theorists of law but rather, to some extent, by historians of law. (If I am right about this claim, then one of the bases for the excellence of Simpson's own essay on the common law may be the fact that he is, among other things, a historian of law.)

In this regard, I find the writing of S.F.C. Milsom, one historian of the common law, to suggest how Wittgenstein's later philosophy may be relevant to educating our own primitive conception of the common law. This does not mean that I find Milsom's account wholly satisfactory or that I think that

---

34. Simpson, *supra* n. 26, at 79-80, 88, 89, 90 (Twining republication, at 10, 16, 17 [with some modifications]).
35. *See* text at n. 27, *supra.*

Milsom has presented us with a full description of the common law. (But he doesn't think that his account is fully satisfactory or complete either.) Rather, when I read Milsom's work, I gain a better sense of how far we still are from achieving a satisfactory view of the common law in its many guises.

And perhaps this is the central message of Milsom's work, for he says again and again that the common law is not one thing, not a univocal system of human thought and activity existing from human epoch to human epoch, but instead is (and has been) many things. Its existence is multifarious, in part because its contexts are (and have been) multifarious.

> It is in the nature of law that what is done in the present must be congruous with the immediate past; and it is therefore in the nature of legal history that the evidence is systematically deceptive. The largest changes cannot be obvious to historians because they could not be obvious at the time. In the thirteenth century, for example, the changes most obvious on the surface of the law are legislative provisions dealing with scattered and seemingly unrelated points of irritation. These were small symptoms of a structural change too large to be knowingly borne, but too piecemeal to be seen; and in the legal records it is hidden behind the changed meaning of some words, the changed operation of some rules. What has really changed is not so much 'the law' as the context; and it is the earlier context that may be lost to historians, overlaid by the later. Perhaps more than in any other kind of history, the historian of law is enticed into carrying concepts and even social frameworks back into periods to which they do not belong.[36]

Here, in the preface to his book, *Historical Foundations of the Common Law*, S.F.C. Milsom tells us that the largest changes in our legal system and our conception of law are both "too large to be knowingly borne, but too piecemeal to be seen." Normally, we do not knowingly change our concept of law, although it certainly may change or evolve. Similarly, we do not usually change the structure of our entire legal system through any sort of conscious or calculated decision, although it is equally true that in fact the structures of legal systems can and do change. These things seem to happen as a result of the interaction of many things, including not only our conscious decisions but also accidents or happenstances, coincidences, gradual accretions that go unnoticed but not unfelt, and a variety of other factors. And we do not combine these factors consciously, as though we possessed a kind of alchemical formula for changing legal concepts or structures; we simply live through them. Living through them, we may not be fully conscious of them, and they are apt not to be obvious or noticeable to us. So, as Milsom says, the records we leave behind are "systematically deceptive" as evidence of our legal concepts and structure, because we are not aware of them fully. Hence, we shall fail to speak to that which those who come after us will most want to know, and our silence allows them to make the same mistakes we make—"carrying concepts and even social frameworks back into periods to which they do not belong."

Milsom's criticism is reminiscent of Wittgenstein in this respect: both appreciate the fact that we normally are not cognizant or conscious of the

---

36. S.F.C. Milsom, *Historical Foundations of the Common Law,* 2d ed., (London: Butterworths, 1981), at vi.

larger contexts in which we think, speak, and act. But then, analogous to the way in which Wittgenstein seeks to make explicit the implicit structure and contours of the criterial and grammatical contexts of our lives, the challenge for a historian or theorist of the law is to make the social and legal contexts of our legal lives and language appear, to elicit them. If these contexts are implicit (as Milsom claims), either we learn how to elicit them or we shall lose them, shall lose their significance for us and our lives. How does Milsom go about trying to elicit them?

He uses what I would call a Wittgensteinian procedure. He asks himself, How can I learn what the law was to those people back then? And he responds by looking for evidence of how they used the law, how they taught the law, how they learned the law—in other words, he looks at all of the kinds of things that I think Wittgenstein would call the "criteria" of their concept of law.[37] For example, Milsom describes the creation and use of the "year books," which are reports of early English cases and which provide us with much of what we know about the early common law.

> They seem to begin as the common-place books of students. ... But in the course of the fourteenth century some organisation seems to take hold: instead of many reports being made of each case there is generally one, and that a more earnest affair less often noting the happy phrase or the anecdote. ... [This reporting by year books then evolved into] an educational routine ... [by which apprentice lawyers] formalised a method of learning about the core of their art.[38]

What do the year books tell us about the law and legal process of those times? About some of their aspects, the year books tell us much; about others, little or nothing. Milsom says that, in the earliest of the year books, "the count itself is often set out in whole or in part, and this ... still engages some of the learner's attention. But usually it is the next step that interests the reporter, and he gives only such summary of the count as is necessary to understand what happens next, which is argument about the defendant's answer, about the plea."[39] Under the ancient mode of trial, the only denial that a defendant could make to the plaintiff's count was a general one, and then both would proceed to the formal decision mechanism (such as wager of law by ordeal or battle). Initially, then, a "general denial" was the only response open to a defendant who wished to contest a plaintiff's cause of action.

But, as trial by jury began to supersede trial by wager of law, or at least became available as an alternative, it would make sense to allow the defendant to plead more specifically the facts in his or her defense. Milsom says, however, that this is not quite how the common law in fact developed. "The

---

37. Michael Oakeshott also illustrates the kind of inquiry that I regard as being essentially Wittgensteinian and criterial:

> ... [I]f political activity is impossible without a certain kind of knowledge and a certain sort of education, then this knowledge and education are not mere appendages to the activity but are part of the activity itself and must be incorporated in our understanding of it. We should not, therefore, seek a definition of politics in order to deduce from it the character of political knowledge and education, but rather observe the kind of knowledge and education which is inherent in any understanding of political activity, and use this observation as a means of improving our understanding of politics.

M. Oakeshott, *supra* n. 5, at 113. *See also* Eisele, "The Activity of Being a Lawyer", *supra* n. 4, at 352.
38. S.F.C. Milsom, *supra* n. 36, at 44-45.
39. *Id.* at 45.

natural reaction to the introduction of the rational jury would be to let him [the defendant] plead whatever facts seemed to tell in his favour,... . In fact[, however,] his freedom was confined by [procedural or pleading] rules which at first sight seem artificial."[40] It appears from the year books that, even with the advent of trial by jury, defendants' lawyers continued to resort to the general denial as a matter of course, either without pleading any special or specific facts in defense, or else pleading them but only as a preamble or a rider to the general denial. The common law at that time, according to Milsom, "was dominated by the ancient pattern of law-suit. For [common law lawyers] the ancient [general] denial, now called the general issue, was paramount; and it must always be made unless there was good reason for departing from it."[41] And apparently to their minds—although not to ours— the rise of trial by jury, the availability of rational argument before a fact-finding body of peers, did not present a reason sufficiently good for departing from this ancient pattern of pleading.

As Milsom puts it, then, the year books frequently do not report or discuss the actual pleading at all; rather, they often discuss what the defendant *might* have pled and how the defense *might* have been stated or formulated. "It follows that year book discussions are not generally about the legal sufficiency of the defendant's facts. They are about the propriety of allowing him to plead them at all, and about the form in which he may do it: is he to add a preamble or rider to the general issue, or to depart from it altogether?"[42] This seems strange to our minds, but it was not unusual behavior from their point of view. Why? Milsom suggests the following possibility:

> The year books, then, and the legal process which they record, lie in the shadow of that ancient unvarying [general] denial. The modern reader can hear real arguments by lawyers who would shine in any age; but often he finds the point of the argument elusive. The difficulty is in his own mind. The terms into which he is trying to translate the argument, the terms of substantive law, were not much in the minds of those arguing. For them the essence of a law-suit was still the formulation of a question to be put to some deciding mechanism, whether wager of law or jury. Practical considerations compelled departures from the old general question. To hindsight [i.e. to our eyes], the important result of these departures was the creation of substantive law. But this was not a focus of attention at the time. The year books astonishingly preserve the true infancy of a modern legal system; but they will not often answer legal questions asked in modern terms.[43]

I have not done justice to the rich detail and liveliness of Milsom's argument here, but perhaps my use of it will suffice to suggest the following connections between Wittgenstein's work in philosophy and Milsom's work in legal history. The changes in context or structure Milsom describes tend to be invisible, both to those who live through them and to those of us who live with their consequences and study them. They seem to be invisible, paradoxically, because they are so large, so all-encompassing, that those living

---

40. *Id.*
41. *Id.* at 47.
42. *Id.*
43. *Id.* at 48.

during that time simply do not notice them or appreciate them, and hence
do not note them in their records, which we who come later use as our evidence of their world. But then, reflecting on this possibility, is it truly so
strange that we might be oblivious to the largest changes in the context or
framework of our lives? For, we might ask, from what perspective, from
what Archimedean point, could we view them? Milsom clearly has no such
privileged position from which to view (or review) these changes, and in
this he again is akin to Wittgenstein, who performs his feats of bringing us to
a consciousness of our implicit circumstances and assumptions from within
the criterial and grammatical weave of our lives.

Also, these changes in the concept and structure of the common law were
not due, by and large, to conscious decisions or social adjustments made by
calculated acts. Rather, they grew out of a variety of actions, omissions,
accretions, accidents, and coincidences. The structure or context of the common law is not something altered by adjusting it or tinkering with it to our
rational delight; rather, it is the result of societal and communal forces and
interactions of which we only know the half of it, if that. (And Wittgenstein
knew this too about language and our lives; we try to over-intellectualize
both.) Milsom's point is that we shall be surprised by what we find in investigating the transformations of the common law, because those same changes
also surprised those who lived within the common law at the time it was
transformed.

> It is a simple starting-point; but the English law did not move from it by a process of
> evolution. A structural change had magical effects. Largely meaning only to enforce
> regularisation of these [local court] customs, the king's court brought to an end the
> feudal jurisdictions that had applied them, and [thus the king's court] had to apply
> the customs itself. But the change of habitat changed their nature. The king's court
> looking from outside the [local feudal] unit could not think in terms of [customary
> feudal] management, only of rules and some abstract right. ... And the entire change
> was in a sense invisible. The canons of inheritance, for example, could be stated in
> the same words after as before. It is just that they did quite different things.
>
> The change of jurisdiction [from local lord to king] therefore produced instant law,
> a system of substantive rules and abstract concepts.[44]

Or, as Milsom says later, "The system could not be altered, only transformed."[45]

Milsom warns us that "the historian of law"—and not just the historian—
"is enticed into carrying concepts and even social frameworks back into periods to which they do not belong."[46] With respect to the common law, he
thinks that this is exactly what has happened: "One of the main things that we
have carried back is our vision of the law as a system of substantive rules having some existence separate from society and requiring separate adjust-
ment."[47] Our vision of law, our concept of law, which sees substantive legal

---

44. *Id.* at 3.
45. *Id.* at 61.
46. *Id.* at vi.
47. *Id.*

rules being applied to facts in the world, is different from (yet related to) the concept of law that we find expressed or implied in the year book descriptions of the early common law. We take law to be a human artifact—something subject to social engineering, or to conscious calculations of utility and cost/benefit analysis, or to rational arguments about justice and equity. Whatever the substantive constraints we see as imposed on law, we see it as something consciously calculated and rationally designed and molded. The early English seemed to see law as being much more dependent upon their customs; they also placed more faith in procedure; and they relied upon a different kind of decision-making mechanism.

> The demurrer to the evidence is one of the clearest examples of the common law having to go back and deal with a matter once deliberately shut out from consideration. The process of pleading made the common law: but it was not a happy juristic invention designed to that end. It was an uncomfortable necessity imposed by the jury, whose fallibility had broken up the comfortable old pattern of a general question to be put to an infallible test. ...

> But this in turn is only an illustration, though a striking one, of the need to consider these institutions of the early common law in their own terms, and not in ours. When it is said, for example, that the writ of error was defective because questions could not be raised about the propriety of evidence given to the jury, we must remember that the excluded questions might be more serious than what we think of as matters of evidence. [Matters of faith or trust, perhaps, not to be put into question lightly or ill-advisedly?] And when it is said, as it too often is, that the year books were inferior to modern law reports because they often did not give the facts or the judgment, it must be remembered that neither was generally important [to students or apprentice lawyers of that time]. The facts and the law are both reflected [at early common law] in the pleading; and the equivalent of today's lawyer seeking a *ratio decidendi* was a year book reader trying to make out whether a particular plea would or would not be upheld on demurrer, or why it should be in this form rather than in that. There was no substantive law to which pleading was adjective. These were the terms in which the law existed and in which lawyers thought [at early common law].[48]

Neither the ancient nor the modern concept of law is better than the other; they are different yet related, just as are the legal processes and issues and activities that are subsumed by each concept. Milsom puts it boldly: "However unsatisfactory to modern eyes looking at it out of its context, the ancient pattern of law-suit in local courts probably did as much justice between the parties to individual disputes as anything we know today."[49]

D. *To Imagine a Legal System is to Imagine a Form of Life*

> It is a property of legal sources, especially from the middle ages, that they will tell the investigator nearly everything except what he wants to know. Business documents are made for those who know the business; and the records of litigation, whether plea rolls which were the courts' minutes, or Year Books which were reports made for the professional or educational purposes of lawyers, are brusque in

---

48. *Id.* at 59.
49. *Id.* at 67.

their unhelpfulness to outsiders. Charters and the like use words which we may
not even recognize as terms of art, let alone guess at the volumes of meaning which
it is the function of terms of art to import. Even legislative acts, even legal treatises,
were addressed to an audience which knew something about the law and which
lived in the society which the law regulated. We have to conjure up both. It is what
was assumed that we need to know, not what was said. ... The law court is miracu-
lously clear in our spotlight. The world around it, largely the world of facts and
wholly the world of ideas, is in the dark.[50]

Among Wittgenstein's many remarks about how we are to accomplish the
tasks set us by his later philosophy, there is the following: "[T]o imagine a
language means to imagine a form of life" (§19 a). I take him here to be urging us to remember that, in investigating any means of expression, any symbol system, any medium for making meaning—which for me includes the
law, and emphatically the common law—we must see implicit in every nook
and cranny of the medium or system the lives of its users and inhabitants.
Their various activities and practices and institutions are formed in part by
means of the language they use; in turn, those matters partially form and
reform that language. These two fields of phenomena—language and forms of
life—are symbiotically related, and we ought not forget it, says Wittgenstein.
So, too, with respect to the common law, says Milsom: we need to describe
and imagine the forms of life from which the law springs. His work goes a
long way toward accomplishing that task. It seems to me to be a task worthy
of anything we should wish to call "legal theory".

---

50. F. Pollock & F. Maitland, *The History of English Law Before the Time of Edward I,* vol. I., (2d ed.
1898), reissued with a new introduction by S.F.C. Milsom, (Cambridge: Cambridge Univ. Press,
1968), at xxv-xxvi, xxvii.

3

The Acceptance of a Legal System

Roger A. Shiner

1. Introduction

The interest of political theory in the acceptance of law is obvious. If one believes that a regime is legitimate only if it governs with the consent of the governed, then the notion of acceptance is deeply linked with the notion of legitimacy, a fundamental concern of political theory. The interest of legal theory in the notion of acceptance is less obvious. I construe it to arise in the following way. One central tradition in legal theory is that of positivistic or content-independent theories of law. Positivism, crudely speaking, is characterized by some form of the Separation Thesis—that the existence of law is one thing and its merit or demerit another. But if it is important for positivistic legal theory to mark the separation of law and the merits of law, then it must also be important to mark the separation between law and the acceptance of law. The existence of law must be one thing and its acceptance as meritorious another. In deference to the separation of existence and merit, positivism tries to find a content-independent account of the validity of law. Equally, in deference to the separation of law and acceptance, positivism tries to find a content-independent account of the acceptance of law. The topic of this paper is whether the separation of law and the acceptance of law is possible. I shall try to suggest, in service of a non-positivistic or content-dependent approach to law, that this separation is not possible. I will attempt to argue on the basis of points which legal positivism itself has acknowledged to form valid constraints on any theory of acceptance. My ambitious thesis is that positivism has presented us with the reasons for rejecting it. Even if that thesis is not made out, I have a less ambitious thesis which I am confident of securing, that the demand for an account of law which permits law to be accepted 'for any reason whatever' is not a theory-neutral demand which might decide between positivism and natural law theory. Rather, it is an expression of a prior commitment to positivism. It is the familiar demand of natural law theory that the convergence of attitudes towards law which makes for acceptance of law must be a convergence for the right kind of reasons; ones that have to do with the value of law.

2. Simple Positivism

Simple positivism claims that it is a contingent truth about some given society how far the law in that society is accepted as legitimate. Note that the

The earliest version of this paper was presented to the Conference on Law, Liberty and Community in 1984 at the University of Victoria. Subsequent versions were presented at the University of Waterloo and the University of Western Ontario, and to the Canadian chapter of the International Society for Philosophy of Law and Social Philosophy. Those whose detailed comments on one or more of these versions have helped me to see many of the errors of my ways are Dick Bronaugh, David Copp, Antony Duff, Barry Hoffmaster, Michael McDonald, Wayne Sumner and Wil Waluchow. I am very grateful to all of them. Some of them will see far more errors still remaining than will others of them; but I guess that happens with friends.

claim here is not that it is a contingent truth how far the law in any given society is legitimate. In one way, whether this latter fact obtains merely contingently is not one issue in the overall debate between positivism and
natural-law theory; it is the issue in the overall debate. In another way, in
some more specific form, this issue of contingency is addressed when we
consider whether law is merely contingently authoritative, or when we consider whether law is merely contingently for the common good. The claim
that it is a contingent truth about some given society how far the law in that
society is accepted as legitimate is a claim about the attitudes of people in a
society towards the law of that society; it is a claim that there is no such
connection of any interest to analytical jurisprudence. Such connections may
be of interest to the sociologist, the psychologist, the criminologist, ... , but
not to the analytical theorist who studies the concept of law.

The phrase 'accept as legitimate' is in the idiolect of this paper almost a
pleonasm. That is to say, to accept the law is to accept it as legitimate; to
accept the law is to accept it as creating obligations ('genuine obligations' is
also pleonastic). We need both nominal and verbal forms. The nominal form
'acceptance of the law's demands', for example, sounds correct and 'acceptance of the legitimacy of the law's demands' awkward. 'He accepts the law'
sounds incomplete, and 'He accepts that the law's demands are legitimate' the
filled-out story.

Support for this thesis about the contingency of acceptance comes from
two places. First, the separation thesis says that a law's status as law has
nothing to do with its content. The separation thesis so understood is a negative thesis, but it has an obvious positive correlate—that the status of a law as
law is a matter of its source or pedigree. The pedigree of a law is dependent
on human intention in the general sense that a given act of law-making, of
pedigreeing, is an intentional act (another pleonasm), whether by an individual or a group of law-makers. But there is no other connection to human
intention, according to simple positivism. The status of any given law as law
is not dependent on its efficacy; a law that is no longer efficacious is still a
law if it has been duly enacted and not duly repealed. It might belong to the
sociology of law to determine why a particular law is not efficacious, or
whether a particular proposed law will be efficacious. But such projects do
not fall within the province of jurisprudence, since they do not have to do
with the determination of what it is for a law to be law. The claim may be
made that efficacy is a necessary condition for the existence of a legal system.
It falls within the province of jurisprudence to make that claim. Simple positivism makes such a claim. The claim is, though, wholly uncontroversial.
Legal theorists almost all agree that efficacy is a necessary condition for the
existence of a legal system. Since the interest of this study is in what divides
legal theorists, little attention will be paid to efficacy here.

The second source of support lies in the notion of laws as commands
backed by sanctions, and the idea that the proper source of law, the sovereign,
is defined in part by the presence of a habit of obedience towards that
sovereign. A 'habit' is a certain pattern of behaviour; we can speak of a habit

of a group when the habits so understood of the members of the group con-
verge. 'Behaviour' here is construed as the 'colourless movements' of
behaviouristic psychology[1]—the movements of human bodies as inert matter,
as opposed to bodily movements considered as the movements of persons.
Thus, that aspect of the life of the norm-subjects of the laws which contributes to the laws being laws is an aspect which can be defined without
reference to human intentionality. The conformity to law which makes a system efficacious also need be interpreted as no more than 'colourless movements'. That a law or set of laws is accepted, on the other hand, is a fact
about the intentional stance of the norm-subjects. If the law's status as law
can be defined without reference to that fact, then the relation of law's status
as law to that fact is one of contingency.[2]

3. Sophisticated Positivism

Simple positivism eschews any connection between the status of the law as
law and the fact of its being accepted by its norm-subjects as making legitimate demands upon them. Simple positivism achieves this disconnection by
characterizing the norm-subjects' conformity to law in terms which prescind
from the intentional aspect of human action. No actual legal philosopher[3]
has defended simple positivism in this stark form. However, we must begin
there in order to understand how sophisticated positivism is to be understood
as an improvement over simple positivism.

Let us recall first familiar arguments from *The Concept of Law*.[4] Austin
defined laws as commands of the sovereign, and the sovereign as a person or
group of persons to whom the bulk of a given society are in a habit of obedience. Hart claims (54ff.) that: i) we should interpret 'habit' in Austin's theory as a convergent pattern of behaviour; ii) that such habits constitute an
example of the external aspect of human life; iii) that habitual behaviour is
significantly different from rule-governed behaviour—social rules differ from
habits in adding to the existence of convergent patterns of behaviour criticism
of deviation, acceptance that deviation is a good reason for criticism, and
the internalization of the pattern of behaviour as a general standard binding on
the group including the individual so internalizing;[5] iv) that Austin's major
error is to omit the 'internal aspect' of rules. The law is an example of a
rule-governed practice, as opposed to a mere aggregate of convergent patterns
of behaviour. Therefore, Austin's theory fails as a theory of law. The point of
my philosophical fiction of simple positivism and its devotion to 'colourless

---

1. C.L. Hull coins the phrase in his *Principles of Behavior* (London: D. Appleton, 1943).
2. Note that this 'behaviouristic' position is a sufficient condition of regarding the existence of law and
   the acceptance of law as contingently connected. It is not a necessary condition. It may be claimed that
   even if we regard the general stance towards law as intentional, that stance may only be contingently
   one of acceptance. I believe that this issue is far from a simple one. I address it later in this paper. For
   the moment, I abide by the attribution to simple positivism of a particularly crude and parsimonious
   position.
3. *A fortiori* and in particular, not John Austin; see below.
4. H.L.A. Hart, *The Concept of Law* (Oxford: Clarendon Press 1961).
5. Hart speaks of the latter as 'implicit' in the two previous elements; I leave unaddressed the question of
   whether the 'internal aspect' of rules is only the third element, or whether it is all three elements, or
   whether it matters which.

movements' should now be clear. Hart takes Austin to be a simple positivist
in the manner described in the previous section. We shall come shortly to
the question of how far Hart's characterization of Austin is adequate, and of
what follows if it is not. Hart also charges Austin with further inadequacies,
which are corollaries of the failure to distinguish rules from habits and the
interpretation of laws as commands of a sovereign. The notion of 'habit of
obedience' clearly has to do with the efficacy of law. Austin explains both
efficacy and obedience in that the coercion afforded by commands backed up
with threats is that in which legal obligation and duty consist. Hart rejects
these further doctrines also. He distinguishes 'being obliged' and 'being
under an obligation' (cf. *CL* 80-1), and claims that Austin shows only why a
subject may be 'obliged' to obey the law, not how he or she may be 'under an
obligation'. The underlying assumption is that properly speaking laws create
obligations; they do not merely oblige. If therefore a theory cannot show
how laws create obligations, but only how they oblige, it must be inadequate
as a theory of law.

So far so good. But now things begin to get more complicated for sophisticated positivism. The first complication is easily absorbed. It cannot be a
requirement of law as a system of obligation-imposing rules that every single
subject of the rules has the internal point of view to the rules. There is no contradiction in asserting that some recalcitrant who has the external point of
view to law nonetheless has an obligation to obey the law. It seems perfectly
proper to substitute for the excessively stringent requirement of unanimity a
lesser requirement that some suitable percentage less than 100% of the group
who are the subjects of the rules having the internal point of view to the
rules is sufficient (whether by itself or in conjunction with other requirements) to show that the rules generally impose obligations on all members of
the group. Moreover, for those who do have the internal point of view, it
seems unreasonable to require that they have it towards each and every rule of
the system, but only to the majority of rules, say, or to fundamental rules in
the hierarchy of rules, rules which give the system its distinctive flavour or
character. A range of cases must be allowed for.

But now there are further complexities. A legal system is in fact not only
an institutionalized normative system, but a very complicated one. Two major
coarse-grained distinctions may be made in its mode of operation. The first is
between the role of citizen and the role of official. The system requires for its
operation and maintenance a body of persons occupying various official roles
within the system, whose responsibilities have to do with the creation, variation, application and enforcement of the rules of the system. The second distinction, a congener of the first, is between two systematically different kinds
of rules of the system, those which directly impose duties upon the subjects or
which provide facilities for the subjects to create and vary legal relations, and
those which control the operations and maintenance of the system by the
officials.[6] It seems paradoxical to say the secondary rules of the system, not

---

6. I realize I am opting here for one construal of the status of facilitating rules. Since they are neither
'rules about rules' nor duty-imposing rules, they do not fit happily into the 'primary rule'/'secondary
rule' distinction, at least as that was made by Hart in ch.V s. 3 of *CL*.

being obligation-imposing rules, are not rules of the system, when in some sense without them there would not be a legal system. A scarcely weaker claim may be made about facilitating rules, in that the existence of formal and institutionalized procedures for the creation of (e.g.) voluntary obligations is a trademark of law. So how might one take these two fundamental distinctions on board without letting go of the idea that a legal system is a system of obligation-imposing rules?

An antecedent commitment to positivism makes the following solution to this problem irresistibly tempting. Positive law gets to exist as positive law by having undergone some appropriate procedure of enactment or recognition— and those terms are to be understood widely enough to satisfy the most enthusiastic devotee of judge-made, common law. But what most obviously goes along with the acknowledgment of this fact is the acknowledgment that a second mode of existence for laws is created, one which is additional to the mode of existence as the product of a social practice embodying the internal point of view. This is the mode of existence through validity, in the sense of creation in accord with procedural rules of recognition (cf. *CL* 97-102). Acknowledgment of this second mode of existence not only seems to accord with the special role of officials and secondary rules, but also with the positivistic requirement of a content-independent test for law—for that a rule is created in accordance with due procedure is so (or not, as the case may be) independently of the content of the rule.

But now the issue of the status of legal rules as obligation-imposing rules has to be reconsidered. For, if it is sufficient for a rule to exist that it is valid, and if it is sufficient for a rule to impose an obligation that it is valid, then it is clearly the case that a rule may impose an obligation through being valid even when no-one has the internal point of view towards that rule. And now we have an apparent substantial tension between the thought that rules impose obligations only if a suitable number of the group whose rules they are have the internal point of view towards the rules and the thought that a rule may impose obligations through existing as valid even when no-one has the internal point of view towards the rule.

Again, sheer facts about how the legal system operates impel the theorist towards the following argument. The central role(s) in the operation of the system is/are the officials' role(s). The central part of their role is the use of the secondary rules. Indeed, unless there are officials and they do meaningfully create, change, apply and enforce the secondary rules to the extent appropriate, there would be nothing to indicate the existence of a legal system rather than a purely customary normative system such as a morality (cf. *CL* 89-96). Thus it seems obvious that:

> There are therefore two minimum conditions necessary and sufficient for the existence of a legal system. On the one hand those rules of behaviour which are valid according to the system's ultimate criteria of validity must be generally obeyed, and, on the other hand, its rules of recognition specifying the criteria of legal validity and its rules of change and adjudication must be effectively accepted as common public standards of official behaviour by its officials. (*CL* 113)

Hart goes on to add that the officials in their capacity as private citizens are in the same position as any other private citizens with regard to the primary rules; that is, they need only obey such rules, as opposed to having the internal point of view towards them. In short, a legal system exists as such when no-one has the internal point of view towards the primary rules, and the officials alone have the internal point of view towards the secondary rules. A censorial concern for the quality of life in a society might lead to hope that the internal point of view will be more widespread, for then the society will be more 'healthy' (cf. *ibid.*). But from the perspective of analytical jurisprudence, the minimal case is undeniably a legal system (*CL* 114).

One more piece of fine-tuning is needed for sophisticated positivism. What kind of attitude constitutes the internal point of view which is required of the officials? It would again be excessive to require that the officials' acceptance had to be a full-blooded commitment to the moral worth of the secondary rules. This is so, not merely because not all secondary rules will raise moral issues—some procedures may be more matters of economic convenience or traditional etiquette than of natural justice.[7] It is so in part because 'acceptance' may be properly taken to cover a range of attitudes other than, and from the moral point of view weaker than, a commitment to moral worth. The underlying reasoning seems at least in part again purely factual—it's just true that officials have a variety of attitudes towards the secondary rules and yet nonetheless regard them as 'common public standards of official behaviour'. But putative factual evidence is not germane to the theoretical issue at stake. A non-positivistic theory which argues that a legal system will not be worthy of the term unless its rules are such as to merit moral commitment will also likely argue as well that the officials will only discharge their duties in a proper spirit when they themselves make a similar moral commitment. Beyleveld and Brownsword, for example,[8] not only require that in general, to be valid, laws must pass a moral test but also that officials must as a minimum make a good-faith attempt to enact laws which pass a moral test; unless the attempt is successful, the officials do not deserve the name. Thus it is an expression of legitimate opposition to positivism to say that officials who have less than a full moral commitment to the 'common public standard' are officials in name only. Positivism therefore has a significant theoretical interest in arguing that a range of attitudes other than full moral commitment nonetheless count as possession of the internal point of view to the secondary rules. We find in fact that this claim is made. Hart (cf. *CL* 198) argues that voluntary acceptance of the system still counts as the internal point of view when it is based on 'calculation of long-term self-interest; disinterested interest in others; an unreflecting inherited or traditional attitude; or the mere wish to do as others do'. Honoré seems to argue for an even weaker requirement—that membership in a group requires understanding of the nature and activities of the group 'minus professed rejection' rather

7. See here Ronald Dworkin, 'Principle, Policy, Procedure', reprinted in *A Matter of Principle* (Cambridge, MA: Harvard University Press, 1985), ch.3.
8. Derek Beyleveld and Roger Brownsword, *Law as a Moral Judgment* (London: Sweet and Maxwell, 1986), ch.8.

than 'plus acceptance'.[9] Sophisticated positivism sees that the theory of law as a set of social rules requires in some form the presence of the internal point of view as well as convergent patterns of behaviour. However, in the spirit of the separation of the existence of law and the merit of law, sophisticated positivism makes the specification of the content of the internal point of view as 'thin' and formal as possible.

In sum, sophisticated positivism's account of the acceptance of law is thus. It is a mistake to think that law is law when it is an entire system of coercive commands. Some persons at least must accept the law as a binding standard for behaviour. But it is sufficient for law that this acceptance be confined to the stance of the officials of the system towards the secondary rules of the system, and that the content of this acceptance be interpreted as thinly and minimally as possible. A range of pro-attitudes falling well short of a full commmitment to the moral worth of the law will satisfy the requirement of acceptance.

4. Anti-positivism

A. The 'Payne Problem'

Sophisticated positivism argued two main theses about the acceptance of law. The first thesis is that the minimum necessary and sufficient conditions for the existence of a legal system are satisfied in the case where no-one has the internal point of view towards the primary rules of the system, and only the officials have the internal point of view towards the secondary rules. 'Have the internal point of view' is equivalent to 'accept'. The second thesis is that 'accept' means no more than 'regard as a common standard of behaviour', and thus may be instantiated by a range of attitudes which may amount to, but which also may fall short of, full commitment to the standards as morally worthy. These two theses contain the essence of sophisticated positivism's account of the acceptance of law.

This position faces an immediate problem, which we may call, after the person who to my knowledge first urged it against Hart, the 'Payne Problem'.[10] The Payne Problem unfolds in two stages. In the first place, it's claimed, Hart's account is simply inconsistent in the treatment of primary rules. Hart is committed to each of the following:

---

9. A.M. Honoré, 'Groups, Laws and Obedience', reprinted in his *Making Law Bind* (Oxford: Clarendon Press 1987), 36.
10. See Michael Payne, 'Hart's Concept of a Legal System' (1976), 18 *William and Mary Law Review* 287-319. Rodger Beehler, 'The Concept of Law and the Obligation to Obey' (1978), 18 *American Journal of Jurisprudence* 120-42, raises essentially the same problem. His paper was published later, and so came to my attention later, than Payne's, though note 7, p.142 indicates it may have been written earlier. The Hodson Problem, as it were, that Hart's minimal legal system is satisfied by a cruel dictatorship (cf. John Hodson, 'Hart on the Internal Aspect of Rules' (1976), 62 *Archiv für Rechts- und Sozialphilosophie* 381-99) I take to be the limiting case of the Payne Problem. Roscoe Hill, 'Legal Validity and Legal Obligation' (1970), 80 *Yale Law Journal* 47-75, is working the same street. However, he represents the problem as being that the analysis of obligation-imposing rules in *CL* ch.5 is irrelevant to the analysis of legal obligation at the 'minimum condition' passage. As will become clear, it is misleading to think of this passage as giving an account of 'legal obligation'—as misleading as to think of Austin as giving such an account.

(a)   If Rule *R* imposes an obligation then *R* is accepted [this follows from the definition of an obligation-imposing rule as presupposing the internal point of view];

(b)   The primary rules in the minimal legal system are not accepted by anyone; and

(c)   The primary rules in the minimal legal system do impose obligations.

These three propositions form an inconsistent set. In the second place, the claim which Hart is implicitly giving up in order to become consistent deprives him of the grounds for saying his minimal legal system is not an Austinian coercive system. He cannot give up (b), for then we would no longer have a minimal legal system. That is, the minimum conditions for a legal system would be stronger than Hart's positivism seems to require. Suppose he tries giving up (a), on the grounds that in the case of a bad man, the law imposes obligations which he does not accept. The point is now made that the law therefore, as Hart admits, coerces the recalcitrant. In the minimal legal system, the ordinary citizens *ex hypothesi* lack the internal point of view, and are therefore in the same position as the bad man—that is, they are coerced by the law into obedience. The claimed difficulty with Austin's theory was that he represented the law as essentially coercive. The minimal legal system is no better. Claim (c) can be retained in the minimal legal system only if either 'obligation' is construed as Austin construed it or, counterintuitively, the acceptance of the secondary rules by the officials really is enough to create a genuine obligation to obey.

We therefore need to re-examine sophisticated positivism's account of the acceptance of law. We will see that it is not possible to avoid an account of law as coercive without abandoning positivism.

B. The 'Hughes Problem'

A theme that appears more than once in *CL* is that there is one phenomenon to which Austin rightly draws our attention, what Hart refers to as the 'relatively passive aspect' (60, 114) of the existence of a legal system. He has in mind what he calls (*id.*) the 'acquiescence' of ordinary citizens in the results of official operations, their 'acquiescing in the rules by obeying them for [their] part only'. In an earlier paper on legal obligation, he attributed to ordinary citizens acceptance of the fundamental constitutional provisions of their society's legal framework.[11] This claim was criticized by Graham Hughes[12] on the grounds of empirical implausibility. Understanding of constitutional law is a technical matter, Hughes argued, and not normally in the ordinary person's intellectual repertoire. Hart refers in *CL* to this criticism as 'just' (248). It thus seems that the stance of the ordinary citizen to the law is more appropriately thought of as 'passive' and acquiescent than as 'active' and accepting.

---

11. Cf. 'Legal and Moral Obligation', in A.I. Melden, ed., *Essays in Moral Philosophy* (Seattle: University of Washington Press, 1958), 93.

12. Graham Hughes, 'The Existence of a Legal System' (1960), 35 *New York University Law Review* 1001-30, at 1011.

Note that there is an inverse relationship between the Hughes Problem and the Payne Problem. The more that one emphasizes the 'relatively passive' aspect of life under law, the more one represents the position of the ordinary citizen under the law as that of a coerced subject, and thus of a person external to the law. The more that one emphasizes the voluntary co-operation of the ordinary citizen in the maintenance of the system, the more one seems to be attributing to the citizen an understanding of the law which that citizen seems not to have. In order properly to understand the acceptance of law it will be important to consider whether there is a way between these two complementary obstacles.

C. Habits of Obedience

We have to return to the basic vocabulary of simple positivism and sophisticated positivism in their theories of the acceptance of law. I shall argue for the following two theses:

(1) that Hart's discussion is infected with an unsatisfactory dualism; and

(2) that the ordinary meanings of the terms in the vocabulary are too unstable to ground a technical philosophical theory.

The *OED* defines a habit as a settled disposition or tendency to act in a certain way. Hart regards a habit as a pattern of behaviour, and the habits of a group as a convergent pattern of behaviour among the members of the group. Austin does not define 'habit', but the 'habit of obedience' which creates sovereignty is one that must be found in 'the generality or bulk' of the members of a society, and must be 'permanent', not 'rare or transient'. Although Austin speaks of 'habits of obedience', he speaks also of laws as rules laid down for the guidance of an *intelligent* being by an *intelligent* being having power over him, and commands as wishes or desires conceived by a *rational* being, that another rational being shall do or forbear.[13] These three conceptions of 'habit' are not equivalent: Hart's is the odd one out. For Hart associates 'convergent pattern of behaviour' with being 'sheep-like' and with being open to description from the 'extreme external point of view' (cf. *CL* 87). I shall show that a concern with these details on my part is not mere obsessive pedantry.

We are concerned here with the general phenomenon of an efficacious legal system, one in which there is conformity to the law's demands. But what does 'conformity' mean here? 'Conformity' in the most minimal sense means simply a mapping of behaviour on to a norm. That is, norm *N* says, 'In circumstances *C* do *A*'; some individual *S* is in *C* and does *A; S* thus conforms to *N*. This minimal characterization is much too weak to capture the conformity to law which forms part of acceptance of law.[14] Let us imagine the

---

13. John Austin, *The Province of Jurisprudence Determined*, Lecture VI (New York: Humanities Press, 1965).

14. This minimal level of conformity is defined by Wayne Sumner to be 'conformity' as such; cf. *The Moral Foundation of Rights* (Oxford: Clarendon Press 1987), 63, 'in order to conform to a rule I

observer in the extreme external point of view observing behaviour. She formulates a description of a pattern of behaviour in the group. She ascertains that a certain pattern of behaviour is commanded by the sovereign.[15] She sees that the description and the command correspond. Is she now entitled to conclude that the pattern of behaviour is a habit of obedience to a command of the sovereign? No. In addition, she has to establish an appropriate kind of connection between the fact of the sovereign commanding a certain pattern of behaviour and the members of the group displaying that behaviour. The connection would have to be in some way or other causal; the counterfactual would have to be supported that if the command had not occurred the behaviour would not have occurred. It is not difficult to imagine how this might go. Suppose the sovereign commanded A-ing. Was there any pattern of A-ing before the sovereign's command? Was there such a pattern after? Did the behaviour cease when the sovereign ceased to command it? Did A-ing resume when the sovereign again commanded A-ing? And so forth.

This conformity to law established by the external observer is what one might call 'ovine conformity' in deference to Hart's reference (CL 114) to a 'deplorably sheep-like' society. Conformity of this kind is not as straightforward as it seems. The ambiguities are highlighted by a recent Gary Larson Far Side cartoon. The picture shows a sheep standing on its hind legs in the middle of a flock with its forelegs raised high and an enthusiastic expression on its face. The caption is, 'Wait! Wait! Listen to me ... We don't have to be just sheep!' Sheep conform their behaviour to the sheepdog in a sense which supposes no more than a causal connection between the activities of the sheepdog and their activities, of the kind discerned by the external observer in the previous paragraph. Sheep are the paradigm of obedience because they never display the range of behaviour which constitutes disobedience. They do not answer back, question or debate orders, ignore orders, make derisive gestures when the sovereign's back is turned, and so forth. They just do what the dog says and what their leader does. As the cartoon brings out, a society of sheep that makes the huge leap up the chain of being to self-consciousness and the capacity for speech and thought does not become any the less 'sheep-like' if all the sheep do is obediently follow their leader.[16] But they are now metaphorically sheep and not literally sheep. In the case of real sheep, the 'habit of obedience' to the sheepdog and the leader is of a piece with the honesty of Wittgenstein's dog.[17] It may presuppose intentional states on the part of the sheep, but the nature of those intentional states is delimited by that fundamental difference between animals and humans Aristotle chose to mark by denying to animals rationality.

---

need not even know that it exists or applies to me'. There is no set of canonical meanings which rule out either his idiolect or mine as mistaken. The important thing is the identification of the phenomenon.

15. I think in fact it is wholly implausible that an observer from the external point of view could identify a 'sovereign', or even a 'command'. But I shall not press the point here.

16. Even when he orders them not to be sheep? Well, really!

17. 'Why can't a dog simulate pain? Is he too honest? Could one teach a dog to simulate pain? Perhaps it is possible to teach him to howl on particular occasions as if he were in pain, even when he is not. But the surroundings which are necessary for this behaviour to be real simulation are missing.', Ludwig Wittgenstein, Philosophical Investigations (Oxford: Basil Blackwell, 1958), s. 250.

The conformity to law that exists in Hart's 'sheep-like society' cannot be construed as 'ovine conformity', nor is the conformity in the Austinian legal world 'ovine conformity'. Remember Austin's emphasis on the intelligence and rationality of sovereign and subject. Hart likewise does not suppose that the citizens of the sheep-like society have no intentional states; he does not even suppose that they have no intentional states towards the law. He supposes only that their conforming to the law is blind, automatic, uncritical— sheep-like for humans, however natural it may be for sheep.

What is the relation between 'ovine conformity' and 'Austinian conformity', the conformity to law that exists in a society where a habit of obedience has been built up by the fact that the norm-subjects will be visited with evil if they do not comply with the law's demands? Hart implies that 'Austinian conformity' is one kind of 'ovine-conformity', but there is conceptual quicksand here. In his criticism of Austin in chapter 4 of CL, Hart faults Austin for leaving out the 'internal aspect' of rules, for not leaving room for the 'critical reflective attitude' towards rules which is an essential part of what it is for behaviour to be rule-governed. Hart, however, wavers between defining the kind of obedience which lacks the internal point of view as 'obedience from any motive whatever [sc. other than the fact that there is law on the matter]' and as the kind of conformity which is found in a 'sheep-like' society of human beings [not of sheep]. Human sheep-like conformity and human conformity 'from any motive whatever' are however very different notions. A morally sensitive anarchist will never obey the law just because it's the law. On the other hand, she might often conform to the law, on those occasions where she is satisfied that it is right to do A in circumstances C when the law requires its norm-subjects to do A in C. Her reasons for doing A in C will be fundamentally unconnected, or at best indirectly connected, with the fact that the law requires its norm-subjects to do A in C. She is on the other hand far from being sheep-like. She conforms to law from some quite specific and articulate motive. The sensitive anarchist exhibits 'indirect moralistic conformity', as it might be called—the conformity to law which involves on each occasion doing what the law requires because one judges such behaviour as morally required independently of whether the law requires it. That is to be distinguished in its turn from 'direct moralistic conformity', where one judges, for whatever reason, that to obey the law as such is the morally right thing to do.

The notion of 'obedience' is in fact doing three quite different jobs in CL, and Hart does not keep them firmly apart. First, 'obey' and cognates, as pp. 19-20 make clear, are terms of art, code-words, for what I am calling 'Austinian conformity', the conformity to law which results from being coerced by threats. Second, 'obey' and cognates are used to refer to 'outward' behaviour describable without remainder from the external point of view, which contains no implication about the intentionality of the entity exhibiting the behaviour. Hart implies this sense when he distinguishes between a 'habit of obedience' as simply a pattern of behaviour and rule-governed behaviour as a pattern of behaviour plus some 'inner' mental accompaniments (cf. 54-60). Third, 'obey' and cognates are used to refer to a pattern of behaviour which may be performed as an expression of a variety of attitudes, while the referrer prescinds from investigation of, or reference to, the actual attitude accompanying the behaviour. Hart's discourse exemplifies this sense when he speaks about obedience 'from any motive whatever' and obedience 'for his part only' (cf. 113-14). Consider again the anarchist who nonetheless conforms to some subset of the laws's demands because she believes they represent genuine moral duties, and performs the required actions under that description. She does not 'obey' the law in the first sense, since she does not obey out of fear of the consequences and is not coerced. Equally, it is a controversial philosophical hypothesis which would analyze the anarchist's behaviour as 'colourless movement' plus 'inner state'; the truth of such a hypothesis does not follow from the accuracy of the description 'she obeyed the law out of moral respect for its demands as such, and not because the law commanded her'.

Hart also deploys two different conceptions of 'habit'. First, to refer to someone as habitually behaving in a certain way refers to the observable externalities of her behaviour, making no reference at all to the inner mental events that are accompanying the behaviour. It is compatible with behaviour being in this sense 'habitual' that there are no accompanying mental events at all, or at least none of any humanly intentional kind—sheep have 'habits of behaviour' in this sense. Second, to refer to someone as habitually behaving in a certain way refers simply to the fact that she regularly behaves that way; nothing is implied about her reasons for behaving that way. For any given habit, there might be a variety of different reasons for behaving that way, but the reference prescinds from investigation into them.

Confusion occurs because Hart maps these two distinctions on to one another in the wrong way. That is, Hart interprets the 'obedience' of Austinian conformity as a 'habit of obedience' in the first sense of 'habit', when he claims that part of the difficulty with the doctrine of 'habits of obedience' is that it leaves law-conforming behaviour comprehensible without remainder from the external point of view. But this interpretation is a mistake. Recall the external observer who establishes a causal connection between the occurrence of behaviour and the commands of a sovereign. A causal connection of that brute kind could as well be established between the occurrence of a pattern of behaviour and the sovereign riding around on her Harley-Davidson. But that is not what Austin has in mind as the relation between the sovereign and the subjects which creates law. Or rather, if we take seriously Austin's references to the intelligence and rationality of subject and sovereign, then he would seem not to have such a relationship in mind. The way that Hart distinguishes between 'habit' as convergent pattern of behaviour and rule-following behaviour implies that both the person with the external point of view and the habit of obedience and the person with the internal point of view to the rules display the same pattern of behaviour, and that can be acknowledged. But it is wrong to represent that fact as saying that both persons 'obey' the law, or both persons conform to the law, but the first person merely 'obeys' while the second person 'obeys' and has the internal point of view to her obeying. For if 'obedience' is a code-word for Austinian conformity, then it is just false that the person with the internal point of view displays Austinian conformity plus has some other 'mental accompaniments'. Austinian conformity is a habit of conscious conformity to the commands of the sovereign under that description. It is not 'mere external behaviour', although and moreover it is incompatible with possession of the internal point of view. Sumner is guilty of the same confusion. In addition to 'conformity' (*supra* n.14), he defines 'compliance' as conformity to a rule at least in part because of one's awareness of it (*MFR* 63)'. The inclusion of the previous term in the definition of the latter term is deliberate; the test for compliance entails the test for conformity but not *vice versa* (*id.*). But how can a test based on self-conscious behaviour 'entail' or include a test based on behaviour that need not at all be self-conscious? The two tests do not stand to each other in entailment relationships. They are simply two quite different and independent tests. The temptation to see the tests related as Sumner sees them arises only because self-conscious behaviour is construed as 'mere' behaviour or 'colourless movement' plus some inner thing else.

Only the influence of philosophical dualism produces the thought of habits of obedience and convergent patterns of behaviour as 'merely external' or observable without remainder from the external point of view. The dualistic picture seems forced upon us by the simple fact that we have to make room for the case of 'outward' conformity to law accompanied by 'inward' repudiation. Bishop Bramhall has a good turn of phrase here. In the context of the religious struggles in England in the seventeenth century, where the pressure to make public religious observances was great even if one was a dissenter, Bramhall is at pains to block the inference from public observance to genuine belief. He writes: 'They confound obedience of acquiescence with obedience of conformity'.[18] The public 'obedience' is the same in each case; the private 'acquiescence' or 'mere conformity' is what makes the difference. We have 'external behaviour' plus one set of 'mental accompaniments' rather than another set of 'mental accompaniments'. But we have to realize that when we speak in such terms of 'habits of obedience' and the like, we are performing an abstraction from the actual intentional behaviour of persons; we are not referring directly to the actual non-intentional behaviour of non-

18. *A Just Vindication of the Church of England from the Unjust Aspersion of Criminal Schism* (Dublin 1674), II.56. A note about 'acquiescence' in Hart. At 197 in *CL* he treats 'acquiescence' as equivalent to 'obedience' (in his technical sense). On p.114 he refers to the ordinary citizen in the minimal legal system as 'acquiescing in the rules by obeying them for his part alone'. It is not clear whether this sentence makes the two terms equivalent or not. At 60 Hart writes that the ordinary citizen 'manifests his acceptance largely by acquiescence'. This is equivocal. If 'acquiescence' is equivalent to 'obedience', and 'obedience' is incompatible with 'acceptance', then the remark at is nonsensical. On the other hand, if the remark ast 60 is legitimate, and 'sheep-like acquiescence' is a form of acceptance from the internal point of view, then it becomes even less clear how Austin so sadly failed in characterizing the nature of law. The *OED* in fact lists as senses of 'acquiesce' and cognates both ones which connote acknowledgment of authority, thus coming close to Hart's 'acceptance', and ones which connote silent or 'mere outward' conformity, thus coming close to Hart's 'obedience'. Thus Hart's slides in the use of 'acquiescence' seem faithfully to reflect ambiguities in the term itself. In general it does not seem unfair to say that one source of difficulty in coming to grips with this part of Hart's theory is caused by his using ordinary fuzzy-edged and imprecise terms as if they were hard-edged technical terms, yet without stating what the hard-edged technical meaning is.

persons, or of a part of a person.

Wittgenstein considers[19] two cases where we 'speak of a man's angry voice, meaning that he was angry, and again of his angry voice, not meaning that he was angry'. He imagines someone saying that 'in the first case the meaning of the description of his voice was much further reaching than in the second case'. That is, the description in the first case 'reaches under the surface' whereas the description in the second case remains on the surface. The first reaches beyond the surface expression to the real anger beneath, whereas the second reaches only to the surface anger. He goes on to say that the differences correspond to a *picture*, not to two genuinely different usages of the expressions in the descriptions. We have a picture of a inner state lying behind overt behaviour; but it does not follow that legitimate usages of terms correspond to the picture. 'We naturally use this picture to express the distinction between "on the surface" and "below the surface" ... But we *misapply* the picture if we ask whether both cases are or aren't on the surface' (emphases both mine). We use the picture naturally to distinguish the 'obedience of conformity' and the 'obedience of acquiescence' or acceptance. But it does not follow that 'conformity' is simply the 'surface' part of 'acceptance'/'acquiesence as acceptance'. If we were to think in those terms, the picture would have taken over. It would have developed a life of its own, and forced our thinking into its pattern. The picture would have become our master, not our servant.[20]

There are two quite different continua of cases here. The first continuum runs from blind, unthinking ('sheep-like', if you insist) conformity at one end to highly self-conscious and articulate conformity at the other end. The second continuum runs from sheer fear of the physical sanction at one end to full commmitment to moral worthiness at the other. That these continua are different is shown by the fact that the external point of view may be found anywhere on the first continuum—both the anarchist and the revolutionary self-consciously and articulately repudiate the authority of law. On the other hand, the point of the second continuum is to show that at some stage one passes from the external point of view to the internal point of view as one progresses along the continuum. Hart's complaint about Austin may be seen as the complaint that Austin locates the intentional stance which helps to create law far too near the beginning of the second continuum. Hart's anti-positivistic opponent will say that the same is true of Hart himself. Note though, that *contra* Hart and Sumner, there is no continuum which runs from mere convergent patterns of behaviour or, in Sumner's sense, mere 'conformity' at one end to convergent pattern of behaviour plus full commitment to moral worthiness at the other. Hart construes his disagreement with Austin as being over where to locate the existence of law on that putative but illusory continuum only because of his thinking of the mind in dualistic terms. The 'pic-

19. 'Notes for Lectures on "Private Experience" and "Sense-Data"' (1968), 77 *Philosophical Review*, 275-320, at 303-4.
20. I have discussed at length elsewhere the deleterious effects of this 'picture' with respect to another complex philosophical problem, that of how to understand the expressive qualities of works of art. See 'The Mental Life of a Work of Art' (1982), 40 *Journal of Aesthetics and Art Criticism* 253-68, *passim*.

ture' of Wittgenstein's discussion has taken over.

We are now in a position to see why it is important to move out from under the shadow cast by philosophical dualism when thinking about the acceptance of law. The notion of a habit as a settled disposition or tendency to act in a certain way is at face value a pre-philosophical or pre-analytic notion. 'Disposition' here does not have to be the technical term of philosophical behaviourism, but merely a reference to the logic of the notion. Now, Hart's vulnerability to the stresses of the Payne Problem and the Hughes Problem is a consequence of his desire to give full weight to the 'relatively passive aspect' of everyday life under the law. I have claimed that the way to a satis-factory account of the acceptance of law will be one which avoids those stresses. I have now shown that Hart's construal of the 'relatively passive aspect' is infected with philosophical dualism. It is tempting now to diagnose that the infection is causing the vulnerability. Perhaps if we cease to think about the 'relatively passive aspect' in dualistic terms, we may be able to construe that aspect in a way which avoids the two Problems, and which thus leads to a more plausible account of the acceptance of law. The price will of course be that such a more plausible theory will be a form of anti-positivism.

D. The Rule of Recognition

The coincidence of the two Problems obtains primarily with respect to the ultimate rule of recognition, that secondary rule which is the source of validity for all the other rules of the system. The ultimate rule of recognition, Hart says, exists only as a complex, but normally concordant, practice of the courts, officials, and private persons in identifying the law by reference to certain criteria (*CL* 107).

It is clear that appreciation of technical questions of constitutional law is reserved for professionals, and thus that whatever stance the ordinary citizen has towards the ultimate rule of recognition it is unlikely to be the full internal point of view. Thus it seems most plausible to represent the stance towards the ultimate rule of recognition of the ordinary citizen as one which requires little in the way of specific mental accompaniments. The price to be paid, and Hart clearly thinks it worth paying, is that the citizen then merely 'obeys' the law, like an Austinian subject.

Let us look more closely at the characterization of the ultimate rule of recognition above. As previous discussion has indicated, whatever intentional stance towards the law we regard as necessary to create law, it has to be one in which the law goes under the description 'the law'. The ultimate rule of recognition is a normally concordant practice of *identification*. What does this mean? Even if we restrict attention momentarily to the officials, the 'practice' does not refer merely to explicit verdicts relating (in Canada) to cases involving the documents specified in s.52(2) of the *Constitution Act* 1982.[21] A court which unhesitatingly rejects an act by a corporation or person

---

21. These documents are the *Canada Act* 1982, a statute of the Westminster parliament, which includes the *Constitution Act* containing the Charter of Rights and Freedoms; thirty other Acts and orders which are schedules to the *Constitution Act;* and any subsequent amendments to the foregoing. As Peter Hogg

on the ground that it infringes a controlling statute is as much participating in the 'concordant practice' of identification as the Supreme Court in a *Charter* case. That is, the Supreme Court displays its acceptance of the ultimate rule of recognition explicitly, by acknowledging a decision as required by the *Charter*. The other court does so implicitly, by applying a rule which is valid by the requirements of the Constitution of Canada. So the practice is misleadingly described as one of 'identification'. It would only be in the rare case that the issue before a court would be resolved by a decision which *identified* a norm as a valid rule. The concordant practice is far more one of the *use* of certain rules rather than others, rules with the proper 'pedigree'. The participants in the practice all agree (are of one mind) that a norm is a valid legal rule just in case it has a certain pedigree, and they agree on what that pedigree is. 'Valid legal rule' here means that the rule is properly applied in, e.g., the adjudication of disputes or in the specification of position. The norm is one understanding of which is properly an essential element in the possession of 'legal expertise'.

We seem now though to have simply shifted the problem, by substituting 'use' for 'identification'. Hart (*CL* 114, 117) uses the expression 'accept and use', almost as if this was a hendiadys. He also (*CL* 59-60) distinguishes legislators making law within their powers, courts applying laws in adjudication, and experts advising under law all three *from* the ordinary citizen who keeps the law, makes claims and exercises power under it, thus manifesting his or her acceptance largely by acquiescing. Peter Hacker objects that the notion of 'using a rule' is 'opaque'; if it means 'constantly consulting the rule book', then it hardly goes along with acceptance, because the tax-evader is likely to be busily consulting the tax rules.[22] I think in fact that a variety of different cases need to be here distinguished. There is certainly a sense in which the officials of the system actively 'use' the secondary rules which regulate their official duties and the primary rules which they apply in the daily execution of their professional duties. There is a sense in which every citizen in every day life makes use of private law—in using public transport whether of civic or private ownership, in making purchases at stores, and so forth. The citizen driver also makes use of a particular regulatory framework. Even though we may not every day write a cheque or make a deposit or buy or sell an investment, our money is every day subject to and (usually) protected by law. Moreover, every citizen benefits from the existence of set and enforceable procedures for the undertaking of voluntary

---

points out (*Constitutional Law of Canada*, 2nd. edn. [Toronto: Carswell Company 1985], 6-7), the wording of s.52(2) says merely that the Constitution of Canada 'includes' these documents. There are a number of other plausibly constitutional documents, including, e.g., the *Supreme Court Act,* which are not on the schedule. There are also those conventions of government which 'are not contained in any authoritative written instrument'. We shall assume any identification problems these further materials are soluble.

22. Cf. 'Hart's Philosophy of Law', in P.M.S. Hacker and J. Raz, eds., *Law, Morality and Society: Essays in Honour of H.L.A. Hart* (Oxford: Clarendon Press 1977) 1-25, at 16. The distinction accountants actually use is between 'tax avoidance', a perfectly legitimate activity and (in the libertarian political morality) even a right, and 'tax evasion', which is criminal. Hacker's point seems to require the tax-evader, for he or she will most likely have the external point of view. However, the tax-avoider seems most likely to be the enthusiastic reader of the Income Tax Act. The tax-evader is a perverse or incompetent tax-avoider.

obligations, even though that diffuse benefit is distinct from the particular benefit gained from embarking on a particular undertaking. Some parts of private law are highly specialized, and only those in certain positions will make use of it—immigration law, the law of libel, copyright law, etc. Every citizen 'uses' in the sense of 'benefits from' 'public good' laws such as laws imposing licensing standards, pollution regulations, safety standards, and so forth. In these cases, it is not the citizen who 'uses', the law in the sense of immediately abiding by the law—that will be the manufacturer, the lawyer, doctor, innkeeper, etc. But the laws daily affect our lives.[23] Every citizen (or the vast majority of citizens) 'uses' the criminal law in a different sense from the regulatory framework. For any who do not break the criminal law abide by it. Only the milk manufacturer abides by milk-purity regulations, though many people benefit from this abiding. But all who do not steal abide by the law against stealing, and so in a sense 'use' it.

In short, the problem is not that the term 'use' is too opaque to describe clearly how citizens stand to the legal system. The problem is rather that citizens stand to the system in many different ways, and this variety is concealed by the deployment of a single term like 'use'. This is, though, a significant result. For, while Hart and Hughes have rightly pointed out that the officials' and the citizens' stances to the law cannot be reduced to one model, Hart has adopted nonetheless one model of what it is to 'accept' the law, the one he finds in the officials as they daily enact their official duties. 'Acceptance' as a state of mind is one determined to exist as a straightforward function of episodes of interaction. Furthermore, the notion of 'habit', with which 'accept' is contrasted, is also ambiguous. Two quite different cases may be distinguished. The first is the case of some personal mannerism of which the person might not at all be aware, such as walking with one's hands joined behind one's back, or (as I'm told I behave) smoothing the hair forward while lecturing. 'Habitual' behaviour in this sense can certainly be 'sheep-like' in the sense of 'mindless'. But when Aristotle in *Nicomachean Ethics* II.6 and elsewhere argued that virtues should be regarded as *hexeis* or 'dispositions', and that a virtue is a disposition to choose according to the mean, he did not mean to urge the moral value of a sheep-like existence. Instead, he meant to depict the virtuous person as the person who had developed the capacity to do the good thing without thinking, who had internalized virtuous behaviour to the point where it had become (as we say) 'second nature'. This second sense of 'habitual', so far from being incompatible with the internal point of view, in fact presupposes it. Hart, however, concentrates only on the first paradigm of 'habit'. It is as least possible that, by his concentration on one paradigm of both 'accept' and 'habit', Hart has presented a false picture of the acceptance of law. I shall now argue that such is indeed the case.

---

23. Soper misleadingly talks of the 'involuntary, passive stance' of those who benefit from public good regulations (*A Theory of Law* [Cambridge, MA: Harvard University Press, 1984], 72). I think the remark is misleading, because our stance towards such regulations when we simply live in an environment which they regulate is neither 'active' (unlike the manufacturer or the environmental activist) nor 'passive' (unlike the residents of the company town who put up with pollution for the sake of jobs).

E. Interacting with the Legal System

It is not difficult to see how the concentration on one paradigm might have arisen. I surveyed above different ways of construing the notion of 'using' a legal system. If we think of 'using' as 'directly interacting' (in some sense), then it is easy for the officials' participation and certain instances of citizens' participation to be the paradigms of 'using'. Being served with a writ, suing for breach of contract, being arrested, voting on a bill, hearing a *Charter of Rights* case, being given a parking ticket, and so forth, will all be instances of directly interacting with the legal system. If this is the model for 'using' the legal system, then it is clearly so that officials of the system 'use' it far more than do ordinary citizens. Moreover, if 'use' is at all closely connected with 'accept', then it is very easy to assume that the system will function only if acceptance of law is found in officials, and that acceptance of law is therefore not required of citizens. For 'use' in this sense of 'direct interaction' with the legal system does not imply 'acceptance' for many activities that citizens might undertake. A black person in South Africa, for instance, may hire a lawyer to pursue such lawful avenues as exist for getting detainees released from prison, while altogether repudiating the internal point of view towards a legal system based on apartheid.[24]

As we saw above, the Hughes Problem forced Hart to reconsider his optimism about citizens' 'acceptance', and to prefer the Payne Problem as the lesser of two evils. He did not take this option arbitrarily. Two other factors combined to make this the plausible-looking option. First, there is the following complex point. Assume arguendo that Austin did indeed set jurisprudence going in the wrong direction by emphasizing habits of obedience to a sovereign, commands backed by threats, and so forth. Austin, we might say, obscured the difference between conformity which is 'sheep-like' or 'for any reason whatever', on the one hand, and conformity from the internal point of view on the other. All the same, Austin was not obtuse. There is, as Hart remarks, a 'vital difference' (*CL* 112) between the behaviour of officials in relation to the law and the behaviour of ordinary citizens in relation to the law. This difference is such that to say that the latter 'obey' the law is pretty much the truth, whereas to say that the officials when carrying out their official duties 'obey' the law distorts enormously the nature of rule-making, -identifying, -applying and -enforcing. Austin was very well aware of that difference, even if he thought that legal rules were commands. Moreover, to say that legal rules are commands of superiors to inferiors is not at all a bad way of marking that difference. Hart tried to combine Austin's insight with his own by thinking of the behaviour of the officials in relation to the law as essentially 'active' and the behaviour of the ordinary citizens in relation to the law as essentially 'passive'. The combination works as follows. One can

---

24. Cf. Michael Payne, 'Law Based on Accepted Authority' (1982), 23 *William and Mary Law Review* 501-28, at 508, who rightly rejects an earlier attempt by myself to argue otherwise on this and other related points (Roger A. Shiner, 'Hart and Hobbes' (1980), 22 *William and Mary Law Review* 201). Even though this latter paper is the ancestor of the present discussion as concerns my own thinking, the view of Hart is quite different.

indeed obey a rule passively/acquiescently, so that Austin's insight can be preserved; it is rules that can be obeyed passively, so Hart's own insight can be preserved. However, acceptance and the internal point of view are clearly incompatible with passive obedience. Therefore, it seems extremely plausible to say that only the active officials really accept the legal system.

F. The Disposition to Accept the Law

Let us review so far the discussion of the acceptance of a legal system. The Hughes Problem is a real problem. Genuine acceptance of the law implies more than mere conformity of external behaviour to the law. It requires some intentional element. But it is counterintuitive to represent the ordinary citizen as interacting with the law in just the way that the official of the system interacts with the law. The citizen's mental stance towards the law cannot be represented as embodying the knowledge of the professional. On the other hand, if it is a mistake to represent the law as a system of coercive commands, then the Payne Problem is a real problem too. One cannot pay the price for avoiding the Hughes Problem that one leaves the citizen as conforming to law only through sheep-like acquiescence or a fear of being visited with evil. Justice is not thereby done to the demand for an adequate account of the internal point of view to law. We need a way of understanding how citizens accept the law which nonetheless preserves the real difference between the role of citizen and the role of official. We need a conception of how the ordinary citizen interacts with the law that manifests acceptance, while acknowledging that this acceptance is not manifested in the way that the officals' daily and continuous intentional operation of the system in accord with its secondary rules manifests their acceptance of those rules.

Let us return to the philosophy of mind and its bearing on the question of the acceptance of a legal system. I have quoted already Wittgenstein's claim that surroundings are necessary to make a particular piece of behaviour an expression of a mental state (cf. *supra* at p. 90 n. 17). Here is a passage from Wittgenstein's *Brown Book*,[25] which makes a similar claim about the idea of voluntary action:

> Acting voluntarily (or involuntarily) is, in many cases, characterized as such by a multitude of circumstances under which the action takes place rather than by an experience which we should call characteristic of voluntary action (157)

Wittgenstein in this passage is primarily concerned to talk about the nature of understanding, and this remark about voluntary action is thrown in by the way. There are in fact two points to be made and this is only one of them. The other is implicit in his discussion of grief in Part II of the *Philosophical Investigations* (at 174, 187), where Wittgenstein says things like 'Why does it sound queer to say: "For a second he felt deep grief"? Only because it so seldom happens?' When one is dealing with a mental state like grief, or

---

25. Ludwig Wittgenstein, *The Blue and Brown Books* (Oxford: Basil Blackwell, 1960).

understanding, or, I want to say, the acceptance of a legal system, not only is one dealing with a state whose logic is that of a disposition existing over time, not that of an episode; one is also dealing with a state whose existence is criterially linked to a certain context. These points are independent though collaborative in the following way. It is true that, for example, a particular episode in a person's life is the expression of grief—tears come to his eyes and he falls silent. But what makes that episode the expression of grief— rather than, for example, dismay or tearful anger—is in part the context in which the episode occurs. A loved one has been lost, there are other similar episodes around the same time, and, most importantly, he is in a culture where grief is expressed thus. Even though tears and silences are stronger candidates for 'natural reactions' than the wearing of black armbands and the closing of businesses, they are still culturally conditioned. Thus, to grieve is to be disposed to certain reactions, and to be so disposed in a certain cultural context.

Concentration on the cases where a person directly interacts with the legal system in constructing the paradigm for 'acceptance' selects as the paradigm an act which is a dateable episode. As a paradigm for the acceptance of a legal system, however, the signing of a contract or the making of an arrest is liable to mislead in two ways—first, these events are episodes rather than dispositions, whereas accepting the law is a dispositional stance, not a date- able episode: second, a genuine signing of a contract, despite what the liber- al paradigm takes it to be, is not a mere episode; it requires a cultural context, in the form of an understood set of rules—not any signature on a piece of paper is a signing of a contract. I want to suggest now how construing accep- tance as primarily a long-term disposition in a social context provides a more satisfactory picture of the 'relatively passive aspect' of law, the everyday stance of citizens towards the law.

Let us look again at some remarks by Hart himself. On p.60 of *CL* he remarks that the ordinary citizen manifests his acceptance of law largely by acquiescence in the results of the officials' activities. Let us call the episodes which count for purposes of determining acceptance 'manifestations' of acceptance, where 'manifesting' means weakly 'giving evidence', not strong- ly 'giving conclusive evidence'. This comment about acquiescence Hart then glosses as the fact that the citizen 'keeps the law which is made and identified in this way, and also makes claims and exercises powers conferred by it'. P.98 and p.107 concede to 'private persons' as well as to officials the ability to identify laws and to use them. Hart also at p.99 refers to the use of legal language in a certain way as being evidence for acceptance, e.g., the use of expressions of the form 'It is the law that ...'. Finally, at pp.136-7 he makes clearly the point that acceptance, or possession of the internal point of view, is quite compatible with the occurrence of law-conforming bevaiour being on some given occasions quite thoughtless and instinctive. Let us apply these points to the case of the ordinary citizen and the law.

One must certainly count in while assessing the acceptance of law by ordi- nary citizens the occasions when they overtly make claims and exercise powers. My argument is an argument against views which count in only such episodes. We must also take seriously as genuine manifestations of acceptance the use of normative language and the keeping of the law. Granting the fact that my view of what the law is does not have the status that my lawyer's does, and that each of those does not have the status that Brian Dickson's does, and especially when he sat as Chief Justice, nonetheless I see no reason not to and every reason to count informal use of normative language as part of the episodes which contribute to the acceptance of law by ordinary citizens. After all, Hart mentions as part of the evidence for a system of rules existing that deviations are regarded as open to criticism, threatened deviations meet with pressure for conformity, and criticism is regarded as legitimate. It is extremely difficult to see how all that could go on without the use of normative legal language.

However, the proposed criterion that really interests me is that of 'keeping the law'. I think Hart is quite right about this, and that he overlooks its significance. To put the matter bluntly, do I not manifest, i.e., give evidence of, my acceptance of criminal statutes every time I do *not* murder, do *not* steal, do *not* assault a policeman in the execution of his duty, do *not* commit contempt of court, and so forth? Here we need to remember the distinction between legal duties and legal prohibitions. When I have a legal duty of care towards my neighbour, I manifest my acceptance of that duty by taking such care—warning her I am mixing explosive chemicals, doing it far from the property line, and so forth. But where the law prohibits something, I manifest my acceptance of that prohibition, not by acting, but by omitting to act. To put out one's hand towards the cookie jar and withdraw it, or to turn down the offer to cut one in on a good caper that one just received in a pub are certainly among kinds of action that manifest acceptance. But why a prejudice in favour of commissions over omissions? I see no good reason. Turning offers down and the like are not dissimilar to criticizing, pressing charges, suing for damages, marrying before witnesses, because they are 'active'. But suppose one simply never steals. The 'passive' nature of that by comparison should not blind us to the fact that *not* stealing, raping, driving while impaired, etc. is in fact *actively* to lead a law-abiding life. If the constraint is that acceptance must be inferred chiefly from what people 'actively' do, it is perverse to count a failure to steal as activity of the relevant kind only if it is accompanied by something like turning down a proposal in a pub.[26]

Likewise, active episodes in relation to public good regulations may be confined to those who bring suit if the regulations are broken or who campaign for tightening or relaxing the regulations. But there is no more reason to deny the attribution to me of acceptance of milk purity regulations, e.g., when all I do is buy milk, e.g., than there is to deny the sleeping virtuous per-

---

26. Sumner claims that 'I conform to a rule prohibiting murder *just in case* I do not commit murder' (*MFR* 63; my emphasis). The material equivalence is a mistake. My not committing murder is compatible with, and even (I am trying to argue) evidence for, my accepting the law. Thus it is possible that I both conform to the law by not committing murder and accept the law. Therefore it is false that if I do not commit murder I conform to the law. The response might be that, by definition, accepting includes conforming though not the reverse. I have already given reasons for doubting this claimed inclusion; see above at p. 93.

son his or her virtue. Although there is room for episodes in the analysis of virtue, their role is more complex than directly to provide the evidence for the possession of virtue. Aristotle distinguishes two aspects in the performance of virtuous acts—the development of the disposition to act virtuously, and the exercise of that disposition on some given occasion by performing a virtuous act.[27] The virtuous person is still virtuous while asleep,[28] and a virtuous act is only centrally so when done by the virtuous person. Precisely the same act done by one learning to be or feigning to be virtuous is 'virtuous' in some derivative (though easily comprehensible) sense.

What makes the sleeping virtuous person virtuous is the truth of a variety of counterfactuals—if she were awake and in such-and-such circumstances, she would act thus and so. The truth to the talk of the 'relatively passive aspect' of the legal system is this—that for most ordinary citizens the occasions on which they directly interact with the legal system are relatively few. I make this concession, though I have given some reasons above for thinking it nonetheless to be a mistake (cf. 96-97, pp. 100-101). But as long as the attribution of the acceptance of law can be supported by the truth of counterfactuals, there is no reason to regard the 'relatively passive aspect' of law as evidence of sheep-like acquiescence. The surrounding cultural context is very different from that of the sheep paddock.

Let us take the hardest possible case for the position offered here. Suppose an ordinary citizen by name Ovid. Ovid has led the following eccentric life. His behaviour has always been in conformity to law; he has never exhibited any of the verbal and non-verbal behaviour which manifests a reflective critical attitude; he has never had any episodic interactions with the law—or else only such a minimal number as to be irrelevant; we might, for instance, permit his mother to have registered his birth. Ovid seems the epitome of 'sheep-like acquiescence'. Ovid is now on his deathbed. Could it be shown, absent a deathbed confession, that Ovid nonetheless was an accepter, not a passive conformer? If dispositional acceptance is to be what counts as acceptance—that is, if to accept is to be disposed to produce episodes manifesting acceptance—then, since *ex hypothesi* Ovid has produced no such episodes, it seems that either I must deny Ovid is a dispositional accepter, which seems to undermine the strategy of using the omission of law-breaking actions as evidence of acceptance, or I must show that Ovid can be recognized as an accepter without widening the notion of acceptance to the point where the distinction between acceptance and 'ovine' conformity is obliterated. I attempt the latter route.

Consider the case of Leo the lion. Leo, like Ovid, is on his deathbed. He has led a zoo-bound life in which he has not once chased an antelope. Yet we know it to be true of Leo that, if he were not in a cage, he would chase antelopes. How do we know this of Leo? We have observed what has happened to Leo's fellow-lions when they have lived in the wild, been released into the wild, and so forth. We also know a certain amount of ethology and

---

27. Cf. *Nic Eth* I.8, II.1; *de Anima* II.1.
28. The truth of this remark is not confined to those specialized occasions where being asleep is the virtuous thing.

physiology. We use all of that information to present a cogent case for it being true that if Leo were not in a cage, he would chase antelopes. Now we compare in the same way Ovid with his fellow citizens. We see those whom we are sure have the internal point of view behaving in the same sort of law-abiding manner as does Ovid. True, we also see and hear them criticizing, and Ovid does not do that. We see them less leery than Ovid is of entanglements with the law. But we are not unintelligent observers of the world's stage. We know what psychological mechanisms make people afraid to criticize other people even when their behaviour suggests they have different normative standards than those other people and would, without such insecurities, criticize them. We also know what makes people afraid of involvement with the law, even though they do as a matter of fact think that all things considered the law is a good thing and they accept that it legitimately imposes obligations to obey. So, although the difference between knowledge of the mind of another and knowledge of the ethology of lions properly leads us to say that, although we can not be certain Ovid is an accepter, we can present a reasonable-looking argument.

And that's all I need. My claim is only that the grammar of acceptance is such that criterially behaviour is evidence of the internal point of view, and that even in Ovid's case, there is reason to say the criteria are met. Ovid may be borderline, in the sense that we can not be sure he is an accepter. But this uncertainty is not chronic Cartesian uncertainty. In principle the logic, the grammar of Ovid's case is no different than the case of Brian Dickson, although the conclusion in the latter case may be much more certain. Inferring acceptance is a matter of inferring the existence of a disposition. Such an inference about doubtful cases is based in the end on behavioural parallels between those about whom we have no doubt that they have the internal point of view and those about whom we have such doubts. We make inferences to the internal point of view and to acceptance, not inference to a mere disposition to manifest certain episodes, because manifesting episodes of that kind just is, in the right circumstances—namely, living in a society with a legal system—criterial for the internal point of view.

One obvious result of using a criterion like the above for the acceptance of a legal system is that, I would say, Canada comes out as being a society in which the legal system is accepted. But, one may feel like objecting, so what? The theory just offered is in fact an account of what it is for a society to be healthy, to accept a legal system in that way. I have not therefore said anything which is inconsistent with Hart's basic account of acceptance. I certainly have not shown what I would need to show to rebut Hart, that this is a theory of acceptance as such, and that a legal system in which there is that minimal level of acceptance which obtains in Hart's 'sheep-like' society is not possible. The objection is sound. I have not yet shown all that. But I have done something which is a necessary step towards showing that—namely, to make some attempt to break the hold on us of the individualist picture of acceptance. As for showing that the theory is a theory of acceptance as such, here is where the speculation comes in. The position I have sketched will become interesting and incompatible with Hart only if one can show that the functions which take one from acceptance by individual members of the group to acceptance by the group, and from acceptance of particular laws to acceptance of the system of laws are stronger than the essentially numerical and aggregative functions of sophisticated positivism. They will have to be instead functions which make the above transitions a matter of nature, not contingency. I shall try to sketch a motivation for such functions by sketching the general theory which deploys them.

Consider the argument about Leo the lion. Why metaphysically is that argument persuasive? Because in the end what it is appealing to is a concept of, if you like, lion nature. It is in the nature of lions, if they are not in cages, to chase antelopes. So also the comparable inference in the Ovid case may be underwritten by a concept of human nature. When we are bringing to bear on the Ovid case what we know of human behaviour, we are bringing to bear what we know of human nature. If, then, it is the natural behaviour of human beings that underwrites grammatically in the way outlined the inference in the Ovid case, then, in acknowledging that to be so, one is acknowledging that human beings are naturally accepters of law, not merely Hartian obeyers. And if that is true, then societies are naturally healthy. 'Normally citizens accept their legal systems' is a non-contingent truth.

I distinguished above (at p. 92) two different senses of 'habit', a sense which was compatible with the behaviour of animals being called 'habitual', and one which was not. An episode in which a gunman points a gun and says, 'Your money or your life', is not in itself evidence of a 'habit of obedience'. Part of the reason why Austin emphasized 'habits of obedience' was his awareness of the two-fold generality of law. Laws differ from the commands of a gunman in being both commands of classes of acts, and commands addressed to classes of people. Law, as Hart emphasized, is also continuous and persistent, not occasional. These facts seem to imply a greater degree of conscious complicity on the part of the law-abiding than the simple model of commands backed by threats allows. Hart's proposal—to include in the analysis of law the internal point of view to law, but say that law, to be law, may be obeyed 'for any motive whatever'—is an attempt to include complicity, but to have it still be a formal notion. The price is an essentially coercive model of law, and moreover one that seems to depend on a separation of mind and body of an implausibly dualistic kind. The view being presented here is one that in a sense reinstates the notion of 'habit' as a way of understanding law-abiding behaviour. The importance of construing the 'habit' as the developed disposition of an intelligent being is that its 'passivity' implies a 'thick' notion of complicity, one that involves acceptance of the legitimacy of the law's demands. It becomes, as it might be put, 'second nature' to us to obey the law. 'Second nature' might be distinguishable from 'first nature'—let us suppose that non-humans only have 'first nature'—but nonetheless for that 'second nature' is 'nature'.

Here it is necessary to investigate seriously what it is to take the internal point of view to law. It is not simply a matter of producing episodes which manifest the internal point of view. It is a matter of a stable, long-term disposition to produce such episodes. I have been arguing that, once this claim is granted, the major motive for, and the major reason for, interpreting the 'relatively passive aspect' of everyday life under the law as a mode of 'sheep-like acquiescence' disappears. Nonetheless, some account is needed of why it might be 'second nature' to obey the law, other than the account which has been ruled out of obedience coerced by threat. Antony Duff has argued that

> we can explain what it is to accept a legal rule, and what the significance of such acceptance, by officials or citizens, is within a legal system, only if we explicate the kinds of significance or value which are internal to this, as to any, kind of rule ... .[29]

He quotes Aquinas on law as an ordinance of reason for the common good and says that (82) 'if law is essentially a rational enterprise of this kind, a legal system ... must be justified to [its citizens] by an appeal which refers to some conception of the common good'. In other words, it is true that simple positivism errs through omitting reference to the internal point of view, and to the acceptance of law. But sophisticated positivism in deeming law to exist even in the minimal legal system where the internal point of view is confined to the officials, in fact no more than simple positivism takes the internal point of view seriously. By construing the internal point of view to law as a matter of the successive production of episodes of interaction, sophisticated positivism omits to take into account what sort of enterprise law is. Law addresses itself to the citizen as much as to the official. It addresses itself to the citizen *qua* rational agent, not *qua* manipulable sheep. It claims to earn acceptance by standards of reason, justice and the common good. But if a stable and functioning legal system exists, and it is not a coercive system, then it follows that it must be accepted. And if a normative system is not a legal system unless it is not coercive, then a normative system is not a legal system unless it is accepted. To point to a largely non-coercive and efficacious legal system is therefore to point to an entity which is paradigmatically a legal system, not merely a healthy example of something which is just as much a legal system even if coercive and not 'healthy'.

5. Conclusion

The most simple, and perhaps most simplistic, account of the acceptance of a legal system is one which reduces acceptance to passive conformity. But if we take seriously the differences between humans and sheep, then we see that there is something deeply misleading about looking at human conformity to law as 'sheep-like'. We also have the sense that to represent the normativity of law as purely coercive is to distort law. It is to imply, what is not the case, that we would have the concepts of law and legality that we have even though history contained nothing but repressive regimes.

However, if we start to take seriously the intentional element in acceptance of law, and we interpret the intentional element in terms of the knowl-

---

29. 'Legal Obligation and the Moral Nature of Law' (1980), 61 *Juridical Review* at 79.

edge of and stance towards the technicalities of law found among officials, it remains hard to see how citizens can accept the law. On the other hand, if citizens do not accept the law but merely conform to its demands, then law remains from the point of view of its citizens a coercive order.

Theory now faces a dilemma. On the one hand, acceptance by citizens cannot be the same as acceptance by officials; on the other hand, acceptance by citizens has to be genuine acceptance. I have suggested that the obstructive force of this dilemma derives from assuming an episodic model for acceptance and consent. If acceptance is construed in terms of a disposition to display law-abiding behaviour, then there is no bar to finding that the ordinary citizen accepts the law. The ordinary law-abiding citizen's interaction with the law is as deliberate and complicitous and as enduring as that of the professional official.

Then we have to ask the question of whether it is plausible to construe such acceptance as simply contingent. Is it purely a matter of historical accident whether a legal system is 'healthy' or 'sheep-like'? If it is a perversion of law that the legal order is a coercive order, then it cannot be contingent that law is accepted. But if that is true, then the merit of law is not separate from its existence. And if that is true, then positivistic or content-independent accounts of law cannot be correct as theories of law.

The insight that legal theory needed to take into account the point of view of those who accepted the law arose within the positivistic tradition. It arose in connection with the insight that to represent law as a system of commands backed by threats is to misrepresent law. But if those insights are valid insights, then legal theory is impelled irresistibly away from legal positivism.

4

Law's Pragmatism: Law as Practice and Narrative

Dennis M. Patterson*

> The more concrete the idea, the greater the probability. The more abstract the medium is, the less the probability; the more concrete, the more. But what does it mean that the medium is concrete except that it either is, or is seen in its approximation to, language, for language is the most concrete of all media.
>
> —*Kierkegaard*[1]

Introduction

The demise of foundationalism, the attempt to find an indubitable ground for claims to knowledge and truth, has been both charted and heralded.[2] Among the views that have been advanced to fill the void left in the wake of foundationalism's demise is pragmatism. Though pragmatism's roots lie in early twentieth century philosophical thought, it has in recent years undergone a renaissance that borders on a rebirth. Legal scholars have been among those in the forefront of that rebirth, championing the revival of pragmatism in the human sciences.[3] But what does it mean to be "pragamatic" about the law? This chapter advances an answer to this question by providing an outline for a pragmatist theory of legal discourse.

The demise of foundationalism in twentieth century philosophical thought is largely reflected in the questions philosophers now ask. In epistemology, for example, debate has shifted from questions regarding the indubitable grounds for knowledge to an attempt to specify the conditions under which one can rightly claim to have knowledge.[4] The inclination to ask, not for the grounds of knowledge, but for the conditions under which assertions of knowledge will be accepted is informed by a distinct view of the relationship between language and the world. This view sees language as constitutive, as the medium through which understanding occurs. Once one accepts this

---

*Professor of Law, Rutgers University School of Law—Camden.
  1. S. Kierkegaard, Either/Or 55 (H. Hong & E. Hong trans. 1987).
  2. The demise of the varieties of *philosophical* foundationalism is described in R. Rorty, Philosophy and the Mirror of Nature (1979). For a critique of foundationalism in ethics, see B. Williams, Ethics and the Limits of Philosophy 1-70 (1985). For a broader view of the demise of modernism, see D. Harvey, The Condition of Postmodernity 3-118 (1989).
  3. For a review of the literature, as well as the presentation of a substantive theory of pragmatic statutory interpretation, see Eskridge & Frickey, Statutory Interpretation as Practical Reasoning, 42 Stan. L. Rev. 321 (1990); see also Eskridge, Gadamer/Statutory Interpretation, 90 Colum. L. Rev. 609 (1990).
  4. As Keith Lehrer has stated:

  > A theory of knowledge need not be a theory about the meaning of epistemic words any more than it need be a theory about how people come to know what they do. Instead, it may be one explaining what conditions must be satisfied and how they must be satisfied in order for a person to know something.

  K. Lehrer, Theory of Knowledge 5 (1990).

view of language, the investigation of the use of language becomes paramount. In other words, the recognition that cognition is a function of language, and not of reason, is the key to abandonment of foundationalism. For if all understanding occurs in and through language, then only the study of language will bring us closer to truth.[5]

It is the thought of Ludwig Wittgenstein which is central to modern philosophy's turn to language. For Wittgenstein, all philosophical problems are ultimately problems of language. This approach is evident in his treatment of what it means to "follow a rule."[6] Consider, for example, the rule of "plus." "75" is the answer to the question "what is 50 + 25?" But how do we know that this answer is correct; what tells us that this is the rule of "plus"? A skeptic might claim that "plus" means "add the numbers up to seventy, but after 70, always add an additional 5." Thus for the skeptic, "80" would be the correct answer to the question "what is 50 + 25?" How do we prove the skeptic wrong? To what do we appeal; what counts as evidence for or against our, or the skeptic's, claim to correctness?

These are the questions that surround the now much discussed problem of "the skeptical paradox" of rule-following.[7] Two distinct philosophical views of the rule-following paradox have emerged from the literature. The first of these is advanced by the principal English-language commentators on Wittgenstein, Peter Hacker and Gordon Baker. They argue that there exists an "internal relation" between a rule and what counts as acting in accordance with it. It is the rule, and nothing else, that determines what counts as a correct application of the rule. The opposing view is the "community consensus" perspective. According to this view, there is a "community consensus" that serves as a mediating device between a rule and what counts as acting in accordance with that rule. Thus, it is not the rule, per se, but the conduct of the requisite social group that determines what constitutes acting in accordance with the rule.

The debate between Baker and Hacker and the community consensus view parallels in many ways the contemporary dispute in legal theory over the indeterminacy of law. As such, the debate over rule-following in the later Wittgenstein may be used to illuminate the current conflict among legal theorists as to whether or not the law can yield "right" answers. Representative of one side of the legal debate is Ronald Dworkin's view that the law can yield "right" answers.[8] Like Baker and Hacker, Dworkin believes that

---

5. The use of the word "truth" is always problematic. At this point, I understand truth to mean the conditions under which an assertion meets adequacy conditions established by some group or discourse.

6. The most recent mention of this problem in the law review literature is Radin, Reconsidering the Rule of Law, 69 B.U.L. Rev. 781 (1989).

7. A recent, select survey of this literature is found in Boghossian, The Rule-Following Considerations, 98 Mind 507 (1989). By alluding to current Anglo-American debates about objectivity in the law, I do not intend to set up a parallel between law on the one hand (Dworkin/CLS) and Wittgenstein scholarship on the other (Baker & Hacker/Community Consensus). I am simply making the point that participants in the legal debates over the nature of objectivity would benefit from a look at the Wittgenstein literature. I have argued elsewhere that the terms of current Anglo-American debates over objectivity are a non-starter and ought to be abandoned. See Patterson, Interpretation in Law: Toward a Reconstruction of the Current Debate, 29 Vill. L. Rev. 671 (1984).

8. R. Dworkin, Taking Rights Seriously, 279-90 (1977).

there is an objective, determinable answer for the question of whether or not the conduct accords with the rule (the law). In contrast to Dworkin's view, there are a number of Critical Legal Studies (CLS) scholars who claim that there are no determinate answers at all.[9] They, like adherents to the community consensus view, believe that the application of law is determined by societal constructs and is, thus, in an ultimate sense, indeterminate.[10] I believe that both of these views are *philosophically* flawed, and I believe that Wittgenstein's arguments demonstrate the flaws in a powerful way.

I shall use the debate over the rule-following paradox as a springboard for the presentation of an original approach to the question of rule-following in law; a view of law as practice and narrative discourse.[11] The later Wittgenstein presents a compelling account of a conventionalist conception of practice.[12] He has, however, little to say about the problem of conceptual change within a practice. While it is an obvious truism that the law changes, the interesting question is whether or not a *philosophical* account of conceptual change can be given.

The account I offer builds upon the philosophy of the later Wittgenstein, in particular his claim that following a rule is a practice. I take that insight and develop it into a conception of law as discursive argument. My claim is that law is an interpretive enterprise whose participants engage in the production of, and debate about, explanatory narratives—narratives that account for the history of the practice and are produced in the service of argumentation about how to resolve legal problems. In short, law is an activity and not a thing. Its "being" is in the "doing" of the participants within the practice.

I. The Problem of Rule-Following in the Later Wittgenstein

No topic in the philosophy of the later Wittgenstein has generated more scholarly debate than Wittgenstein's remarks on rule-following. One problem for scholars attempting to find a unitary thesis on rule-following in the later

---

9. For discussion, see Langille, Revolution Without Foundations: The Grammar of Scepticism and Law, 33 McGill L. J. 451 (1988).

10. By "indeterminate" I mean that there is no preexisting connection between a concept and individual judgments that a certain state of affairs is an instance or example of that which is picked out by the concept. Without a determinate link between concept and application, judgment is a species of violence. See H. Caygill, The Art of Judgment 395 (1989) ("The text bears witness to a binding which is prior to law—an act of binding which is also a realization—and which does not efface differences but congregates them in the furtherance of life evoked by the beautiful.")

11. The present article represents the development of an orientation begun in Patterson, Wittgenstein and the Code: A Theory of Good Faith Performance and Enforcement Under Article Nine, 137 U. Pa. L. Rev. 335 (1988). There, I assessed the concept of good faith from the perspective of Wittgenstein's account of meaning and understanding. Notwithstanding my best efforts to remain within the pure Wittgensteinian framework, I often found myself unable to retain a non-revisionist stance toward the Wittgenstein corpus. The present article is an explicit attempt to move beyond Wittgenstein. It does, I suspect, demonstrate that, despite my best efforts, I have succumbed to the urge to do philosophy.

12. By "conventionalism" I mean a group practice that revolves around standards of conduct and behavior that are appealed to by members of the group as a ground for conduct and criticism. Further, the meaning of the standards and *what the standards are* is subject to revision and question. For a full discussion of recent philosophical approaches to conventionalism, see Patterson, An Introduction to Conventionalism, 10 W. New Eng. L. Rev. 43, 51 n.36 (1988).

Wittgenstein is that his remarks on the topic are both varied and widely scattered. His most sustained treatment of the problem of rule-following is found in sections 185–242 of *Philosophical Investigations.*[13] No account of Wittgenstein's position(s) on rule-following is complete without paying serious attention to his sustained treatment of the topic in these sections.

The problem of rule-following is really two problems. First, there is what Saul Kripke labels Wittgenstein's "sceptical paradox":[14] one can never know whether one's current use of a word coheres with one's past use, for one's current use of a world (or calculation of a sum) can always be shown to be in accord with any number of different rules.[15] Thus:

> [t]here can be no such thing as meaning anything by any word. Each new application we make is a leap in the dark; any present intention could be interpreted so as to accord with anything we may choose to do. So there can be neither accord, nor conflict. This is what Wittgenstein said in § 202.[16]

I shall label the thesis for this problem, which Kripke finds in Wittgenstein, the "overdetermination thesis."[17] The problem can be articulated in general terms as the relationship between acts and possible descriptions of them. Any practice is a finite set of behavioral moves (acts). For example, the practice of gardening is a complex repertiore of behavioral sequences that involve constant repetition and variation (e.g., watering, pruning, etc.). The overdetermination thesis posits that any given act, say watering the garden, need not necessarily be described as being in conformance with a rule of gardening (e.g., "water the vegetables regularly"). Rather, it might also be explained as behavior in accordance with a host of other rules which are part of wholly different practices (e.g., in a collectivized state, watering a private garden could be a political act.)[18]

The second problem of rule-following is the question of whether or not any system of rules is, by itself, capacious enough to both determine, and allow the participants in a practice to know, when and under what circumstances they are acting in conformity with a given rule. This problem of "underdetermination" is a familiar one in law,[19] and one which reaches its

---

13. L. Wittgenstein, Philosophical Investigations §§ 185-242 (G. Anscombe trans. 3d ed. 1968). A complete understanding of Wittgenstein's remarks on rule-following and private language requires an analysis of at least two other major portions of the text, §§ 143-84 and §§ 243-315 (this latter group being the remarks on private language).

14. S. Kripke, Wittgenstein on Rules and Private Language 4 (1982).

15. Id. at 7.

16. Id. at 55.

17. I borrow the overdetermination/underdetermination distinction from Michael Rosen. Rosen, Critical Theory: Between Ideology and Philosophy, *in* The Need for Interpretation: Contemporary Conceptions of the Philosopher's Task 90, 111-13 (S. Mitchell & M. Rosen, eds. 1983).

18. It is important to see that the overdetermination thesis is a *logical* one. That is, it need not be the case *in fact* that there is available to an agent another repertoire of behavior in which the agent might be engaged. All that is required is that there exist an *in principle* possibility of some other explanatory framework.

19. H.L.A. Hart describes the "underdetermination" problem as precipitating "something in the nature of a crisis in communication." H. Hart, The Concept of Law 123 (1961).

expressive zenith in the claim of certain CLS adherents that law is "indeterminate."[20]

The scholarly literature has yielded two "solutions" to the "problems"[21] of underdetermination and overdetermination. The first solution is posited by Gordon Baker and Peter Hacker in their book, *Scepticism, Rules & Language*.[22] Baker and Hacker argue that a rule and its applications are internally related through the medium of grammar.[23] Understanding a rule means understanding its grammar. There is no "interpretation" that "mediate[s] between a rule and its application."[24] Rather, reality and grammar are coextensive.[25]

The second solution is offered in the community consensus reading of Wittgenstein's remarks on rule-following. This view is well represented in the comments of Norman Malcolm: "[F]or Wittgenstein the concept of a rule presupposes a community within which a common agreement in actions fixes the meaning of a rule."[26] Thus, "[o]nly someone who had been a member of a community in which there was the *institution* of sign posts, could be said to *take his direction* from a sign post."[27] This view is supported by a number of passages in which "Wittgenstein stresses the point that a language can exist only if there is *agreement* between persons in their applications of the language."[28]

Baker and Hacker believe the community consensus reading of Wittgenstein is incorrect because it exploits the social aspects of rule-following at the expense of the internal relation between a rule and its applications. As they put it:

> The pivotal point in Wittgenstein's remarks on following rules is that a rule is *internally* related to acts which accord with it. The rule and nothing but the rule determines what is correct (PI § 189). This idea is incompatible with defining 'correct' in terms of what is normal or standard practice in a community. To take the behavior of the majority to be the criterion of correctness in applying rules is to abrogate the internal relation of a rule to acts in accord with it.[29]

The choice between the two readings of Wittgenstein has important implications for jurisprudence. If a judicial decision cannot be said to be a

---

20. See, e.g., Singer, The Player and the Cards: Nihilism and Legal Theory, 94 Yale L.J. 1, 61 (1984) (law is indeterminate because it cannot mechanically yield answers to interpretive questions). For a discussion of the relationship between the indeterminacy thesis and wider trends in post-modern theory, see C. Norris, Paul deMan: Deconstruction and the Critique of Aesthetic Ideology 125-48 (1988).
21. The words "solution" and "problem" are in quotes to indicate that, for some, these are only pseudo-problems yielding pseudo-solutions.
22. G. Baker & P. Hacker, Scepticism, Rules & Language (1984).
23. Id. at 123-24.
24. Id. at 128.
25. Id. at 135.
26. N. Malcolm, Nothing Is Hidden: Wittgenstein's Criticism of His Early Thought 175 (1986); see also, Malcolm, Wittgenstein on Language and Rules, 64 Phil. 5, 8 (1989) (arguing that "community consensus" is what determines how to "go on" with a practice or a rule).
27. Id. at 172.
28. Id. at 173.
29. G. Baker & P. Hacker, Wittgenstein: Rules, Grammar and Necessity 171-72 (1985).

necessary result of the application of a preexisting rule, then the decision
can be attacked, at least prima facie, as a subjective choice having nothing
to do with the rule. An example of such an attack can be seen in Dworkin's
persistent critique of positivism; viz., his claim that the judicial phenomenology of positivism commits its proponents to the view that judges exercise
strong discretion in deciding novel cases at law. In its latest formulation,
Dworkin criticizes positivism as necessitating a system in which

> [j]udges must decide . . . novel cases as best they can, but by hypothesis no party has any
> right to win flowing from past collective decisions—no party has a *legal* right to win—
> because the only rights of that character are those established by convention. So the
> decision a judge must make in hard cases is discretionary in this strong sense: it is left
> open by the correct understanding of past decisions.[30]

This is precisely the sort of charge Baker and Hacker level against the
community consensus interpreters of Wittgenstein: "On this account [the
community consensus view], there is, in effect, *no* explanation of what it is
to apply a rule correctly. That would require pinning down a single interpretation of the rule over the entire (infinite) range of its application, and this,
it is argued, is impossible."[31] Further, Baker and Hacker are strident in their
criticism of the community consensus view regarding objectivity:
"[I]ndependently of a given rule it is unclear how to determine in advance
what the community disposition is in respect of hitherto unencountered
cases. Although both views aim to establish an objective standard of correctness in the face of sceptical doubts, the form of objectivity looks distinctly
flaccid."[32]

Read from a jurisprudential perspective, I hope to show that it is possible
to fuse the discordant voices in this debate. The community consensus
reading of Wittgenstein does suffer from some critical weaknesses that the
"internal relations" thesis highlights. On the other hand, Baker and Hacker's
claim that "[t]he rule and *nothing but* the rule determines what is correct"[33]
cannot, at least in law, but sustained. First, I shall detail the claims each side
makes for its reading of Wittgenstein. I shall then seek to enrich the view of
each by incorporating Wittgenstein's remarks on practices. It is Wittgenstein's
pragmatism with respect to practices that will, I hope, prove to be the fibre
that links these now discordant voices.

II. The Community Consensus View

The paradox to which the community consensus interpretation responds
is found in section 201 of *Philosophical Investigations:*

30. R. Dworkin, Law's Empire 115 (1986).
31. G. Baker & P. Hacker, supra note 27, at 69.
32. Id. at 71.
33. G. Baker & P. Hacker, supra note 34, at 172 (emphasis added).

This was our paradox: no course of action could be determined by a rule, because every course of action can be made out to accord with the rule. The answer was: if everything can be made out to accord with the rule, then it can also be made out to conflict with it. And so there would be neither accord nor conflict here.[34]

The community consensus reading of section 201 is rooted in the claim that, for Wittgenstein, "there are always, on the basis of any normal training in and exposure to others' applications of the concepts involved, indefinitely many equally viable interpretions of which rule it is that we are intended to follow."[35] Consider, for example, Wittgenstein's discussion of how one would continue the series "0, 1, 2, 3, 4, 5, ..."[36] The pupil is instructed to continue the series by adding by 1 until he reaches 1000 and then adding by 2 thereafter. If he continues the series after 1000 with 1004, 1008, 1012, we say that he has gotten it wrong; he has failed to follow the rule we gave him. But, "[s]ince the pupil's answers are compatible with myriad possible rules, how can we ever be certain that a pupil has grasped the rule we meant?"[37]

Following a rule correctly requires that it be performed in a manner consistent with that of any other similarly situated member of the community. As Christopher Peacocke puts it, "what it is for a person to be following a rule, even individually, cannot ultimately be explained without reference to some community."[38] Rule-following is a matter of habit insofar as behavior (or the requirement to act or refrain from acting) in accordance with a rule is a process of being socialized (trained) to act a certain way.[39] From this perspective, rules cannot be understood acontextually; the social, or contextual, element is central to the community consensus view.

How then, if there is no internal means for fixing the meaning of a rule, is its meaning determined? The community consensus readers of Wittgenstein point to section 202 and Wittgenstein's assertion that "'obeying a rule' is a practice."[40] It is only in practices (established ways of acting) that the common ways of "going on" with rules get settled. Knowing what a rule requires in a given case is a matter of assessing the function of the rule within a practice. Mastering a rule is part of mastering "a technique—a technique is part of a social practice, institution or custom."[41]

Malcolm develops this aspect of the community consensus reading in his analysis of Wittgenstein's remarks in section 198 of *Philosophical Investigations*. Wittgenstein writes that "a person goes by a sign post only in so far as there exists a regular use of sign posts, a custom."[42] In other words, in order for there to be rules about sign posts, there must first be a community

---

34. L. Wittgenstein, supra note 18, § 201.
35. C. Wright, Wittgenstein on the Foundations of Mathematics 23 (1980).
36. L. Wittgenstein, supra note 18, §§ 143, 185.
37. S. Shanker, Wittgenstein and the Turning-Point in the Philosophy of Mathematics 15 (1987).
38. Peacocke, Reply: Rule Following: The Nature of Wittgenstein's Arguments, *in* Wittgenstein: To Follow a Rule 73 (S. Holtzman & C. Leach eds. 1981).
39. See C. McGinn, Wittgenstein on Meaning 24 (1984).
40. L. Wittgenstein, supra note 18, § 202.
41. R. Fogelin, Wittgenstein 162 (1976).
42. L. Wittgenstein, supra note 18, § 198.

in which there is an institution of sign posts.[43] To react to the sign post in
the "normal" or "required" way, there must be a response to sign posts that
is consistent with some social training. Without the training, there would be
no "normal" response: the training is the embodiment of normalcy, its
genesis. This point is affirmed by Wittgenstein in his statement that
"[f]ollowing a rule is analogous to obeying an order."[44] What constitutes a
correct response to the order must be assessed against the background of the
training that supplies the contextual foreground for the meaning of the order.
For example, unless one was trained in military tactics, the order "soften the
beachhead before deployment of troops" would be open to any number of
interpretations: the order and its many possible meanings would "hang[] in
the air."[45]

The community consensus reading of the alleged skeptical paradox of
section 201 of *Philosophical Investigations* is consistent with much that
Wittgenstein has to say about related notions such as practice, custom, and
institution. Despite its plausibility, however, Baker and Hacker present
powerful objections to this "social gloss" on Wittgenstein's position. It is to
these objections that we now turn.

III. Rules and Internal Relations

Baker and Hacker uncharitably describe the community consensus reading
of section 210 as a "caricature" of Wittgenstein's remarks on rule-following.[46]
The reason for their disparaging characterization lies in their belief that, for
Wittgenstein, there must be an *internal* relation between a rule and acts that
accord with the rule.[47] By their view, only *the rule itself* can be a source of
its meaning: "To take the behavior of the majority to be the criterion of
correctness in applying rules is to abrogate the internal relation of a rule to
acts in accord with it."[48] In short, the fact that the majority acts in a certain
way does not constitute the standard for acting in according with the dictates
of a rule. At most, it merely serves to show that most people, most of the
time, act in accordance with the rule.[49]

On this view, the notion of "correctness" is logically unrelated to the
behavior of any member of the community. The justification for any application of a rule is the internal relation exemplified by the grammar of the
rule. Applying the rule correctly is a matter of grammar; correct application
means no more than applying a rule in accordance with its grammar. Thus,
there cannot be, and need not be, any external (social) *justification* for a
claim that a particular extension of the rule is mandated or warranted. The
"justification" is in applying the rule correctly:

43. N. Malcolm, supra note 31, at 172.
44. L. Wittgenstein, supra note 18, § 206.
45. Id. § 198.
46. G. Baker & P. Hacker, supra note 34, at 171.
47. Id. at 117-72.
48. Id. at 172.
49. Id.

What *justifies* called rubies 'red'? Red is this ○ colour; and rubies are this ○ colour, i.e. red! Saying 'rubies are red' is a correct application of this rule for the use of 'red'. What *makes* is correct? Nothing. That is what we call 'applying "red" correctly.' There is no room for justification.[50]

It is not true, as the community consensus view asserts, that correctness in rule-application is reducible to, or is no more than, "a notion of assertion-conditions for correctness and incorrectness. . . ."[51] It is simply not enough to say that one "acts as everyone else does" in applying a rule. Such a claim misses the internal relation between a rule and its extension. Knowing what a rule requires and what accords with it is "akin to intending and knowing what will fulfil one's intention. . . ."[52]

Examples of what counts as following a rule "are no more *applications* of the rule explained than is an ostensive definition of 'red' (by pointing at a tomato) and application (predication) of 'red.' "[53] There must be a "canon of correct use,"[54] which is made manifest in the application of a rule. For example, no explanation of a rule containing the phrase "one metre" can be correct unless some *further* explanation is given of the uses to which measuring rods are put. The rule, coupled with the teaching or instruction in its application, makes manifest the internal relation between the rule and its extension. The fact that rules for the use of measuring rods are "used in justifying, correcting, and sometimes even in applications . . . is not a matter of collective dispositions, but of a normative practice, which may be collective, but need not be."[55]

One particular objection Baker and Hacker level against the community consensus view is significant, at least for present purposes; the problem of objectivity. The power of this objection lies in its simplicity, as an example will illustrate:

If the leader of the community instructed his people to sacrifice to the gods on midsummer's day, they may well miscalculate the day, and later discover that they had misapplied the law (equally, just one of them might make this discovery, and despite his being right, be disbelieved by the rest).[56]

Simply stated, the problem of objectivity is what to count as correct application of a rule if the rule is to be judged *solely* by reference to what the community takes the rule to be. If that is the reference point, then is there not an unstable link (the community's consensus) between a rule and its extension? Baker and Hacker are correct to press their claim that interposing a notion of community consensus between a rule and its applications severs the internal relation between a rule and its extension. As they put it:

---

50. G. Baker & P. Hacker, supra note 27, at 83.
51. Id. at 72.
52. Id.
53. Id. at 73.
54. Id.
55. Id. at 73-74.
56. Id. at 74.

In place of that internal relation the community view substitutes the notion of community *agreement,* which is not an *internal property* of the rule. Community agreement shows that the members of the community are all playing the same game, as it were, but that they should agree in applying the rules of the game is not itself one of the rules of the game. It is a framework condition within which the community game is possible. But that acting thus-and-so *is* acting in accord with *this* rule is no more a matter of what people are disposed to do than the fact that *p* is that fact that makes the proposition that *p* true is a matter of what people are disposed to believe.[57]

If the community consensus view is correct, then it is human agreement that decides what is true and false and not the world. As Baker and Hacker see it, such a formulation of the relationship between a rule and what accords with it collapses the distinction between meaning (which humans create) and truth (which is determined by the world).[58] Maintaining the distinction between meaning and truth requires that there be "a certain constancy in the results of following a rule. . . ."[59] There can be no such constancy unless the internal relation between a rule and what accords with it remains unsevered. This is precisely what the community consensus view fails to do. By interposing consensus between a rule and its extension, both objectivity and the truth/meaning dichotomy are destroyed.

What the community consensus reading fails to account for is the "stipulative" nature of the relationship between a rule and its extension. A rule stipulates, in itself, its own content: the content (the extension) is "fixed (not open)."[60] One does not discover that " $2 + 2 = 4$." Getting "4" is "a *criterion* for following the rule of [plus]."[61] To do otherwise is, quite simply, to make a mistake.

For Baker and Hacker, past applications of a rule (one source of content for the community's view of what a rule requires), do not count in any future judgment of correctness in rule applicaion. They write:

The suggestion that my past *applications* of a rule are the evidence that *I* must go on to 'discover' or 'determine' what I mean by 'W' (or what 'W' means), what I understand by 'W', or what a rule for the use of 'W' I am now following, is surely absurd.[62]

The thrust of this last shot at the community consensus view is that rule-following is not a matter of *"Praxis."*[63] Past applications do not in any way constrain present contexts. What the rule requires now is the same as what it always required, that is, application of *the rule.* Only "[t]he rule-sceptic thinks that what counts as doing the same thing is determined here by

---

57. Id. at 75.
58. Id.
59. Id. at 76.
60. Id. at 79.
61. Id. at 77.
62. Id. at 79.
63. While Baker and Hacker state that "[f]ollowing a rule is a *Praxis,"* id. at 88, it is difficult to make sense of their claim. They deny that there is *any* necessarily social element to rule-following, stating that "[the community consensus view] wrongly takes Wittgenstein's conception of a practice to be necessarily a *social* practice (as if 'social practice' were a pleonasm)." G. Baker & P. Hacker, supra note 34, at 164.

precedent."[64] Again, "[t]he rule and nothing but the rule determines what is correct."[65] Rule-following is not social; it is grammatical. The internal relation between a rule and what accords with it is isomorphic and closed. Precedent teaches us nothing about what a rule does or does not require. Only the rule can do that. Precedent is nothing more than the history of correct and incorrect applications of what the rule requires; it is merely illustrative and not determinative of correct application.

IV. Law, Rules, and Interpretation: An Overview of the Argument

Reduced to its simplest terms, the argument between Baker and Hacker and proponents of the community consensus view is over the appropriate criterion of choice for how to "go on" with a rule; i.e., apply a rule in the future. If Baker and Hacker are correct in their claim that the rule and only the rule determines what will count as "acting in acccordance with the rule," then assessing the propriety of any claim for what a rule requires in a given case that resorts to a source of authority outside the parameters of the rule itself constitutes an unwarranted undermining of the internal, normative force of the rule.[66]

In contraposition to Baker and Hacker, the community consensus position locates the interpretive criterion for correct application of rules outside the canonical form of the rule. The community of rule-followers determines *both* what its rules are (the answer to overdetermination) and what their content will be (the answer to underdetermination). The community consensus view is problematic, however. While the content of the rules, what they require in particular cases, is set in advance, it is always subject to revision. It is this aspect of the community consensus view with which Baker and Hacker take issue: if what is required by rules is always subject to revision, then the purveyors of the community consensus approach do not know the meaning of the word "rule." Rules require or prohibit actions *in advance;* they are not retrospective. It is inherent in the concept "rule" that what is permitted or mandated be known in advance so that actors can conform their conduct to what the rules require. It will not suffice to decide, after the fact, what the rules *ought to be read* as requiring. For Baker and Hacker, it must be the case that ex post facto determinations of what is required for conduct to count as "following a rule" are illegitimate (beyond the bounds of consideration). This makes a great deal of logical sense. How can it be said that "X was following A" when we only known what A requires after X has acted? If this were the state of affairs, then the best that could be said is that X acted in a manner that, after the fact, can be described as having been in accord with A. X could not, however, *really* have been "following A" at the time he acted because, prior to acting, we could not have known what A required.

---

64. G. Baker & P. Hacker, supra note 27, at 87.
65. G. Baker & P. Hacker, supra note 34, at 172.
66. Cf. Raz, Authority, Law and Morality, 68 The Monist 295 (1985) (arguing that the arthoritative nature of law is undermined by appeals to evaluate arguments beyond the "source" of law.

These are strong arguments indeed for the necessity of recognizing the internal relation between a rule and its extension. I shall demonstrate, however, that while it is true that there is an internal relation between a rule and its extension in law, it is not the case that what a rule requires can be determined solely by reference to that internal relation. For, as the community consensus view makes clear, determining what a rule requires in a given case is essentially a *social* question, though in a manner distinct from that described by the proponents of the community consensus view. In brief, I will argue that the determination of what a legal rule requires is arrived at through the disclosure of the *point* of the rule in a legal system, a "disclosure" that is essentially a matter of social anthropology.[67] In order to follow a rule, we must know the reasons why the rule exists as part of the normative structure of law. The point of the rule, which is socially determined, constitutes the internal relation that links together the divergent factual contexts that comprise the extension of a rule. Community consensus does not, by itself, determine what constitutes acting in accordance with a rule. Rather, what constitutes acting in accordance with a rule is determined by the point of the rule and is analytically and socially specifiable apart from the rule. Thus, it is indeed true that there is necessarily a social element to rule-following, but it is not true that community consensus alone decides what constitutes acting in accordance with a rule.

The claim that the meaning of a legal rule is determined by the point or purpose of the rule begins with the notion of a "practice." Following Rawls, practice may be defined as "any form of activity specified by a system of rules which defines offices, roles, moves, penalties, defenses, and so on, and which gives the activity its structure."[68] While it is true that games and law are both rule-governed practices, there is an important difference between the two that is not often recognized.[69] The difference is in the nature of the rules governing each. For example, chess is a game comprised solely of rules for the movement of the pieces. There is nothing to chess qua game that is not stated in the rules. In other words, the game is identical and coextensive with the sum of its rules. This is so because all the rules of chess are constitutive rules.[70]

Unlike games, however, law is comprised of prescriptive as well as constitutive rules.[71] While it makes no sense (it is a category mistake) to say, vis-à-vis chess, that "the rule of castle has negative consequences," it makes perfect sense in law to say "stealing from your neighbor is wrong." The difference lies in what Hart describes as "the critical reflective attitude" that

---

67. Recognition of this fact is perhaps the greatest contribution of Peter Winch to the importance of Wittgenstein's thought to social theory. See P. Winch, The Idea of a Social Science and Its Relation to Philosophy 62 (1958).
68. Rawls, Two Concepts of Rules, 64 Phil. Rev. 3, 3 n.1 (1955).
69. In the analysis that follows, I have profited from the insights of T. Morawetz, Wittgenstein & Knowledge: The Importance of On Certainty 53-58 (1978).
70. Morawetz, The Concept of a Practice, 24 Phil. Stud. 209, 209-10 (1973).
71. The rule "no will is valid without the testator's signature" is a constitutive rule. Constitutive rules state conditions for something being what it is, e.g., a valid will. Prescriptive rules state "ought" requirements, e.g., the rule prohibiting assault.

is a necessary element of social rules.[72] The critical reflective attitude constitutes the "internal point of view"[73] that participants in a legal system have toward their own conduct and that of others. When conduct is criticized, appeal is made to a rule for justification of the criticism. But the character of the appeal in the practice of law is different from a claim for violation of a rule in a game. In chess, when one says "X has violated the rule for moving the bishop diagonally," no appeal beyond the rule need be made. The rule is the sole justification for the claim of violation. The only justification necessary or possible is the comment, "That's how the game is played."

In contrast to games, normative practices like law provide for the evaluation of conduct by reference to norms that are analytically antecedent to the rules that embody them. Norms are embodied in legal rules that are comprised of concepts having the character of "open texture."[74] This marks the essential difference between games as practices and law as a practice. In law, claims of justification for what counts as "acting in accordance with a rule" must necessarily go beyond (behind) the rules to the norms that are the ground of justification for the rule. It is the norm, the *point* (reason) of the rule, that serves as the criterion for what does and does not count as acting in accordance with the rule. As J. L. Austin showed that it is proper to ask after the *point* for an utterance,[75] it is likewise constitutive of the practice of law to ask the interpretive question "What is the point of the rule?"

These considerations suggest that something is missing in the debate between Baker and Hacker and the community consensus view on the nature of following rules. It *is* true, as Baker and Hacker maintain, that there is an internal relation between a rule and its extension, but this relation is not, as Baker and Hacker suggest, *in* the rule itself.[76] It is not the case that there is no conceptual space within which community consensus, or anything else, can do work. Grammar does not completely fill the conceptual space of understanding; understanding the rule is not accomplished simply by understanding its grammar. Baker and Hacker claim that: "In so far as grammar is shared among the speakers of a single language, reality will be a public and community-wide creation of grammar. But in so far as grammar is a collection of decisions or stipulations, reality will depend upon us."[77] This characterization of the relationship between grammar and understanding creates a false dichotomy that serves as a rhetorical ploy in the argument for an unseverable internal relation between a rule and its applications. It is *not* the case, however, that a community consensus reading of the relationship between a rule and its applications need reduce rule-following *solely* to community consensus. In other words, the community consensus view need not be a thorough-going reductionist argument for rule-following. Rather,

---

72. See H. Hart, supra note 24, at 56.
73. Id. at 86-96.
74. See Waismann, Verifiability, *in* Logic and Language 122, 125-30 (A. Flew ed. 1965).
75. J. Austin, How to Do Things with Words 94-131 (1962).
76. G. Baker & P. Hacker, supra note 34, at 172 (stating that "[t]he rule and nothing but the rule determines what is correct (PI § 189)").
77. G. Baker & P. Hacker, supra note 27, at 135.

what "relates" the instances that can be said to fall under a rule with the rule itself is the norm that is the *point* of the rule in the practice of law.

For their part, the community consensus theorists are right to claim that rule-following is essentially a social enterprise. But, as Baker and Hacker suggest, it is conceptually untoward to reduce rule-following to mere consensus. Rather, the point of the rule is a social construct without which the rule would have no point and would be unintelligible.

Thus, with respect to law, there is a relationship between the grammar of rules and community consensus that is dialectical. The grammar of the rule enables us to understand what counts as "following the rule"; however, the grammar is erected upon an edifice of social practice which is itself subject to criticism and reconceptualization.

All of this is perfectly consistent with Wittgenstein's remarks about practices and rule-following. In section 43 of Philosophical Investigations, Wittgenstein remarks that "the meaning of a word is its use in the language."[78] This remark serves as an invitation to see language not merely as *expression* but *action:* the idea that we use words to *do* things.[79] Language games are activities comprised *both* of words and of acts. Understanding language requires attention to the point of its use(s) in context. Only by giving our attention to the *reasons* why norms are part of discourse, including legal discourse, can we make any sense of what they require when they are applied in concrete cases.

This would appear to be what Wittgenstein himself envisaged when he took up the question of doubt: "If you tried to doubt everything you would not get as far as doubting anything. The game of doubting itself presupposes certainty."[80] To doubt means to raise questions from a perspective within the practice; it is to ask questions about what is going on (e.g., claims of knowledge) from within a shared perspective. Without (some) agreement in judgments, there would be no communication and no critique.[81] But the possibility of critique, and thus the reformulation of grammar, is inherent in all social practices. To deny this, as Baker and Hacker seem to, is unwarranted.

V. Purpose, Meaning, and Interpretation in Law

In the previous Section, I advanced the claim that discerning the meaning of a legal rule is a matter of seeing the purpose of the rule within the practice

---

78. L. Wittgenstein, supra note 18, § 43.
79. Strawson makes this point in his review of Philosophical Investigations where he writes:

> Variants on 'use' in Wittgenstein are 'purpose' 'function' 'role' 'part' 'application'. . . . The general aim is clear enough: to get us away from our fascination with the dubious relation of naming, of meaning, and to make us look at the speaking and writing of language as one human activity among others, interacting with others; and so to make us notice the different parts that words and sentences play in this activity.

> Strawson, Review of Wittgenstein's Philosophical Investigations, *in* Wittgenstein: The Philosophical Investigations 22, 25 (G. Pitcher ed. 1966).

80. L. Wittgenstein, On Certainty § 115 (G. Anscombe & G. von Wright eds., D. Paul & G. Anscombe trans. 1969).
81. L. Wittgenstein, supra note 18, §§ 241-42.

of law. I should now like to defend that claim through the use of several examples.[82] My goal is to choose relatively simple examples to support the general descriptive claim that legal argument is always directed at constructing a purpose or rationale for law. Without this rationale, law would be unintelligible. It is the effort to clarify the point of legal norms that drives legal argument.

A. Form and Matter

Many concepts, and certainly all social and political concepts, have a formal and a material element. By formal element I mean that which makes something what it is and not something else. As stated in the Introduction to this Article, the distinction between formal and material elements is heuristic. My use of these terms implies no metaphysical claims about the nature of reality *sub specie aetermitatis*.[83] The distinction serves merely to highlight certain aspects of conceptual understanding.

The distinction can be illustrated with a simple rule. For example, "All automobiles, bicycles and other wheeled vehicles must stop at red lights."[84] Let us suppose that, when the rule was promulgated, it was empirically the case that all "vehicles" had wheels which, in normal use, touched the ground. Suppose that one day a "vehicle" is designed which rides not on rubber tires but on a cushion of air. Does the rule cover such a "vehicle"?

By resort to the formal element of the rule, we know that the point of the rule is the regulation of traffic in the interests of safety and the like. The *reason* for the rule, which arises in a particular way of life, is the basis upon which we make the judgment that this object is a "vehicle" for the purpose of this rule. Without the formal element, we could not make such a judgment.[85]

Whether a concept is moral or non-moral will depend upon differences in the formal element. My reason for this assertion is not to argue that there is no distinction between description and evaluation, but rather to argue that the relationship between the formal and the material elements of both descriptive and normative concepts is the same. Form determines matter.

A favorite philosophical example of this point is the table. What makes a table a table? Tables serve a multiplicity of functions and are the subjects of

---

82. Absent from this Part is any discussion of the conflict of interpretations. I will, however, address this subject in Part X.
83. In contrast to my view, see Weinrib, Legal Formalism: On the Immanent Rationality of Law, 97 Yale L.J. 949, 957-66 (1988). In Weinrib's view, "[f]orm is not separate from content but is the ensemble of characteristics that marks the content as determinate, and therefore marks the content as content." Id. at 958. Unlike the view advanced here, Weinrib's concept of "law" as form and content is *distinctly* metaphysical. Law has "juridical significance" (immanent *metaphysical* rationality) of which "positive law may provide only a *defective* [relative to its metaphysical form] rendering of the juridical [form]. . . ." Id. at 957 (emphasis added). See also Weinrib, The Intelligibility of Law, *in* The Rule of Law: Ideal or Ideology? 59-84 (A. Hutchinson & P. Monahan eds. 1987).
84. This example is taken from E. Hirsch, Jr., Validity in Interpration 124-25 (1967).
85. Notice that what is common to these vehicles is not their *empirical* similarities (criteria), but the fact that the point of view from which they are collected is the *single* thing that brings them together. The *point* of collocation is the formal element.

various language games. Tables are used for eating, for meetings, for piling things, for writing, etc. The language games of tables include stacking, counting, comparing, and selling. All of these activities are what we do with objects called "tables." The reasons we have tables are, "as it were, the guiding principle for deciding what are tables and what are not, or what new constructions will be accepted as tables."[86]

Language games are the practical activities into which and out of which we weave the concept of a table. Taken together, these language games exemplify the grammar of the word "table." The unity of the things we do with tables (e.g., eating, sitting, setting, stacking, etc.) is exemplified by the grammar of the word "table." That is why "[g]rammar tells us what kind of object anything is."[87]

One important feature of the form/matter distinction is the fact that there is no necessary or entailment relation between formal and material elements. Wittgenstein recognized this fact and evinced his recognition in the concept of "family resemblance."[88] But Wittgenstein did not go far enough in recognizing that essence is in grammar and not, as Aristotle thought, in the world.[89] The formal element of "table" does not require that a table be a particular height, depth, or shape in order to be a table. Such a requirement may arise in the course of a particular language game (e.g., choosing a table for a specific purpose), but there is nothing in the formal element itself that selects one group of characteristics over another *for a specific purpose*. All that is required is that the material elements belonging to the proffered "table" satisfy the social need for tables.

One might object, asking: "But can't a chair serve as a table? Can't it perform the function of a table and, thus 'be' a table?" The very form of the question contains its own answer. Surely it is possible to treat a chair *as a* table, or a table *as a* chair. But, as Stanley Cavell reminds us, "[w]hat can *serve as a chair* is not a chair, and nothing would (be said to) serve as a chair if there were no (were nothing we called) (orthodox) chairs. We could say: It is part of the grammar of the word 'chair' that *this* is what we call 'to serve as a chair'."[90]

B. *Form, Matter, and Rule-Following*

Conceptual form determines what will and will not count as an example of the form. Form determines matter, but not ontologically. The position

---

86. J. Kovesi, Moral Notions 3 (1967); see also S. Cavell, The Claim of Reason: Wittgenstein, Skepticism, Morality, and Tragedy 71 (1979) (discussing the grammar of "chair"); Sellars, Aristotle's Metaphysics: An Interpretation, *in* W. Sellars, Philosophical Perspectives 73-124 (1967).
87. L. Wittgenstein, supra note 18, § 373.
88. Id. § 67 (stating that the features of things that bear the same name will have no *one* thing in common, but will exhibit a variety of shared or overlapping features).
89. The mistake Wittgenstein makes is to locate similarity recognition at the level of criteria. The concept of "family resemblance" is an expression of the view that we see things as "the same" because they share certain features in common. This view is mistaken. In my opinion, we see things as "the same" because they have the same role in a situation or language game. The key to similarity recognition is the formal element and not, as Wittgenstein thought, criteria.
90. S. Cavell, supra note 91.

advanced here does not advocate looking for formal properties *in the object.* Such an approach fails to recognize that form is an object of reason, not the senses.[91] We no more sense with our minds than we reason with our fingers.[92] The making of one or the other of these regrettable moves engenders bad metaphysics.

This Part expands upon the argument for the conceptual distinction between the formal and the material elements of concepts by tying that dichotomy to the issue of rule-following. The connection lies in the fact that it is by virtue of the formal element of a concept that a rule can be followed. As previously stated, the "point" of a rule is a crucial element in understanding what conduct can be considered to fall within the rule. To take this inquiry a step further, it is important to realize that the point of a rule is the reason underlying the formal element in the concept as it is expressed by or contained in the rule under question. Thus, the meaning of a rule is a function of the formal element which is itself the verbal formulation of the reason underlying the rule. In short, a rule is a verbal formulation of a reason, and the reason is the formal element of the rule. For the moment, I shall concentrate on the concept of the point of a rule, as opposed to a group of rules, with an eye toward developing the relationship between the formal element in rule-following. Again, my claim is that, without a formal element, no rule can be followed. A correlative point is that the meaning of a rule is a function of its point or purpose and that this point is coextensive with the formal element.

To make my point, I can do no better than return to H.L.A. Hart's famous example of the "vehicle" in the park.[93] As you may recall, Hart's focus was on the interpretation of the rule: "No vehicles are allowed in the park."[94] In his debate with Lon Fuller,[95] Hart maintained that words have a settled or "core" meaning and that it is by virtue of this core of settled meaning that communication is made possible. If the meaning of the concept in question were debatable, then judicial discretion would resolve questions of "penumbral" meaning.[96]

For his part, Fuller disputed the core/penumbra distinction. Fuller claimed that meaning was a function of the purpose of the rule. His position is captured by his rhetorical question: "[I]s it really ever possible to interpret a word without knowing the aim of the statute?"[97] Without knowledge of

---

91. Hume made the same mistake, in a different way, when he complained that vice was not a "matter of fact." D. Hume, A Treatise of Human Nature 468 (L. Selby-Bigge ed. 1888). Hume's mistake was his failure to recognize that vice is an object of reason and not the senses. We "know" what vice is because we know its formal element.
92. See J. Kovesi, supra note 91, at 19 ("We do *not* perceive with our reason any more than we know with our fingers. . . .").
93. Hart's argument was first advanced in a debate with Lon Fuller in the Harvard Law Review. Hart, Positivism and the Separation of Law and Morals, 71 Harv. L. Rev. 593 (1958), *reprinted in* H. Hart, Essays in Jurisprudence and Philosophy 49 (1983).
94. Id. at 607.
95. Fuller responded to Hart in Fuller, Fidelity to Law, 71 Harv. L. Rev. 630 (1958).
96. Hart, supra note 98, at 606-15.
97. Fuller, supra note 100, at 664.

purpose, no understanding of a statute is possible. In Fuller's view, statutory meaning is coextensive with legislative purpose.

Within the context of the form/matter distinction, it is easy to reconcile the seemingly incommensurable positions of Hart and Fuller. Hart's "core meaning" is nothing more than a function of the formal element in standard contexts. The reason we understand the meaning of the word "vehicle" is because, in hearing it, we attribute to it (it calls to mind) the contexts in which the word is used.[98] Use means context, and core meaning is nothing more than contextual, standard use.

Fuller's interpretive purposiveness exposes the Benthamite element in Hart's thought.[99] Hart seems to say that when the core of settled meaning runs out, a jduge is inexorably forced to create meaning where none existed before (judicial legislation). Fuller objects to this move. The judicial obligation, according to Fuller, is to discern meaning from the point of view of the statute. Hart's rejoinder, though direct, is somewhat curious. He states:

> We are invited to include in the "rule" the various aims and policies in the light of which its penumbral cases are decided on the ground that these aims have, because of their importance, as much right to be called law as the core of legal rules whose meaning is settled. But though an invitation cannot be refuted, it may be refused and I would proffer two reasons for refusing this invition. First, everything we have learned about the judicial process can be expressed in other less mysterious ways. We can say laws are incurably incomplete and we must decide the penumbral cases rationally by reference to social aims. I think Holmes, who had such a vivid appreciation of the fact that "gentle propositions do not decide concrete cases," would have put it that way. Second, to insist on the utilitarian distinction is to emphasize that the hard core of settled meaning is law in some centrally important sense and that even if there are borderlines, there must first be lines.[100]

What Hart fails to see, and Fuller sees all too well, is that settled meaning is settled because contexts of use are regular. Without settled contexts of use, there would be no such thing as core meaning. We can agree with Hart that "laws are incurably incomplete"[101] without rejecting as "mysterious" Fuller's claim that meaning is a function of purpose. Secondly, Hart is correct in asserting that there must be lines in law. Fuller would not dispute this. His complaint is not with the drawing of lines per se, but rather with Hart's analysis of how lines should be drawn.

My purpose in discussing this debate is not to take sides, for I find merit in both positions. The interesting point, however, is that these apparently conflicting positions are both reconcilable and explicable within the framework of formal and material elements. Hart's "core meaning" and Fuller's "purpose" both exemplify the logic of the formal element. Core meaning is

---

98. See L. Wittgenstein, supra note 18, § 43 (stating that "the meaning of a word is its use in the language").

99. For an insightful discussion of the pragmatic and ontologoical presuppositions of Bentham's view of the common law, see Simpson, The Common Law and Legal Theory, *in* Legal Theory and Common Law 8, 16-18 (W. Twining ed. 1986).

100. Hart, supra note 98, at 614.

101. Id.

a function of settled contexts of use. "Vehicle" means a car because the point of many rules isolates this configuration of (material) elements as "vehicle" (e.g., automobile registration and inspection, the auto club, autobahn, auto-glass, auto tire, auto fuel, etc.). Likewise, the point of having vehicle inspections is to keep the road and other drivers safe from the hazards of dilapidated vehicles. The concept of a "vehicle inspection" is unintelligible apart from a way of life where vehicles are driven on roads by persons who have some interest in their own safety and the safety of others. What *counts* as a proper inspection can only be discerned from the point of view of these (conventional) interests.[102]

Thus, in answering the question "May a statue of a vehicle be placed in the park?" appeal must be made to the formal element of the rule. It is proper to ask what *the point* of the rule is, why the legislature has promulgated it, and what reason(s) there is for making this rule part of the law. To ask these questions is to ask for the formal element. A preliminary answer to the question may be found in settled contexts of use, Hart's core meaning. But the better answer, the complete answer, is found in the purpose of the rule. Without knowledge of the formal element, a court asked to apply the rule can only guess at its meaning.

C. Examples of Form, Matter, and Rule-Following

These general remarks on rule-following can be amplified through a further legal example. Take the common law rule of contract, the idea that no contract is enforceable absent consideration. How does one comprehend the meaning of "consideration"? To begin, we might offer a definition or state a rule; better still, we might look at some examples of what has, in the past, "counted" as consideration. As we go through the examples, it is important to note how they are united, i.e., what it is that brings them all under the rubric "consideration."

A and B each have children in the Happy Trails Nursery School. Each morning A and B take their children to school prior to the commencement of classes at 8:00 a.m. From there, they both proceed to their respective jobs at the same office. On day at their office, A offers to pick up B's child the

---

102. D.W. Hamlyn presents a strong case for this view in the context of perception. The very idea of visual discrimination presupposes a scheme of concepts. Without concepts, "whatever information is availabe in the stimulus array . . . will not be available *to the perceiver* unless he has the concepts necessary to make that possible." D. Hamlyn, In and Out of the Black Box: On the Philosophy of Cognition 98 (1989). Perception is a function of knowledge and knowledge is a matter of concepts.

[T]he perception of something as F cannot, logically, take place without the knowledge of what it is for something to be an F.

But to have that understanding is to have the concept of F, and it is put to use in some way in perceiving whatever it is as F. To put the matter in a slightly different way—to have a concept of F is to know what it is for something to be an F. To know what it is for something to be F involves knowing that an indeterminate list of things are so—things such as that being F involves being. . . , or that such and such range of things are F. But it is important that that list is indeterminate. One cannot lay down a determinate set of knowings—that which are necessary and sufficient for knowing what it is for something to be F. To perceive something as F nevertheless entails having that knowledge.

Id. at 92.

next morning and take him to school. B is thankful and tells A that he appreciates the favor. A's promise to B is unenforceable because B did not give A anything in return for A's promise. There has been no reciprocal offer of *value* by B., i.e., B has not offered *consideration.*

Jones is interested in purchasing a lawn tractor and goes to the Acme Tractor Co. for that purpose. After haggling with a salesman for an hour, the salesman promises to sell Jones the top-of-the-line model for ten percent off list price. Jones promises to pay that amount and signs a contract to that effect. The contract is enforceable because, among other things, each side has offered the other consideration.

An initiate into the practice of contract law would, at this point, be able to say at least two things about consideration:

1. consideration is something of value given in exchange for a promised performance; and
2. each side of a bargain must offer consideration in order for the contract to be enforceable.

With these two attributes of consideration in mind, can we decide whether or not the following agreement is enforceable as a contract?[103]

> A widow promises to repay a debt owed by her deceased husband in exchange for the creditor bank's cancelling the estate's debt. The husband's estate is without assets, and no part of the cancelled debt could ever have been collected.[104]

The obvious question is whether or not the widow's promise to pay her deceased husband's debt is an example of "consideration." Can we elaborate on the meaning of consideration by describing its predicates? How do we know which of its predicates are accidental and which are essential? A view that the widow's promise of repayment is consideration is only intelligible within the context of a theory of contract which has at its core a concept of contract as bargain. Only in recognizing the practice of contract as a system of rules with bargain theory at its center can we decide whether or not the widow's promise serves as consideration.[105]

---

103. C. Fried, Contract as Promise 28-31 (1981).
104. Id. at 31.
105. Notice that I said *a* concept of contract as a bargain and not *the* concept of contract as bargain. Compare the concept of contract as bargain with the benefit/detriment test of consideration employed in Hamer v. Sidway, 124 N.Y. 538, 27 N.E. 256 (1891). In *Hamer,* the New York Court of Appeals decided the question of whether of not an uncle's promise to pay his nephew $5,000 if the young man refrained from alcohol and tobacco until his 21st birthday was enforceable against the uncle's estate.
   The court found that the "detriment" imposed upon the nephew (his abstention from conduct he had a right to pursue) was sufficient to support a determination that the promise was enforceable. The point is not that the New York Court of Appeals *called* "consideration" something different than did the Restatement test of a bargain. Rather, the point is that the conception of contract as bargain makes the concept of consideration intelligible. The meaning of consideration is a function of the conceptual presupposition of contract as bargain. The very intelligibility of consideration is tied to *this* (as opposed to some *other*) conception of contract.

Let me return to my general claim that the meaning of a legal rule is a function of the point or purpose of the rule. The rule that no contract is enforceable without consideration cannot, on its own or in conjunction with a definition of consideration, tell us whether or not a contract is enforceable.[106] The constituent components of consideration are determinable only when we have elaborated the point of the rule requiring consideration. The rule of consideration is unintelligible until one realizes that it is "grounded" in a particular conception of contract law—the bargain theory. It is only against the background of the bargain theory that we can make sense of the question of whether or not "X" is consideration. The answer will be determinable only after we recognize the purpose of consideration and its role in contract law.

VI. All Justification Must Come to an End—but Only Temporarily

If anything is central to the later philosophy of Wittgenstein, it is the distinction between reasons and causes. Of the former, he had much to say. Of the latter, he could not disparage enough the psychological theories of his day, particularly their proponents' wish to explain meaning as a mental phenomenon.[107] For Wittgenstein, meaning is a public process, a socially created phenomenon. To know the meaning of a word is to give a correct linguistic performance in appropriate contexts.

In this Part, I will elaborate upon the claim that the meaning of a legal rule is a function of its point or purpose. What I offer will, in some quarters, be seen as a sociology of law—and in a sense it is, if one understands sociology as the description of what participants in legal discourse actually do.[108] In another sense, what I offer is a phenomenology of legal practice. I will describe, first in general terms and then by way of example, the *constructive* aspects of purpose. In addition to illustrating that the phenomenology of judging is more a *collective* than an *individual* enterprise, I will illustrate how that collective enterprise contributes to the construction of legal meaning. In short, attribution of purpose is constructive and dialogical; constructive in the sense that the source of purpose is multiple, not unitary, and in the sense that legal meaning is produced through dialogical encounter among participants in legal discourse.

The general philosophical claim that lies at the center of the theory of law as narrative discourse is that the meaning of the activities of rational agents

---

106. In other words, contra Hegel, the idea of contract cannot be understood in itself, for itself. See G. Hegel, The Philosophy of Right § 80 (T. Knox trans. 1977) (stating that "[t]he classification of contracts and an intelligent treatment of their various species once classified is not here to be derived from external circumstances but from distinctions lying in the very nature of contract").
107. For an extensive and extremely well-informed treatment of this topic, see generally S. Hilmy, The Later Wittgenstein 190-226 (1987) (noting Wittgenstein's rejection of meaning as a mental phenomenon).
108. For a discussion of the connection between Wittgenstein and Karl Llewellyn on the central role of description in jurisprudence, see Patterson, Law's Practice (Book Review), 90 Colum. L. Rev. 575 (1990).

cannot be understood apart from the agents' own perceptions and self-descriptions of the activity under question. In other words, the meaning of a practice is an *internal* phenomenon. It is within the practice, and by virtue of the acts of the participants in the practice, that the practice has meaning. Without purposeful activity, there would be no practices. Practices are creatures of reason and function as conventions. It is, therefore, against the specifics of a practice that claims for actions consistent with the practice are validated. Our perception of the objectivity of any particular decision is a function of the degree to which the act in question is in conformity with the demands of the practice as understood by the participants.

It is perhaps paradoxical to assert that a practice has standards against which claims of conformity are measured and, at the same time, to claim that those standards are a function of the needs, wants, desires, and purposes of the participants. This is precisely my claim, however. Claims of consistency with the practice are measured against the practice, but the participants in the practice determine what those standards are and will be. I shall now present arguments in support of each of these claims.

Concepts are not theories.[109] The relationship between concepts and actions is one of reasons and justifications. Purposeless activity is unintelligible as action, for no action is intelligible apart from some reason or justification for the act undertaken.[110] But not just *any* concept will explain the meaning of an agent's action. If the explanation is not one the agent would accept, at least in principle, then the explanation must be rejected, for it fails to capture the meaning of the act in question.

But why insist that any proffered explanation of action be one the agent would, in princple, accept as a rationale for her action? Let me return to the notion rejected at the outset; the idea of concepts as theories. I am *not* saying that actions are not to be *causally* explained by concepts. My claim is that there exists no set of concepts that explain an agent's activity better than those in which the agent finds her activity intelligible.[111] Regularity or pattern

---

109. See Hacker, Language, Rules and Pseudo-Rules, 8 Lang. & Commun. 159, 170 (1988) ("Understanding a language does not involve constructing a theory of any kind, but mastery of an array of skills or techniques in the use of words.").
110. As Alasdair MacIntyre has stated:

> Unintelligible actions are failed candidates for the status of intelligible action; and to lump unintelligible actions and intelligible actions together in a single class of actions and then to characterize action in terms of what items of both sets have in common is to make the mistake of ignoring this. It is also to neglect the central importance of the concept of intelligibility.

MacIntyre, After Virtue: A Study in Moral Theory 195 (1st ed. 1981)
111. I do not deny that texts can be read in contexts that create meanings unknown to the authors of those texts or beyond the cultural milieu out of which those texts were produced. What I do claim, however, is that it is a fundamental mistake to fail to consider the self-understanding of the participants in a discourse. The limitation here is one of representation: if the framework within which a practice is redescribed is not *in principle* cognizable by the subjects of the description, it must be rejected as meaningless. Why? Because meaning is neither in the text nor in the head (of the described participants). Meaning is what the discursive participants do with their texts. Compare C. Altieri, Act & Quality: A Theory of Literary Meaning and Humanistic Understanding 155-56 (1981) (stating that meaning is the intention an author can accept on redescription) with Ricouer, The Model of The Text: Meaningful Action Considered as a Text, *in* P. Ricouer, Hermeneutics and the Human Sciences 218 (J. Thompson ed. & trans. 1981) ("The depth semantics of the text is not what the author intended to say, but what the text is about, i.e., the non-ostensive reference of the text.").

in behavior, coupled with a hypothesis about what the regularity could amount to, is not understanding. No theory of regularity can hope to make sense of behavior until and unless its proponent is willing to construct the theory in a manner consistent with a subject's self-understanding. Of course, when this is done, the need for an explanatory theory disappears.

Consider the cancellation of debts and gift-giving. If A loans money to B and then decides not to demand payment, what are the observed regularities? A gives a pile of paper (money) to B; B acquires material objects by giving the paper to third parties; and B never returns the paper or its equivalent to A. Without knowing more, four possible explanations of these behavioral regularities are possible:

1. A made a gift of money to B, which B then spent;
2. A loaned money to B and they orally agreed that B would pay it back to A at 10 percent interest per annum, and B has refused to repay the loan;
3. Same as 2 except that A has forgiven B's obligation; or
4. A was repaying a debt to B which required no further action on B's part.

In order to determine which of these four possible explanations is appropriate in relation to the activity of A and B, an observer must understand the concepts of loan, gift, repayment, contract, breach, etc. The meaning of the actions of A and B are unintelligible apart from these terms. They are, as it were, merely "brute facts." It is the practice of lending money or making a gift that makes the action intelligible. But, and this is important, if A and B had no notion of gift-giving and explained their behavior relative to the practice of lending money with a promise of repayment, it would be a *misunderstanding* of their actions to explain it in any other terms, e.g., gift-giving. Money-lending is not a *theory* that explains the actions of A and B. Rather, it is the framework within which these actions are intelligible. To describe the actions of A and B in any other terms is to misconstrue *the meaning* of their actions. Understanding a practice and understanding the concepts that comprise the practice are one and the same thing.

One possible objection to my general philosophical claim that the meaning of legal rules is unintelligible apart from contexts of use (wherein the point of the rule is made manifest) is the fact that words can often be understood apart from context.[112] In short, the claim is that literal semantic meaning is a feature of linguistic practice, and thus of legal practice as well.

The fact that words can be understood apart from context in no way impairs the substance of my argument. I do not dispute, for example, the claim that Lord Russell's famous sentence, "the present King of France is bald," is understandable by a competent speaker of English. But understanding is not enough. The statement must also be *intelligible*. If I called upon a

---

112. See, e.g., Schauer, Formalism 97 Yale L.J. 509, 527-28 (1988).

student for the facts of *Hadley v. Baxendale* and she responded with Lord Russell's famous sentence, I would not know what to say, how to respond to her statement. I would understand her utterance, but it would not be intelligible; I would not know what *she* meant by it.[113]

It simply will not do, as proponents of semantic formalism maintain, to make the obvious point that words and sentences have meaning apart from their contexts of use. No one would dispute this. What is disputed is the claim that one can build a theory of law (formalism) on such an edifice. Bare semantic meaning exists as a feature of linguistic practice because the contexts in which the words were first learned provide the background necessary for the recognition of meaning by the listener. The meaning of words is a function of training in the contexts of use.[114] The traning provides the foundation for meaning and makes meaning possible. Without training in contexts of use, words would have no meaning. Thus, when a sentence is uttered in an inappropriate context, the *sentence* is understood because the listener associates the sentence with the contexts in which it was learned.[115] The reasons the sentence is unintelligible is because, in the situation in which the listener finds himself, he cannot find anything with which to link the utterance. In answer to the question, "[o]n what occasion, for what purpose, do we say this,"[116] the listener is forced to say "none." Thus, the statement may be understandable and yet still be unintelligible.

VII. Wittgenstein's Tailor

It is now time to return to the dispute between Baker and Hacker and the community consensus readers of Wittgenstein's remarks on rule-following. Recall, if you will, that the basic disagreement between these two readings of Wittgenstein is over the extent to which the conduct of the community of rule-followers contributes to the meaning of the rules. For Baker and Hacker, *no* contribution is allowed. As they put it, "the rule and only the rule determines what counts as 'following the rule.'"[117] In other words, the extension of a rule is a function of its internal relation.

For their part, the community consensus readers of Wittgenstein claim that it is *only* in a community of rule-followers that the extension of a rule comes to light. The community consensus readers take the position, exemplified by Malcolm, that "the concept of following a rule implies the concept of a *community* of rule-followers."[118] In short, far from agreeing with Baker

113. This, I take it, is the point Wittgenstein makes when he says: "If a lion could talk, we could not understand [verstehen] *him*." L. Wittgenstein, supra note 18, at 223e (emphasis added). We would understand the utterance, but not what the lion meant by it.
114. L. Wittgenstein, Zettel § 419 (G. Anscombe & G. von Wright eds, G. Anscombe trans. 1967) (stating that "[a]ny explanation has its foundation in training").
115. Rorty, How to Interpret Actions, *in* Rationality, Relativism and the Human Sciences 81 (J. Margolis, M. Krausz & R. Burian eds. 1986) ("But when we interpret isolated sentences and events, we supply the standard contexts in which they occur.").
116. L. Wittgenstein, supra note 18, § 489.
117. G. Baker & P. Hacker, supra note 34, at 172.
118. M. Malcolm, supra note 31, at 156.

and Hacker that the rule and only the rule determines what will count as part of its extension, the community consensus reading indicates that, without a *community* that follows the rule, the notion of "following" the rule makes no sense at all.

Can there be an internal relation between a rule and its applications that is socially determined? I think this is possible and I believe Wittgenstein thought so as well. In his *Lectures on Aesthetics*,[119] Wittgenstein discusses several practices that are governed by rules, including tailoring. Wittgenstein's remarks on the practice of tailoring reveal much about the relationship between rules and practices.

> In the case of the word 'correct' you have a variety of related cases. There is first the case in which you learn the rules. The cutter learns how long a coat is to be, how wide the sleeve must be, etc. He learns rules—he is drilled—as in music you are drilled in harmony and counterpoint. Suppose I went in for tailoring and I first learnt all the rules, I might have, on the whole, two sorts of attitude. (1) Lewy says: 'This is too short.' I say: 'No. It is right. It is according to the rules.' (2) I develop a feeling for the rules. I interpret the rules. I might say: 'No. It isn't right. It isn't according to the rules.' Here I would be making an aesthetic judgement about the thing which is according to the rules in sense (1). On the other hand, if I hadn't learnt the rules, I wouldn't be able to make the aesthetic judgement. In learning the rules you get a more and more refined judgement. Learning the rules actually changes your judgement.[120]

In considering these remarks, one cannot help but notice that Wittgenstein's emphasis on the relationship between a rule and its interpretation is compatible with, yet in an important way different than, his comments in *Philosophical Investigations*. In *Philosophical Investigations*, he says that "[i]nterpretations by themselves do not determine meaning."[121] The reason for this is clear: interpretations of rules only make sense in practices where there is an established way of "going on" with the rule such that the interpretations of a rule will have something that will moor them to the practice.

Different types of practices, however, have different rules and, more importantly, different criteria for what does and does not constitute "following the rule." Wittgenstein comments:

> On the other hand we can contrast different kinds of formula, and the different kinds of use (different kinds of training) appropriate to them. Then we *call* formulae of a particular kind (with the appropriate methods of use) "formulae which determine a number y for a given value of x", and formulae of another kind, ones which "do not determine the number y for a given value of x". ($y = x^2$ would be of the first kind, $y \neq x^2$ of the second.) The proposition "The formula. . . . determines a number y" will then be a statement about the form of the formula—and now we must distinguish such a proposition as "The formula which I have written down determines y", or "Here is a formula which determines y", from one of the following kind: "The formula $y = x^2$

---

119. L. Wittgenstein, Lectures and Conversations on Aesthetics, Psychology and Religious Belief (C. Barrett ed. 1972).
120. Id. § 15.
121. L. Wittgenstein, supra note, 18, § 198.

determines the number y for a given value of x". The question "Is the formula written down there one that determines y?" will then mean the same as "Is what is there a formula of this kind or that?"—but it is not clear off-hand what we are to make of the question "Is $y = x^2$ a formula which determines y for a given value of x?" One might address this question to a pupil in order to test whether he understands the use of the word "to determine"; or it might be a mathematical problem to prove in a particular system that x has only one square.[122]

The discussion of rules in *Philosophical Investigations* is addressed to the emptiness of skepticism and is aimed at showing that rules make sense in practices and that only through use is the meaning of a rule made manifest. In his remarks on tailoring in *Lectures on Aesthetics,* Wittgenstein seems to have a different point in mind. Instead of focusing on which rule to apply, Wittgenstein draws our attention to the *application* of rules that participants in the practice agree are the rules of the enterprise. There is a distinction between knowing the rules of a practice and being a competent practitioner; a practitioner exercises "aesthetic judgement" whereas a nonparticipant does not. Although learning the rules is *necessary* to having aesthetic judgment, *knowing the rules* of tailoring is not enough to make someone a competent tailor.

VIII. Law as Practice

A. Law as Thing, Law as Activity

The implications of Wittgenstein's description of the relationship between language and reality for law are significant. To the extent there is law, we can only know it relative to our practices; the activities we identify as "law." "Law" is not law merely because we call it "law," nor is what we call "law" law because it comports with an a priori Idea of Law.[123] What we call "law" is law because it is that activity by which we institutionally organize collective argument about how we should live. Law is a medium of intelligibility; it is a way of making sense of our collective and individual experience.

As an institution, law gives meaning to utterances which they would not have, but for the institution.[124] In other words, the meaning of the law cannot be separated from the institution of law. Consider John Canfield's discussion of this concept in connection with the simple declaration "he can swim the river."

> In the case of "He can swim the river," the background "institutions" of warfare, a chief assigning battle roles or tasks, and so on, are parts of the surroundings necessary for the making of the assertion in that language game. One might be inclined to deny this. For couldn't we imagine that these cultural patterns or roles are absent, and yet the assertion "He can swim the river" is made sensibly, and made, moreover, as governed

---

122. Id. § 189.
123. For a discussion of this distinction in the context of Wittgenstein's position vis-a-vis nominalism and realism, see Bambrough, Universals and Family Resemblances, *in* Wittgenstein: The Philosophical Investigations 186 (G. Pitcher ed. 1968).
124. It should be noted, however, that the same can be said of all institutions.

by exactly the same criterion as governed it in the original example? For instance, "He can swim the river" might be said in the "narration circumstances" mentioned above. But, to argue the other side, "He can swim the river" as uttered in the narration circumstances does not make the same assertion as it does when uttered in the preparing for warfare circumstances. "He can swim the river," in the warfare use makes the assertion it makes because it is said in a particular cultural surrounds, and because it has, therefore, certain implications and a certain portent. It engages in a certain way with the life of the people. Hence, it seems these particular cultural surrounds, or at least quite similar ones, are a necessary condition for the utterance to be the move it is in that language game.[125]

Canfield's example effectively demonstrates the Wittgensteinian antipathy to generalization. Like the sentences that express them, there is no unitary, singular meaning to concepts.[126] Language use occurs in situations (contexts); it is in and through these activities that understanding occurs.

Generalization abounds in contemporary jurisprudence. For example, in A Theory of Law,[127] Philip Soper advances the claim that legal theory is at a "dead end" because it continues to ask the sterile question "What is law?"[128] To eradicate the sterility of modern legal theory, Soper recommends that we change the question from "What is law?" to "What is law that I should obey it?"[129] One reason to change the question, according to Soper, is that no modern legal theorist holds the view that "law is somehow 'out there' with a unique essence awaiting discovery."[130]

Soper is wrong on both counts. The question "What is law?" remains viable because legal theory has yet to advance an adequate conception of law as an activity and not a thing. In addition, if anyone in modern legal theory advances an "essentialist" conception of law, it is Ronald Dworkin. Dworkin's distinction between concepts and conceptions, first advanced in Taking Rights Seriously and reemphasized in Law's Empire, can only be read as an attempt to promote the Kantian distinction between an Idea and its representations. It is hard to see how else passages like the following can be read:

Suppose I tell my children simply that I expect them not to treat others unfairly. I no doubt have in mind examples of the conduct I mean to discourage, but I would not accept that my 'meaning' was limited to these examples, for two reasons. First I would expect my children to apply my instructions to situations I had not and could not have thought about. Second, I stand ready to admit that some particular act I had thought was

---

125. J. Canfield, Wittgenstein: Language and World 55 (1981).
126. As Wittgenstein put it in *The Blue Book:*

> The idea that in order to get clear about the meaning of a general term one had to find the common element in all its applications has shackled philosophical investigation; for it has not only led to no result, but also made the philosopher dismiss as irrelevant the concrete cases, which alone could have helped him to understand the usage of the general term. When Socrates asks the question, "what is knowledge?" he does not even regard it as a *preliminary* answer to enumerate cases of knowledge.

L. Wittgenstein, The Blue and Brown Books 19-20 (1958).
127. P. Soper, A Theory of Law (1984).
128. Id. at 1.
129. Id. at 7.
130. Id.

fair when I spoke was in fact unfair, or vice versa, if one of my children is able to convince me of that later; in that case I should want to say that my instructions covered the case he cited, not that I had changed my instructions. I might say that I meant the family to be guided by the *concept* of fairness, not by any specific *conception* of fairness I might have had in mind.[131]

If law does not have some Archimedean perspective from which to assess competing claims, then how is there ever objectivity in law? To put the point differently, if the point of law is not imposed from without,[132] then from whence does it arise?

B. Law as Narrative

To conceive of law as an activity and not as a thing is to approach law as a way of making sense of the world; that is, as a medium of understanding. James Boyd White's characterization of law as "a continuing and collective process of conversation and judgment"[133] is a powerful metaphor. Its power lies in its ability to picture law as a process of becoming. Law is more like painting than archaeology; it is more a process of creation than pure discovery. But what is it that is painted in this conversation?

Let us return to the idea of the form of law. I said that to understand the point of a legal concept it is necessary to know its form. As I described it, the form of a legal notion is that which makes it intelligible. Thus, knowing the meaning of a legal notion means understanding or "grasping the *point* or *meaning* of what is being done or said"[134] by someone employing the concept. Law is a form of social relations: we associate with others through the medium of law. It is a means of ideational expression. Like all cultural forms, law has a history or, to put it better, histories. It is to these that we appeal when we engage in the practice of law.

1. Easy Cases. But must we always appeal to legal history in support of a claim in law? Surely not. And therein lies the distinction between hard and easy cases. The easy case is the one which can be decided by reference to a rule, the extension of which clearly covers the case and against the application of which no good reason can be advanced. Examples of such cases abound in the reporters; one might mention going against a red light, a promissory note signed by the maker, and dozens, nay thousands, of others.

It is in these easy cases that Baker & Hacker's reading of Wittgenstein's rule-following provides a complete description both of what rule-following is like in actual practice and what Wittgenstein likely would have said about easy cases in law, had he thought about law. There *is* an internal relation between a rule and its applications, but contra Baker and Hacker, that relation is in and through the concept embodied in the rule.

---

131. R. Dworkin, supra note 8, at 134 (1977).
132. For example, Dworkin's "best" interpretation of the practice of law.
133. J. White, When Words Lose Their Meaning 264 (1984).
134. P. Winch, supra note 72, at 115 (1958).

For example, consider the rule, "[a]n offeree's power of acceptance is terminated when the offeree receives from the offeror a manifestation of an intention not to enter into the proposed contract."[135] What is the meaning of the word "receive"? Does the rule require that the offeror personally communicate the revocation to the offeree? Is it sufficient that an agent of the offeree perform the act of communication? Need the notice be in writing? What if the offeree gets the news from a third party unrelated to the transaction?

The point of the rule generates the form of the concept of "receive" and provides the internal relation between the rule and what will count as "receiving notice." The point of the notice requirement is to prevent a detrimental change of position on the part of the offeree in reliance upon the offer which, if accepted before notice of revocation, could lead to injurious reliance upon the (withdrawn) offer.[136]

I wish to stress that the concept of "receipt" as used in the rule is unintelligible apart from its relation to the (institutional) practice of law. As Peter Winch puts it: "[t]o give an account of the meaning of [the] word is to describe how it is used; and to describe how it is used is to describe the social intercourse into which it enters."[137] The "fact" that someone in any given case received notice of revocation is the result of interaction between the institution of contract and doings in the world. The "fact" that "'x' received notice of revocation" is what Anscombe and Searle refer to as an "institutional fact."[138] Without the social practice of contract, there would be no "notice" to be "received."

2. Hard Cases. Not all cases are easy cases, and it is in distinguishing easy from hard cases that the role of community consensus in legal argument will be clarified. Consider *Riggs v. Palmer.*[139] Elmer Palmer's grandfather, Francis Palmer, executed a will in which he left his estate to three persons: his grandson Elmer and Elmer's two aunts, Mrs. Riggs and Mrs. Preston.[140] When Elmer's grandfather remarried, Elmer feared his grandfather might change his will and, to preclude this possibility, murdered his grandfather.[141] Elmer was convicted of murder and sent to prison.[142]

Elmer's aunts sued in New York to prevent Elmer from taking anything under his late grandfather's will.[143] The New York Statute of Wills said nothing about devisees being precluded from inheriting because they murdered the testator. On the basis of that silence, a New York trial court

---

135. Restatement (Second) of Contracts § 42 (1981).
136. See Dickinson v. Dodds, 2 Ch. D. 463 (C.A. 1876).
137. P. Winch, supra note 72, at 123. For a different view of "internal," see L. Wittgenstein, supra note 134, § 4.123 ("A property is internal if it is unthinkable that its object should not possess it.").
138. See Anscombe, On Brute Facts, *in* G. Anscombe, 3 Collected Papers (Ethics, Religion and Politics) 22-25 (1981); J. Searle, Speech Acts 50-53 (1969).
139. 115 N.Y. 506, 22 N.E. 188 (1889).
140. Id. at 508, 22 N.E. at 188.
141. Id. at 508, 22 N.E. at 189.
142. Id. at 515, 22 N.E. at 191 (Gray, J., dissenting).
143. Id. at 508, 22 N.E. at 188.

dismissed the aunts' complaint.[144] On appeal, the New York Court of Appeals held, in a split decision, that the principle, "no man shall profit by his own wrong," precluded the enforcement of the will in Elmer's favor.[145] In dissent, Judge Gray argued that, because Elmer had received the punishment for murder and was duly incarcerated, it would be unjust to impose additional punishment upon him.[146] In short, Judge Gray advanced the principle, "no man shall be punished unjustly," in order to contend that Elmer should receive his inheritance just as if his grandfather had died of natural causes.[147]

It seems to defy practical legal experience to say that there is one "right" way to answer the question posed by the *Riggs* case. Instead, most participants in the practice of law, the group Brian Simpson refers to as the "caste of lawyers,"[148] would say that each reading of the appropriate legal materials[149] in *Riggs* is plausible and that there is no way to decide which reading is "the best." And yet, pace CLS, if the community of lawyers cannot agree on which reading of the legal materials is "right," doesn't that mean that the law is "indeterminate"?

The position of these CLS theorists is reminiscent of the "outsider" of which Alasdair MacIntyre speaks.[150] With no Archimedean point from which to judge the adequacy of legal arguments, all we can do is appeal to the history of our collective practice and make sense of where we are going by reference to our understanding of where we have been. If law is an activity, and the caste of lawyers a community, then the two readings of the legal materials advanced in *Riggs* should be seen as two plausible narratives of the point of our practice, each pointing in a different direction.

The direction chosen will be the result of dialogue among the members of the community: courts, lawyers, and scholars. It is out of this dialogical encounter among the participants in the discursive practice of law that the point of law is determined.[151] The great debates in law, debates about the point or purpose of the law, are collective arguments about where we ought

---

144. Id. at 515, 22 N.E. at 191 (Gray, J., dissenting).
145. Id. at 513, 22 N.E. at 190.
146. Id. at 519, 22 N.E. at 129 (Grey, J., dissenting).
147. Id. at 519.
148. Simpson, supra note 104, at 20.
149. One can only agree with Charles Silver that Dworkin is simply incorrect in his contention that "'the dispute about Elmer was not about whether judges should follow the law or adjust it in the interests of justice. . . . It was a dispute about what the law was, about what the real statute the legislators enacted really said.'" Silver, Elmer's Case: A Positivist Replies to Dworkin, 6 Law & Phil. 382 (1987) (quoting R. Dworkin, supra note 35, at 20).
150. A. MacIntyre, Short History of Ethics 266 (1966).
151. This is not to say that all applications of law require such a dialogical encounter. What counts as "following a rule" is often a relatively simple matter. If this were not the case, then ordinary citizens having little or no knowledge of legal materials would live in a Kafkaesque nightmare. This is not an apt description of our condition.

On a different plane, it reaffirms the truth of Llewellyn's insight that legal knowledge is not reducible to a structure constitutive of law. See Patterson, Law's Practice, supra note 113, at 592-600. Since the time of Hobbes, legal theorists have maintained that the validity of law was a function of structure or source. For Hobbes and Austin this could be traced to the command of the sovereign; for H.L.A. Hart, to the Rule of Recognition; for Hans Kelsen, to the *Grundnorm;* and for Dworkin, to a structure of embedded principle. See Postema, "Protestant" Interpretations and Social Practices, 6 Law & Phil. 283, 317-18 (1987) (discussing Dworkin's theory of interpretation of the nature and practice of law).

to take the law. As collective argument, law is the premier activity, for it affords us the opportunity to shape our collective future. As such, the activity of law is charged with the utmost opportunity and, more importantly, responsibility.

IX. Tradition, Practice, and Narrative

T.S. Eliot believed that the appreciation of a poet "is the appreciation of his relation to the dead poets and artists."[152] Clearly, tradition is at the center of Eliot's view of poetry. Tradition plays a similar role within a conception of law as narrative.[153] As with poetry and art, the law reproduces itself through the participants in the practice. The question then becomes how it is that law reproduces itself.

The understanding of the practice of law as narrative is internal. Understanding the practice means knowing how to "go on" with the repertoire of behaviors identified as the practice. "Going on" means taking the existing world of the practice and absorbing "new items in that world, to move around with a certain ease in the web of relationships created by it."[154]

Narrative is the nerve of historical reason. The key to a narrative account of law is not to reveal a preordained pattern in law's past, but to create a discursive intelligibility out of temporal unity. In short, accounting for the coherence of law "primarily involves narrating the process of its development, highlighting the rhyme and reason therein."[155]

Practices carry their own internal standards and rules. To become an initiate into a practice means accepting the authority of the standards articulated and adhered to by the practitioners at the time of initiation.[156] That initial acceptance, however, does not preclude subsequent critique of the practice. As Amelie Rorty has recently noted, "[R]easons do not end with embeddedness."[157]

So what does narrative provide in the way of illuminating legal argument? It suggests that the way law changes is through the advancement of stories or accounts of the practice that have an internal unity that captures the significant elements of the practice while pointing in a direction different from the current understanding of the enterprise. For instance, can there be any doubt that Fuller and Perdue's essay on the reliance interest in contract suggests a radical reinterpretation of the practice of contract law?[158] Their

---

152. Eliot, Tradition and the Individual Talent, *in* T.S. Eliot, Selected Prose of T.S. Eliot 38 (1975); see also, R. Shusterman, T.S. Eliot and the Philosophy of Criticism 83-85 (1988) (discussing Eliot's "literary constellation" theory, according to which new authors build on the tradition of old authors, thus augmenting the body of art and criticism).
153. For a general discussion on the importance of tradition to law, see Krygier, The Traditionality of Statutes, 1 Ratio Juris 20 (1988); Krygier, Law as Tradition, 5 Law & Phil. 237 (1986).
154. Postema, supra note 188, at 304.
155. Carroll, Art, Practice and Narrative, 71 The Monist 140, 150 (1988).
156. See A. MacIntyre, supra note 187, at 177.
157. A. Rorty, Mind In Action: Essays in the Philosophy of Mind 288 (1988).
158. Fuller & Perdue, The Reliance Interest in Contract Damages: 1, 46 Yale L.J. 52 (1936); Fuller & Perdue, The Reliance Interest in Contract Damages: 2, 46 Yale L.J. 373 (1937).

"story" was and is a powerful narrative because it takes all of the "elements" that the participants agree to be what we refer to as "contract" and casts them in a new light. The power of the narrative is a direct function of its ability to conceptualize the subject matter in a way previously unseen by the participants, yet in a form that most agree still captures the point of the practice.

My suggestion is that the whole of law is the production of one narrative after another. Every innovative case, law review article, and judicial opinion is an account of the past practice of the law and the advancement of reasons and arguments in support of a claim for the point (form) of law. Of course, each individual focus (a constitution, a statute, the common law) will have unique features that set it apart. Nevertheless, the unity of law as a discursive enterprise will be the primary element of narrative and will lie at the center of arguments over the point of law.

X. A Representative Narrative

One of the classic rules of contract law is that there is a duty to read.[159] The doctrine generally states that, regardless of whether or not one reads the contract, the affixing of one's signature has the legal effect of binding one to the terms contained in the agreement.[160] This rule has been applied to a variety of cases including standardized form contracts[161] and contracts written in a language which the signer was unable to read.[162]

In this Part, I focus attention on standardized form contracts or, as they have come to be known, "contracts of adhesion."[163] The law on contracts of adhesion is particularly useful for assessing the cogency of a conception of law as narrative. I say this because the question of the enforceability of contracts of adhesion has been the subject of much academic writing.[164] Yet no consensus exists as to the extent to which these contracts should be enforced.

A contract of adhesion is one that is presented to a party on a take-it-or-leave-it basis. The contract usually consists of a form, composed in various print sizes, and containing an excess of what has euphemistically come to

---

159. See generally Calamari, Duty to Read—A Changing Concept, 43 Fordham L. Rev. 341 (1974) (overview and analysis of the duty to read doctrine).

160. See, e.g., National Bank v. Equity Inv., 81 Wash. 2d 886, 506 P.2d 20 (1973) ("The whole panoply of contract law rests on the principle that one is bound by the contract which he voluntarily and knowingly signs.").

161. See, e.g., Lewis v. Great W. Ry., 157 Eng. Rep. 1427 (Ex. 1860) (denying a claim for bailee's loss of the parcel because bailor failed to file a claim within the narrow window allowed by a written contract which bailor had neglected to read).

162. See, e.g., Landry Loan Co. v. Avie, 147 S. 2d 725 (La. Ct. App. 1962) (binding a French-speaking illiterate as co-signer on a promissory note despite the fact that he had made his 'X' without understanding the nature of the liability undertaken).

163. The term "contrats d'ahesion" has been traced to R. Saleilles, De la Declaration de Volonte 229 (1901), and was introduced into American jurisprudence in Patterson, The Delivery of a Life-Insurance Policy, 33 Harv. L. Rev. 198, 222 (1919).

164. See, e.g., Rakoff, Contracts of Adhesion: An Essay in Reconstruction, 96 Harv. L. Rev. 1174 (1983) (arguing that standardized form terms, because of the balance of power between commercial organizations and individuals, should be presumptively unenforceable).

be known as "boilerplate." Much of this boilerplate is never read by the parties who sign these contracts. This is largely due to the fact that there is simply no reason to read the contract. Even if one were to take the time to read the contract, it is almost always the case that the party proffering the document will either simply refuse to alter, or will lack the requisite authority to alter, the terms of the contract.[165]

The traditional common law of contracts reveres the sanctity of the written agreement.[166] A natural consequence of such reverence is the emergence of a duty to read rule: "one having the capacity to understand a written document who reads it, or, without reading it or having it read to him, signs it, is bound by his signature."[167] The reason, or at least one reason, for the rule is clear: "no one could rely on a signed document if the other party could avoid the transaction by saying that he had not read or did not understand the writing.[168]

When parties enter into a contract, each has individual motivations and expectations. As a general matter, the law does not guarantee a party to a contract a remedy in the event the other party's performance fails to live up to the expectations of a hopeful contractual partner. Contract law does not guarantee results; it simply provides a vehicle whereby two parties can strike a deal on mutually agreed terms with the ability to engage the state's power of enforcement (or to award damages) in the event one of the parties fails to live up to the *terms* of that bargain (as opposed to one party's subjective expectations).

The form contract ("contract of adhesion") has altered the classical view of contract, or so it would seem. Insurance contracts, loan agreements, and retail installment sales contracts are everyday, familiar examples of a contract of adhesion. Nothing remotely recognizable as "bargaining" enters into the picture. The form contract is presented by the seller-drafter on terms that are the product, not of the party presenting the document, but of an industry that circulates model forms that impose a unitary structure on a corner of commerce.[169] Should adhesion contracts be treated differently than "normal," contracts? If so, how far should the courts go in policing the terms of the agreements and on what basis?

These and other questions are raised by *C & J Fertilizer, Inc. v. Allied Mutual Insurance Company.*[170] The plaintiff in *C & J Fertilizer* was a 37-

---

165. See Farnsworth, Contracts § 4.26 (1982). This happens frequently with national franchisees, and the courts generally enforce the standardized contract. See Zapatha v. Dairy Mart, 381 Mass. 284, 408 N.E.2d 1370 (1980) (court declines to find franchise agreement unconscionable).

166. Several commentators describe the historical embrace of the writing by describing the sanctity of the written contract as *inviolate*. See, e.g., Birnhaum, Stahl & West, Standardized Agreements and the Parol Evidence Rule: Defining and Applying the Expectations Principle, 26 Ariz. L. Rev. 793, 793 (1984).

167. Rossi v. Douglas, 203 Md. 190, 199, 100 A.2d 3, 7 (1953). The rule in the first Restatement is that: "One who makes a written offer which is accepted, or who manifests acceptance of the terms of a writing which he should reasonably understand to be an offer or proposed contract, is bound by the contract, though ignorant of the terms of the writing or of its proper interpretation." Restatement (First) of Contracts § 70 (1932).

168. J. Calamari & J. Perillo, The Law of Contracts 410 (3d ed. 1987).

169. See Rakoff, supra note 202, at 1222-48.

170. 227 N.W.2d 169 (Iowa 1975).

year-old farmer who owned and managed a fertilizer plant.[171] The plaintiff
had two insurance contracts with the defendant insurance company, Allied
Mutual, which covered him for losses resulting from, among other things,
burglary.[172] In each policy, "burglary" was defined as follows:

> [T]he felonious abstraction of insured property (1) from within the premises by a person
> making felonious entry therein by actual force and violence, *of which force and violence
> there are visible marks made by tools, explosives, electricity or chemicals upon, or
> physical damages to, the exterior of the premises at the place of such entry. . . .*[173]

On Monday morning, after a weekend when the premises were checked
and found to be secure, the plaintiff discovered that his building had been
burglarized and that a quantum of chemicals had been removed.[174] The trial
court found that the burglar had gained entrance to the area where the
fertilizer was stored by breaking the lock on the *interior* door.[175] Any
perplexity on the part of the plaintiff as to how a burglar could gain entrance
without leaving any marks on the exterior door was dispelled by an investi-
gator who demonstrated how the *exterior* door could be opened without
damaging the door, or even leaving any marks.[176]

The insurance company, however, refused to pay the claim, arguing that
the break-in did not meet the definition of "burglary" in the policies.[177] The
case was tried to the bench and a judgment entered for the defendant
insurance company, the judge holding that the definition of "burglary" in
the policies was "unambiguous" and thus binding on the parties.[178] There
being nothing in the record to support a finding of "felonious entry" as
defined in the contract, the trial court's ruling was, in its view, inexorable.[179]

In reversing the trial court's judgment in favor of the insurance company,
the Iowa Supreme Court moved first to consider evidence extrinsic to the
contract, evidence which it claimed "throws light on the situation of the
parties."[180] The evidence is exactly what one would expect. The insured
never look at the policies after he got them; he expected that he was covered
for all break-ins that were not "inside jobs." Further, the plaintiff and the
agent who sold him the policy never discussed any details of coverage, and
the agent who sold him the policy expressed shock at the company's denial
of the claim.[181]

The majority's entire opinion, and the reasons it adduces in support of its
conclusion that adhesion contracts are not enforceable if they are inconsistent
with the reasonable expectations of the insured, is built upon the assumption

---

171. Id. at 171-72.
172. Id. at 171.
173. Id.
174. Id.
175. Id. at 172.
176. Id. at 171.
177. Id.
178. Id.
179. Id.
180. Id. at 172.
181. Id. at 172-73.

that adhesion contracts should be specially treated. In support of this claim the court marshalled the following (material) elements:

1. it is generally recognized that insureds do not read their contracts;[182]
2. assent is a fundamental element of contract;[183]
3. the law of contracts attempts the realization of reasonable expectations;[184]
4. mass advertising creates an expectation of "protection";[185]
5. the principles of (classical) contract law were formulated at an early time when parties were of equal bargaining strength and negotiated on a face-to-face basis.[186]

The majority's opinion is built on the claim that, because empirical reality (the reality of the world of insurance) has changed, the law must be responsive to that fact. This is a fundamentally different conception of law than that advanced by the dissent in *C & J Fertilizer*. The dissent never gets past the problem of contractual (lingustic) ambiguity. As the dissent sizes up the case, the fact that the language was unambiguous means that the contract should be enforced according to its terms.[187] Further, according to the dissent, "Once this indisputable fact is recognized, plaintiff's arguments virtually collapse."[188]

More important than the details of two opinions is the fact that the majority opinion reflects the triumph of legal realism and the death of the orthodox view of contract (if not the orthodox view of law).[189] In support of the argument that form determines matter, it is important to see that what counts as an enforceable clause in a contract is a function of divergent conceptions of the "point" of contract law. If the point of contract law is to enforce an agreement that one had an opportunity to read but chose not to (the *First Restatement* view),[190] then parol evidence should be barred when offered to explain an unambiguous term, and it should be of no consequence that one had certain expectations with respect to any particular agreement.[191]

At the global level, the majority opinion supports the view that the individual circumstances and persona of the parties is critical to the adjudication of their claims. This presupposition dominates the majority's view

---

182. Id. at 174.
183. Id.
184. Id. at 176.
185. Id. at 178.
186. Id. at 173.
187. Id. at 183.
188. Id.
189. See generally Grey, Langdell's Orthodoxy, 45 U. Pitt. L. Rev. 1 (1983) (discussing in detail, orthodoxy and contrasting views of Legal Realism). See also Patterson, Good Faith, Lender Liability, and Discretionary Acceleration: Of Llewellyn, Wittgenstein, and the Uniform Commercial Code, 68 Tex. L. Rev. 169, 186-211 (1989) (discussing Llewellyn's Code jurisprudence in light of the classical (Langdellian/Willistonian) conception of contract).
190. Restatement (First) of Contracts § 70 (1932).
191. See Restatement (Second) of Contracts § 215 (1979). This section, which states the current common law rule, prohibits the introduction in evidence of just the sort the majority uses in *C & J Fertilizer*.

of the form of contract law as the enforcement of the agreement of the parties in a manner consistent with the reasonable expectations of the (economically) weaker party. According to this view, the point of contract law is, in part, paternalistic—the protection of the (informationally, economically, etc.) disadvantaged party.

Which is the "better" view? Which view is more (less) "just"? What is the "right answer" to the question posed by *C & J Fertilizer*? What is the "best constructive interpretation" of the issues at stake in *C & J Fertilizer*? Isn't the case really just the expression of two diametrically opposed political visions?

For different reasons, I don't believe that any of these questions are at all useful in accounting for what lawyers *do*. There are no "right" (single) answers in law. The materials out of which arguments are fashioned are themselves multivocal, that is, capable of a multitude of readings, both individually and collectively. As I have said, lawyers take the (historical) materials and articulate a narrative that participants in the dicourse recognize as having a coherence, an internal rhythm. It is the task of the lawyer to articulate that narrative and render clear both its internal coherence and relevance to present problems.

The power of a narrative, however, is contingent upon the extent to which it figures in other narratives. As Bruno Latour says of scientific "facts":

> [A] fact is what is collectively stabilised from the midst of controversies when the activity of later papers [for our purposes, judicial opinions, law review articles, addresses, etc.] does not consist only of criticism or deformation but also of confirmation. The strength of the original statement does not lie in itself, but is derived from any of the papers that incorporate it.[192]

If no form of representation (narrative) is privileged, then isn't one story as good as another? There can be no doubt that many legal narratives are "politically" motivated in the sense that they represent a particular vision of social life. But that is what I have been arguing all along: law is an institutional forum for the advancement of arguments (narratives) about how we are to live. The judgments of the participants in the discourse are the product of arguments which occur "within an institutionally defined structure of opportunities and possibilities."[193] The task of the committed discursive participant is to make of the institutionally defined possibilities for argument what she will. The denser the institutional history, the greater the possibilities for argument. In the words of Jean-François Lyotard:

> [T]he people are only that which actualizes the narratives: once again. They do this not only by recounting them, but also by listening to them and recounting themselves through them; in other words, by putting them into "play" in their institutions—thus by assigning themselves the posts of narratee and diegesis as well as the post of narrator.[194]

192. B. Latour, Science in Action 42 (1987).
193. R. Beiner, Political Judgment 148 (1983).
194. J. Lyotard, The Postmodern Condition 23 (G. Bennington & B. Massumi trans. 1984).

Conclusion

What are the implications for legal pragmatism of a narrative conception of legal discourse? Perhaps the clearest implication is that vocabulary—the categories with which we make sense of experience—must be the primary focus of attention. One cannot reject the false dichotomy of objectivism and relativism yet retain the notion that the ways in which we divide up the world can somehow be compared along a neutral continuum of measurement. The success or failure of our conceptual schemes must be judged, not relative to "the world" or "reality" (moral or otherwise), but with respect to the degree to which problems are solved (or dissolved), efficacious doctrinal schemes identified, or, at the level of political action, "by providing piecemeal nudges and cautions in respect to particular projects at particular times."[195]

Pragmatism of the sort argued for here is surely to be criticized for the seeming lack of grandeur in its hopes for the power of theory. While not advocating a position "against theory," the perspective advanced here is humble with respect to the possibilities of "grand narratives."[196] It would be a mistake to attack pragmatism at the level of humility, however, for the position is itself a realistic expression of the recognition that metatheoretical claims to truth are philosophically indefensible. Pragmatism's merit lies the recognition that our collective energies are better spent working within the limits of the possible rather than attempting to transcend the infinite.

195. Rorty, Philosophy as Science, as Metaphor, and as Politics, *in* The Institution of Philosophy 27 (A. Cohen & M. Dascal eds. 1989).
196. For discussion of the demise of grand narratives in postmodernity, see J. Lyotard, supra note 233.

PART TWO

Rules

5

Reconsidering the Rule of Law

Margaret Jane Radin

I. Introduction

The ideal of "the rule of law, not of men"[1] calls upon us to strive to ensure that our law itself will rule (govern) us, not the wishes of powerful individuals. According to this traditional ideal, government must be by "settled, standing Laws," not by "Absolute Arbitrary Power."[2] Although the Rule of Law ideal is central to our legal tradition, it is deeply contested. Among those who affirm the traditional ideal there is no canonical formulation of its meaning, and critical theorists argue that the Rule of Law is mere ideology that should be jettisoned. In this essay I suggest that it is too soon to throw out the Rule of Law wholesale, but that at minimum the concept should be reinterpreted.

By way of concrete introduction to the complex of problems I mean to examine, consider *Robinson v. Diamond Housing Corporation.*[3] *Robinson* was one of Judge J. Skelly Wright's famous decisions remaking modern landlord-tenant law in the early seventies. Judge Wright decided that the landlord, Diamond Housing Corporation, could not end Mrs. Robinson's month-to-month tenancy if its termination was motivated by retaliation against Mrs. Robinson for having successfully asserted the habitability defense of "illegal contract."[4] The result was that if a tenant lives in housing that seriously violates the housing code, he or she has a right to stay there, rent-free, until the landlord either fixes up the premises or proves economic compulsion to exit the landlord business. As Judge Wright put this, perhaps not fully mindful of the irony, precedent and the housing code "guarantee the right of a tenant to remain in possession without paying rent when the premises are burdened with substantial housing code violations making them unsafe and unsanitary."[5] In a ringing peroration, Wright declared that

---

1. For obvious reasons, because I am considering the Rule of Law in today's context, I shall rephrase the ideal as "the rule of law, not of individuals." Yet we must not forget that when the ideal developed, and during most of its long history, it was inconceivable that any individuals who were not "men" could be a part of political life.
2. J. Locke, *Of the Extent of the Legislative Power,* § 137 in Two Treatises of Government (P. Laslett rev. ed. 1970) (3d ed. 1698) (emphasis omitted). The formulation of the term "the Rule of Law" is sometimes credited to the nineteenth-century British jurist Albert Venn Dicey, who elaborated upon three characteristics of "the rule or supremacy of law": absence of arbitrary power on the part of the government; ordinary law administered by ordinary tribunals; and general rules of constitutional law resulting from the ordinary law of the land. *See* A. V. Dicey, Introduction to the Study of the Law of the Constitution 179-92 (1908).
3. 463 F.2d 853 (D.C. Cir. 1972).
4. The District of Columbia Court of Appeals had recently recognized the "illegal contract" defense in Brown v. Southall Realty Co., 237 A.2d 834, 837 (D.C. 1968). Successful assertion of this defense meant that a tenant's promise to pay rent was unenforceable.
5. *Robinson,* 463 F.2d at 865. Wright conceded that he would be "deeply troubled" if his ruling led to "many families living indefinitely in substandard housing without paying rent," *id.* at 869, but he apparently believed that giving the landlord the legal choice of either repairing the premises or being unable to charge rent would result in an increase in habitability at no increase in rent.

this result is "required . . . by respect for the separation of powers and the rule of law."[6]

It is this claim about the underlying ideal of the Rule of Law that prompts me to bring up the *Robinson* case here. My guess is that a great number of legal observers thought the Rule of Law required the case to come out the other way, in favor of the landlord's previously unquestioned right to end a month-to-month tenancy on proper notice. Can the Rule of Law impose any limitation of the "arbitrary power" of individual decision makers? Is the Rule of Law a good way to go about trying to achieve government by law?

I begin with an attempt to make clear exactly what *is* the Rule of Law, and the way in which its meaning is contested because of differences in emphasis of its instrumental and substantive aspects. Having noticed the fact that the main formulations of the Rule of Law do agree upon an assumption that law consists of rules, I move on to an inquiry into the nature of rules. Specifically, I consider a social practice conception of rules, commonly attributed to Wittgenstein,[7] which holds that rules can only be claimed to exist when there is community agreement in practice. To put this conception roughly, agreement in action does not *follow* from there being a pre-existing rule; agreement in action is the only basis for claiming that there *is* a rule.

I then consider the implications for the Rule of Law once this social practice conception of rules is accepted. First, I show how the traditional ideal of the Rule of Law is connnected with a certain traditional conception of the nature of rules, which I shall call "formalist." Then I ask the more specific question which is the main focus of this essay: Does the social practice conception of rules render the Rule of Law impossible? I argue that the social practice conception of rules does indeed render the traditional Rule of Law impossible, because of the link between the Rule of Law and the traditional conception of rules. I believe the Rule of Law can survive as a coherent ideal if it receives a modern interpretation, however, and I conclude by suggesting a possible avenue for such reinterpretation.[8]

II. The Rule of Law as a Contested Concept

Before reconsidering the Rule of Law in light of a social practice conception of rules, we must try to define the elements of the Rule of Law. The complex of ideas thought to comprise the Rule of Law is not completely canonical. We can, in fact, readily distinguish two main contested views: a primarily

---

6. *Robinson,* 463 F.2d at 871.

7. The view I discuss is often attributed to Wittgenstein, but no view can be attributed to him uncontroversially. As I discuss below, *see infra* pp. 797–810, my reading of Wittgenstein is broad and neo-pragmatic in character, but a narrower, more analytic reading is preferred by many.

8. The task of working out the required reinterpretation in detail, and exploring its connections with reinterpreted central aspects of political theory, awaits further work. The complete analysis would involve theories of the person, the state, and community, and theories of the proper roles of citizens, legislators, and judges in the well-developed polity. For another piece of the picture, see Michelman, *Law's Republic,* 97 Yale L.J. 1493 (1988) (presenting a modern interpretation of government by law through reinterpretation of the political theory of civic republicanism and exploration of the conundrum of government-of-laws versus government-by-the-people).

instrumental version and a more substantive version. The instrumental version holds that the Rule of Law is a prerequisite for any efficacious legal order. The substantive version holds that the Rule of Law embodies tenets of a particular political morality.[9] These versions are illustrated by two of the best modern attempts to address the Rule of Law, those of Lon Fuller[10] and John Rawls.[11] Although labels oversimplify, I think it will be appropriate to characterize Fuller's version as instrumental[12] and Rawls's version as substantive.[13]

A. The Instrumental Conception of the Rule of Law, or "How to do Things with Rules"

Lon Fuller claimed that the Rule of Law is part of the "internal" morality of law.[14] I interpret this to mean that the complex of ideas associated with the term "Rule of Law" is essential for the efficacy of any system of legal rules. This instrumental conception of the Rule of Law is presented in Fuller's engaging parable of King Rex,[15] who failed to make law by ignoring

---

9. To avoid possible misunderstanding, I should say here that the view I refer to as substantive is substantive only in an attenuated sense. As elaborated below, see infra notes 22-33 and accompanying text, the view I call substantive merely asserts that having a system of rules of a certain type by itself serves substantive values, such as fairness and respect for persons. On its fact, at least, the view I call substantive does not make the stronger claim that, in addition, in order to fulfill the Rule of Law ideal the rules must themselves be good rules. Ronald Dworkin's recent view of the Rule of Law is indeed "substantive" in this more robust sense, but I believe Dworkin's view departs from the main parameters in which the Rule of Law has previously been conceived. See R. Dworkin, A Matter of Principle 11-12 (1985) (the "rights conception" of the Rule of Law "requires, as part of the ideal of law, that the rules in the rule book capture and enforce moral rights").
10. See L. Fuller, The Morality of Law 33-94 (rev. ed. 1969).
11. See J. Rawls, A Theory of Justice 235-43 (1971).
12. I do risk mischaracterizing Fuller's view by calling it instrumental, because Fuller himself apparently believed that his formulation embodied other values besides instrumental efficacy. See infra note 17. For another account of the instrumental conception of the Rule of Law, see J. Raz, The Rule of Law and Its Virtue, in The Authority of Law: Essays on Law and Morality 210-29 (1979), although Raz in the end turns toward the substantive conception in important respects. Cf. Michelman, Justification (and Justifiability) of Law in a Contradictory World, in Justification in Law, Ethics, and Politics 71, 72 (J. Pennock & J. Chapman eds. 1986) (XXVIII) (characterizing legalist justification as implying a law that is general, external to the case to be decided, rationally applicable to cases, and transcending individual deciders).
13. Other accounts that stress the substantive aspect of the Rule of Law are F. Hayek, The Political Ideal of the Rule of Law (1955) (characterizing the liberty produced by the Rule of Law in terms of the laissez-faire market regime—private property and freedom of contract); J. Lucas, The Principles of Politics §§ 24-25 (1985); R. Sartorius, Individual Conduct and Social Norms (1975). Cf. Moore, The Semantics of Judging, 54, S. Cal. L. Rev. 151, 293 (1981) [hereinafter Moore, Semantics]; Moore, A Natural Law Theory of Interpretation, 58 S. Cal L. Rev. 277 (1985) [hereinafter Moore, Theory of Interpretion] For a discussion of Moore's ideas, see infra notes 100-110 and accompanying text.
14. Fuller entitled his chapter on the Rule of Law "The Morality That Makes Law Possible." He did not explicitly elaborate on why he thought his analysis rested on anything properly called morality. He did seem to think that government by rules is necessary before the question of justice can be meaningfully posed:

> The internal morality of the law demands that there be rules, that they be made known, and that they be observed in practice by those charged with their administration. These demands may seem ethically neutral so far as the external aims of law are concerned. Yet, just as law is a precondition for good law, so acting by known rule is a precondition for any meaningful appraisal of the justice of law.

> L. Fuller, supra note 11 at 157.
15. For the parable of King Rex, see id. at 33-38.

the eight elements of the Rule of Law. These eight elements compromise the "morality that makes law possible":

1. Generality. Roughly, there must be rules, cognizable separately from (and broader than) specific cases, such that the rules can be applied to specific cases, or specific cases can be seen to fall under or lie within them.
2. Notice or publicity. Those who are expected to obey the rules must be able to find out what the rules are.
3. Prospectivity. The rules must exist prior in time to the actions being judged by them.
4. Clarity. The rules must be understandable by those who are expected to obey them.
5. Non-contradictoriness. Those who are expected to obey the rules must not simultaneously be commanded to do both A and not-A.
6. Conformability. The addresses must be able to conform their behavior to the rules.
7. Stability. The rules must not change so fast that they cannot be learned and followed.
8. Congruence. The explicitly promulgated rules must correspond with the rules inferable from patterns of enforcement by functionaries (e.g., courts and police).

I believe this list can be boiled down to two principles: first, there must be rules; second, those rules must be capable of being followed.

The requirement that there must be rules encompasses what Fuller meant by generality. Generality implies that the rules are broader (more general) than specific cases or particulars, which can be brought within them, or seen to be comprehended, subsumed, or covered by them. All particulars of specific cases that fall under the rule are covered by the rule. If a rule commands, "No one under 21 is allowed in a saloon," then it applies necessarily to all people under 21 and to all saloons.

Thus, here the familiar idea that like cases ought to be treated alike (consistency) is seen to be an attribute of the formally general nature of rules. Consistency here means simply that every particular item that *is* within the extension of the operative words in the rule must be *recognized* as being within the extension of the words, and hence within the purview of the rule. We are not allowed to pick out only certain people under 21 or only certain saloons and say our rule applies only to them, simply because the rule's general nature precludes this. Similarly, the familiar idea that the discretion of judges and other functionaries should be limited in applying or interpreting the rules is, in Fuller's view, likewise seen in a formal guise. The generality of rules (that is, their very status as rules) is negated if functionaries are able to treat one item that comes within the extension of the operative words— hence falls under the rule—differently from another. If functionaries can treat different minors or saloons differently (without showing that they aren't "really" minors or "really" saloons), then we don't have the "rule" we thought we had.

The requirement that the rules must be capable of being followed encompasses all the rest of Fuller's list. In order to be capable of being followed by the addressees, rules must have certain characteristics, which I think can also be boiled down to two. Let me colloquially call these two requirements "know-ability" and "perform-ability." In order for those to whom the rules are addressed to *know* what they are commanded to do, the commands must be public, congruent, and non-contradictory, clear enough to understand, and they must not change too fast. In order for the addresses to *do* what is commanded of them, in response to the commands, the commands must be prospective (not retroactive), not contradictory or non-congruent, and not physically, mentally, or circumstantially impossible for the human beings addressed to follow.

This is indeed an instrumental conception of the Rule of Law,[16] which could more colloquially be called "how to do things with rules."[17] All of Fuller's requirements are directed toward there being rule-like commands that can successfully induce desired behavior (whatever it is) in the addressees.[18] Substantive ideals, like fairness or democracy, and autonomy or dignity of persons, are not explicitly raised. Neither are democratic procedural traditions, like the separation of powers or the access to courts and jury trials. It seems that if a Nazi regime wanted to accomplish its heinous goals by means of rules, it would perforce make its commands conform to these requirements.[19]

This conception of the Rule of Law assumes that law consists of rules. In Ronald Dworkin's terms, this conception is premised upon a model of rules.[20]

---

16. It is apparent, however, that Fuller himself objected to the type of instrumentalist reading I have given his work, for he chose to reply to the instrumentalist reading of his early reviewers in the revised editions of *The Morality of Law. See* L. Fuller, *supra* note 11, at 187-244 (chapter V is titled "A Reply to Critics"). Fuller tried to clarify his views after all of his reviewers argued that "the alleged internal morality of law is merely a matter of efficacy." *Id.* at 201. In his attempted clarification he spoke about the law as a *"facility* enabling men [sic] to live a satisfactory life in common," *id.* at 223 (emphasis in original), and about "'an interactional theory of law,'" that characterizes law as a joint normative enterprise of lawmakers and law-followers. *Id.* at 237. Fuller's concluding plea for legal philosophy to turn away from conceptualism and positivism and toward "the social processes that constitute the reality of law," *id.* at 242, makes clear that he was groping for a pragmatic theory of law.

17. After so dubbing the instrumental conception, I discovered that there is a book with this title. *See* W. Twining & D. Miers, How To Do Things With Rules: A Primer of Interpretation (1982).

18. What motivates the addressees to conform their behavior to these rule-like commands is a separate issue. Traditionally, of course, a primary motivator is penal sanctions.

19. *See e.g.,* J. Raz, *supra* note 13, at 211 ("A non-democratic legal system, based on the denial of human rights, on extensive poverty, on racial segration, sexual inequalities and religious persecution may, in principle, conform to the requirements of the rule of law better than any of the legal systems of the more enlightened Western democracies."). It should be noted that Fuller was unwilling to commit himself unequivocally to this implication of the instrumentalist conception. He often noted that the Nazi regime itself was not law-like, *see, e.g.,* L. Fuller, *supra* note 11, at 40-41, and he may have thought that truly bad regimes would never be law-like.

20. R. Dworkin, Taking Rights Seriously 14-80 (1977) [hereinafter R. Dworkin, Rights]. In his later work, Dworkin refers to the "rulebook model of community." *See* R. Dworkin, Law's Empire 209-15 (1986). Although he does not elaborate on the connections between this model of community— roughly, a positivist social contract position—and the notion that law consists of rules, they seem to be related.

Implicit in the understanding of law as rules, and of the Rule of Law as a guide to the efficacy of those rules, are two sets of philosophical problems. The first focuses on the individual as a rule-follower. Fuller's instrumental conception of the Rule of Law presupposes that the law controls its subjects by providing incentives to structure behavior. Thus, although not included on Fuller's list, it is clear that there must be a ninth and tenth requirement: (9) addressees of rules must be rational choosers; (10) addressees must be suitably motivated, perhaps by penal sanctions, perhaps by opportunities for reward. The addressees must be such as *can* respond by following the rules, if the rules have the two characteristics of know-ability and perform-ability. The addressees must further be such as *will* respond, if they are motivated to do so by their desires to obtain rewards or avoid punishment. The problems of choice and motivation are not my concern here, however, and I set them aside.

Instead, my focus will be on the second set of philosophical problems. These revolve around the very concept of rules itself. Does it make sense to think, as Fuller apparently did, that rules are general in the sense of being logically prior to action, and that they apply formally to particular actions that fall under them? These are the issues raised by the social practice conception of rules. But before addressing these issues, it will be helpful to examine the substantive conception of the Rule of Law.

B. The Substantive Conception of the Rule of Law, or "How to Foster Liberty and Constrain Leviathan"

John Rawls claims that the Rule of Law is an aspect of his overall scheme of "justice as fairness." The Rule of Law is formal justice—"the regular and impartial administration of public rules"[21]—applied to the legal system. It promotes liberty, the prime value in justice as fairness. Indeed, perhaps Rawls may be read as making the stronger claim that the Rule of Law is *required* for liberty.

Rawls proposes a rationalist model of law, from which he draws out one version of the traditional complex of ideas that comprise the Rule of Law. Here is his seminal defintion of a legal system: "A legal system is a coercive order of public rules addressed to rational persons for the purpose of regulating their conduct and providing the framework for social coopera-tion."[22] This conception encapsulates many of the traditional precepts of the Rule of Law, in that, as Rawls explains, the precepts are derivable from it.[23] A lot is packed into these carefully chosen words. In the following paragraphs I shall unpack them slightly.

"A legal system is a coercive order of public rules": In Rawls's conception (as in Fuller's), the law consists of rules. To regulate conduct, and thereby

---

21. J. Rawls, *supra* note 12, at 235.
22. *Id.*
23. *Id.* at 236.

achieve the social cooperative necessary for justice, rules must have certain characteristics associated with the Rule of Law:

1. "Ought implies can." The addressees must have the ability to conform, and the authorities must act in good faith. Impossibility of conformance, therefore, must be recognized as a defense.
2. Similar treatment of similar cases. This includes the requirement of consistency, and imposes limitation on judicial discretion.
3. "*Nullum crimen sine lege*" (no crime without law). Laws must be known and expressly promulgated, with clear meaning. There must be no retroactivity. Laws must be general and not bills of attainder. Severe offenses must be narrowly construed.
4. Natural Justice. There must be structures for achieving truth and correct enforcement: trials, hearings, rules of evidence, due process. Judges must be impartial and independent. Trials must be fair, open, and not "prejudiced by public clamor."[24]

Rawls advances two arguments for a connection between these precepts of the Rule of Law and the fundamental substantive value, liberty. First, he argues that absence of these characteristics will cause a chilling effect. To the extent that rules are vague, or that like cases are not treated alike, or that judicial process is irregular, "the boundaries of our liberties are uncertain." And when these boundaries are uncertain, "liberty is restricted by reasonable fear of its exercise."[25] Hence, if rational persons in the original position are choosing a legal structure to promote their paramount value—liberty—they will choose the Rule of Law because of the need for predictability, determinateness, and certainty of legal consequences.

The second argument advanced by Rawls for a connection between the Rule of Law and liberty is characterized by Rawls as "Hobbes's thesis."[26] The scheme of social cooperation, which has as its purpose the enhancement of liberty over the conditions prevailing in the state of nature, requires the precepts of the Rule of Law. This is so because, under Hobbesian assumptions, the problem of social cooperation is the problem of the "n-person prisoner's dilemma." It benefits each person to restrain herself if all others cooperate, but it benefits her even more to act in self-interest while all others cooperate. Hence, there are strong incentives for each to act against the scheme of social cooperation, but only if she thinks she can get away with it while everyone else cannot. (If all can cheat and get away with it, the system reverts to the state of nature, which is everyone's least preferred choice.) A coercive sovereign is necessary to remove the incentives of self-interested individuals to break the rules that all should see are in their interest so long as all obey. "The existence of effective penal machinery serves as men's [sic]

---

24. *Id.* at 239.
25. *Id.*
26. *Id.* at 240.

security to one another."[27] Hence, even an "ideal theory" of justice requires an account of penal sanctions as a stabilizing device.[28] Once the rational choosers in the original position have recognized the necessity of a coercive sovereign that can enforce penal sanctions, they must also recognize the necessity of restraining this Leviathan. In order to control Leviathan, the Rule of Law is needed: "the dangers to liberty are less where the law is impartially and regularly administered in accordance with the principle of legality."[29]

Moreover, the principle of liberty leads to the principle of responsibility, which in turn leads again to the Rule of Law. The principle of responsibility requires the Rule of Law to include all the traditional defenses in the criminal law, not just the instrumental aspects of notice and non-retroactivity needed for instrumental efficacy of rules. "[U]nless citizens are able to know what the law is and are given a fair opportunity to take its directives into account, penal sanctions should not apply to them."[30]

This description should make clear why I refer to Rawls's argument as a substantive conception of the Rule of Law (even though he too is "doing things" with rules). His conception of liberty—the negative liberty of traditional liberalism—is held to be required for achieving justice in society; the precepts of the Rule of Law are held to be strongly connected with that substantive value. Although the list of precepts—generality, consistency, notice, perform-ability, and congruence—is roughly the same as in the instrumentalist conception, the justification offered is quite different. The Rule of Law is grounded not on the bare claim of efficacy of behavioral control, but on the specific political vision of traditional liberalism. Liberty is the core value; overreaching by Leviathan is the danger on one hand, and disintegration of social cooperation because of the prisoner's dilemma is the danger on the other.

There is one traditional element of the Rule of Law in its substantive guise that is not explored by Rawls, yet it looms large in American jurisprudence. This element is the commitment to the separation of powers, and the connected ideas about judicial review and the constrained role of the judge. This commitment also figures in the instrumental conception from the instrumental point of view: rules as applied must not differ from the rules as made (Fuller's precept of "congruence"). Otherwise, the system gives conflicting commands and fails in its purpose of guiding behavior of the

27. *Id.* In a later work, Rawls makes clear his view that if a liberal political order is to be stable over time, it must rest on moral consensus and not be merely a Hobbesian *"modus vivendi."* Rawls, *The Idea of an Overlapping Consensus,* 7 Oxford J. Legal Stud. 1, 9-12 (1987). It is unclear, however, whether this development of Rawls's views would modify his treatment of the Rule of Law in *A Theory of Justice.* J. Rawls, *supra* note 12, at 235-43.

28. Rawls characterizes his theory of justice as an "ideal theory" in the sense that everyone is presumed to act justly. In general, this means that all principles dealing with the errors, complexities, and injustices of the real world are not properly a part of the theory. This excludes civil disobedience and revolution, as well as the theories of corrective justice and punishment. J. Rawls, *supra* note 12, at 8-9.

29. J. Rawls, *supra* note 12, at 241.

30. *Id.* According to Rawls, the principle of responsibility is not based on the idea that punishment is primarily retributive or denunciatory, but that punishment exists for the sake of liberty itself. *Id.*

addressees. In a system committed to the institutions of courts and judicial review as ways to apply law, this instrumental point takes the form of insisting that judges be constrained so that they strictly "apply," and do not "make," the law. In the substantive conception of the Rule of Law the constrained judicial role is more central because it is held to be required for democracy, a core substantive value.

The point is put in typical fashion by Rolf Sartorius:

> If courts were to have the authority to make law, they would constitute a legislative elite in a very pure form indeed. But the very arguments which favor majority rule as the form of legislative decision procedure as against some form of nondemocratic elitism imply that the law-making power should be the exclusive province of the majority. They militate against entrusting a judicial elite with the awesome power to make the law as well as apply it.[31]

Those who are versed in the debate surrounding judicial review in American jurisprudence will recognize that this strong statement is simplistic and leaves untouched many famous puzzles. One is the counter-majoritarian difficulty—the problems surrounding the idea that the majority in creating a constitution can be understood to have constrained its own quotidian legislative actions by a broader vision, to be guarded by the judiciary. Another is the working-out of the idea that where there are "gaps" in the law, judicial law-making (subject to legislative override) may be perfectly consistent both with congruence and democracy. A third is the curious tendency to emphasize limiting the power of the judiciary rather than the equally nondemocratic organs of the executive branch. Nevertheless, Sartorius's statement well captures the force of the distinction between "making" and "applying" law, and the constrained conception of the judicial role, in the substantive conception of the Rule of Law.

C. A Contested Concept

At this point I hope it is clear that much of the complex of ideas called the Rule of Law is two-faced. My discusison so far has shown that the central precepts of the Rule of Law can be defended either instrumentally, as necessary to make a legal system work to structure behavior, or substantively, as necessary to fairness, human dignity, freedom, and democracy. The ambiguous precepts include generality (no bills of attainder); treat like cases alike (consistency); notice; non-retroactivity; perform-ability (no impossible or conflicting commands); and congruence (limit discretion of enforcement functionaries). Hence, the Rule of Law itself is deeply ambiguous, a contested concept. Someone who stresses the instrumentalist aspect might affirm that a rule-bound dictatorship evidences the Rule of Law; someone who stresses the substantive aspect would not.

Having elaborated the instrumentalist and substantive conceptions, we can also see the connection between the Rule of Law and liberal legalism.

---

31. R. Sartorius, *supra* note 14, at 175-76.

As far as I can tell, legalism means the decision of particular cases by means of general pre-existing rules.[32] Then liberal legalism is the variety of legalism exhibited by liberalism, or found in liberal ideology. If this is correct, the instrumental conception of the Rule of Law is simply legalism, and the substantive conception is the (or a) liberal form of legalism.

Aside from the surface correlation in the lists of precepts, it is apparent that the two conceptions do have much philosophical underpinning in common, including five important assumptions: (1) law consists of rules; (2) rules are prior to particular cases, more general than particular cases, and applied to particular cases; (3) law is instrumental (the rules are applied to achieve ends); (4) there is a radical separation between government and citizens (there are rule-givers and appliers, *versus* rule-takers and compliers); (5) the person is a rational chooser ordering her affairs instrumentally.

Nevertheless, the two conceptions *are* different. The instrumental conception is a model of government by rules to achieve the government's ends, whatever they may be. The substantive conception is a model of government by rules to achieve the goals of the social contract: liberty and justice. The instrumental conception purports to be more general and ahistorical; the substantive is more clearly bound up with our particular modern ideological heritage.

III. Traditional Formalism and the Rule of Law

Now I can zero in on the connection between the Rule of Law and traditional formalism—roughly the view that a unique answer in a particular case can be conclusively derived from application of a general rule. I begin by recounting several traditional senses of formalism, and considering their connection with traditional conceptions of the Rule of Law. Then I review the social practice ("Wittgensteinian") critique of the traditional conception of rules as formally or logically prior to particulars. This will bring me to the crucial issue of whether a switch to a Wittgensteinian view of rules makes any difference to our conception of the Rule of Law.

A. Sense of Traditional Formalism

1. Formal connection between rule and particulars. Traditionally, legal "formalism" is the position that a unique answer in a particular case can be "deduced" from a rule, or that application of a rule to a particular is "analytical." (The scare quotes indicate that philosophical arguments about language have made the traditional understanding of these concepts just as problematic as "rule" itself. I shall return to this issue in the next section.) The connection between the rule and its application is, in other words,

---

32. *See* R. Unger, Law in Modern Society 52-57, 176-81 (1976); *cf.* J. Shklar, Legalism 1 (1964) (defining legalism as "the ethical attitude that holds moral conduct to be a matter of rule following, and moral relationships to consist of duties and rights determined by rules").

formal. Perjoratively, this is mechanical jurisprudence, or the computer model of judging. In this model, judges do not judge; they are only black boxes, who function to juxtapose the rule and the particular so the formal connection can be declared.

2. Formal connection between foundations and rules. There is another way that the term "formalism" traditionally has been used. This "formalism" is the view that there exists a mind-independent reality consisting of certain first principles either of fact or value. These first principles form a logical, analytical, "foundation" for the law. A natural law theory would be formalist in this sense if it claimed that legal and moral rules are real and are there for us to discover, for example, or if it claimed that legal rules are deducible from a foundational set of real values. In this foundationalist kind of formalism, the crucial formal connection is between the structure of the universe and the rules of law. It is thus different from the mechanical jurisprudence kind of formalism, where the crucial formal link is between rules and the application of those rules to particulars.

3. Formal connection between words and things. In a famous metaphor, H.L.A. Hart suggested that legal rules have a "core" of certainty and a "penumbra" of uncertainty.[33] Hart declared that in the penumbra, judges must "legislate." A common understanding of the core/penumbra distinction—although probably not Hart's own understanding of it—is that in the core, formal deductive application of rules to particulars is possible.[34] If we do assume that formal application to particulars is possible within the core of a rule, then we can characterize a third sense of traditional formalism: formalism in semantics.[35] If there is a set of particulars, comprising the core meaning, to which a rule is applicable analytically or through deduction, it must be true that the *words* in the rule have an analytic connection with at least a subset of the particulars falling within these words' extensions. For example, if a rule contains the word "vehicle," then for the rule ever to be formally applicable there must be some subset of cases involving objects that are seen to be vehicles through deduction or some sort of analytic connection alone.[36]

---

33. Hart, *Positivism and the Separation of Law and Morals*, 71 Harv. L. Rev. 593, 607 (1958).
34. Hart said that "[i]f a penumbra of uncertainty must surround all legal rules, then their application to specific cases in the penumbral area cannot be a matter of logical deducation," *id.*, leaving it open to question whether logical deducation is what we do in core cases. Hart's general view of rules and language should more likely be interpreted, however, as incorporating the Wittgensteinian critique. *See, e.g.,* Hart, *Definition and Theory in Jurisprudence,* 70 Law Q. Rev. 37 (1954). *See infra* notes 76-77 and accompanying text.
35. *See* Moore, *Semantics, supra* note 14, at 152, 157.
36. The example of the word "vehicle" appearing in a statute was debated by Hart and Fuller in their *Harvard Law Review* exchange in 1958. *See* Hart, *supra* note 38, at 607; Fuller, *Positivism and Fidelity to Law,* 71 Harv. L. Rev. 630, 662-63 (1958). It is drawn from the case of McBoyle v. United States, 283 U.S. 25, 26-27 (1931) (reversing defendant's conviction for theft of an airplane under the National Motor Vehicle Theft Act because the word "vehicle" as used in the statute could be read to include only those contrivances "capable of being used 'as a means of transportation on land'").

The notion of an analytic connection between a word and its extension raises thorny problems in the theory of reference.[37] Yet some logical positivists may have thought word-meaning could be analytic in this way. Formalism in semantics may assume that the extension of a word can be logically determined by connection with a list of necessary and sufficient criteria, and thus that there is a formal connection between a word and the things to which it applies once the criteria are known. The necessary and sufficient criteria could be conventional artifacts of language. For a thorough reductionist, however, the criteria would be deducible from foundational sense-data, and formalism in semantics would lead back to formalism in metaphysics.

4. Formal realizability and the formalist conception of rules. In the traditional conception of the nature of rules, a rule is self-applying to the set of particulars said to fall under it; its application is thought to be analytic. It is often said that rules are logically prior to the particular cases that fall under them. Another way of putting this is to think that somehow the applications to particulars are already present in the rule itself. For example, if a rule says that no one under 21 is allowed in a saloon, then the application of the rule to Sally, who is in Joe's Saloon on her sixteenth birthday, is analytic or formal. The result that Sally must be excluded follows immediately from the rule itself and Sally's specific circumstances, and is unaffected by any other previous applications of the rule or other circumstances.

Under the traditional conception of rules, the property of analytic self-application, thought to inhere in rules, is sometimes called "formal realizability."[38] When a directive or command is formally realizable, its application is deductive or analytic. In other words, it deserves to be called a "rule." To the extent that legal directives are formally realizable they are to be implemented by mechanical jurisprudence. In my view, rules would be formally realizable to the extent that the words in them are formally realizable. Thus, traditional formalism in the conception of rules leads back to traditional formalism in semantics. Formal realizability is an asserted characteristic primarily of words, and only secondarily of rules.

B. *Traditional Formalism and the Rule of Law*

The traditional understanding of formal realizability correlates with the demand for clarity in both the instrumentalist and substantive versions of the Rule of Law. The traditional view has been that in order for people to

---

37. Of course, we can retain our common understanding that words have a core of certain meaning (some objects are unmistakably vehicles) without a formalist explanation of the source of this certainty. One way to do this is through Wittgenstein's essentially pragmatic view that words have meaning by virtue of being embedded in a form of life.

38. The notion of formal realizability is rooted in German jurisprudential thought. Duncan Kennedy finds the term in Rudolph von Ihering's *Spirit of Roman Law.* Kennedy, *Form and Substance in Private Law Adjudication,* 89 Harv. L. Rev. 1685, 1687-89 (1976), *citing* R. von Ihering, Der Geist des Romischen Recht 50-55, 84 (1883). Though Kant did not use the term "formal realizability," he apparently thought that law could not exist without it. *See, e.g.,* I. Kant, *Perpetual Peace,* in Kant on History 85, 91-92 n.4 (L. Beck ed. 1963) ("[T]he possibility of a formula similar to those of mathematics is only legitimate criterion of a consistent legislation.").

know what the law is so that they can conform their behavior to it, it is necessary for the law to consist, to the fullest extent possible, of formally realizable rules. Directives that are not formally realizable are sometimes called "standards."[39] If in the previous example of the rule about presence in saloons we substituted the words "no one who has not reached maturity and responsibility" for "no one under 21," it would be deemed a "standard" and not a "rule." The prevalence of "standards" in the law poses problems for the notion that clarity of command depends upon formal realizability.

The traditional understanding of formal realizability as the crucial property of rules also correlates with the traditional conviction that the Rule of Law demands that judges "apply" rather than "make" the law. If rules do not tie judges' hands with their logical and analytic application, the traditional view is that judges will have personal discretion in how to apply the law. This will undermine congruence and confuse those who are supposed to follow the rules. It will diminish the efficacy of the system (in the instrumental view) and the liberty of the rule-followers (in the substantive view). It will also confer on judges a realm of "arbitrary power" and undermine democracy.

The Rule of Law as it comes down to use in the liberal tradition is committed to the model of rules, and this means, under the traditional conception of rules, that it is committed to traditional formalism. One reason for this, as Rawls saw, is that this model of law readily connects with aspects of the Hobbesian view of the nature and purposes of social cooperation. Because everyone is always motivated to "defect," government by majority rule reduces to accommodation among shifting coalitions of self-interested individuals. The government is a Leviathan to be restrained. Yet, if judges can ignore the legislative "bargains" of these shifting coalitions, then judges are even more in need of restraint than legislatures. Hence, the role of the judges is tightly constrained. Judges should be mere tools of implementation of the underlying "contract" that guarantees social cooperation and prevents "defection" and degeneration into the state of nature.

The underlying "contract," that justifies the existence of government at all, can be thought of as a "constitution." Most of the time judges should function as tools to implement what the legislature enacts, but when legislatures overstep the bounds of justified government, judges must function as tools of the underlying constitutional "contract" and intervene to strike down the offending legislation. In view of the very great danger posed by judges, the Hobbesian theorist needs an ironclad system of rules to restrain them. Rules, in the traditional formalist sense, must determine the decisions of judges to the fullest extent possible, on pain, otherwise, of losing the underlying justification for the whole legal system.

---

39. This use of the term "standard" was apparently introduced by Duncan Kennedy, Kennedy, *supra* note 43, at 1688, and has been adopted by a number of critical writers. *See, e.g.,* Schlag, *Rules and Standards,* 33 UCLA L. Rev. 379, 382, n.16 (1985). Unfortunately it causes confusion because other writers do not use the term "standard" in this way. *See e.g.,* R. Dworkin, Rights, *supra* note 21, at 22 (using "standard" as a general term referring to rules, principles, policies, and others). *See infra* note 83 and accompanying text.

Although Rawls is not a thoroughgoing Hobbesian theorist by any means, his conception of a legal system coheres with this motivation for commitment to the model of rules.[40] It appears that any form of traditional liberalism, with its commitment to means/ends rationality and to methodological individualism, will be drawn to the traditional conception of rules as the means to structure incentives so as to achieve maximally the individual behavior desired by the state.

IV. The Wittgensteinian Conception of Rules and Its Consequences (if any)

A. The Wittgensteinian Social Conception of Rules

A Wittgensteinian view of words, and of the rules containing them, suggests that there is no such thing as traditional formal realizability, or in other words, that the traditional formalist conception of rules is wrong. The Wittgensteinian view of rules may be characterized as both a social and a practice conception. It is a social conception because in this view rules depend essentially on social context, and it is a practice conception because rules also depend essentially on reiterated human activity.

If we assume that the traditional formalist conception of rules is what we mean by the word "rule," the Wittgensteinian perspective may also be characterized as a species of rule-skepticism. A number of assertions may be encompassed in skepticism about rules in the traditional formalist conception of them. These assertions are skeptical answers to a set of problems about rules and rule-governed action. One problem is in determining when it can be said that someone is "applying" a rule. How do we *know* the rule is being "applied"? The skeptic says, "We can't really tell." We cannot identify any formal or logical criterion by which we can determine whether or not someone is following a rule. The problem is important for a distinction that is crucial to the Rule of Law—the distinction between the existence of the rules and their application by rule-appliers, such as judges.

A second problem is how we should understand the notion that rules are "binding." In what consists the "binding-ness" of rules? The skeptic says, "This bond cannot be shown." We cannot demonstrate any formal or logical nexus between the rule and the rule-follower's behavior in response to it. The problem is important for the coherence of the conception of a legal system as a "system of coercive rules" binding on citizens.

A third problem is how we should understand "ruleness" itself. I have suggested that traditional formal realizability is a conception of rules that asserts that rules are analytically applicable to particulars insofar as they contain words with precise, determinate extensions. The skeptic says, "Traditional formal realizability cannot be shown to exist." We cannot demon-

---

40. Recall Rawls's quintessential definition: "A legal system is a coercive order of public rules addressed to rational persons for regulating their conduct and providing the framework for social cooperation." J. Rawls, *supra* note 12, at 235.

strate that application of a rule is analytic or deductive. This problem is important for the idea that a rule is logically prior to particulars falling under it and can be seen to apply of its own force to any individual cases falling under it.

I think Wittgenstein in *Philosophical Investigations*[41] is fairly read as rejecting the traditional conception of rules in favor of a social practice conception in which agreement in responsive action is the primary mark of the existence of a rule.[42] I also think Wittgenstein is fairly read as a rule-skeptic in the three senses I just suggested.[43] There is no way to tell deductively or analytically when a rule is being followed; there is no special state that describes the binding-ness of rules; and traditional formal realizability is not the right way to conceive of the nature of rules.

The relevant passages in *Philosophical Investigations* are three sequences of remarks: on continuing an arithmetic series according to a certain formation rule; on reading; and on obeying a rule.[44] The questions Wittgenstein addresses are both internal and external. That is, with respect to continuing a series, he is interested both in what happens when someone can say, "Now I can go on" and what happens when others can say, "Now she's got it." Likewise with reading: What licenses "Now I am reading" or "Now she's reading"? The discussion of rules in the third sequence is a generalization of these two examples. The internal questions are: What is the inner experience of obeying a rule? In what consists the determined-ness or binding-ness on me? The external questions are: How can other people tell when someone is obeying a rule? In what consists the knowledge or recognition of rule-application?

To all of these questions Wittgenstein gives skeptical answers. In the introspective portions of his analysis, Wittgenstein considers suggestions that the binding-ness might be a mental state or process or disposition,[45] a special experience or feeling or inner sensation,[46] a kind of derivation or being guided,[47] a causal or "super-strong" connection,[48] or a way of grasping

---

41. L. Wittgenstein, Philosophical Investigations (G.E.M. Anscombe trans. rev. ed. 1968) [hereinafter L. Wittgenstein, Philosophical Investigations]. *See also* L. Wittgenstein, Remarks on the Foundations of Mathematics 391-437 (G.E.M. Anscombe trans. rev. ed. 1978) (another version of Wittgenstein's investigation on rules).

42. The proper reading of Wittgenstein's later work is hotly disputed in the secondary literature. Among those whose readings seem most congenial to me are Peacocke, *Reply: Rule-Following: The Nature of Wittgenstein's Arguments,* in Wittgenstein: To Follow a Rule 72 (C. Leich & S. Holtzman eds. 1981); P. Strawson, Skepticism and Naturalism: Some Varieties 75-95 (1983); S. Kripke, Wittgenstein on Rules and Private Language (1982). For opposing readings, see G. Baker & P. Hacker, Skepticism, Rules & Language (1984); C. McGinn, Wittgenstein on Meaning (1984).

43. In characterizing Wittgenstein as a rule-skeptic, we must remember that he does not say there can be no such thing as a rule, only that the traditional formalist conception is the wrong way to think about how rules work. Wittgenstein's skepticism about rules has been compared with Hume's skepticism about induction. *See* P. Strawson, *supra* note 48, at 14-21; S. Kripke, *supra* note 48, at 62-68. In a reading that seems to me reasonable and interesting, Kripke understands Wittgenstein's *Philosophical Investigations* as propounding a skeptical paradox about rules. *See also* Yablon, *Law and Metaphysics* (Book Review), 96 Yale L.J. 613 (1987) (reviewing Kripke for a legal audience).

44. L. Wittgenstein, Philosophical Investigations, *supra* note 47, §§ 143-242.

45. *Id.* §§ 146, 152-154.

46. *Id.* §§ 155, 157, 159-160.

47. *Id.* §§ 162-163, 172-173, 175.

48. *Id.* §§ 169, 176-177, 197.

in a flash or in a direct sense.[49] Wittgenstein rejects these attemtps to capture
the essence of the rule-follower's subjective experience of binding-ness. His
conclusion is that the rule-follower acts without reasons,[50] without choice,[51]
blindly, as a matter of course.[52] Following the rule is "simply what I do."[53]

In external portions of his analysis, Wittgenstein replies to his introspective suggestions, from the point of view of how we observe someone else
following a rule. His conclusions are similarly skeptical. All we can say when
we think someone is following a rule is that it seems natural.[54] For someone
to apply a rule correctly is simply to do it "as we do it."[55] The decisive factor
in knowing whether someone has followed a rule "is not his [the rule-
follower's] inner experience but the *circumstances* under which he had it."[56]

The result of this skeptical deconstruction of the formalist notion of rules
is that rule-following must be understood to be an essentially social phenomenon. Rule-following can only be understood to occur where there is reiterated human action both in responding to directives and in observing others
respond. Only the fact of our seemingly "natural" agreement on what are
instances of obeying rules permits us to say there are rules. The rules do not
cause the agreement; rather, the agreement causes us to say there are rules.[57]
As Wittgenstein says, "The word 'agreement' and the word 'rule' are *related*
to one another, they are cousins."[58] As Wittgenstein also says, this is "not
agreement in opinions but in form of life."[59] Rules are not logically prior to
uniformity of action in response to them; rather, uniformity of action is prior
to the existence of rules.

This view of rules is irreducibly social and rejects the traditional formal,
logical, analytic, or deductive understandings of rule-application.[60] The form
of life called rule-following is a practice, and the practice is a form of
agreement among members of a social group. It is not possible to obey a rule
"privately,"[61] nor is rule-following something that can be done by "only *one*
man, only *once*."[62]

---

49. *Id.* §§ 191-192.
50. *Id.* § 211. That there is no identifiable reason for one's experience of "binding-ness," no essence of
"binding-ness," should of course not be misunderstood to mean that one cannot have reasons for
following a rule.
51. *Id.* § 219. Similarly, that there seems to be no choice about whether or not one has the experience
of "binding-ness" should of course not be misunderstood to mean that one cannot choose whether
to follow a rule or to disobey it.
52. *Id.* § 238.
53. *Id.* § 217.
54. *Id.* § 185. *Cf.* S. Kripke, *supra* note 49, at 92-96; P. Strawson, *supra* note 48, at 75-80.
55. L. Wittgenstein, Philosophical Investigations, *supra* note 47, § 145.
56. *Id.* § 155 (emphasis in original). *Cf. id.* § 180 (calling words a "signal" of mental state, not a
description of it).
57. S. Kripke, *supra* note 49, at 96.
58. L. Wittgenstein, Philosophical Investigations, *supra* note 47, § 224 (emphasis in original).
59. *Id.* § 241. *Cf.* S. Kripke, *supra* note 49, at 96-98.
60. I believe the appropriate Wittgensteinian conclusion is that, along with the concept of rules, the
concepts of formality, logic, analyticity, and deduction cannot mean what we have thought them to
mean; even these categories are irreducibly social. *See infra* note 77 and accompanying text.
61. L. Wittgenstein, Philosophical Investigations, *supra* note 47, § 202. Wittgenstein also notes that "to
think one is obeying the rule is not to obey the rule." *Id.*
62. *Id.* § 199 (emphasis in original).

In the Wittgensteinian view, an action is *determined* by a rule when the action seems a "matter of course,"[63] and "disputes don't break out."[64] How do I know when I am following a rule? When I feel the answer is automatic or self-evident. But my subjective feeling of "binding-ness" could be mistaken.[65] How do I know when I'm *really* "applying" a rule? When everybody else also would have felt compelled to do as I did. How do we know someone else is following a rule? When we all would have felt bound to do as she did.

Although the Wittgensteinian view thus certainly admits that there can be action determined by a rule, it is not the kind of determined-ness required by the traditional concept of formal realizability. Formal realizability (the traditional formalist conception of the nature of rules) asserts that only the words of the rule and the action of one person with regard to one set of particulars are relevant in questions of rule-following. This Wittgenstein denies. If formal realizability would allow for the possibility of obeying a rule privately or only once, then formal realizability is merely what Wittgenstein would call a "philosophical superlative."[66]

There are still rules, of course; rules are an important practice of ours. But traditional formal realizability is not the right way to understand "rule-ness."

B. Consequences (if any) for the Model of Rules and the Rule of Law

1. Does our conception of rules matter? One might say, "So what?" Under the Wittgensteinian view there are still obvious cases or rules and rule-following; whether we hold the traditional view of rules or the Wittgensteinian view makes no difference for our conceptions of the model of rules and the Rule of Law.[67] The "So what?" response is particularly appealing to those who read Wittgenstein more narrowly than I do. I take a view that aligns him with modern pragmatism. His insistence that meaning cannot be separated from "use"—from reiterated human activity, *practices,* embedded in and helping to constitute a "form of life"—seems, when given the central weight I believe it deserves, to make clear his intellectual affinity with pragmatism.[68] Yet those who read Wittgenstein more narrowly understand

---

63. *Id.* § 238.
64. *Id.* § 240: "Disputes do not break out (among mathematicians, say) over the question whether a rule has been obeyed or not. People don't come to blows over it, for example. That is part of the framework on which the working of our langauge is based (for example, in giving descriptions.)." *Id.*
65. *See supra* note 67 and accompanying text (rule-following does not depend solely on one's private experience of it).
66. L. Wittgenstein, Philosophical Investigations, *supra* note 47, § 192.
67. For a sophisticated view of rules that has fully incorporated the Wittgensteinian perspective, and yet sees no important practical effects for our conceptions of law and the Rule of Law, see F. Schauer, Playing by the Rules: A Philosophical Analysis of Rule-Based Decison-making (Oxford Clareden, 1991).
68. This view of Wittgenstein is explicit in the work of Richard Rorty, *see* R. Rorty, Philosophy and the Mirror of Nature 367-68 (1979) [hereinafter R. Rorty, Mirror of Nature], and is implicit in the views of many other modern critics of foundationalism and the traditional dichotomies of fact and value, theory and practice, and the like. What may be distinctive in the modern wave of pragmatism is the degree of emphasis placed on the social construction of reality. For a lucid description of the basic tenets of pragmaticsm as well as some elaboration of a modern pragmatic view of law, see Grey, *Holmes and Legal Pragmatism,* 41 Stan. L. Rev. 787 (198).

him merely to have been making an analytic point about language, and rules couched in language, to the effect that no rule can determine the scope of its own application. They deny that Wittgenstein means that there is something essentially social or "communitarian" about rules.[69]

If we thus interpret Wittgenstein narrowly we might think that everything remains the same. Law still consists (entirely or in important part) of a set of rules authoritatively laid down and implemented by judges who apply, but do not make, the rules. The only difference would be conceptual: we just change the way philosophers, inside their own heads, understand rules. In other words, if we think that all we change is our internal philosophical view of *rules* when we become Wittgensteinian, then the "So what?" response seems initially plausible.

The "So what?" response also seems initially plausible under a broader view of the role of practices. If one is inclined to treat practices as so "brute" and "given" that they cannot be interpenetrated by what we say or think about them, then the practice we call philosophy (or theory, or conceptual schemes) is radically separate from every other practice. When we reconceive meaning in terms of practice, all our practices (except philosophy) remain unchanged. So again, as with the narrow analytic view, any Wittgensteinian change is internal to philosophy.[70]

Wittgenstein's statement that we know there are rules when "disputes don't break out" provides a way to reinterpret the idea that rules have a "core" of certain application, as well as a "penumbra" of doubt, without resort to traditional formal realizability. In this reinterpretion, the core signifies our observance of rule-responsive behavior that feels compelled or blind or "a matter of course"; the penumbra signifies our observance of disputes breaking out or the absence of the feeling of compulsion. The core is roughly coextensive with our ability so say, "We all think that's self-evident." We can all recognize action under a rule when we eject sixteen-year-old Sally from Joe's saloon in response to the directive, "No one under 21 is allowed in a saloon." Under the Wittgensteinian view someone who doesn't see this result as self-evident will be considered insane or from Mars; and this is just as

---

69. See G. Baker & P. Hacker, *supra* note 48, at viii (arguing against Kripke); C. McGinn, *supra* note 48, at 9 (same).

70. The most vociferous exponent of this view, at least in law reviews, is Stanley Fish. *See, e.g.,* Fish, *Dennis Martinez and the Uses of Theory,* 96 Yale L.J. 1773, 1775 (1987) (discussing the dichotomy between theory and practice and arguing that the two cannot interact). Fish is clearly wrong that judging is a "brute" practice of this kind; judging as a practice also includes ideals about judging, critiques of judging, understandings about the role of judging in the polity, etc. *See infra* notes 89-90 and accompanying text (interaction between rhetoric and the world). I even think that Fish is wrong about the practice of baseball. Part of the reason Orel Hersheiser is a better pitcher than Dennis Martinez is his attention to "theory"; his detailed notes about hitters' propensities and past performances enable him to make better decisions about how to pitch to them, and these decisions are a part of the practice of baseball.

   The primary complaint against these Fish-like views is that if practices are so "brute," so always-already given, we cannot make space for critique and social progress. On this reading, Wittgenstein seems like an apologist for the status quo. *See, e.g.,* R. Unger, Passion: An Essay on Personality 11-12 (1984). *But cf.* H. Pitkin, Wittgenstein and Justice 46 (1972). Maybe, in the end, whether we read Wittgenstein in the broad, holistic way I prefer, in which the theory/practice dichotomy is dissolved and the practices of conceptualization and critique can interpenetrate many (all?) others, is perhaps a matter of personal temperament.

strong a form of social control as being thought irrational or deficient in deductive powers.

Even if we accept a slightly broader view of Wittgenstein, the philosophical change might still seem not to imply any significant differences in practice. A Wittgensteinian reinterpretation is just as possible, and just as necessary, for all the concepts allied with the traditional conception of "rule" as it is for the conception of "rule" itself. If the traditional conception of a "rule" amounted to a mistaken "philosophical superlative," then so too have our conceptions of "formal connection," "analyticity," "deduction," and so on. But it is possible to think of "formalism" not in the traditional sense of a logical connection existing independent of a social setting and history of application, but instead as decisionmaking by uncontroversial reasoning.[71] It is possible to think of "analyticity," "deduction," and "logical connection," all as similarly embedded in an ongoing practice in which completely uncontroversial results are reached by what we "naturally" think of as rational procedures under the circumstances.

Does a Wittgensteinian reinterpretation of all of these concepts prevalent in the traditional Rule of Law change anything? At least, doesn't it leave untouched everything practical, everything that we can observe or that has significance for us and our lives? When the phlogiston theory was rejected, it did not change the fact that fire will burn us. Even if we admit that the formally realizable rules required by the Rule of Law rest on a social practice, a brute unquestionable agreement in a form of life, don't all our reasons for requiring formally realizable rules (clarity, notice, congruence, stability, prospectivity, restraint of judges) remain the same?[72]

Perhaps Wittgenstein himself would say, if we could ask him, that this is the correct way to understand his reinterpretations. After all, he was not one to think that the form of life called philosophy had much influence on our larger forms of life. Nevertheless, if this would be his position, I think it too modest.[73] We should not hastily conclude that commitment to the Wittgensteinian understanding of rules, at least to the broader, neo-pragmatist view of Wittgenstein I prefer, would be irrelevant for our views about law and the Rule of Law. But neither should we hastily conclude that because there is no such thing as traditional formal realizability, everything is indeterminate or up for grabs. We shall have to proceed in a more cautious and more piecemeal manner. As Wittgenstein might say, we must "look and see."

We can begin by noticing that the Wittgensteinian limitation of rules to situations in which "disputes don't break out" does not help lawyers much. Disputes *do* break out among lawyers and judges, and litigants *do* come to blows, at least metaphorically. If our only way to find out what result is compelled by a rule is to be part of a community that recognizes action as

---

71. *See* Grey, *Langdell's Orthodoxy,* 45 U. Pitt. L. Rev. 1, 8 (1983) (characterizing formalism in this way).
72. For a thoughtful argument to this effect, see F. Schauer, *supra* note 73, §§ 8.5, 8.6.
73. In other words, if Wittgenstein professed this Fish-like view, *see supra* note 76, he would be untrue to himself.

rule-following, then there is no way to bring any truly disputed cases—in which neither side changes its position even after being confronted by what the other side believes to be completely uncontroversial reasoning—under pre-existing rules, as the Rule of Law requires.

Perhaps a Wittgensteinian would not want to think of law as consisting *only* of rules. Of course, truly disputed cases can indeed come under reasonable judgment, or whatever faculty our practice recognizes as making appropriate judgments in disputed cases. But if by "our practice," we mean "our *legal* practice," then our practice is at odds with the Rule of Law ideal that is supposed to describe and govern it.

A stubborn commitment to the model of rules as essential to the Rule of Law explains why legal theorists go to such lengths to try to show that even "hard cases" have pre-existing determinate answers.[74] Hart's declaration that judges "legislate" in hard cases is unorthodox in the liberal tradition because it tends to undermine the commitment to the model of rules. It is not surprising that Hart urges us to think such hard cases are few and far between. To the extent that law, when we "look and see," is the terrain of "disputed" cases, the pragmatic Wittgensteinian view seems to tell us we had better find another model (other than rules) for what law "is."

2. Compromise positions on the model of rules. Perhaps, then, a Wittgensteinian reinterpretation requires us to divide law into domains, consisting of rules and other things, and to reconceive the Rule of Law in light of this complexity. A number of prevalent views (although they may have rested originally on the traditional conception of rules) present themselves as candidates for appropriate reinterpretation. The challenge, of course, is to characterize those "other things"—the domain of law that does not consist of rules—as "lawlike" in a sense that is politically acceptable to us.

The Wittgensteinian interpretation of the core/penumbra distinction can divide legal directives into domains of formal realizability vel non, but, as Dworkin complains, waving one's hand at the penumbra and simply announcing that we should recognize that judges "legislate" is not politically acceptable.[75] One who believes that rules (and words) have cores and penumbras would argue that we need all attributes of the Rule of Law to make sure that in at least the core cases, the formalist result is properly implemented. This strategy supposes that part of the legal realm instantiates formalism and the precepts of the Rule of Law, while the balance is given over to the "discretion"—the "Absolute Arbitrary Power"—that the traditional Rule of Law, in both its instrumental and substantive conceptions, decries. In the "discretionary" areas we cannot be manipulating behavior by means of known pre-existing rules (the instrumentalist view) nor can we be fixing the structure that enhances negative liberty (the substantive view). Unless we decide by fiat that the penumbra is insignificant compared to the

74. *See, e.g.,* R. Dworkin, Rights, *supra* note 21, at 81-130.
75. *Id.* at 44-45.

core,[76] this strategy gives up a good deal to the abyss of absolute arbitrary power, the elimination of which is supposed to be the *raison d'être* of the social contract.

Ronald Dworkin's bifurcated model of law is aimed at answering this kind of criticism of Hart. When Dworkin attacked the model of rules he attributed to legal positivism, he did so by dividing up the general category of "standards" into "rules," on the one hand, and "principles, policies and other sorts of standards" that "do not function as rules," on the other.[77] His argument was that the model does not fully describe what the law is, because law also consists of principles; and that rule-application does not fully describe what judges do, because judges also use principles.[78] Moreover, the use of principles determines one right answer to legal questions even though principles lack formal realizability, because in using principles the judge should apply the best interpretation of the entire body of past legal authoritative acts, where that interpretation rests on the best political theory available to explain and justify law as an enterprise.

Can Wittgensteinian reinterpretation stop with this reinterpreted version of Dworkin? There are a number of important objections, only two of which I raise here.[79] First, in actual practice, in the form of life we call the law, it makes no sense to say that right answers are available in principle when in reality there is no agreement on the answers; the disputes stubbornly remain when all the arguments are done. If those who are subject to judicial decisions cannot confidently predict the outcome, then Dworkin has not succeeded in preserving the Rule of Law virtues for the area in which "disputes break out"; he is susceptible to the same criticism he levelled against Hart. Second,

---

76. This appears to be Hart's approach. *See* Hart, *supra* note 38, at 614-15.

77. *See* R. Dworkin, Rights, *supra* note 21, at 22.

78. Dworkin asserted that there is a "logical difference" between rules and principles. Rules are applicable either/or, all-or-nothing, whereas principles have "weight." *Id.* at 26-27. Further, rules set out necessary conditions for their application but principles do not; in theory, a rule can be completely stated with all exceptions, but a principle cannot. *Id.* at 25-26. Although the notion of a "logical difference" can be given a Wittgensteinian reinterpretation, references to "logical difference" in conjunction with the idea of a complete statement of a rule with all its exceptions strongly suggest that Dworkin held the traditional conception of rules. In Dworkin's more recent work, Law's Empire, *supra* note 21, he has turned toward interpretative theory, which renders shaky the idea that any rules could be self-evidently applied in the way assumed by the traditional conception of rules. As far as I know, however, Dworkin has not explicitly reinterpreted his rules/principles distinction.

79. There is by now a large secondary literature on Dworkin and it is not my aim to add to it. In that literature, the lines of critique of Dworkin that I think are most significant are those relating to (1) the role of community and dialogue in legal meaning and decision making, *see, e.g.,* Michelman, *Foreword: Traces of Self-Government*, 100 Harv. L. Rev. 4, 66-73 (1986); (2) the role of political practice in law, *see e.g.,* Bruns, *Law as Hermeneutics,* in The Politics of Interpretation 315 (W. Mitchell ed. 1983); and (3) the problem posed for coherence theory by indeterminacy and widespread conflict in the law, *See, e.g.,* Altman, *Legal Realism, Critical Legal Studies, and Dworkin,* 15 Phil. & Pub. Aff. 205, 217 (1986). I am sympathetic also to Stanley Fish's critique, suggesting that Dworkin's dimensions of "fit" and "soundness" take apart fact and value in a way Dworkin acknowledges should be rejected along with the old paradigm supporting positivism. *See* Fish, *Working on the Chain Gang: Interpretation in the Law and in Literary Criticism,* in The Politics of Interpretation 271, 284-85 n.5 (W. Mitchell ed. 1983).

   In addition I believe there is an important critique that is underrepresented in the Dworkin literature. Contrary to the Critical Legal Studies critique that law is indeterminate and incoherent, it seems to me that law and its institutions may indeed exhibit integrity or coherence—for example, as they did with respect to racism and sexism—and yet be coherently wrong. A main task for nonfoundationalist theory is to find room for this kind of judgment.

when we really do "look and see" what law is like as a practice or a form of life, it is much more complicated than simply applying authoritative directives that are either rules or not-rules.

At this point we might turn to the distinction between "rules" and "standards" described by Duncan Kennedy and adopted by a number of critical writers.[80] Kennedy's claims are more complex than Dworkin's because Kennedy "continuum-izes" the dichotomy.[81] A directive can tend toward "rule-ness" (formal realizability) or be relatively standard-like. Thus the semantic underpinning of the formal realizability dimension must be complex: we must assume that words vary along a continuum from extremely vague (or otherwise indeterminate) to completely determinate. This vision may be adequately Wittgensteinian in its understanding of language (or may be reinterpreted to be), but it still seems to leave out something important in its conception of law as consisting of verbal directives of one kind or another. In order to be true Wittgensteinians, at least on the neo-pragmatic understanding of him, we must find a way to say things about law as an activity or form of life containing practices other than the giving and following of verbal directives.

3. On the connection between philosophy and normative social activity: the repercussions of reconceiving rules. Although I speculated earlier that perhaps Wittgenstein himself wouldn't have thought that philosophical changes in our conception of rules would make much difference to us in real life, I think that view is too simplistic. At least on the pragmatic view of Wittgenstein that I find congenial, theory and practice cannot remain so separate; our conceptual schemes and human activity cannot be held apart.[82] Deep inner shifts in theoretical practices (like the "conversation" of philosophy[83]) must have repercussions in other kinds of practices (like legal decisionmaking). In this section I suggest how far-reaching the inner shifts must be if we accept the Wittgensteinian view of rules. Later I speculate on how those shifts might be allied to a more pragmatic reinterpretation of the Rule of Law.

The philosophical consequences we must accept if we accept the pragmatic Wittgensteinian view of rules are, I think, these: the tendency of "applying" rules to coalesce with "making" rules; the tendency of the "rule" to coalesce with the "particulars falling under it"; the idea that rules are contingent upon whole forms of life and not just specific acts of a legislature; and the essential mutability of rules.

---

80. *See supra* note 44 and accompanying text; Kennedy, *supra* note 43, at 1687-1701; *see also* Schlag, *supra* note 44, at 429-30 (accepting the rules/standards distinction and arguing that the distinction has been institutionalized in legal argument so as to form a dialetic incapable of resolution).

81. *See* Kennedy, *The Stages of the Decline of the Public/Private Distinction,* 130 U. Pa. L. Rev. 1349, 1352-53 (1982).

82. *See* H. Putnam, Reason, Truth and History 66-69 (1981); Radin, *Market-Inalienability,* 100 Harv. L. Rev. 1849, 1884-87 (1987) (exploring the consequences of using only market rhetoric to talk about human affairs).

83. R. Rorty, *Pragmatism, Relativism, and Irrationalism,* in Consequences of Pragmatism 160 (1982) [hereinafter R. Rorty, *Pragmatism*]; R. Rorty, Mirror of Nature, *supra* note 74, at 389-94.

From a Wittgensteinian perspective, making rules and applying rules cannot be radically separate activities. A rule would cease to exist if we (the relevant community) stopped apprehending it as a rule and stopped recognizing ourselves and others as acting under it. This view of legal rules would contrast with one aspect of the positivist view formulated by H.L.A. Hart. Hart drew a sharp distinction between primary rules of obligation, which can be valid whether or not people obey them, and the rule of recognition, whose existence depends upon the observed actions and public commitments of the legal community.[84] For a Wittgensteinian it seems the distinction cannot be quite so sharp. The rule of recognition itself certainly depends upon community agreement in practice, but so too (even if in a less direct sense) must the notion of validity. If a primary rule were never followed, at some point it would become questionable whether we were justified in thinking it to be a rule.

If we fail to follow a rule we undermine its existence as a rule. Thus when we do follow a rule we reaffirm its existence. Every time we apply a rule we also make it. Moreover, because a rule depends upon the existence of a social practice, it seems than an essential part of rule-application in a legal context is predicting the behavior of the community of judges and other legal actors, including (it seems) one's own behavior if one is a legal actor. (At least this is true for the kind of rules Hart collectively called rules of recognition.) This is a very different picture of rule-application than the one embedded in the traditional formalist conception of rules, where the point of a rule is to close off contingencies related to one's own or others' behavior.

If we accept the Wittgensteinian view of rules, there can also be no radical distinction between a rule and the particulars falling under it. This seems to deny the generality (in Fuller's sense) of rules. In a Wittgensteinian view, rules depend upon the practice of decisions that the relevant community accepts as rule-like. Rules do not wholly pre-exist the particular applications of them in practice, because people must actually follow rules before we can say rules exist.

More broadly, a switch to the Wittgensteinian view of rules must profoundly affect our views about law and the Rule of Law because the Wittgensteinian view makes the existence of legal rules contingent not just upon the acts of legislatures or other authoritative entities, but also upon the surrounding social context, the content of an entire form of life. Of course, rules can come into being partly because we have specific practices (legislation, judging, agency promulgation) that formulate them. In order to find out what rules exist by virtue of these practices, we must "look and see" what the practice is.[85] But that which makes any directive rule-like relates not only to

---

84. *See* H.L.A. Hart, The Concept of Law 97-107 (1961).
85. According to Hart, for example, we would look and see if our rule of recognition validated the particular rules in which we were interested. Hart's rule of recognition, which has its being only in the acceptance of legal actors as manifested in their actions and in their continuing public commitments, is essentially pragmatic. (In fact, Hart wondered whether it even should be thought of as a "rule." *See* H.L.A. Hart, *supra* note 91, at 107-14.)

its promulgation according to an essentially social existing practice, but also to the content of surrounding social activities and understandings. Rules are created and continue to exist not only because a legislature says so, but also by virtue of their being embedded in our *nomos*. A judge's decision in response to a rule responds necessarily to the community as a whole and not just to what the legislature has said.[86]

Finally, if we accept the Wittgensteinian view we must recognize that rules are not immutable. Whether an activity is seen as rule-like is contingent upon material social context and agreement. Over time the "same" action in response to the "same" directive can go from being compelled by a rule to not being compelled by a rule, or vice versa. The traditional notion of law as rules cannot readily accommodate the idea that the contours of the law may shift through no legislative or official act but merely through social change. At what point in the process of coming-to-be-rule-like do we treat something as law?

The point of "the Rule of Law, not of individuals" is that the rules are supposed to *rule*. The easiest (most "natural") way to achieve that in our historical and philosophical context is to assume that rules apply to particular cases in an analytical or self-applying way. "Individuals"—judges, police, administrators—are needed to make sure these self-evident applications are carried out, but these individuals are not supposed to *rule*. They are to be rule-bound, merely instrumental functionaries.

Once we admit that rules are mutable and inextricable from material social practice, we will at least experience a psychological change in the way we perceive our roles as legal actors. This alone may have subtle but pervasive consequences in our practices. For example, suppose the majority of lawyers and judges come to see legal decisionmaking as pragmatic work in the sense described by Duncan Kennedy. Kennedy describes the interaction between the views and desires of the legal actor and the "normative power of the field." Even though the actor will sometimes find the field to be "impacted"— perceive it to be stubbornly rule-like—this cannot be read from the face of the legal materials. Often what looks at first to be rule-like will turn out not to be. I agree with Kennedy that on some not-quite-conscious level good lawyers know this. But if conscious awareness of this malleability in response to legal work—this non-pre-existing-ness of the law—replaces the prevailing positivist rhetoric about decisions predetermined by the plain meaning of rules, the character of our practice will change in ways we cannot now predict very well.[87]

If we do come to think of rules in a different way—anti-formalist, non-foundationalist, contingent, socially constructed—I think the change in

---

86. And because acting under a rule re-affirms the *nomos* that treats any particular directive as binding, judging can never be choice-less or value free. When rules exist only because we continue to apprehend them as rules, it can be argued that we are morally responsible even for "mere" rule-application. Cover explored this responsiblity in R. Cover, Justice Accused (1975), and Cover, *supra* note 94, at 53-68.

87. *Cf.* R. Rorty, *Pragmatism, supra* note 90, at 174-75 (discussing the unforeseeability of the consequences of pragmatism).

thought would not be irrelevant, but rather would be incompatible with the traditional ideal of the Rule of Law. Will this shift in our conception of rules allow us to form a better conception or interpretation of the Rule of Law? Or will it force us to abandon the concept of the Rule of Law altogether? I think it is too soon to counsel abandonment.

V. Toward Reinterpretation of the Rule of Law

Suppose we drop both the notion that law is mediated through formal rules in the traditional sense (accepting Wittgensteinian reinterpretation of formalism), and the broader idea that law consists essentially of verbal directives like rules and standards, apart from the practice in which they are embedded (accepting a more far-reaching reinterpretation). We will still find it deeply normatively appealing to conceive of ourselves as a people governed by its law rather than by arbitrary individual power, because conceiving of ourselves this way I take to be constitutive of ourselves as a political community.[88] The enduring normative appeal of the Rule of Law is the reason I pursue reinterpretation. The reinterpretation I want to pursue (barely beginning in this essay) turns toward a view of law that emphasizes practice as well as words. It is a view that turns toward pragmatism, seeking to view law a a pragmatic normative activity. In this view, hermeneutics— the view of interpretation and meaning as holistic and practice-based—forms the epistemology of law.

The work of Robert Cover is suggestive for the reinterpretation I seek. Cover is perhaps the quintessential modern anti-positivist. He claims that the role of judges is rightly law-creating ("juris*generative*"). Thus, he stands on its head the traditional slogan that judges should apply rather than make law.[89] When judges slip into the old rhetoric and claim to act not as people but as functionaries whose hands are tied, they "substitut[e] the hermeneutic of jurisdiction for the hermeneutic of the text."[90] In other words, they refuse to take responsibility for their actions by taking refuge in their role as rule-followers. "Judges are people of violence";[91] one way of being violent is to disavow responsibility for the consequences of their functionary behavior.

In Cover's view, judges are not functionaries but rather constitute an interpretive community. Law-creation is not unique to them; it inheres in all interpretive communities. In interpretive communities, "applying" and "making" law coalesce. As a community applies its law, it continuously [re-]makes it.[92] Law is not the creature of the state but the mark of an

---

88. *See* Michelman, *supra* note 9, at 1499-1503 (discussing the way we conceive self-rule and law-rule).
89. Cover, *supra* note 94, at 53-60.
90. *Id.* at 58.
91. *Id.* at 53.
92. Even the new Dworkin of Law's Empire, *supra* note 21, would, it seems, readily acquiesce to this last statement. "[Hercules] does not amend out-of-date statutes to suit new times. . . . He recognizes what the old statutes have since become." *See, e.g., id.* at 350. (Unlike Cover, however, Dworkin is resolutely statist; he seems to write on the heroic assumption that we are one interpretive community expressing itself through the state.)

interpretive community. Law is not made by legislatures (or judges) alone. Under the sway of the positivist model of law as rules, the role of the state has been to crush all law contrary to that of the state. This Cover deplores. For Cover, to act rightly as a judge is to refuse to use the violence of one's office to enforce the law of the state against the law of various dissenting communities, while at the same time recognizing and taking responsibility for the fact that the law of the community of judges can come into conflict with, and is not intrinsicallly privileged over, the law of other interpretive communities.

Like Cover's theory of law, hermeneutic social theories have rejected foundationalism, formalism, and the idea that a rule could be applied by one person, only once, apart from a group in whose interpretive practice the rule is embedded. Hermeneutic theories have also rejected the notion that there can be application without interpretation, or interpretation without politics and value, or politics and value without commitment.[93] These theories view interpretation as holistic, pragmatic, and historically situated. Because of these features, hermeneutic theory bears an affinity with the turn toward coherence theories and pragmatism in ethics and metaphysics. Hermeneutic theory thus seems more promising than the new non-foundationalist "natural law" for legal theorists who seek to exorcise formalism.

A pragmatic reinterpretation of the Rule of Law would at least deny that law consists of formally realizable rules in the traditional sense. More controversially, perhaps, I believe such a reinterpretation would deny that law consists quintessentially of rules at all, as well as the notion that rules are separate from cases and logically pre-exist their application. Such a reinterpretation would also deny the strict division of people into rule-givers and rule-followers, and the conception of judges as rule-appliers rather than rule-makers.

How would these broad theoretical features play out into a substantive conception of the Rule of Law that can supersede the traditional one? One task in answering this question is the one I left aside in this essay: the remaking of the supporting theories of the person and of politics.[94] In the meantime, we can set out to "look and see," readjusting our theory and thus the interpretation of our practice at each step along the way. Thus I suggest that we explore how each precept of the Rule of Law might be reinterpreted. If we can retain the entire complex, or most of it, but with new philosophical underpinnings, we shall retain the Rule of Law as a central normative commitment of our legal system. For those who accept the new interpretation, however, its meaning and import for the form of life we call law may be very different.

---

93. *See* Hermeneutics and Praxis xiii-xvi (R. Hollinger ed. 1985); R. Rorty, Mirror of Nature, *supra* note 74, at 315-21; Garet, *Comparative Normative Hermeneutics: Scripture, Literature, Constitution,* 58 S. Cal. L. Rev. 35, 38-39 (1985).

94. *See supra* notes 9-46 and accompanying text. *See also* Michelman, *supra* note 9, at 1502 (arriving at something close to the same point as I do through reinterpretation of politics).

I suggest we begin by reconsidering the Rule of Law precepts clustering around notice, non-retroactivity, and the separation of powers. In the instrumental view of the traditional model of rules, a law must not be retroactive because it cannot be the cause of conforming behavior unless it precedes the behavior. A law must be made public because it cannot be the cause of conforming behavior if the addressees do not know about it. In the substantive view of the traditional Rule of Law, fairness is the value underlying the requirements of non-retroactivity and notice. These precepts both rest on the idea that it is unfair to base adverse government interference with individual interests on the individual's failure to conform to rules the individual cannot fairly be charged to have known in advance of the non-conforming behavior, either because the rule has not properly been made public (the notice precept) or because the rule has not yet been enacted at the time of the conduct (the non-retroactivity precept). What the pragmatic approach can add to this traditional view is a broader understanding of what constitutes sufficient publicity or notice, and a reinterpretation of retroactivity in light of the idea that rules are not made merely by legislatures or other authoritative entities.

In the pragmatic view, a rule will be public whenever strong social agreement exists in practice, regardless of whether a legislature or a court has spoken.[95] Similarly, if a rule exists normatively even without specific legislative enactment (as, for example, would a rule against intentional homicide), then later legislative confirmation would not necessarily mean that it would be unfair retroactive application to punish earlier transgressions.[96] Moreover, where the line of evolution of legal interpretation is clearly foreseeable, it would not be unfair to hold people to what they can see is the emerging interpretation.[97]

The Rule of Law precepts concerning separation of powers and the nature of the judicial role pose a more complex issue. If we accept the Wittgensteinian view of rules, we must reject the conception of the separation of powers that pictures a rigid distinction between the legislature as rule-maker and

---

95. In Keeler v. Superior Court, 2 Cal. 3d 619, 470 P.2d 617, 87 Cal. Rptr. 481 (1970), the California Supreme Court decided that a man who assaulted his ex-wife when she was nine months pregnant and killed the fetus, with intent to do so, could not be prosecuted for murder because common-law judicial precedent did not clearly give notice that killing an unborn baby could result in a murder prosecution. *Id.* at 636, 470 P.2d at 628, 87 Cal. Rptr. at 492. A pragmatic view would make us confront the unspoken social context—an abortion issue the Court did not wish to discuss—by asking: is our contemporary *nomos* one in which the killing of an unborn nine-month fetus by assault on the mother recognizable to us as murder?

96. For example, if defendant assaults with intent to kill and the victim dies fourteen months later, it is fair to abolish the common-law year and a day rule and prosecute defendant for murder. The defendant can be fairly charged with knowing that if the victim dies the crime is murder, and we do not mind the "chilling effect" on people's liberty to assault with intent to kill. *See* United States v. Jackson, 528 A.2d 1211, 1216-20 (D.C. 1987).

97. An interesting passage in the Hart and Sacks materials suggests that Buick Motor Co. could not object on notice and non-retroactivity grounds to Cardozo's decision in MacPherson v. Buick, 217 N.Y. 382, 389, 111 N.E. 1050, 1053 (1916) (holding the manufacturer liable to the ultimate consumer for injury caused by its negligence), because Buick could not reasonably maintain that it was justified in behaving negligently in light of the old (and decaying) doctrine limiting recovery to those in privity of contract with the manufacturer. H. Hart & A. Sacks, The Legal Process 575 (tent. ed. 1958).

the judges as rule-appliers; indeed, we must reject, as well, the more general distinction between government as rule-maker and citizens as rule-followers. But this does not mean that there is no difference between the judicial role and the legislative role. The pragmatic view must certainly accept that the distinction is normatively important in the political tradition of our community.

In the pragmatic normative understanding, our constitution is not merely a document but rather that which "constitutes" us as a political community.[98] We are constituted both by commitment to majority rule and by counter-majoritarian commitments. One way to understand this constitutional dualism is to see it as a reflection of the tension between our understanding of our present state and our understanding of social ideals toward which progress is possible. In this pragmatic view of politics, we are always attempting to accomplish a transition from today's nonideal world to the better world of our vision, and its is a transition that never ends.[99] Moreover, our visions and our nonideal reality paradoxically constitute each other: what we can formulate as being better depends upon where we are now, and the way we understand where we are now depends upon our vision of what should be.

To the extent we live in present imperfect reality, majority rule is normatively appealing, and so is conventionalism in our understanding of morals and politics. To the extent we live in our visions of a better world (even though such visions must be contingent upon our present circumstances), judgment against the majority is normatively appealing where the majority has transgressed those visions, and so is some form of transcendence of conventionalism in our understanding of morals and politics. Because our constitutional tradition partakes of both tendencies, we constitute ourselves both by conventional reality and by vision. Our understanding of the separation of powers can be reinterpreted in light of this constitutive tension.

We might say that often legislatures are responsible for fidelity to convention, and judges for fidelity to vision. More important, perhaps, is recognition that legislatures and judges must interact in pursuing our vision. Consider, for example, civil rights in the modern era. The Court led the way in *Brown v. Board of Education,*[100] but in *Bell v. Maryland,*[101] it was able to let civil rights legislation carry the weight of progress toward the vision of social equality. The interaction of courts and legislatures in the modern development of the law of landlord and tenant is an equally good although less

---

98. An important issue is whether "we" are indeed one political community. *See infra* note 127. It seems to me that "we" are one community on the issue of whether $2 + 2 = 4$, but perhaps we are many diverse communities on other issues more readily regarded as ethical, religious, or political. The pragmatic normative significance of our having a constitution is to deny at least the furthest reaches of such pessimistic irreconcilable pluralism. We are one in at least some sense(s).

99. *See* Radin, *supra* note 89, at 1875-76.

100. 347 U.S. 483 (1954). It is important to recall that traditional concerns about neutral principles and the Rule of Law made *Brown* controversial when it was decided. For an eloquent pragmatic defense of the Court's decision, see Black, *The Lawfulness of the Segregation Decisions,* 69 Yale L.J. 421, 424-28 (1960).

101. 378 U.S. 226 (1964).

celebrated example. Judges like J. Skelley Wright could move forward on their understanding of fair treatment of tenants in principle, but it was for legislatures to tell us what exactly might count as retaliatory eviction or breach of the implied warranty of habitability.[102]

Independence and impartiality are traditional aspects of the judge's role as a functionary separate from the legislative power; these elements of the Rule of Law are supposed to ensure that judges stay within their task of rule-applying. But independence and impartiality can refer to moral autonomy and a commitment to judgment in light of one's own moral understanding of the nature of community—not just to formal separation from the interests of the legislature or the litigants. Robert Cover, for example, regards independence for a judge in the same way as the independence characterizing a person of moral integrity who faces choices that impact on other people's lives, not as merely formal independence of a functionary whose hands are tied.[103]

In such an anti-formalist view of the judge's role, judges are an interpretive community conscious of their obligation to act as independent moral choosers for the good of a society, in light of what that society is and can become. The law, as long as it is part of a viable and developing community, is neither "found" nor "made," but continuously re-interpreted. There are still rules. But there are no rules that can be understood apart from their context; nor are there rules that can be understood as fixed in time.

VI. Conclusion

In *Robinson v. Diamond Housing Corporation,* Judge Wright did not see himself as a functionary implementing pre-existing formal rules. Yet he did see himself as acting in accord with the Rule of Law. If we are receptive to the reinterpretation I have begun to sketch, I think we may now see at least how he was trying to act in accord with the Rule of Law. Judge Wright recognized that in order even to know what his own prior cases "held" and their bearing on the case before him, he had to formulate a normative understanding of what the legislature and courts were doing by promulgating and enforcing a housing code. What they were doing depended not just on the words of the code, but also on the social context of housing in the District of Columbia community at the time, where (it seemed to Judge Wright, at least) landlords were commercial enterprises controlled by powerful groups

---

102. When Judge Wright decided Robinson v. Diamond Housing Co., 463 F.2d 853 (D.C. Cir. 1972) (the case with which I introduced the problem of the Rule of Law in this essay), he could point to legislation enacted subsequent to the events at issue to support his result. The legislation Judge Wright looked to was in turn based upon earlier court decisions. *Id.* at 857 n.1. For many other examples of pragmatic interaction between legislatures and courts, see G. Calabresi, A Common Law for the Age of Statutes (1982).

103. *See, e.g.,* Cover, *supra* note 94, at 58-59 (advocating a "natural law of jurisdiction" which "implies the articulation of a legal principle according to an independent hermeneutic"); R. Cover, *supra* note 95, at 171 (exploring the moral predicament of anti-slavery judges who nevertheless enforced the fugitive slave laws in the era before the Civil War). *See especially id.* at Part III ("The Moral-Formal Dilemma").

and tenants were poor and powerless. What the code meant depended also on the broader social context of the Vietnam era.[104]

Within this context, Judge Wright understood the normative force of the law as affirming not only that there should be safe and sanitary housing for people, but also that people themselves should be involved in bringing this about by enforcing their housing rights in court. If he had allowed a situation to continue in which tenants would immediately lost their homes whenever they tried to invoke the law to improve those homes, the aspect of the law calling for community participation would be a cruel hoax, and the group upon whom it was perpetrated would become even more alienated from the community as a whole. In light of his obligation to support his community, Judge Wright saw the law as working against this alienating result. The Rule of Law ideal itself persuaded Judge Wright to see the law this way.

One could fault Judge Wright for not going further and enjoining the landlord to repair the house, rather than arriving at the ironic result that the tenant's right to habitable housing meant she could stay indefinitely in uninhabitable housing for free. Perhaps even the iconoclastic Judge Wright could not imagine bucking the traditional disfavor for affirmative injunctions. Perhaps it was relevant that in this particular case there was no need for such an injunction because Mrs. Robinson had in fact stopped living in the unsafe and unsanitary house before final disposition on appeal. One could also fault Judge Wright for taking too sanguine a view of the economic situation, if he thought that market forces would necessarily prevent landlords from sticking tenants with the increased costs of making housing habitable.[105]

I do not think, however, that we should fault Judge Wright merely because he did not adhere to the traditional conception of law as static formal rules. His action in trying to keep open tenants' avenues of redress and thereby keep the community open to tenant participation, while at the same time not depriving landlords of the expected monetary gain afforded by property ownership, seems quite law-like. It seems so, that is, when law is understood to mean not just a set of rules laid down but rather to include an evolving complex of political commitments to the flourishing of the community and the individuals in it.

In the view of law as a pragmatic normative practice, law does not disappear. But it is always open to people to recognize, in various ways, that the law in the statute books is not the real law. Some practices are so deeply accepted that they seem like immutable rules. Life according to rules is not impossible but quite routine, as Wittgenstein saw. It is only that, if we take

---

104. In a letter to Professor Edward H. Rabin, Judge Wright said, "I was indeed influenced by the fact that, during the nationwide racial turmoil of the sixties and the unrest caused by the injustice of racially selective service in Vietnam, most of the tenants in Washington, D.C. slums were poor and black and most of the landlords were rich and white." Rabin, *The Revolution in Residential Landlord Tenant Law: Causes and Consequences,* 69 Cornell L. Rev. 517, 549 (1984).

105. The citation of Bruce Ackerman's theoretical article on the economic effects of housing code enforcement as if it were an empirical study of the D.C. housing market is indeed a weakness in Judge Wright's opinion. *See Robinson,* 463 F.2d at 860, *citing* Ackerman, *Regulating Slum Housing Markets on Behalf of the Poor: Of Housing Codes, Housing Subsidies and Income Redistribution Policy,* 80 Yale L.J. 1093 (1971).

the pragmatic and hermeneutic view of law, our understanding of rule-following must be reconstituted so that we know that rules are neither formal in the traditional sense, nor eternal, nor existing independently of us; and so that we know that every application of them is a reinterpretation. We must know that each time we feel ourselves to be rule-followers we are rule-creators as well.

Whether or not the term "the Rule of Law" should be dropped becomes another pragmatic question, a matter of judgment about its ideological baggage. Is the term indelibly linked in our usage with the ideas that law is instrumental and consists of pre-existing formal rules applied in a value-free manner? Or can its precepts be reinterpreted in the way I have begun to suggest? If we can use the term in this new way, it seems that we would at least have to drop the slogan, "the Rule of Law, *not* of individuals." If law cannot be formal rules, its people cannot be mere functionaries.

6

Wittgenstein and the Sceptical Fallacy

Gene Anne Smith

Introduction

Legal theorists have become increasingly interested in whether or to what extent the later writings of Wittgenstein[1] support scepticism about the possibility of rational objectivity or determinacy in legal reasoning and discourse. Some critical legal theorists have explicitly relied upon Wittgensteinian arguments to support arguments for radical scepticism.[2] More recently, anti-sceptical theorists have argued that reliance by critical theorists upon Wittgensteinian arguments involves a serious misinterpretation.[3] I shall in this essay add my voice to those already making this argument.

However, the factual issue of whether or to what extent Wittgenstein has been misinterpreted is not, of course, the whole question. Equally significant is the extent to which Wittgenstein's writings have, by and large, been ignored in the entire debate surrounding the issue of scepticism in legal theory. The danger, therefore, is not merely the danger of wrongly attributing to Wittgenstein views that he did not hold. More serious is the failure to appreciate the importance for legal theory of the profound philosophical insights which have, for many, marked Wittgenstein as "the first philosopher of our age".[4]

Although I agree that Wittgenstein does not draw the sceptical conclusions which would support nihilistic or anti-rational legal theorists, it is equally important to recognize the extent to which he shares what might be seen as a sceptical starting point with those same theorists. Wittgenstein's scepticism, however, was only directed to some commonly held philosophical or theoretical claims and presumptions. His great contribution was to show that these theoretical presumptions are the result of *philosophical* confusions. For him, dispelling this confusion did not result in pragmatic or practical scepticism. Rather, it showed most forms of such scepticism to be themselves products of the original confusion. This is why he believed most

I would like to express my gratitude to my colleagues Louis Romero, Wanda Wiegers and Ken Norman for their helpfulness and generosity in reading and commenting upon earlier drafts of this essay.

1. I rely in this paper upon L. Wittgenstein, *Philosophical Investigations,* trans. G. E. M. Anscombe (Oxford: Basil Blackwell, 1958). For a brief account of the distinction between the linguistic theory of Wittgenstein's early period and that of his later period which I shall appeal to in this paper and discuss in some more detail below, see D. Patterson, "Wittgenstein and the Code: a Theory of Good Faith Performance and Enforcement Under Article Nine" (1988), 137 *U. Penn. L. Rev.* 335 at 356-69.

2. See B. Langille, "Revolution Without Foundation: The Grammar of Scepticism and Law" (1983), 33 *McGill L.J.* 451 at 454-65. Langille has described the extent to which "strong interdeterminacy critics" (citing, among others, J. Boyle, Mark Tushnet, Sanford Levinson and Stanley Fish) rely upon Wittgensteinian arguments, with or without citing Wittgenstein, in order to justify their views.

3. See, e.g., Langille, *supra,* n. 2 and Patterson, *supra,* n. 1. These writers also appeal to Wittgenstein's theory of language to support particular interpretive approaches to legal questions. Langille appeals to Wittgenstein to support an interpretative approach to the Canadian Constitution. Patterson offers a Wittgensteinian interpretation of the "good faith" provisions of Article Nine of the *Uniform Commercial Code.*

4. Langille, *id.,* at 455, citing also P. F. Strawson, "Review of the *Philosophical Investigations*" (1954), 63 *Mind* 70 and Hacker, *Insight and Illusion,* revd. ed. (New York: Clarendon Press, 1986), preface.

forms of scepticism to be nonsense.[5]

It is important, I believe, to understand and to acknowledge the sense in which Wittgenstein's analysis does rest upon insights which the sceptical theorists share, for it is only then that it is possible fully to appreciate why the sceptical conclusions drawn by such theorists are mistaken. Moreover, properly understood, the sceptical aspects of Wittgenstein's arguments do have important implications for legal theory, for they support a deep distrust of abstract and acontextual analysis and argument which we cannot afford to ignore.

I begin, in Part I of this essay, with a brief outline of the foundations of the arguments for radical scepticism which I believe to be widely reflected in the literature and which I accordingly attribute to a hypothetical sceptical theorist whom I shall call "The Sceptic". I illustrate this position by reference to the writing of Allan C. Hutchinson.[6] I argue that the sceptical foundations of The Sceptic create a dilemma for him, for the same arguments which seem to establish the radical indeterminacy and ultimate irrationality of legal discourse ultimately undermine the intelligibility of political and social discourse as well.

The analysis of the Wittgensteinian arguments in Part II is intended to show that The Sceptic's dilemma is based upon a fallacy. I will in this part attempt to illuminate the nature and extent of Wittgenstein's own theoretical and philosophical scepticism as this is reflected in three Wittgensteinian arguments: the paradox of rules, the private language argument and the concept of family resemblances. The first of these, the paradox of rules, has received by far the most attention from legal theorists and is also, in this context, the most complex of the three arguments. It will accordingly receive the lion's share of my attention as well. I will argue that while Wittgenstein's insights in relation to this argument do not assist the position of radical practical scepticism, they do support distrust of abstract, acontextual theoretical analysis and also cast doubt upon a particular *theoretical* account of reasoning in general and of legal reasoning in particular which views rational argument and justification as a mechanical deductive process.

I conclude that because the sceptical foundations, reinterpreted in light of Wittgenstein's arguments, should not be understood as casting doubt upon the possibility of objectivity and rationality in legal discourse, they leave untouched the questions of legal legitimacy upon which The Sceptic mistakenly thought these arguments to be decisive.

I. The Sceptic's Dilemma

I have chosen Hutchinson's recently published collection of theoretical essays[7] to illustrate the basic position and foundational arguments of radical

---

5. Langille, *supra*, n. 2, at 486-7.
6. A. C. Hutchinson, *Dwelling on the Threshold, Critical Essays in Modern Legal Thought*, (Toronto: The Carswell Company Limited, and London: Sweet and Maxwell Limited, 1988). See *infra*, text accompanying notes 7-25.
7. *Id.*

philosophical scepticism as this position is reflected generally in legal philosophical literature.[8] In these essays, Hutchinson argues for the impossibility of objective rationality in discourse generally and in legal discourse in particular. He believes that language is radically indeterminate and unstable rendering objectivity in interpretative argument impossible and illusory. For him, all— philosophy, rationality and language—is and can be nothing but the expression of subjectively held personal preference. All, therefore, is politics. Accordingly, I shall use Hutchinson's arguments to illustrate the position of "The Sceptic".[9]

The Sceptic's argument has three main themes. The first theme is the characterization of legal liberalism (sometimes, "mainstream lawyers") as irredeemably committed to a particular concept of "Formalism". The second and third themes are the arguments of anti-Rationalism and Deconstruction. Together these arguments purport to undermine the cogency of Formalism and thereby to destroy the logical foundation for legal liberalism.

"Formalism", as Hutchinson defines it, has two major components:

> that there is a defensible distinction between legal reasoning and open ideological debate and that such legal reasoning itself represents a defensible and workable scheme of social justice.[10]

While this notion of "formalism" is "higher and more abstract" than "crude rule-formalism", the two are at heart the same.

> First, both recognize and consider realizable the responsibility of the decision-maker to eschew personal preference and to be guided by the dispositive force of the law: each defers to and feels bound by the appropriate legal norm....In both instances, it is "the law" that resolves the dispute and not "the lawyer". Secondly, both defend any decision by reference to an implicit vision of social justice.[11]

In short, the version of "formalism" under attack by The Sceptic is not merely the narrow conceptualism or the blind following of inappropriate rules which all "mainstream lawyers" deplore in judicial writing. Rather, it is any belief in any form of objectivity, or any basis for deciding which is dis-

---

8. See *supra*, n. 2. Although the central arguments of this essay are directed against the general sceptical position I shall here describe, I will also more specifically address arguments of two particular theorists in addition to Hutchinson. These are Mark Tushnet, *infra*, text accompanying n. 45-51, and Saul Kripke, *infra*, text accompanying n. 63-74. Tushnet and Kripke are particularly important because they both attribute radically sceptical conclusions to Wittgenstein. I shall try to show why their conclusions are mistaken.

9. It is important to acknowledge that it is not Wittgenstein's writings which have inspired Hutchinson's scepticism. His mentors are primarily the continental philosophers, Jacques Derrida and Michel Foucault. I intend here to set out only the barest outline of Hutchinson's argument in order to indicate the sceptical presumptions from which his argument proceeds. It is impossible in the context of this essay to make a full argument for the accuracy or even the reasonable fairness of my interpretation of Hutchinson. Certainly, he often denies that he is committed to radical scepticism. See Hutchinson, *supra*, n. 6 at 43, 46-9. While I believe that these denials are inconsistent with Hutchinson's general arguments, it is not essential to my argument in this essay to pursue that point, for I believe that in any case the arguments which I here outline, in varying forms and degrees, are reflected widely in the literature of scepticism. Accordingly, while I appeal to Hutchinson as both inspiration and illustration for the sceptical arguments here presented, I shall attribute the sceptical conclusions only to the hypothetical theorist, "The Sceptic".

10. *Id.*, at 25.

11. *Id.*, at 25.

tinguishable from personal preference.

"Anti-Rationalism" takes the form of an attack upon what is described as "the Rationalist tradition" in philosophy. "Formalism," Hutchinson tells us, is "only a symptom of a much more profound malaise. The villain of the piece is the Rationalist tradition which has dominated our thinking (and our thinking about thinking) for so long."[12] This tradition is identified as a faith in Absolute, ahistorical Truth, a "metaphysical dream of providing a complete and unassailable explanation of everything for all time"[13] and a reliance upon the abstract power of Reason to discover it. It is "the attempt to escape our finitude and its thoroughly contingent contexts and to establish a body of principles that are unconditionally valid for all persons at all times."[14]

The Sceptic equates the Rationalist tradition with "the Enlightenment"[15] and the philosophies of Descartes, Kant and Locke. Hutchinson believes that these philosophers are committed to a notion of truth "unconditionally valid for all persons at all times".[16] In the Rationalist tradition, "abstract reflection is given priority over experiential engagement."[17] Legal theorists caught in its web remain committed "to the possibility of developing a theory of legal interpretation that is built around an impersonal and determinate application of immanent rationality."[18]

The Sceptic argues that the Rationalist claims for Absolute Truth are discredited by the realization that philosophy itself is grounded in historical circumstance which cannot be transcended.[19]

From the idea of historical contingency, The Sceptic draws two related conclusions. One is that claims of "detached reason" and therefore of "objectivity" are suspect. The second is that philosophy and *politics* are therefore inextricably intertwined. There are vested interests and hidden value commitments in all claims of objective rationality.[20]

The Deconstruction argument is a further development of the acknowledgment of historical relativity and the claim for the impossibility of rational objectivity which makes all analyses disguised political assertions. In Hutchinson, the deconstruction thesis (attributed to Derrida[21]) is to be under-

---

12. *Id.*, at 27.
13. *Id.*, at 37.
14. *Id.*, at 27.
15. A. MacIntyre, *After Virtue*, 2d ed. (Notre Dame: University of Notre Dame Press, 1984).
16. Hutchinson, *supra*, n. 6 at 27.
17. *Id.*, at 28.
18. *Id.*, at 29.
19. "The history of philosophy is philosophy *tout court*. To understand a philosophical proposal and its career, it is important to appreciate its historical context; it can only begin to make sense in terms of an agenda of pressing issues, the methodologies on offer, the bounds of political propriety and the like. To put it crudely, philosophers begin and end with their own prejudices as understood within the larger social context of available values".
    "The critical upshot of this argument (i.e., the inextricable relation of philosophy and history) is that modes of thinking and discourse are themselves revealed as contingent. The great systems of philosophy and styles of theorizing about the human condition are not fixed nor immutable. *Id.*, at 32.
20. *Id.*, at 33.
21. Hutchinson's seems to be an overly simplistic view of Derrida's theory which more fundamentally also attacks the idea that meaning can be situated contextually, since context is itself boundless. See Patterson, *supra*, n. 1 at n. 58 for a summary of Derrida's claim and critiques of his theory. Patterson concludes: "Derrida's claims for the boundless nature of context have no purchase on non-totalizing theories of social knowledge of the type advocated by the later Wittgenstein nor, for that matter, speech act theories such as those of Austin, Searle and Grice."

stood as an attack upon the belief that words, or texts, have "embodied meanings".

> For deconstruction, referentiality and meaning are not so much non-existent as profoundly problematic. The attempt to demonstrate and defend any theory of embodied meaning is ruthlessly revealed as leading down the blind alley of foundational thought. No interpretation is right or wrong and no mode of linguistic signification can achieve interpretive hegemony.[22]

Significant conclusions are seen to follow from the claim that meanings are not "embodied". The first, in the paragraph quoted above, is that no interpretation is right or wrong. Moreover,

> The deconstructive critique of embodied meaning ....puts language and texts up for political grabs or, to be more accurate, makes it "open to interested appropriation".[23]

For The Sceptic, once the claims of "absolute Rationality and Truth", and of objectivity in theories of meaning are abandoned, nothing is left but *politics*. Hutchinson tells us that "to acquire and exercise a language is to engage in the most profound of political acts."[24] Words, texts, communications generally, have no objective meaning. All is interpretation. And interpretation is purely subjective.

However, a moment's reflection reveals that The Sceptic has a problem. His arguments prove too much. The Sceptic set out to appeal to theoretical argument in order to discredit legal discourse in favour of politics. But his arguments are equally cogent against the possibility of rational resolution of true value debates. Accordingly, they cast as much doubt upon the possibility of meaningful political discourse as they do upon the possibility of meaningful legal discourse. The Sceptic begins to see political debate itself as "ad hockery"[25]. He is likely to espouse a somewhat surprising commitment to democratic majoritarianism, for if value decisions *cannot* be made objectively, then voting may seem to him the only non-arbitrary alternative.

In short, in basing his attack on legal liberalism upon a rejection of a theory of absolute, ahistorical Truth and Rationality and a theory of "embodied meanings", The Sceptic has implicitly undermined any rational basis for and thereby rendered unintelligible not only legal discourse, but also theoretical discourse, on the one hand, and political discourse on the other. This is The Sceptic's dilemma.

II. The Sceptical Fallacy

I believe that while many of the sceptical insights with which The Sceptic begins are both valid and important, that he is mistaken in drawing from

---

22. Hutchinson, *supra*, n, 6, at 36.
23. *Id.,* at 39.
24. *Id.,* at 288.
25. *Id.,* at 297.

those insights the radically sceptical conclusions which for him make objective judgment and rational debate impossible. I intend, in this part of this essay, to try to describe the kind of mistake I believe The Sceptic to be making and, further, to show that he is indeed mistaken.

I propose to begin by describing in a schematic way the form, or logical structure, which I believe that sceptical arguments often assume in philosophical discussions. This description will suggest, in an abstract way, the nature of the sceptical fallacy to which I believe The Sceptic has fallen victim. I will then turn to a more specific and concrete analysis, in this light, of three "sceptical" arguments of Ludwig Wittgenstein.[26]

First, then, some suggestions about the structure of sceptical arguments: Imagine a stage in our intellectual history at which there is a generally held theoretical belief that some commonly perceived phenomenon, P, is caused by entities known as X's. At least in intellectual circles this theory may seem so intuitively plausible or be so ingrained that the idea that P is not caused by X may be, for some period, simply inconceivable. Then, one day, a great and original theorist emerges to espouse 'X-scepticism'. That is, she argues persuasively: 1) that there is good reason to doubt that X's exist at all in the way the 'X-theory' presupposes, and 2) in any case, even if X's existed, when we more closely examine our experience of P we see that X could not be the cause of or the explanation of P. Conceiving of this event in such a schematic and abstract way, it might appear that the only natural or expected intellectual response to 'X-scepticism' would be to discard our 'X-explanations' and seek a new theoretical explanation for P. However, if the society's intellectuals were sufficiently "hung up" on the *picture* of X's causing P, *and* they were intellectually persuaded by 'X-scepticism', then an equally likely, although importantly mistaken, response might be for them to become 'P-sceptics'.

Because we have disassociated ourselves from the compelling "picture" which holds these intellectuals captive, we can readily recognize that if P were a fairly common phenomenon in ordinary life and discourse, this could lead to some problems for 'P-sceptics' and one might expect them to experience some difficulty in maintaining their 'P-scepticism'. They might in non-reflective moments continue to act as if they "believed in" P and might even devise a pragmatic theory explaining why it is useful to act "as if" P were "real" or "legitimate" in ordinary life, even though we know that this is not "really" so. Again, in the abstract, it is obvious that this intellectual move would be a serious mistake, because, by grasping only half the message of 'X-scepticism', 'P-sceptics' would not only have acquired a mistaken and confused scepticism about P, they would also have missed the enlightenment of the new and better theoretical explanation of P which the arguments for 'X-scepticism' might entail.

Wittgenstein made three related arguments relevant to the issues The Sceptic is concerned about: the paradox of rules,[27] the argument of the impos-

---

26. Wittgenstein, *supra,* n. 1.
27. See subsection A, *infra.*

sibility of "private languages",[28] and the theory of "family resemblances"[29]. Each of these could be characterised as an argument for 'X-scepticism'. Each, in fact, argues for a kind of scepticism closely analogous if not identical to premises upon which The Sceptic's position is based. But Wittgenstein was not a 'P-sceptic', for he took seriously the second part of our schematic argument for 'X-scepticism', *viz,* that even if X's existed they could not cause or explain P. Indeed, properly understood, this is the point of the arguments. I intend to offer a brief summary of each of these arguments in order to show how it might be understood in this light, and how looking at it this way might cause one to hesitate before embracing the sceptical conclusions which inform The Sceptic's writing.

A. *The Paradox Of Rules*

There is a great deal of current interest in legal theory circles in what Brian Langille[30] calls Wittgenstein's "rule following critique", for this argument is seen to have special relevance for traditional theories of law and of legal reasoning. It is common for the discussion to begin with consideration of this passage from paragraph 201 of *Philosophical Investigations:*

> This was our paradox: no course of action could be determined by a rule, because every course of action can be made out to accord with the rule. The answer was: if everything can be made out to accord with the rule, then it can also be made out to conflict with it. And so there would be neither accord nor conflict here.[31]

In his essay, Langille explains the way that critical scholars[32] have relied upon this passage:

> ...the strong indeterminacy critic reads Wittgenstein as denying that language itself can constrain because it is always malleable and open to the politics of context. Furthermore, rules themselves do not guide, determine, or direct what results flow from them. That is, nothing is in the text or the rule—all of the action is with the reader. In short we do not have rule by law (language or text) but rule by the politics of our judges (readers).[33]

This sounds very much, of course, like the position of The Sceptic, although the direct source of The Sceptic's scepticism is not the writing of Wittgenstein. Indeed, scepticism about 'rules' seems to be at the heart of Allan Hutchinson's critique of "formalism" and closely related to Hutchinson's rejection of "embodied meaning".[34]

However, Langille argues compellingly that Wittgenstein did not himself understand the rule following critique to entail scepticism as to our ability to

---

28. See subsection B, *infra.*
29. See subsection C, *infra.*
30. Langille, *supra,* n. 2 at 489-498.
31. Wittgenstein, *supra,* n. 1 at para. 201.
32. Langille's primary example is Mark Tushnet, "Following the Rules Laid Down: A Critique of Interpretivism and Neutral Principles" (1982), 96 *Harv. L. Rev.* 781.
33. Langille, *supra,* n. 2 at 465.
34. See *supra,* text accompanying n. 7-25.

follow rules, or as to the determinacy or stability of language. Langillle supports this interpretative claim by citing, *inter alia,* the following passage which immediately follows the above quoted portion of paragraph 201 and continues its argument:

> 201....It can be seen that there is a misunderstanding here from the mere fact that in the course of our argument we give one interpretation after another; as if each one contented us at least for a moment, until we thought of yet another standing behind it. What this shews is that there is a way of grasping a rule which is *not* an *interpretation,* but which is exhibited in what we call " obeying the rule" and "going against it" in actual cases.[35]

It is not enough, of course, simply to show that Wittgenstein did not himself draw all of the sceptical conclusions from his argument which the critical scholars rely upon. Langille focuses his own argument, quite legitimately, upon the *non-sceptical* and positive account of "rule following" which Wittgenstein offered, of rule following as the mastery of a technique, a community practice. While we, too, must ultimately come back to this, I want first to look more carefully at what might be seen as Wittgenstein's negative argument,—at the particular theoretical account of rule following which he was challenging, and at the nature of the challenge.[36] I believe that until there is better understanding among legal scholars of the nature of Wittgenstein's sceptical challenge, his positive account will continue to be unpersuasive to those held captive by the picture of language and rules which he is challenging. It is *because* they remain captives of this picture that critical scholars wrongly interpret Wittgenstein's arguments as 'P-sceptical'.

For The Sceptic, I believe that it is because *he* is entranced by the picture that Wittgenstein seeks to challenge that he so glibly lumps together all possible claims for objectivity or rationality in legal argument under the pejorative term "formalism".[37] The Sceptic implicitly, if not explicitly, believes that only abstract rules and deductive reasoning can yield objectivity and rational justification. If doubt is cast upon the primacy of a deductive and abstract mode of "rule following" this, for him, entails doubt about the possibility of objective justification at all. A better understanding of Wittgenstein's insight will, I believe, show this conclusion to be fallacious.

In order to understand both the negative and the positive aspects of Wittgenstein's rule following critique, it is important to understand that Wittgenstein was attacking a particular theory of language—of meaning, intention, and understanding—which *presupposed* that all understanding is

---

35. Wittgenstein, *supra,* n. 1 at para. 201.
36. To express the issues in terms of my schematic account of sceptical arguments, we might say that Langille is primarily concerned to show that Wittgenstein was not himself a 'P-sceptic' and that he offered a theory of language which was not 'P-sceptical', for he did not doubt the effectiveness or stability of language or the possibility of following a rule. I agree with Langille here and his argument is important to my general thesis. However, I want to focus, perhaps more than Langille does, upon what I perceive to be Wittgenstein's 'X-scepticism', for I believe that it is equally important, and that it has its own implications for legal theory. Indeed, I am perhaps more ready than Langille to accept that some of the conclusions about the nature of legal reasoning drawn from Wittgenstein's insights by critical legal scholars are correct.
37. See *supra,* text accompanying n. 10-11.

fundamentally a matter of interpreting and following given abstract rules, concepts or definitions, which have been learned and which one then interprets and applies to new contexts. According to this picture, when such rules are properly interpreted and applied, they uniquely determine the correct meaning, ascription, description, or outcome, in the new situation. This picture presumes that normal concept formation is a matter of grasping a particular rule, perhaps a verbal formula or definition, and that concept application is a deductive mental process which involves interpreting and applying these rules to specific contexts.

Wittgenstein tried to show that this account could not be correct. In this sense Wittgenstein's argument *is* sceptical of a particular notion of rule following. He argued that the particular mental activities which we describe as interpreting and deducing are not and cannot be fundamental to or presupposed by our use of language. They do not account for our abilities to communicate or for the stability and constancy of language. Rather, they are themselves activities in which we can and do meaningfully and confidently engage only because we have already mastered a language which in turn gives the activities of interpretation and deductive rule following a role and a meaning. One might say that Wittgenstein has shown that the ability to follow a rule in this deductive and self conscious sense is itself parasitic upon having already mastered a technique which is not itself rule following, interpretation or deduction in the same sense. Accordingly, rule following cannot be the basic or fundamental ability in terms of which our ability to use language is itself explained.

While this argument is not intended to and does not cast doubt upon our abilities either to interpret and apply rules self-consciously or to use language meaningfully, it is nonetheless important in itself in relation to those theories of law and legal reasoning which seem to presume that the ability to follow an abstract rule *is* somehow fundamental and therefore makes sense prior to and independently of particular linguistic contexts. To some extent it is this point that the critical scholars Langille discusses have identified and relied upon. In this they seem to me to be at least half right.

In order to understand the nature of the theoretical account with which Wittgenstein was concerned, (an account, it must be appreciated, to which he had himself been drawn, and whose power he therefore appreciated), it is necessary to start with the idea of abstract concept formation, for this is closely related, in Wittgenstein's argument, to the notion of forming and following a rule.

It is natural, and in important respects true, to say that I have learned to describe objects as 'red' or to identify them as 'tables' by applying to them general abstract concepts ('redness' and 'tableness') which I have abstracted from my past specific experiences of red things and tables. It is the fact that I have grasped the general and abstract concept that enables me to make such ascriptions and identifications correctly, even in circumstances substantially different from any that I have encountered before.

Our ability to make such ascriptions with both considerable confidence and usual success suggests to us a theoretical picture of how this must be possible. We imagine that there is some aspect of all the things we have learned to call 'red' or 'table', as the case may be, which is both the same in all cases (for it justifies our ascriptions of redness and tableness in each past instance) and is also something more than the sum of all our finite past experiences (for it will apply to previously unencountered circumstances which are, possibly in ways previously unimagined, distinct from our previous experiences.) We assume, moreover, that this abstract quality of 'redness' or 'tableness' is itself an object of experience, for it is this concept that we must appeal to, and match up against our new experiences in order to ascribe redness or tableness to them. It is such a concept that we "grasp" when we recognized what is meant by a description of something as red, or as a table.

It is this *account* of grasping a concept and not, of course, our obvious ability in *some* sense to 'grasp a concept' which Wittgenstein meant to challenge. He believed that it is false and that it is misleading.

The challenge to this picture (the argument for 'X-scepticism') takes a number of forms in *Philosophical Investigations* and I want to distinguish two separate lines of argument. The first raises doubts about whether I *have* anything which could count as the concept of 'redness' or of 'tableness' *in the sense that this theory seems to require,* viz., as an introspectable mental experience or event which I can match up against new experiences. It is intended to raise doubt about the existence or reality of 'X's', and is therefore a challenge to the *truth* of the 'X-theory'. The second is an argument that even if there were concepts in the sense required by the picture, it is difficult to see how this could in any way account for my confidence and success in ascriptions of redness and tableness to newly encountered objects. This argument challenges the *explanatory power* of the 'X-theory'. While it is the second more abstract and "logical" line of argument which is the more familiar to sceptical theorists, and therefore the one to which I shall direct more attention, it is important to look briefly, first, at the first line of argument, which is in form the more uniquely Wittgensteinian and is also, in my view, the more compelling.

This line of argument is semi-empirical.[38] Wittgenstein asks us to *look at* (or reflect upon) our experience in teaching concepts and in making ascriptions and identifications and to *notice* that we do not in fact, for the most part, teach or appeal to fully defined or transcendent abstract concepts. When we look at our experience we see that we do not actually have or appeal to concepts in the way that the theory presupposes.

Consider these passages in which Wittgenstein is debating with his imaginary interlocutor[39] about how one might teach someone a concept by means of an ostensible definition —or by giving examples:

38. See Wittgenstein, *supra,* n. 1, at para. 66: "...don't think, but look!"
39. In *Philosophical Investigations* Wittgenstein presented much of the argument in the form of a dialogue with an imaginary interlocutor whose comments are usually distinguished in the text by quotation marks.

208.....How do I explain the meaning of "regular", "uniform", "same" to anyone?—
I shall explain these words to someone who, say, only speaks French by means of
the corresponding French words. But if a person has not yet got the *concepts* I shall
teach him to use the words by means of *examples* and by *practice*.—And when I do
this I do not communicate less to him than I know myself.....

210. "But do you really explain to the other person what you yourself understand?
Don't you get him to *guess* the essential thing? You give him examples,—but he has
to guess their drift, to guess your intention."—Every explanation which I can give
myself I give to him too.—"He guesses what I intend" would mean: various interpretations of my explanation come to his mind, and he lights on one of them. So in
this case he could ask; and I could and should answer him.[40]

The last sentence of paragraph 210 is crucial to Wittgenstein's argument,
and I believe that it is also compelling: "...he could ask; *and I could and
should answer him.*" There is *nothing* that I, who understand the concept
'red', "tell myself" that I cannot also "tell" the person I am trying to teach. I
teach my pupil by way of concrete examples and explanations, exhortations to
correct his mistake, etc. There is no mysterious something more that he must
grasp, after he has understood all of this. It is possible, of course, that he
might misunderstand, but if he articulates or exhibits a misunderstanding, I
can correct it. Furthermore, there are no misunderstandings which cannot, in
principle, be articulated or exhibited. There is nothing that I 'grasp' in my
understanding of 'red', or 'the same', which somehow *transcends* the concrete contextual examples and explanations of the concept in use and cannot
be captured by them.

The other semi-empirical argument is related. The picture, or theory, which
Wittgenstein was challenging assumes that the concept of 'redness' which I
grasp somehow already includes all possible future experiences of redness.
This is part of the idea of the transcendence of the concept. Wittgenstein
challenged the factual assumption, here, that subsequent recognition and
identification of things as 'red' has already been mentally predetermined by
our concept in the way that this picture suggests. Here he was challenging the
idea that in grasping a concept I have already "drawn the boundaries" of
anything that might come within or under that concept; that I have acquired
an "unformulated definition" which I could, if necessary put into words and
which would, itself, *settle* the appropriateness of all conceivable future uses
of the concept. Wittgenstein argued that if we attend to our actual experiences here we will discover that we do not appeal to such definitions to settle
what, in the future, we are prepared to call 'red' or 'table'. In fact, he suggested, we are normally far more certain about what ascriptions we are prepared to make, in particular cases, than we are about what "definitions" we
are prepared to accept, and we will readily abandon a particular definition
which we might provisionally have accepted, if it is necessary to accord with
our practice. In other words, if we attend to what we actually do we will discover that our ability to formulate and use abstract and transcendent
definitions is parasitic upon our ability to apply concepts (make confident

40. Wittgenstein, *supra*, n. 1 at paras. 208-210.

and correct ascriptions and identifications in normal cases), *rather than the other way around.*[41]

> 79.....
>
> And this can be expressed like this: I use the name "N" without a *fixed* meaning. (But that detracts as little from its usefulness, as it detracts from that of a table that it stands on four legs instead of three and so sometimes wobbles.)
>
> Should it be said that I am using a word whose meaning I don't know, and so am talking nonsense?—Say what you choose, so long as it does not prevent you from seeing the facts. (And when you see them there is a good deal that you will not say.)[42]

There is a two-fold point here. One is that one is able to use concepts unproblematically in most contexts without having recourse to, or even being able to come up with, a verbal formula which would itself have determined the correct application in those cases.[43] The other point is that there may, of course, be cases in which we do have to decide what to say—in which there is a doubt, given our previous understanding and experience, about what we should say in *this* case. This experience casts doubt upon the theoretical account which Wittgenstein is challenging, for the picture of "concept" which that account entails would seem to make the concept itself determinative of every possible application. Here we are asked to note that there are many *imaginable* circumstances in which we have no ready answer as to whether the concept should apply. No matter how well defined our concept of redness or tableness may be, it will not be determinative of all *possible* cases. However, the fact that there may be doubt in such cases does not mean that there is doubt in all cases. Indeed, it is because we do know what we should say in normal circumstances that we are able to identify doubtful cases as doubtful, say why they are doubtful, and reasonably consider and decide how we wish to treat such cases.[44]

These semi-empirical arguments: about what we can and do teach when we teach a concept; about our inability to provide definitions for all concepts we employ and the limited relevance for us of the definitions we do provide; and about the fact that we do not seem to have drawn boundaries in advance

---

41. See *id.,* paras. 78-80 for passages in which Wittgenstein attempts to *show* us the way in which our endorsement of or commitment to an abstract definition may fluctuate depending upon our experiential judgments.

42. *Id.,* at para. 79.

43. This is the point about the difference between knowing and saying in paragraph 78:

    78. Compare *knowing* and *saying:*
    how many feet high Mont Blanc is—
    how the word "game" is used—
    how a clarinet sounds.
    If you are surprised that one can know something and not be able to say it, you are perhaps thinking of a case like the first. Certainly not of one like the third.
    There are many other passages of *Philosophical Investigations, id.,* also relevant here. Consider, for example:
    150. The grammar of the word "knows" is evidently closely related to that of "can", "is able to". But also closely related to that of "understands". ("Mastery" of a technique.)

44. Also relevant here are paragraphs 84, 85, and, best of all, 87. These are quoted below. See text accompanying n. 55.

for all possible uses of a concept; all combine to cast doubt on the existence of mentally experienced fully determinant and transcendent 'concepts' such as the theory presupposes.

But of course none of these arguments was intended to cast doubt upon our confidence and ability to use concepts in a consistent, stable and confident way. The conclusion of linguistic indeterminacy seems compelled by the arguments only to those theorists who see the force of the arguments for 'X-scepticism' yet remain wedded to the picture entailed by the 'X-theory'.

Wittgenstein's second line of argument, more abstract and also more familiar to sceptical theorists, challenges the explanatory power of the X-theory. There are basically two tributary branches to this line of argument. The first challenges the coherence of the theory's account of concept formation. It suggests that not only do we not find transcendent concepts when we introspect, but it seems at best problematic and at worst impossible to explain how we *could* acquire a concept which transcends our finite experiences from those experiences considered merely in themselves. I shall refer to this argument as "the induction puzzle". The second line of argument attempts to show that even in cases in which we can come up with a rule, or definition, such a rule could not *in itself* account for our conceptual abilities. This is the problem of the infinite regress of interpretations.

As I have indicated, the first of these lines of argument is really one form of the problem of induction. I believe that it is this aspect of the problem which is illustrated by Mark Tushnet's example, borrowed from Peter Winch and discussed by Langille:

> Consider the following multiple choice question: "Which pair of numbers comes next in the series 1, 3, 5, 7? (a) 9, 11; (b) 11, 13; (c) 25, 18." It is easy to show that any of the answers is correct. The first is correct if the rule generating the series is "list the odd numbers"' the second is correct if the rule is "list the odd prime numbers" and the third is correct if a more complex rule generates the series. Thus, if asked to follow the underlying rule—the "principle" of the series—we can justify a tremendous range of divergent answers by constructing the rule so that it generates the answer that we want.[45]

Although Tushnet may himself want to draw more radical conclusions from this example, a point to which we will return below, the example does very nicely illustrate the point that a finite series does not and cannot in and of itself generate a "rule", in the sense of a regular pattern which will uniquely determine what the next occurrence in the series ought to be. The short numerical sequence used as an example is obviously ambiguous in this regard, but it is important to recognize that the *theoretical* ambiguity which Tushnet is concerned with would not be eliminated by merely lengthening the pattern. It would still be possible in the abstract with respect to any conceivable candidate for the next numbers in the series to find some rule, formula or

---

45. Tushnet, *supra*, n. 32 at 822. Tushnet indicates that this example is suggested by Peter Winch, *The Idea of a Social Science and Its Relation To Philosophy* (London: Routledge and Paul, 1958) at 29-32, who in turn draws on Wittgenstein. Langille quotes more extensively from this passage from Tushnet's article in Langille, *supra*, n. 2 at 464.

regularity which covered the given series plus the proffered candidates. It would also be possible to find a rule which covered the given series and excluded the same proffered candidate.[46] The 'right' answer for the next candidates in the sequence (i.e., what shall count as continuing the same pattern which the given series illustrates) is not and cannot be generated by the sequence *itself.*

However, Tushnet does not leave the matter there. He continues:

> There is, however, something askew in this anarchic conclusion. After all, we know that no test maker would accept (c) as an answer to the mathematical problem; and indeed we can be fairly confident that test makers would not include both (a) and (b) as possible answers, because the underlying rules that generate them are so obvious that they make the question fatally ambiguous. Another example may sharpen the point. The examination for those seeking driver's licenses in the District of Columbia includes this question: "What is responsible for most automobile accidents? (a) The car; (b) the driver; (c) road conditions." Anyone who does not know immediately that the answer is (b) does not understand what the testing enterprise is all about.

> In these examples, we know something about the rule to follow only because we are familiar with the social practices of intelligence testing and drivers' education. That is, the answer does not follow from a rule that can be uniquely identified without specifying something about the substantive practices.[47]

It is my view that Tushnet is entirely right in drawing this particular conclusion from his example. No finite, acontextual, abstract series *in itself* can yield a general rule which will uniquely determine the next item in the sequence. Rather, the pattern, ('rule' or 'principle' governing the sequence) must come from the context (or, as Tushnet says, "the social practice") in which regularity, or pattern is sought, and discussed, in the first place. It is context in which the regularity is generated as a pattern, for it is only in context that there is a reason for viewing this series as reflecting a pattern at all. It is the context, the social practice, the *point* of looking for regularity at all, which tells us *which* regularity is relevant.

But it is important to be cautious about what "sceptical" conclusions are thought to follow from this. Tushnet concluded the first passage quoted above[48] with these remarks:

> Thus, if asked to follow the underlying rule—the "principle" of the series—we can justify a tremendous range of divergent answers by constructing the rule so that it generates the answer that we want. As the legal realists showed, this result obtains for legal as well as mathematical rules. The situation in law might be thought to differ, because judges try to articulate the rules they use. But even when an earlier case identifies the rule that it invokes, only a vision of the contours of the judicial role constrains judges' understanding of what counts as applying the rule. Without such a vision, there will always be a diversity of subsequent uses of the rule that could fairly be called consistent applications of it.[49]

---

46. The latter may seem less obvious, but Kripke's ingenious account of the "paradox" shows that this is so. See, *infra,* text accompanying n. 63-74 and in particular n. 64.
47. Tushnet, *supra,* n. 32 at 822-823.
48. See text accompanying n. 45.
49. Tushnet, *supra,* n. 32 at 822.

But what Tushnet's argument has shown is not that considered acontextually the series "can justify any range of answers." It has shown that considered acontextually it can *justify* no answer at all, for every possible answer can be shown both to fit and not to fit some possible rule, and there is no basis (and therefore no "justification") for choosing one potential "rule" over another. Moreover, the fact that no unique rule can be derived from the abstract and acontextual consideration of a series of numbers does not mean that it is therefore merely a matter of personal preference which rule is relevant.[50] It means simply that it is a matter of context, and is determined by the point or purpose of seeking a rule at all. Nor is context itself a matter of personal choice. It is given by the circumstances in which the question arises and by the community practice which determines what is relevant in those circumstances.

It is helpful in analyzing Tushnet's argument to distinguish two kinds of ambiguity which he has identified: theoretical ambiguity and actual ambiguity. Theoretical ambiguity is revealed when we try to discover pattern or regularity in the given series considered acontextually, as merely an abstract series, considered in itself. Part of Tushnet's point is that every series is irresolvably ambiguous in this sense, for it will yield an infinite number of possible rules and no basis for choosing among them. Actual ambiguity, on the other hand, depends entirely upon context, and does not suffer from the same kind of intransigence.

It is important to note that the numerical example that Tushnet cites is not only theoretically ambiguous, as explained above, but it is actually ambiguous as well, for there are two 'right' answers to the test question, even after one has taken context fully into account. This is the point of Tushnet's comment that a test maker would not include both (a) and (b) as possible answers. The inclusion of both (a) and (b) *in this context* makes the question actually ambiguous. The inclusion of (c) as a choice, however, is only theoretically, and not actually, ambiguous, for context rules it out as an acceptable answer. As Tushnet says, "We know that no test maker would accept (c) as an answer."

The power of Tushnet's puzzle is more apparent than real because it combines these two very different notions of ambiguity. Actual ambiguity is a real problem. The test question will not work until it is resolved. But, of course, it can be resolved, merely by lengthening the series given. We may be misled by the example of actual ambiguity to conclude that theoretical ambiguity creates an even greater difficulty, because it is more sweeping and it is irresolvable. In fact, of course, it creates no difficulty at all.[51]

---

50. Although the main force of Tushnet's argument is simply that context is essential to rule derivation, at some points in the argument he seems to come close to drawing the further odd and unjustifiable conclusion that this means that judges can "do whatever they want". See Tushnet, *id.,* at 824. But this, of course, would require that the judge disassociate herself not only from a particular context, but from any context at all. Yet the point of the argument is to show that this is not merely impossible, as a practical matter, but is conceptually incoherent. Rule following loses its meaning when abstracted in this way.

51. It is interesting to note that Hutchinson has himself fallen into this very trap in discussing Tushnet's puzzle in a recently published reply to Langille's article. After describing the theoretical ambiguity Tushnet identified in determining which two numbers come next in the series which begins "1,3,5,7...", considered abstractly, Hutchinson makes these comments:

Does Tushnet himself think that his puzzle casts doubt upon the possibility of rule following? I do not think so. He concedes, in the first passage quoted, that if we are *given* the relevant rule, (e.g. "list the odd numbers") we are then able to determine the "right" answer. His second example, moreover, illustrates the power of context itself to tell us what the "right answer" is.

These examples do not illustrate anything about the radical indeterminacy of language in general or of rules in particular. They do illustrate the very Wittgensteinian point that meaning is highly contextual. Although they do cast doubt upon the 'X-theory', they do not lead to any conclusions of 'Pscepticism'.

There is one final aspect of the Wittgensteinian critique which must be mentioned here. This is the idea of an infinite regress of definitions, or interpretations. It is this idea which is the focus of the remarks in paragraphs 201 and 202 of *Philosophical Investigations* with which we began this discussion.[52] It is the final leg in the challenge to the explanatory power of the 'Xtheory'.

Recall that the theory which Wittgenstein was challenging is the idea that when I understand a word, follow a rule, or apply a concept to a new context, I call up a mental image (perhaps a chart or an arrow[53]) or a verbal formula or definition which *itself* instructs me how to respond to the particular case. What this theory assumes is that *all* understanding is deductive —following a rule, or going by a sign-post.

Wittgenstein's argument was not that a chart, an arrow, a verbal formula or definition could *never* assist me. Rather, he sought to show that *all* comprehension could not be ultimately a matter of "interpretation" in this sense, for we would then be led to an infinite regress of interpretations. The interpretation would itself have to be understood and this would require yet another interpretation, etc.[54]

Where does all this leave the student of mathematics or law? The only Langillean answer must be..—who knows? If "precedent" and "intention" are no guide, the hapless student is on her or his own. In such circumstances, it makes no sense to require a following of existing practice when the character of such practice is the very matter in issue. Even to advise a choice for elegance or symmetry seems self-defeating and question-begging. Whatever the case in mathematics, the legal situation is doubly or even trebly problematic. (Hutchinson, "That's Just the Way It Is: Langille on Law" (1989), 34 *McGill L.J.* 145 at 157.)

The question which one must ask Hutchinson, however, is this: whatever the case in *law,* what difficulty does Hutchinson think that this puzzle creates for the student of *mathematics?* Is it not obvious that it creates no difficulty whatsoever for the student of mathematics? Moreover, if there is a difficulty for law, it is not one of theoretical ambiguity. It can only be one of actual ambiguity. There will, of course, be many problems of actual ambiguity in law, but it is important to recognize that Tushnet's example does not speak to them. It does not illustrate the universality or the intransigence of actual ambiguity. Nor, for that matter, does the puzzle say anything at all about the possibility of challenging particular presumptions which may operate in any particular context. The induction puzzle does not show this to be problematic. It merely shows that the challenge will itself, of necessity, emanate from some context, and cannot be merely abstract and acontextual if it is to be coherent.

52. See *supra,* text accompanying n. 31.
53. Wittgenstein, *supra,* n. 1 at para. 86.
54. This is closely related to the point made in paragraph 152 where Wittgenstein is investigating (*id.,* at paras. 143-155) what it is to "know how to go on" i.e., to give the next number in a series:

> 152..."B understands the principle of the series" surely doesn't mean simply: the formula "a{n} =..." occurs to B. For it is perfectly imaginable that the formula should occur to him and that he should nevertheless not understand. "He understands" must have more in it than: the formula occurs to him. And equally, more than any of those more or less characteristic *accompaniments* or manifestations of understanding.

Wittgenstein sought to resolve this puzzle by showing us, first, that the logic, or grammar, of 'explanation' and 'interpretation' is in fact different than the theory supposes, and second that there is a way of knowing, understanding, etc., which is *not* an interpretation. It is the mastery of a technique. Moreover, it is fundamental, in the sense that the explanations and interpretations could not themselves assist us unless we had already acquired understanding (acquired a language) in this more fundamental sense.

The first point takes us back to much earlier passages in *Philosophical Investigations*. These may be most helpful in this context:

84. I said that the application of a word is not everywhere bounded by rules. But what does a game look like that is everywhere bounded by rules? whose rules never let a doubt creep in, but stop up all the cracks where it might?—Can't we imagine a rule determining the application of a rule, and a doubt which it removes—and so on?

But that is not to say that we are in doubt because it is possible for us to *imagine* a doubt. I can easily imagine someone always doubting before he opened his front door whether an abyss did not yawn behind it, and making sure about it before he went through the door (and he might on some occasion prove to be right)—but that does not make me doubt in the same case.

85. A rule stands there like a sign-post.—Does the sign-post leave no doubt open about the way I have to go? Does it shew which direction I am to take when I have passed it; whether along the road or the footpath or cross-country? But where is it said which way I am to follow it; whether in the direction of its finger or (e.g.) in the opposite one?—And if there were, not a single sign-post, but a chain of adjacent ones or of chalk marks on the ground—is there only *one* way of interpreting them?—So I can say, the sign-post does after all leave no room for doubt. Or rather: it sometimes leaves room for doubt and sometimes not. And now this is no longer a philosophical proposition, but an empirical one.

86. [The example discussed here is a language-game played with the help of a table, and a schema of arrows for reading the table, etc.]
....Can we not now imagine further rules to explain this one? And, on the other hand, was that first table incomplete without the schema of arrows? And are other tables incomplete without their schemata?

87. ...."But then how does an explanation help me to understand, if after all it is not the final one? In that case the explanation is never completed; so I still don't understand what he means, and never shall!"—As though an explanation as it were hung in the air unless supported by another one. Whereas an explanation may indeed rest on another one that has been given, but none stands in need of another—unless *we* require it to prevent a misunderstanding. One might say: an explanation serves to remove or to avert a misunderstanding—one, that is, that would occur but for the explanation; not every one that I can imagine.

It may easily look as if every doubt merely *revealed* an existing gap in the foundations; so that secure understanding is only possible if we first doubt everything that *can* be doubted, and then remove all these doubts.

The sign-post is in order—if, under normal circumstances, it fulfils its purpose.[55]

---

55. *Id.*, at paras. 84-87.

Wittgenstein was in these and other passages trying to *show* us that the logic, or grammar, of "explanation" or "interpretation" is more limited than the 'X-theory' supposes. An explanation can meaningfully be offered only to remove an actual doubt or misunderstanding. Its role is exhausted when that doubt or misunderstanding is dispelled. Explanations and interpretations, as well as the doubts and misunderstandings they address, depend for their coherence upon an established context—a logic or grammar which gives them meaning. These passages relate, of course, to other passages in which Wittgenstein addresses the idea of profound scepticism. These might be summarized by saying that while it is always possible to doubt or to misunderstand, it is not possible always to doubt or misunderstand, for in order for the doubt or misunderstanding itself to be coherent, it must presume a context and a language.

> 133. ....For the clarity that we are aiming at is indeed *complete* clarity. But this simply means that the philosophical problems should *completely* disappear.[56]

If all understanding is not, then, a matter of interpreting, what is it? Wittgenstein's answer is contained in passages which immediately follow the passages in paragraph 201 with which we began this discussion.

> 201....It can be seen that there is a misunderstanding here from the mere fact that in the course of our argument we give one interpretation after another; as if each one contented us at least for a moment, until we thought of yet another standing behind it. What this shews is that there is a way of grasping a rule which is *not an interpretation,* but which is exhibited in what we call " obeying the rule" and "going against it" in actual cases.
>
> Hence there is an inclination to say: every action according to the rule is an interpretation. But we ought to restrict the term "interpretation" to the substitution of one expression of the rule for another.
>
> 202. And hence also 'obeying a rule' is a practice. And to *think* one is obeying a rule is not to obey a rule. Hence it is not possible to obey a rule 'privately': otherwise thinking one was obeying a rule would be the same thing as obeying it.[57]

"There is a way of grasping a rule which is not an interpretation." "Obeying a rule is a practice." And recall the reminder in paragraph 78 that "one can know something and not be able to say it." The argument here is that all our knowledge is ultimately mastery of technique. It is like knowing how a clarinet sounds. This is, I believe, the meaning of Wittgenstein's seemingly sceptical comments in paragraphs 217-219:

> 217 "How am I able to obey a rule?"—if this is not a question about causes, then it is about the justification for my following the rule in the way I do.
>
> If I have exhausted the justifications I have reached bedrock, and my spade is turned. Then I am inclined to say: "This is simply what I do."

56. *Id.,* at para. 133.
57. *Id.,* at paras. 201-02.

219. ....
When I obey a rule, I do not choose.
I obey the rule *blindly.*[58]

Wittgenstein is not saying here that obeying a rule is ultimately like a leap in the dark.[59] I would make a leap in the dark if asked to make a move in a game I do not understand, hum a tune I do not know, or play an instrument I do not know how to play. If asked to hum a tune I do know, I do this "blindly" not in the sense of a leap in the dark, but in the sense of being unable, at some point, to *say* how I do it.

Justifications run out not because what we do is ultimately unjustified. Rather, they run out ultimately because we have justified all that needs to be justified in a particular context at a particular moment. This is not a regrettable limitation of our abilities. The need for justifications, like the need for explanations and interpretations, is itself contextual and temporal. A request for a "justification" *in the abstract* is not merely a demand for the regrettably unattainable; it is logically incoherent. It does not set too high a standard for rationality, it sets an unintelligible one. Wittgenstein explained the mistake we are likely to make in this regard in the passage quoted earlier from paragraph 87:

It may easily look as if every doubt merely *revealed* an existing gap in the foundations; so that secure understanding is only possible if we first doubt everything that *can* be doubted, and then remove all these doubts.[60]

He was saying, of course, that we will be *misled* if we think of explanations or justifications in this way.[61]

Wittgenstein's view is summarized in these passages which immediately precede the troublesome paragraph 201:

198. "But how can a rule shew me what I have to do at *this* point? Whatever I do is, on some interpretation, in accordance with the rule."—That is not what we ought to say, but rather: any interpretation still hangs in the air along with what it interprets: and cannot give it any support. Interpretations by themselves do not determine meaning.

---

58. *Id.,* at paras. 217, 219.
59. As Saul Kripke, for example, seems to interpret these passages. See Saul A. Kripke, *Wittgenstein on Rules and Private Language* (Cambridge: Harvard University Press, 1982) at 10, 17, 55.
60. *See supra,* n. 55.
61. A good example of this mistake is illustrated by the following footnote in Tushnet's article, where he is discussing Dworkin's interpretative theory of adjudication:

....Dworkin's analysis might alternatively be read as a call for a metatheoretical defense of interpretivism—that is, for a demonstration that a suitably flexible interpretivism is the mode of judicial decision making that best accords with our broader vision of a just society. This alternative project recalls an anecdote about Indian cosmography. A traveler, it is said, asked a wise man to describe the earth's place in the universe. The wise man replied that the stars were on a bowl above the earth, that the earth rode on the back of an elephant, and that the elephant stood on the shell of a huge turtle. But what, asked the traveler, does the turtle rest upon? "Ah, after that it is turtles all the way down," was the reply.

Tushnet seems to be suggesting that *no* "interpretation" could satisfy us, for any "interpretation" can only create a need for a new "interpretation", "all the way down." See Tushnet, *supra,* n. 32 at 791-92 n. 32.

"Then can whatever I do be brought into accord with the rule?"—Let me ask this: what has the expression of a rule—say a sign-post—got to do with my actions? What sort of connexion is there here?—Well, perhaps this one: I have been trained to react to this sign in a particular way, and now I do so react to it.

But that is only to give a causal connexion; to tell how it has come about that we now go on by the sign-post; not what this going-by-the-sign really consists in. On the contrary; I have further indicated that a person goes by a sign-post only in so far as there exists a regular use of sign-posts, a custom.

199. Is what we call "obeying a rule" something that would be possible for only *one* man to do, and to do only *once* in his life?—This is of course a note on the grammar of the expression to "obey a rule".

It is not possible that there should have been only one occasion in which someone obeyed a rule. It is not possible that there should have been only one occasion on which a report was made, an order given or understood; and so on.—To obey a rule, to make a report, to give an order, to play a game of chess, are *customs* (uses, institutions).

To understand a sentence means to understand a language. To understand a language means to be master of a technique.[62]

The significance of these references in Wittgenstein's account to "customs, uses and institutions" is perhaps best brought out by making a brief foray into Saul Kripke's fascinating account of the rule following critique which he calls "the Wittgensteinian paradox", and describes as "perhaps the central problem of *Philosophical Investigations*".[63]

Kripke illustrates Wittgenstein's paradox with the example of the mathematical function of addition. He imagines that having learned how to add, I am confronted for the first time with a calculation I have never done before. For anyone, he points out, there are bound to be some new instances of addition, since one can only have done a finite number of calculations before. Suppose, therefore, that I set out to calculate for the first time "68+57". Before this I have only added smaller numbers. Because I know how to add smaller numbers, but I have never added *this* sum before, I have no available "rule" which tells me explicitly "68+57= 125". I must look for the rule in

---

62. Wittgenstein, *supra*, n. 1 at paras. 198, 199. These passages are also quoted by Langille, *supra*, n. 2 at 489-90.

63. Kripke, *supra*, n. 59 at 7. Kripke describes this paradox as "a new form of scepticism....the most radical and original sceptical problem that philosophy has seen to date, one that only a highly unusual cast of mind could have produced." (At 60.) Kripke's description of this aspect of Wittgenstein's argument as a "paradox" is significant, for it reveals Kripke himself as one who appreciates better than many the power of Wittgenstein's arguments in support of 'X-scepticism', and yet one who is ultimately unable to escape the power of the theoretical picture which Wittgenstein's arguments were meant to dispel. Wittgenstein's successful challenge to the picture results in "paradox" only if one believes that the picture *must*, in some sense, be accurate. Although Kripke himself acknowledges that Wittgenstein offered a "solution" to this "paradox", he also thinks that the solution is itself a "sceptical" one. It is "sceptical", as far as Kripke is concerned, because it leaves untouched the conclusions of 'X-scepticism', with which it begins. A "straight" solution, for Kripke, would show that 'X-scepticism' is itself a mistake. (At 66-67.)
   Many have written critically of Kripke's argument, including Langille, *supra*, note 2. The most complete argument is that of G.P. Baker and P.M.S. Hacker, *Scepticism Rules and Language* (Oxford: Basil Blackwell, 1984). My own critique is, I believe, consistent with but somewhat distinct from both of these. For a more sympathetic account of Kripke's argument see Charles M. Yablon, "Law and Metaphysics" (1987), 96 *Yale L.J.* 613.

what I have done before. Kripke argues that we *should* be able to reflect upon our previous experiences of adding to find this rule, because even in previous cases, I perceived myself *as adding*, and not, for example, simply coming up with random solutions which turned out to be correct. That is, I understood at the time that my results were necessitated in some way by my understanding of addition. Therefore, I must have perceived myself as following directions which I gave myself which compelled the particular results I achieved in the past. I should therefore now be able to retrieve these directions by recalling my past experiences and they should in turn justify my giving the answer "125" in the present case.

It is clear that what Kripke is looking for is something in my past experience which represents what I "meant by plus" in those earlier cases, and which will now compel and justify the correct answer when applied in this new case.

Kripke imagines a "bizarre sceptic", however, who suggests that applying what I did in the past, I could now conclude that 68+57=5. The sceptic claims that I can find no justification for my insistence that based upon my understanding of addition, 68+57=125.

Applying Wittgenstein's argument, Kripke shows that there is *no* interpretation of the meaning of "plus" or "addition" which accompanied the experience of what I have done before,—no instruction which I previously gave myself—, which itself logically dictates or guarantees the way in which it is to be applied in this new instance. I did not have the particular sum "68+57=125" expressly in mind at the time that I calculated previous sums. The argument is that if in order to calculate this sum I now must rely upon some verbal formula, present in the past instances, which will dictate the correct result and only this result, I will not be able to *find* this formula by reflecting upon my past experience. Telling myself to do "the same" that I have done in previous cases is no help, for the question just is, what is "the same", given that I am now faced with a new, never before experienced, set of numbers? Kripke sets out the puzzle this way:

> But of course the idea is that, in this new instance, I should apply the very same function or rule that I applied so many times in the past. But who is to say what function this was? In the past I gave myself only a finite number of examples instantiating this function. All, we have supposed, involved numbers smaller than 57. So perhaps in the past I used 'plus' and '+' to denote a function which I will call 'quus' and symbolize by '⊕'. It is defined by:
>
> $$x \oplus y = x+y, \text{ if } x,y < 57$$
> $$= 5 \text{ otherwise.}$$
>
> Who is to say that this is not the function I previously meant by '+'?[64]

It is clear that Kripke's paradox turns, to some extent, upon the same inductive problem that fascinated Tushnet. This aspect of the paradox could

---

64. *Id.*, at 8-9.

be put this way: to illustrate a function which we shall for the moment designate by "*", set out any series of equations, as long as you like so long as none of the numbers on the left hand side is larger than 57. We might have, for example: 1*1=2; 12*15=27; 35*42=77; 7*9=16; etc., etc. The inductive puzzle shows us that these examples, considered only in themselves, do not determine that 68*57=125. The examples do not tell us, that is to say, that "*" means "+" in the series set out.

However, we have already seen that while this is true, it is not, as Kripke appears to think, *in and of itself,* puzzling. Indeed, we might easily imagine a game in which we define "*" as Kripke has defined "quus". There would be a *point* to this, so long as it worked coherently in the game.[65] In other words, there could well be contexts in which a rule like "quus" would be perfectly sensible. The sceptic's hypothesis is not *necessarily* "bizarre". It becomes "bizarre" only when one assumes that what would be perfectly possible in the abstract, so long as context has not yet been identified, remains a possibility within a specific defined context. However, once we move within a particular context, the sceptic's hypothesis is not merely "bizarre", it will have ceased to be a possibility. It will be clearly wrong as an interpretation of what I meant within that context.

If, bearing this in mind, we then ask how we know that we were, in particular past instances, using the '+' function and not the '*' function, the answer seems clear: *context* would tell us so.[66] We would recall *why* we had been performing this function, what others were doing and saying in response to us, what its purpose or function had been. If we reflect upon the role which addition plays in our lives, then it will follow that 68+57=125 (and not 5) because otherwise the *point* of adding (in the *previous* instances) would be altered or defeated when we come to larger sums. Within some contexts a function may drastically change when it reaches a certain level (as in the game 'Blackjack') but in others this would be ruled out by the logic of the enterprise in which we are engaged. It would be ruled out by the point of addition. In short, if we look at past practice not merely as isolated and abstract instances of performing a mathematical function, but as an activity in which we were engaged with others, we will discover, in that practice, a logic which will determine, in this new instance, that 57+68=125. Wittgenstein would call this logic the "grammar" of the "language game" in which we are engaged when we add.

Kripke does not consider this kind of answer to his puzzle, because he seeks something which was going on privately in my mind when I was in past instances adding, which itself justified my past results and which also transcends them and requires the result, 68+57=125. He seeks an "interpretation" of "+" which takes the form of mental instructions I gave myself in the past and which I can now again appeal to. But he always considers such

---

65. In thinking of this, I was reminded of the card game "Blackjack" or "21" in which the winning hand is the one in which the face value of the cards comes closest to a total of 21 without exceeding that sum. Any hand which exceeds that sum automatically loses.

66. If it did not, then our past practice might itself have been *actually* ambiguous. E.g., we might have been in the process of learning the game, not yet fully understanding how this function would finally fit in.

instructions as themselves 'acontextual'.[67]
Thus, for the purpose of this book, at least, Kripke accepts the Wittgensteinian arguments for 'X-scepticism' that if we look we will not find this private mental definition or interpretation which accompanied and yet transcended my past practice. Having assumed, however, that we can escape the *inductive* problem only if we can appeal to such a 'concept' he then draws the 'P-sceptical' conclusion, that I can never, personally, be "justified" in my belief that my sums are correct.[68]
As Langille points out,

> Kripke believes this to lead to the paradox that language is "impossible". The only way out is the appeal to a "community *consensus*" which chooses or selects the correct "interpretation" from the many available. It is a "sceptical conclusion" to a sceptical argument.[69]

Kripke's conclusion that the paradox cannot be resolved except by appeal to "community consensus" for the proper interpretation of the rule, suggests that the interpretation of a rule is a matter of arbitrary choice and would support The Sceptic's view that language, (and even mathematical rules) are "up for grabs". But Wittgenstein's argument is not that language is impossible. Nor is it, as Kripke thinks, that as an individual, I simply make leaps in the dark (which fortuitously happen to be correct most of the time) when I add new sums, or apply concepts in new situations. It is that language is a practice, a technique, that we learn. It depends upon a *given* community of understanding and established practices, to be sure.[70] But this is required not in order to *verify* my judgments. It is required to give the context in which I can make meaningful judgments at all.[71]
Because the practice must be an established one, with point, function and consistency, in order to yield the logic or "grammar" which makes meaning

---

67. For example, Kripke considers a reply to the sceptic that in the past I did not merely rely upon a finite number of examples of addition, but, rather, that I "learned and internalized instructions for—a *rule* which determines how addition is to be continued....I proceeded according to an *algorithm* for addition that I previously learned." (Kripke, *supra*, n. 59 at 15-16.) This cannot extricate us from the sceptic's problem, he argues, because if we seek to expound such a rule in terms of the concept of counting, for example, the sceptic's puzzle simply recurs at another level.
68. This conclusion is, of course, attributed to Wittgenstein. See these passages in Kripke, *id.*,

> We can put the problem this way: When asked for the answer to '68+57', I unhesitatingly and automatically produced '125', but it would seem that if previously I never performed this computation explicitly I might just as well have answered '5'. Nothing justifies a brute inclination to answer one way rather than another. (At 15.)
> The sceptical argument, then, remains unanswered. There can be no such thing as meaning anything by any word. Each new application we make is a leap in the dark; any present intention could be interpreted so as to accord with anything we may choose to do. So there can be neither accord, nor conflict. This is what Wittgenstein said in paragraph 202. (At 55.)
> ...Wittgenstein's main problem is that it appears that he has shown *all* language, *all* concept formation, to be impossible, indeed unintelligible. (At 62.)

69. Langille, *supra*, n. 2 at 465, n. 58.
70. See Langille, *id.*, at 491-497.
71. This view of the role of community, in Wittgenstein's writing, in determining the meaning of a rule, is the subject of some controversy. See Norman Malcolm, "Wittgenstein on Language and Rules" (1989), 64 *Philosophy* 5. Malcolm disputes the position taken by G.P. Baker and P.M.S. Hacker that the relationship between a rule and what it requires is essentially an "internal" relationship. Malcolm believes that it is a question of communal consensus. Baker and Hacker argue that communal agreement has only a limited significance in that *shared* language games assume "a framework of agreement in

possible, the one thing that Wittgenstein's argument shows conclusively is that language is not "up for political grabs". This is not to deny, of course, that language, like anything else, can be used for political purposes. But the notion that we can "mean" anything we like, as a matter of personal whim, in our use of language, is shown by Wittgenstein's argument to be nonsense.

The conclusion that language is impossible only follows if we are captives of the picture of language (or of mathematical calculation) as "rule following" which it is the point of the paradox to dispel. Kripke's move is from 'X-scepticism' to 'P-scepticism'. But this move is a particularly implausible one for Kripke to make, for, by taking his example from mathematics, he has shown that even our ability to perform simple mathematical functions *cannot* be a matter of "rule following" if this is understood as the mental process of interpreting an acontextual self-interpreting verbal formula which we have given ourselves whenever we have added sums and which itself determines a particular outcome. Therefore, in the move to 'P-scepticism', Kripke must conclude not only that language is indeterminate, but that mathematics, even the simple practice of addition, is indeterminate (or "impossible"), as well.

Kripke is led to gulp and swallow this implausible result because he is unable to discard the notion that addition is a matter of mentally following or applying a rule which we must interpret. And since interpretations of rules (at least in relation to new instances) are not "given" by the rules themselves he concludes that the activity of addition is itself somehow contingent upon the particular "interpretation" which the community happens to have "accepted".

But the "sceptical solution" regarding mathematical addition is not only implausible in an intuitive sense (in making mathematical functions more contingent, or a matter of choice, than we think they are), it seems impossible on Kripke's own account. It is no solution at all. Recall that the paradox required us to apply the addition rule (or, more accurately, our understanding of "plus") to a new instance not explicitly encountered before. The point of the paradox is that there is nothing *in the rule* (or in the "concept of addition" or "the meaning of 'plus'" which we have grasped) which tells how it is to apply to new instances. Therefore, for an "accepted community interpretation" *of the rule* to provide a solution for this dilemma, there would have to be a separate discoverable community interpretative practice for every conceivable mathematical sum. There would have to be a discoverable community

---

behaviour." (G.P. Baker and P.M.S. Hacker,*Wittgenstein: Rules, Grammar and Necessity* (Oxford: Basil Blackwell, 1986) at 249, quoted in Malcolm, at 16.) In general, however, a practice itself, they argue, must be *sharable* but need not be *shared*. Thus they believe that for Wittgenstein a community, *per se*, is not a necessary condition for a language. Malcolm argues that meaning must as a matter of logic be independent of what an individual speaker believes and that "this independence condition can be satisfied only if there is a community of speakers who use the sign in a customary way." (At 28.) I should not like to dispute with Malcolm, Baker or Hacker about what Wittgenstein himself actually thought about this. However, it is my view that the analysis I have presented here supports only the double point (consistent with the Baker/Hacker position) first, that meaning is inherently *sharable* (and therefore not "private" in a sense that would render this impossible) and second, that most language games of any degree of complexity do, as a contingent matter, depend upon a community of agreed practice for their logic or grammar.

practice for *every application* of a rule. But surely, no such practice can be discovered in the vast majority of possible instances. Moreover, in any case, neither our ability to add in new instances nor the ability of others to verify our sums in any way involves the sort of empirical inquiry that this analysis would seem to entail.

The picture Kripke paints is one of an individual who acts instinctively but with unjustified confidence ("blindly") *until* his practice has been *verified* by community agreement. This, in my view, is a misunderstanding of Wittgenstein's remarks in paragraph 219.[72] Wittgenstein's point was not that the individual's confidence is *un*justified. Nor was it that the individual, if asked a proper question calling for justification (e.g., "Why did you put down 5 and carry one, rather than putting down one and carrying 5?") could not provide one.

The more plausible "solution", surely, is that adding is not a matter of mental rule following in the sense suggested at all. We are not able to add because we first learn an abstract and acontextual rule (or the meaning of "plus") and then mentally interpret it to apply it to new situations. Rather, to say that we know the meaning of "plus" is just to say that we know how to add. We know how to add because we are taught how to add, largely by trial and error, and we see the point of adding in a wide variety of contexts. Try to imagine teaching a child to add by teaching an abstract rule first. Being a member of an adding community (a community in which adding is a practice that has a point) is a condition of our being able to add, and is therefore a condition of our understanding of the word "plus". But this is not because the community has chosen a particular interpretation (from an infinite range of possibilities) for every possible application of the 'plus' function. We must once more recall Wittgenstein's reminder in paragraph 78:

> 78. Compare *knowing* and *saying:*
>
> > how many feet high Mount Blanc is—
> > how the word "game" is used—
> > How a clarinet sounds.
>
> If you are surprised that one can know something and not be able to say it, you are perhaps thinking of a case like the first. Certainly not of one like the third.[73]

Being master of a technique, knowing how to do something, does not entail being able to follow a rule which we recite to ourselves and then must "interpret". Scepticism about rule following should not lead to scepticism about the possibility of language or of mathematics. What it does lead to is scepticism of a view of language that supposes that using words requires mental acts of rule following and a view of rationality which presupposes that all rational thought is a matter of applying or following abstract rules which "determine" specific outcomes. It casts doubt, in short, upon the presumption that rational, logical thinking is always or ultimately a deductive mental pro-

72. See *supra*, text accompanying n. 58.
73. Wittgenstein, *supra*, n. 1 at para. 78.

cess. But this is not to cast doubt on the possibility of rational, logical thinking. To suppose that it does is to move illegitimately from 'X-scepticism' to 'P-scepticism'.

Nor was Wittgenstein's point sceptical about the possibility of following a rule. In an appropriate context a rule may be determinate of proper practice. However, the ability to recite, interpret and follow a formula is not fundamental to our ability to understand. It is, rather, parasitic upon already having a language and upon understanding and being able to play a language game in which such a rule has a function or logic.

Thus, we may, of course, acquire and use abstract general concepts or verbal formulae. We might, for example, learn the meaning of a word by looking up a definition in a dictionary. We might be told mathematical formulae for performing specific mathematical functions (e.g., "the square of the hypotenuse of a triangle equals the sum of the square of the two sides"). We are able to use these formulae meaningfully in new instances. We must be able to interpret and apply them. Understanding a definition, for example, depends, as Wittgenstein tried to show, upon already knowing a language. It depends upon knowing how to play a language game in which we understand the role and context of the proffered definition. Without this, the definition would tell us nothing.

29. Perhaps you say: two can only be ostensively defined in *this* way: "this *number* is called 'two'". For the word "number" here shews what place in language, in grammar, we assign to the word. But this means that the word "number" must be explained before the ostensive definition can be understood.—The word "number" in the definition does indeed shew this place; does shew the post at which we station the word. And we can prevent misunderstandings by saying: "this *colour* is called so-and-so", "This *length* is called so-and-so", and so on. That is to say: misunderstandings are sometimes averted in this way. ....

Whether the word "number" is necessary in the ostensive definition depends on whether without it the other person takes the definition otherwise than I wish. And that will depend on the circumstances under which it is given, and on the person I give it to.

And how he 'takes' the definition is seen in the use that he makes of the word defined.

30. So one might say: the ostensive definition explains the use—the meaning—of the word when the overall role of the word in language is clear. Thus if I know that someone means to explain a colour-word to me the ostensive definition "That is called 'sepia'" will help me to understand the word.—And you can say this, so long as you do not forget that all sorts of problems attach to the words "to know" or "to be clear".

One has already to know (or be able to do) something in order to be capable of asking a thing's name. But what does one have to know?[74]

---

74. *Id.*, at paragraphs 29-30. See also paragraph 31:

....the words "This is the king"....are a definition only if the learner already 'knows what a piece in a game is'. That is, if he has already played other games, or has watched other people playing 'and understood;—*and similar things*....We may say: only someone who already knows how to do something with it can significantly ask a name.

I think that Wittgenstein wanted to *distinguish* between "knowing how to go on" on the basis of our acquired knowledge and experience of the grammar or logic of linguistic usage, from the "knowing how to go on" which is doing what a formula tells us to do. The former is basic. Unless we can do *this*, nothing else is possible. Other uses, creative uses, abstract formulae, definitions, etc. are parasitic upon our having this ability. Therefore, the former cannot depend upon the latter. Rather, the reverse is true. We could not apply and understand formulae unless we already knew "how to go on" in non-formulistic ways. This is the paradox of rules. The formula *itself* can tell us nothing.

The paradox of rules shows this in two ways: first, by showing that our capacity for meaningful and correct linguistic usage need not and does not normally involve the use, application or interpretation of abstract formulae *at all;* second, by showing that we could not follow formulae, apply abstract definitions and concepts, or engage in the interpretative activity this might involve, unless we *already* knew how to go on *linguistically* in the general way in the usual case.

If we restrict the description "following a rule" to cases like following a formula, then Wittgenstein's message is that most cases of going on the same way (using language, obeying commands, complying with requests, adding and subtracting sums) are not cases of "rule following" at all. Our acquired ability to use language, our knowledge of the logic and grammar of ordinary language usage is not abstract in this way.

The ability to abstract—to use verbal formula, to follow a rule, is *secondary* to our knowledge and facility with linguistic usage.

Similarly, the "formalism" upon which The Sceptic focuses is indeed untenable insofar as it is understood to imply that words, or rules, *in the abstract*, "in themselves", are determinative of unique results. However, the Wittgensteinian arguments show that the idea that rules might be meaningful in an abstract and acontextual way itself reflects an untenable theory, or picture, of language and of meaning. Therefore, nothing about the general indeterminacy of language (or, indeed, of rules, considered in context) is entailed by the rejection of that theory. To suppose that it is is to move illicitly from 'X-scepticism' to 'P-scepticism'.

B. The Private Language Argument

A full discussion of Wittgenstein's argument about the possibility of a private language would require a book, and I would not in any case be the one to write it. It would, moreover, take us into a discussion of the epistemology of sensations (e.g., pain) which is not fruitful in this context. However, as Kripke correctly argues, the private language argument is in one of its aspects simply an application of Wittgenstein's point about rules. What Wittgenstein wanted to dispel is the idea that meaning in communication is a function of something that occurs in the mind of the speaker which the listener must induce from the speaker's words and behaviour. This is another "picture" which holds our imaginations captive. The reason that it seems so compelling is that we feel that its truth must be assumed in order to explain the instances in which we *mis*understand one another. The possibility of misunderstandings makes us think that we can never do better than guess what another speaker means when she speaks. If we are captives of this picture, we generally think that we often make "educated" guesses, but sometimes we imagine that we might *always* be mistaken, or, at any rate, that it is possible that we never fully or perfectly understand, but can only come reasonably close to devising a speaker's "true" meaning. This picture is in itself a sceptical one, for it suggests that true meaning is locked up in people's heads, ultimately unattainable.

Wittgenstein's argument is that meaning could not be something going on privately in a person's mind when she speaks because, (1) often no plausibly relevant mental act even occurs, and (2) even if it did, it could not have the consequences of *meaning*. While I *might* form a mental image of, say, a red square when I say the word "red", I do not necessarily do so. Moreover, even if I did, how would that contribute to my *meaning* "red" (and not, say, "square")? Meaning is custom, use. It consists in the way words function in what Wittgenstein called "language games", the infinitely various practices of usage we learn when we learn a language. The same word, with identical mental images accompanying it, might occur in a wide variety of contexts, with very different meanings from context to context. It is the context, the function that language is performing, which makes these distinctions of meaning possible. This is what Wittgenstein means by a "language game".

21. Imagine a language-game in which A asks and B reports the number of slabs or blocks in a pile, or the colours and shapes of the building-stones that are stacked in such-and-such a place.—Such a report might run: "Five slabs". Now what is the difference between the report or the statement "Five slabs" and the order "Five slabs!"?—Well, it is the part which uttering these words plays in the language-game. No doubt the tone of voice and look with which they are uttered, and much else besides, will also be different. But we could also imagine the tone's being the same—for an order and a report can be spoken in a *variety* of tones of voice and with various expressions of face —the difference being only in the application.[75]

Language is therefore irreducibly institutional, or communal.[76] There could be no misunderstandings if there were not understandings, common accepted language practices. To use language is to engage in a language game, the context and rules of which are established by a community which, in Wittgenstein's terminology shares a "form of life"[77]. Moreover, language games are concrete and they are functional. They have a point. There could be no "meaning" which others *could not* understand, for there would be nothing in which such meaning could then consist. There would be no basis for saying that one "meant" one thing rather than another.

Wittgenstein offered this illustration:

75. *Id.,* at para. 21, and see also, para. 23.
76. In the sense discussed *supra,* n. 71.
77. Wittgenstein, *supra,* n. 1, at para. 23.

> Can I say "bububu" and mean "If it doesn't rain I shall go for a walk"?—It is only in a language that I can mean something by something. This shews clearly that the grammar of "to mean" is not like that of the expression "to imagine" and the like.[78]

This argument has an important consequence for The Sceptic's brand of scepticism. On the one hand, it does support the idea that language is in an important sense "contingent", for it depends upon the practices of an existing community, and there is no reason to presume that all or perhaps any of those are "necessary". However, it in no way supports the view that language is "up for grabs" and is, in this sense, "political". Language cannot, except in a very limited and parasitical way, be a matter of individual choice. We might, of course, personally choose to alter certain specific uses of vocabulary. Feminists' arguments for and some success in attaining gender neutral usage illustrate this. But the possibility of this kind of control and change is itself fully parasitic upon a larger context of established practices which both makes it possible for us to make sense of this alteration in practice, and which gives it a point.[79] That is, this sort of deliberate adoption of linguistic practice is only possible because it is itself a move in a language game that is already established and understood. The established community of understanding, which is *not* a matter of individual and personal choice, (and, of course, is not a matter of communal choice, either) is the very condition for those limited choices about language usage which we can make. As Wittgenstein pointed out, one must already be master of a language before she can understand an ostensible definition.[80]

The argument that meaning is not a matter of a private mental act, but rather of the function or use of language in the context of established community practice is not an argument *for* scepticism of the possibility of objectively correct understandings or interpretations, it is an argument *against* that scepticism. Because there is no meaning to one's words apart from the function they perform, the language game one is playing, meaning cannot be an *unattainable* something locked up in a person's mind. The idea that someone might *always* mean something different or something more than you or I do, or than she might be able to explain to us, when *she* describes lemons as "yellow", is incoherent, for there is nothing in which that 'something more' *could consist*. Radical subjectivity in meaning and interpretation is incoherent.

---

78. *Id.*, n. at bottom of English page 18.
79. A similar point can be made about creative use of language, which is common in poetry but may occur in even the most prosaic contexts. The idea of "community practice" should not be understood as an entrenchment of the "status quo". Both challenge and creativity are possible, and, indeed, may themselves be established practices! Nonetheless, creative use is parasitic upon established use. It is established use which makes it possible *and* gives it a point.
80. Wittgenstein, *supra*, n. 1 at para. 33. And see also para. 31: "We may say: only someone who already knows how to do something with it can significantly ask a name."

C. Family Resemblances

Many people are familiar with this Wittgensteinian passage:

66. Consider for example the proceedings that we call "games". I mean board-games, card-games, Olympic-games, and so on. What is common to all of them?—Don't say: There *must* be something common, or they would not be called "games"—but *look and see* whether there is anything common to all.—For if you look at them you will not see something that is common to *all,* but similarities, relationships, and a whole series of them at that. To repeat: don't think, but look!—Look for example at board-games, with their multifarious relationships. Now pass to card-games; here you find many correspondences with the first group, but many common features drop out, and others appear. When we pass next to ball games, much that is common is retained, but much is lost.—Are they all "amusing"? Compare chess with noughts and crosses. Or is there always winning and losing or competition between players? Think of patience. In ball games there is winning and losing; but when a child throws his ball at the wall and catches it again this feature has disappeared. Look at the parts played by skill and luck; and at the difference between skill in chess and skill in tennis. Think now of games like ring-a-ring-a-roses; here is the element of amusement, but how many other characteristic features have disappeared! And we can go through the many, many other groups of games in the same way; can see how similarities crop up and disappear.

And the result of this examination is: we see a complicated network of similarities overlapping and criss-crossing: sometimes overall similarities, sometimes similarities of detail.

67. I can think of no better expression to characterize these similarities than "family resemblances"; but the various resemblances between members of a family: build, features, colour of eyes, gait, temperament, etc. etc. overlap and criss-cross in the same way.—And I shall say: "games" form a family.

And for instance the kinds of number form a family in the same way. Why do we call something a "number"? Well, perhaps because it has a—direct —relationship with several things that have hitherto been called number; and this can be said to give it an indirect relationship to other things we call the same name. And we extend our concept of number as in spinning a thread we twist fibre on fibre. And the strength of the thread does not reside in the fact that some one fibre runs through its whole length, but in the overlapping of many fibres.[81]

This passage certainly supports one kind of non-essentialist view of language. And its message is important and relevant in relation to many kinds of "formalistic" arguments that may be and have been offered as legal arguments. It also has a special message for philosophers who imagine that it is not only possible, but important, to discover the essential meaning of, for example "law" which will explain and legitimize its use in the wide variety of contexts in which it occurs. These are the theorists who try to derive a grand "theory of law" which will capture this meaning.

---

81. *Id.,* at paras. 66 and 67. There is another point in this passage which is worth mentioning. That is Wittgenstein's insistence, "Don't say: There *must* be....*Look and see!*" The passage quoted, of course, illustrates the wisdom of that imperative. Wittgenstein shared The Sceptic's scepticism of *abstract* rationalism. But this did not, of course, render him philosophically mute. It suggested a better way of doing philosophy.

However, the family resemblances argument does not in any sense other than that support the view that language is "indeterminate". It is not an argument, for example, that the meaning of the word "game" is somehow vague, or indeterminate. In fact, the argument assumes that the uses of the word "game" which it cites *are correct,* not that there is "no correct or incorrect" use. If this kind of argument is behind Hutchinson's claim that because meanings are not "embodied", no interpretation is correct or incorrect, then the conclusion simply does not follow. What the argument shows is not that ring-a-ring-a-roses and chess are not both games. It shows that our undoubted ability to say that they both are does not presuppose that the word "game" has a single core meaning. The fact that a thread does not have a single fibre running through it is no reason to feel insecure about using thread to sew the buttons on our pajamas. Wittgenstein went on to say:

> 70. "But if the concept of 'game' is uncircumscribed like that, you don't really know what you mean by a 'game'."—When I give the description: "The ground was quite covered with plants"—do you want to say I don't know what I am talking about until I can give a definition of a plant?[82]

Again, to move from scepticism of an essential core meaning to scepticism of the possibility of understanding is to move illicitly from 'X-scepticism' to 'P-scepticism'.

III. Conclusion

By way of conclusion, I want to sound a warning about the relationship between the Wittgensteinian insights I have propounded and the critical project in which The Sceptic is engaged. It is tempting but would be facile to suggest that my argument, if accepted, shows that the entire critical project is based upon a profound mistake, and can therefore be ignored. In fact, this is only half wrong.

The arguments I have made attempt to show that The Sceptic's scepticism about language and rational argument is mistaken and that the mistake is the result of an illicit move which I characterized as the move from 'X-scepticism' to 'P-scepticism' in my schematic account of a sceptical argument. The Sceptic moves from rejection of "the enlightenment project" and its notions of abstract and absolute truth to a rejection of the possibility of objective rationality at all. This is a move from rejection of a particular *epistemological theory* to denial of the possibility of knowledge at all. Despair over the possibility of absolute, once and for all time, ahistorical "explanations" or "justifications" is based upon an incoherent concept of what an explanation or justification is, and therefore upon an incoherent account of the nature of objective rationality. Similarly, he seems to leap from scepticism about a particular *theory* of meaning to scepticism about the possibility of objective meaning at all.

But this only shows that The Sceptic is wrong to be a 'P-sceptic'. He is

---

82. Wittgenstein, *supra,* n. 1 at para. 70.

wrong, in other words, to think that language is radically "indeterminate" in the sense that he expounds—that any communication is open to any interpretation and that language is in that sense "up for political grabs". He is wrong to think that all theory is "political" (unless this is given a vacuous sense) and that all value decisions can be nothing more than an expression of personal preference, or majority preference.

But The Sceptic's 'X-scepticism' may be right. He is right in rejecting, if he does, a version of "rationalism" that thought that we could make *abstract* determinations of what "the good", "the beautiful" and "the real" are, which would themselves settle ethical, aesthetic and logical debates. He is right in rejecting, if he does, the possibility of objective practical (or legal) reasoning that is "algorithmic",—based upon some notion of a mechanical deductive process of following abstract rules. He is right in rejecting, if he does, a theory of meaning which makes the possibility of communication depend upon the existence of an "essential" or core meaning of words which is acontextual.

These insights are important in legal theory. Their significance is not, however, as The Sceptic thinks, that they show "objectivity" in legal reasoning to be impossible, but that they call into question a particular kind of *theoretical* justification of the *legitimacy* of adjudicative decision making. 'X-scepticism' creates problems for such theories of legitimacy, for once the theoretical picture (and it is only that) of adjudication as a deductive rule following process is discredited, then so too are those theories of legitimacy (which I associate with legal positivism) which rely upon that picture.

Critical scholars, however, are not the only ones to recognize this. It is the motivation, as well, behind the move toward interpretative theories of legal reasoning. If my versions of the Wittgensteinian arguments are correct, then The Sceptic and others cannot reject these theories out of hand, for, although they do not reflect 'P-scepticism', (they assume that objectivity is possible in language and in reason) they do accept 'X-scepticism' (and therefore reject "the Rationalist tradition", as The Sceptic has characterized it.) Therefore, the issue of whether they can give an account of adjudication upon which a theoretical justification for its legitimacy can be based is an issue on which the jury is still out, and a debate which cannot be avoided by the kind of arguments upon which The Sceptic relies.

The Sceptic relies upon radical scepticism to discredit all possible claims for the legitimacy of legal reasoning, for he believes that he has shown that it cannot be *in any sense* objective and is therefore indistinguishable from the bare exercise of personal political preference by a judge. This is 'P-scepticism' and it is unconvincing. But worse than that, it diverts The Sceptic from the true task to which he claims to be committed. The arguments for profound scepticism and linguistic indeterminacy are attempts to defeat all theoretical justifications for legitimacy at one blow by showing, *a priori*, that none *can* succeed. When this argument fails, as it does, the important arguments about legitimacy *remain to be made*. And The Sceptic, failing to perceive this, does not address them. Moreover, in light of his own sceptical conclusions, he *cannot* address them, for his scepticism precludes the rational debate which this would require. This is The Sceptic's dilemma.

7

No Easy Cases?

Andrei Marmor

Of all the various aspects of legal positivism, it is those bearing upon a theory of adjudication which have prompted its critics' fiercest attacks. Legal positivism is taken to be committed to the thesis that a distinction exists between (so called) 'easy' cases—where the law can be identified and applied straightforwardly—and 'hard' cases—where the issue is not determined by the existing legal standards. Most critics are united in their rejection of this dichotomy, but divided by the two main routes they follow. The more familiar one, first outlined by Professor R.M. Dworkin, sets out to deny that hard cases are not regulated by legal standards. The other objection, and the one I wish to consider here, strives to show that the distinction itself is illusory since in all relevant respects, there are no easy cases as the positivist presumes.

This essay forms an attempt to repudiate the latter argument. I shall begin by explaining and supporting the view that legal positivism is indeed committed to the distinction between easy and hard cases, while describing in what sense this is true. I will then proceed to defend the distinction against the various arguments which have been raised to undermine it.

1. A scarecrow called Formalism

Legal positivism does not constitute a single, unified doctrine. A wide range of diverse, and sometimes even conflicting, views about the nature of law belong to this jurisprudential school. These differences, however, do not affect our present discussion; even a rough formulation of some of the main tenets of legal positivism would suffice to show the distinction between easy and hard cases to be a thesis with which legal positivists cannot dispense.

The postulate that there must be easy cases derives from two interrelated theses held by legal positivists. The so called *social thesis,* formulated at its most abstract level, contends that the law is basically a matter of social fact. The *separation thesis,* by and large entailed by the former, insists upon the existence of a conceptual separation between the law as it is and the law as it ought to be. According to this view, determining what the law is—that is, identifying a given norm as a legal norm—does not depend upon moral or other evaluative considerations about what it ought to be in the circumstances. Surely, this entails that it must be possible to *identify* the law, and consequently to apply it, without recourse to considerations about what the law is there to settle. Otherwise, if it takes moral considerations about what the law is there to settle in order to be able to identify what the law is, law

---

I am indebted to Professor R. Dworkin and Professor J. Raz for their illuminating comments on a draft of this essay.

could no longer be construed as conceptually independent of morality. Nor could it be considered a matter of social fact; the identification of facts does not require reference to considerations about what those facts ought to be.[1]

The idea that law must comprise hard cases, also follows from the social thesis, though in a rather complex manner.[2] The topic of this essay renders it unnecessary to spell out these considerations in any detail. Suffice it to say that hard cases manifest the logical consequences of legal gaps. There is a gap in the law whenever the legal issue under consideration is not completely settled by the existing (i.e. identifiable) legal standards. In such cases, a judicial decision about the issue is a partly *creative* activity, involving considerations about what the law ought to be. If such a decision is followed as a precedent, new law is thus created.

The distinction between easy and hard cases suggests a particular view of the role of interpretation in adjudication. The concept of interpretation is typically meant to designate a (partly) creative activity. It has to do with determining the meaning of that which is in some relevant respect unclear or under-determined. Put somewhat loosely, one could say that interpretation adds something new, previously unrecognized, to that which is being interpreted. Thus, the distinction between easy and hard cases entails that legal positivism rejects the view that law is always subject to interpretation. In their interpretive activities, judges participate—to a greater or lesser extent—in the process of creating the law. first, however, there must be a law to interpret.[3]

Of course, the fact that the distinction between easy and hard cases is entailed, or rather required, by the separation thesis cannot be of much help in the present context. The argument offered by the line of criticism under discussion is that the latter should be rejected precisely because the former is indefensible. What we should ask then, is whether the distinction between easy and hard cases has any conceptual basis which is independent of the legal positivist doctrine. The most prominent attempt to propound such a foundation is Professor H.L.A. Hart's thesis of the distinction between the core and *penumbra* of concept-words, a distinction which he placed at the root of judicial reasoning. Consider this, by now very famous passage:

> A legal rule forbids you to take a vehicle into the public park. Plainly this forbids an automobile, but what about bicycles, roller skates, toy automobiles? What about aeroplanes? Are these, as we say, to be called 'vehicles' for the purposes of the rule or not? *If we are to communicate* with each other at all ....[and] behaviour be

1. The most recent, and to my mind illuminating, positivist account which shows the necessity of easy cases is to be found in Professor raz's analysis of the authoritative nature of law. He argues that the only way to acknowledge someone's authority over another is to take his directives to be a reason for action which replace the reasons on the basis of which the authority was meant to decide. Hence it must be possible for the alleged subjects of the authority to be able to identify the authoritative directives as such, without recourse to the condiserations on the basis of which he was meant to decide. See J. Raz, "Authority, Law, and Morality", (1985), 68 *Monist* 295. See also M. Moore, "Authority, Law, and Razian Reasons" (1989), 62 *Southern California Law Review* 827 (hereafter "Razian Reasons") at 890-893, where one of Moore's objections to the Razian analysis of law is based precisely on the point that it rests on the possibility of thre being easy cases. Moore's arguments are discussed in detail below.

2. Cf. J. Raz, *The Authority of Law*, (Oxford: Clarendon Press, 1979) (hereafter *The Authority of Law*) at 53-77.

3. As we shall see in detail below, the views which attempt to repudiate the distinction between easy and hard cases rest on the assumption that interpretation is always required to determine the applicability of a rule to a given set of facts.

regulated by rules, then the general words we use—like 'vehicle' in the case I consider— must have some standard instance in which no doubts are felt about its application. There must be a core of settled meaning, but there will be, as well, a penumbra of debatable cases in which words are neither obviously applicable nor obviously ruled out. [My emphasis][4]

This short passage epitomizes Hart's thinking on our present subject. Simple as it sounds however, it has been gravely misunderstood. This essay sets out to defend the view encapsulated in this passage, in two ways. first, I shall try to undermine the various criticisms put forward against it. Second, I hope to demonstrate that Hart's insight here is well entrenched in a highly sophisticated conception of meaning and language, namely, that of Wittgenstein.

The gist of Hart's thesis may be summed up as follows: The formulation of legal rules in a natural language makes their meanings depend, primarily, on the meanings of the concept-words used in these formulations. Since the meaning of a concept-word consists (inter alia) in its use, there must always be standard instances in which the application of the concept-word is unproblematic. This is what Hart calls the core of meaning. But most of the concept-words in our language do not have a determinate meaning, they are vague. Hence the application of concept-words to the facts will always involve some borderline cases, what he coins the penumbra, consisting in the absence of agreement in judgments as to the question whether the word applies or not.[5] In these cases, the fit between facts and concept-words is an issue which must be determined according to various non-linguistic considerations, like the presumed purpose of the rule, for example. But, and this is the controversial point, when the facts do fall under the core of the pertinent concept-words of the rule in question, the application of the rule is obvious and unproblematic, and this is what is meant in (the rather unfortunate) jurisprudential jargon by the term 'easy' case.

It is important to bear in mind, however, that the view presented here is very schematic; adjudication is of course much more complex a practice than Hart's simple example might be understood to suggest. The following are only a few examples: first, most of the rules confronting a judge are already, directly or indirectly "loaded", so to speak, with previous interpretations (e.g., in case similar rules have been construed in a certain way). Second, in instances requiring extraction of the rules from precedents, their formulation would typically be much more difficult to determine. Third, the individuation of legal rules often depends upon other legal rules or fragments of them (e.g. a rule determining the amount of income tax for a certain level of earnings must be supplemented by the rules defining 'income', 'tax', etc.).

Notwithstanding these complexities, and many others I haven't mentioned, it would be a mistake (or at least premature at this stage) to dismiss Hart's

---

4. H.L.A. Hart, "Positivism and the Separation of Law and Morals", in *Essays in Jurisprudence and Philosophy* (Oxford: Clarendon Press, 1983) 49-87 (hereafter "Positivism and Morals") at 63. (First published in (1958), 71 *Harvard Law Review* 593.)
5. It should be noted that the disagreements are irresolvable according to *linguistic* standards. There is nothing in the idea of vagueness to prevent agreement in judgments which is based on considerations not pertaining to the meaning of the concept-word in question.

distinction between easy and hard cases as overly simplistic. In particular, it would be misguided to suggest that Hart's thesis is necessarily inadequate as adjudication is not merely a matter of applying rules. firstly, it should be realized that Hart isn't offering a comprehensive theory of adjudication based on the distinction between easy and hard cases. The distinction is meant to illuminate one important aspect of judicial reasoning which, however, is by no means, the only one. Secondly, one can hardly deny that the application of rules is at least the core of judicial reasoning. No reasonable account of the latter could be provided, without an explication of what understanding, following and applying a rule consist in. It still remains to be seen whether complexities of various kinds cast any doubts on this basic model as it is suggested by Hart, but this should not prevent anyone from taking the basic model seriously, despite its apparent simplicity.

Before embarking on our main project though, that is examining Hart's thesis in detail, several somewhat crude misconstruals should be set aside. first, one cannot repeat too often the warning that the terms 'easy' and 'hard' cases are potentially misleading. The distinction has nothing to do at all with the amount of intellectual effort required to decide a legal case, nor is anything of the sort implied by this distinction. As Raz once pointed out, deciding an easy case in e.g. tax law (i.e., a case which is wholly determined by the legal standards) might be much more difficult than deciding many another hard case.[6] Nor is there any intended implication here that the application of the law in easy cases is in some way 'mechanical' or 'automatic', as is sometimes suggested. There is nothing mechanical about the application of a rule to a particular case, nor there is necessarily anything utterly complex or difficult about solving most of the hard cases. If any distinction were to be drawn between more and less 'mechanical' applications of rules, it would pertain to the complexity of the operations required by the rule, and not to the distinction between easy and hard cases, in the sense being use here.[7]

More importantly, the distinction between easy and hard cases (whether in legal positivism in general or in Hart's particular version of it) is sometimes associated with a philosophical scarecrow called judicial Formalism. The latter is taken to suggest that the application of rules is a matter of *logical inference* expressible in terms of analytical truths, while the positivist doctrine that there are easy cases is taken to endorse of some type of Formalism. Needless to say, Formalism is then easily undermined and the entire move is considered a serious critique of legal positivism.[8] The truth is that Formalism is so obviously false as to require some explanation why it would be associated with Hart's doctrine in the first place. It's easily discernible that whatever it is that connects a rule to its application cannot consist of logic or

---

6. J Raz, *The Authority of Law, supra* n. 2 at 182.
7. For example, think of the difference between carrying out an order to continue an arithmetical series, say n + 2, compared with a more complicated one, e.g. $13 + n^2 \times 0.5$, both of which would be 'easy' cases.
8. See: M. Moore "The Semantics of Judging" (1981), 54 *Southern California Law Review*, 151 (hereafter "The Semantics of Judging") at 155-163.

analyticity.[9] The move is even more perplexing when we recall that it was Hart himself who repeatedly exposed this fallacy of Formalism.[10]

To pinpoint what seems to lie at the source of this confusion, consider Hart's example once again. A legal rule forbids the entrance of vehicles into the public park; Hart's contention that 'plainly this forbids an automobile' is understood to be a statement made *true by its very meaning,* hence an analytical truth. Given this construal, the view that in easy cases the legal conclusion is logically deduced from certain premises, i.e., rule formulations and statements expressing the classification of the pertinent particulars, would seem easily attributable to Hart. But in fact the whole picture here is confused.

The concepts of logical inference and analyticity apply only to the interrelations between rules or expressions, not to their application to the world, as it were. As Hart put it, "logic is silent on how to classify particulars"[11] but it is precisely this classification to which his distinction between core and penumbra pertains. In other words, we must keep separate, what might be called, rule-rule, and rule-world, relations; logic and analyticity pertain only to the former, but not the latter kind of relations. The fact that in both cases the criteria for correct use are semantic, should not obscure this crucial difference. Suppose someone is pointing at a red object in front of him, saying 'This is red'. When asked to justify this assertion, one can only appeal to the *meaning* of 'red'; one would say that this is what 'red' means, thus appealing to *a rule* about how a word is used in English. But surely, it makes no sense at all to say that we have a logical inference here, or that the ostension expresses an analytical statement. (This is unlike the statement "bachelor = unmarried man" which does not concern the application of rules (or expressions), but the semantical relation between them.)

In short, Formalism is a scarecrow; neither Hart nor any other legal positivist must subscribe to the view that the application of legal rules is a matter of logical inference. This is not to say that Hart's distinction between easy and hard cases is unproblematic, but only that one should concentrate on the serious worries, and that Formalism is not one of them.

2. The Hart-Fuller debate.

Professor Fuller's objections to the Hartian distinction between easy and hard cases may still constitute the most elaborate criticism of this thesis, one deserving of a close examination. According to Fuller,[12] Hart's thesis is based on three assumptions, of which he accepts none. first, Hart maintains the

---

9. This should not be confused with a different thesis, namely, that the law of universal instantiation ((x)Fx infer Fa) ultimately mediates between the rule and its application. For a rejection of this idea see Baker & Hacker, *Wittgenstein: Rules, Grammar and Necessity,* (Oxford: Blackwell, 1985) (hereafter *Rules, Grammar and Necessity* at 92-93.

10. Positivism and Morals, *supra* n. 4, at 67; see also H.L.A. Hart, "Problems of the Philosophy of Law" in *Essays in Jurisprudence and Philosophy, supra* n. 4, at 88-119, 100-106. (First published in Edwards (ed.) *Encyclopedia of Philosophy* vol. 6 at 264-276)

11. "Positivism and Morals", *supra* n. 4, at 67.

12. L. Fuller, "Positivism and Fidelity to Law—A Reply to Professor Hart" (1958), 71 *Harvard Law Review,* 630, (hereafter "A Reply to Hart") at 661ff.

view that the interpretation of a legal rule is a matter of interpreting the con-cept-words it deploys. Second, that the interpretation of concept-words in legal rules is (or ought to be) determined by the ordinary use of these terms in natural language. Hart's third alleged assumption, possibly taken to be entailed by the previous two points, is that the meaning of concept-words is not sensitive to the particular legal context in which these words are meant to function.

Fuller's main criticism, then, is aimed against these three assumptions. But he also attributes to Hart the view that unless these assumptions are maintained, "we must surrender all hope of giving an effective meaning to the ideal of fidelity to law."[13] Fuller accordingly attempts to add another level of criticism in showing that the ideal of fidelity to law is not jeopardized by a rejection of the allegedly Hartian position.

Let us take a closer look at the details of Fuller's account. Hart's first alleged assumption, that the interpretation of a legal rule is purely a matter of determining the concept-words it deploys, forms the target of Fuller's most vigorous attack:

> The most obvious defect of his theory lies in its assumption that problems of inter-pretation typically turn on the meaning of individual words.

> If the rule excluding vehicles from parks seems easy to apply in some cases, I sub-mit this is because we can see clearly enough what the rule "is aiming at in general" so that we know there is no need to worry about the difference between Fords and Cadillacs.[14]

By way of demonstration, Fuller asks us to consider whether the rule exclud-ing vehicles from the park would apply to a group of local patriots who want to mount a truck used in World War two on a pedestal in the park as a memo-rial. "Does this' truck, in perfect working order, fall within the core or the penumbra?" he then asks.[15] Now the point here is actually twofold: first, that understanding a rule is always a matter of determining its *purpose*, and that it is only in the light of this purposive interpretation that one can judge the rule's application to the facts of a given case to be relatively easy or difficult. Second, since the purpose of a rule can only be determined in view of con-siderations as to what the rule is there to settle, 'it is in the light of this "ought" that we must decide what the rule "is".'[16]

The basis for the criticism of Hart's second alleged assumption is some-what more obscure, partly because it is not fully stated. Instead, we are left with a vague disavowal of 'common usage' as the basis for the analysis of meaning, something which is thought to ignore or underestimate the "speak-er's purpose and the structure of language".[17] In all, this is meant to imply that Hart's concept of interpretation is based on an inadequate theory of

---

13. *Id.* at 664.
14. *Id.*, at 661-663.
15. *Id.*, at 663.
16. *Id.*, at 666.
17. *Id.*, at 669.

meaning. Since Fuller does not discuss the kind of theory of meaning Hart supposedly relied upon, nor does he elaborate on the grounds for its inadequacy, one is left somewhat in the lurch. In any case, the question whether Hart's thesis is based on a particular conception of meaning, and to what extent, is an interesting one in its own right, and I shall discuss it in the sequel.

Hart's third alleged assumption as Fuller outlines it, and accordingly Fuller's objection to it, in fact, amount to a misunderstanding. The idea that concept-words used in the formulation of legal rules ought to be interpreted so as to assign them the same meaning in each and every occurrence, irrespective of the particular context in which the rule functions, is one which quite obviously ought to be dismissed outright. There is no reason to contend that the word 'vehicle', for instance, should be assigned exactly the same meaning in the rule forbidding the entrance of vehicles in the park, and, e.g., a rule concerning the insurance of vehicles. But the real question is, whether Hart is committed to maintain the contrary. The answer to this, I think, is quite obviously "No!" To begin with, Hart can only be taken to be committed to the view that the *core* of concept-words, as opposed to their penumbra, remains constant across different rules. Thus, he would say that, e.g., an ordinary automobile must be taken as a standard example of 'vehicle' if anything is, so that any rule concerning 'vehicles' must be taken to apply *inter alia* to ordinary automobiles. Conversely, it is quite clear that he would not hold this true with respect to the question whether bicycles are also 'vehicles' for the purposes of different rules. But even this point, (which Fuller seems to ignore) should not be overstated. Hart was very much aware of the fact that numerous concepts are 'family resemblance' concepts, in which case even their core, i.e., standard examples, might vary from case to case. (This point shall be explained in greater detail below.)

Furthermore, there is no need to deny that in some unusual circumstances a judge might face the possibility that applying a rule to a given case in keeping with the core of the pertinent concept-word would lead to unacceptable results, and hence decide, for example, that even an ordinary automobile was not a 'vehicle' for the purposes of the rule at hand. The question is whether in this case the judge can be properly said to have *applied* the rule or not, and this clearly depends on the soundness of the point which is raised by Fuller's first objection (and perhaps also the second). We are thus left with Fuller's first two objections, and I shall begin by considering the second.

Recall that what we are faced with is the question whether Hart's distinction between core and penumbra commits him to any particular theory of meaning, and to what extent. It is a biographical fact, based on Hart's own account,[18] that he has been greatly influenced by various philosophers of language, particularly Wittgenstein and J.L. Austin. But I would suggest that as someone who has learnt from (the later) Wittgenstein, Hart would have avoided any attempt to construct, what is usually called, a *theory* of meaning for a natural language. Pointing out the futility and the misconceptions which

---

18. See the introduction to his *Essays in Jurisprudence and Philosophy, supra,* n. 4.

would be involved in such a project is one of the main insights of Wittgenstein's later work,[19] and there is no evidence to suggest that Hart has ever dissented on this point. On the contrary, Hart seems to share Wittgenstein's view that an adequate account of meaning and language must not obscure the fact that the meaning of our concepts is completely overt and manifest in their use. In other words, as long as the idea of a theory of meaning is understood in its contemporary sense (e.g. Davidson's), namely, as a quasi-scientific explanation of meaning, it should not be assumed that Hart had any such theory in mind.

Wittgenstein's impact is, however, most evident in Hart's treatment of the indeterminacy of sense, which is at the root of his distinction between core and penumbra. Hart is usually understood to have adopted Wittgenstein's view's here, and it might be instructive to trace some of these ideas back to their source. The requirement that sense be determinate was propounded by Frege (and the early Wittgenstein), and preoccupied him for various theoretical reasons. In general, he thought an ideally scientific language would have to be one in which all expressions had a determinant sense. By the latter he meant the following: A word/sentence would have determinate sense if and only if about every possible object there is a definite answer to the question whether it is within the extension (or reference) of the word/sentence or not. It is worth mentioning that Frege did not consider this requirement to be satisfied in our natural languages. On the contrary: he saw natural language as hopelessly contaminated by vagueness.[20]

The later Wittgenstein not only discarded this Fregeian version of the requirement for the determinacy of sense but was even anxious to show that the requirement itself made no sense whatsoever. It is only if one presumes that there is more to the meaning of an expression than what is perspicuous in the practices of using it and explaining its meaning, that it would make sense to impose this requirement on any language, be it natural or scientific.[21] However, as this presumption is utterly mistaken—as Wittgenstein strove to demonstrate throughout the *Philosophical Investigations*[22]—he came to realize that Frege's notion of the determinacy of sense is intrinsically incoherent.

Does this mean that all the words in our language are vague? That of course depends on what we mean by 'vague'. If the latter is taken to mean that sense is indeterminate (i.e. in the Fregeian sense), then properly speaking, the answer should be "No!" As Baker and Hacker put it "if there is no such thing as determinacy of sense, there is no such thing as absence of it."[23] This, however, should not be taken to mean that no meaningful content can be

19. Cf. P.M.S. Hacker, *Insight and Illusion*, (revised ed.) (Oxford: Clarendon, 1986), (hereafter *Insight and Illusion*) ch. 6. See also C. McGinn, *Wittgenstein On Meaning*, (Oxford: Blackwell, 1984), (hereafter *Wittgenstein On Meaning*) at 29.
20. See M. Dummett, *The Interpretation of Frege's Philosophy* (London: Duckworth, 1981), at 31-35, 48, 316, 440.
21. See G. Baker & P.M.S. Hacker, *Wittgenstein: Meaning and Understanding—Essays on the Philosophical Investigations* (Oxford: Blackwell, 1980) (hereafter *Meaning and Understanding*) at 225.
22. L. Wittgenstein, *Philosophical Investigations*, trans. by G.E.M. Anscombe (Oxford: Blackwell, 1958), 2nd ed., (hereafter *Philosophical Investigations*).
23. *Id.*, at 225.

given to the idea of vagueness. If we understand vagueness to mean that in the practice of applying a word there are irresolvable disagreements in judgment over certain areas of its application, then it is obviously true that most concept-words are vague. Yet in order to be more accurate, vagueness should be distinguished from 'open texture' and 'family resemblance'. The former term (coined by Waismann[24]) is meant to designate the *possibility* of vagueness. Even terms which are not vague, are potentially so, since one can always imagine circumstances where there would be irresolvable disagreements in judgments as to the word's applicability. That Wittgenstein would subscribe to the view that most of the words in our language are at least possibly vague is quite undisputable,[25] yet one would be on safe grounds in presuming that he would not have attached a great significance to this fact: "The sign-post is in order—if, under normal circumstances, it fulfills its purpose".[26]

More importantly, vagueness should be distinguished from 'family resemblance'. The latter designates a concept-word which is applied to various phenomena where "these phenomena have no one thing in common which makes us use the same word for all."[27] Instead, these phenomena are linked to each other by numerous and complex *similarities,* which Wittgenstein illustrates by the famous metaphor of 'family resemblance'. And it is only due to these similarities that distinct phenomena are called by the same concept word.[28] The idea that our language comprises 'family resemblance' concepts is perhaps one of Wittgenstein's least controversial contributions to philosophy of language, and there is no need to expand on it here. What we do have to address here, however, is the question whether the distinction between vagueness and 'family resemblance' has any bearing on Hart's thesis.

On the one hand, we can see that there is this difference: In the case of vagueness, the standard examples would share something which makes us use the same word for them all, whereas in the case of 'family resemblance' we would face multifarious standard instances which do not share any single defining feature. This of course, makes the distinction between core and penumbra more intricate in the latter case. On the other hand, Hart's thesis remains basically untouched by this difference. Any concept-word, whether vague or one of 'family resemblance', must have standard examples which manifest agreement in judgments about its applicability. Although no single defining feature shared by all the standard examples can be specified in the latter case, this does not mean that they are not standard examples. Suppose we cannot find any one feature due to which we call chess, football and patience, all 'games'; does this mean that any of them is not a standard exam-

---

24. This is not to imply that Wittgenstein would subscribe to Waismann's analysis of 'open texture'. See G. Baker & P.M.S. Hacker, *An Analytical Commentary On Wittgenstein's Philosophical Investigations* (Oxford: Blackwell, 1980), (hereafter "*Analytical Commentary*") at 170.
25. *Philosophical Investigations,supra* n. 22, s. 187.
26. *Id.,* s. 87.
27. *Id.,* s. 65.
28. *Id.,* s. 67. To be sure, it is not maintained by Wittgenstein that the instances of family resemblance concepts do not have any features in common to them all; but only that these are not *defining* features, namely, that it is not due to these features that we call these instances by the same concept-word. All games, for instance, might share the feature that they involve the activities of human beings; but this is not why we call, e.g., football, patience, and chess, 'games'.

ple of 'game'? Clearly not; on the contrary, this only shows the crucial importance of the idea that a great deal of agreement must exist as to what the
standard examples of our concept-words are. In the absence of such agreement, the successful employment of 'family resemblance' concepts would
have remained a total mystery.

Thus we can see that vagueness, open texture and 'family resemblance', all
support the thesis that the concept-words we employ must have a core of
meaning, i.e., standard examples which manifest agreement in judgments
about the word's applicability. These standard examples are used in our
every-day explanations of what words mean, and we often have no better
explanation of the meaning of a word than pointing at its standard examples.
Furthermore, standard examples provide the *criteria* for correct understanding
of expressions in our language. Under normal circumstances, someone who
denies the applicability of a word to its standard examples manifests that he
hasn't mastered its use. And vice versa: since understanding the meaning of
an expression consists in one's ability to use (and explain) it correctly, the
ability to specify the standard instances of its applicability can usually be
taken to manifest that one has understood the meaning of the expression.

Notably, at some point Fuller seems to be challenging the picture of meaning depicted here. As an example, he takes the word 'improvement' in the
sentence "All improvements ought to be promptly reported ...." which he
claims 'is almost as devoid of meaning as the symbol "X".'[29] He then goes on
to demonstrate the disambiguation of 'improvement' in this sentence according to various assumptions about communication intentions and context, with
a particular emphasis on the purpose of the pertinent rule. All this is taken to
demonstrate something like a profound context dependence of meaning in
general.[30]

Fuller's discussion here is rather confused though. If a word is 'almost as
devoid of meaning as the symbol "X"', then it cannot be disambiguated.
Disambiguation can only take place when an expression has several possible
meanings, not when it is devoid of meaning. In other words, either a word has
meaning, in which case it can be used, and hence it must also have standard
examples, or it is devoid of meaning, in which case it simply cannot be used.
Words can be more or less vague, but not more or less without meaning at all.
What Fuller's example would seem to demonstrate, then, is that the word
improvement is perhaps a 'family resemblance' concept and hence has multifarious standard examples. This in itself, as we have seen, has no bearing
whatsoever on Hart's thesis.

3. The argument from defeasibility.

Let us return to Fuller's first and most important objection to Hart's thesis.
As we have seen, he claims that Hart's thesis is intelligible only against the
assumption that the interpretation of a legal rule is a matter of determining the

---

29. L. Fuller, "A Reply to Hart", *supra* n. 12 at 665.
30. *Id.*, at 667-668.

concept-words it deploys, an assumption to which he objects forcefully. Fuller's objection comprises two main theses: first, that understanding a rule must always involve an understanding of its particular purposes. Second, and as a consequence of the fact that determining the purpose of a rule typically involves considerations about what the rule is there to settle, "it is in the light of this ought that we must decide what the rule is."[31]

In the following, I shall concentrate on Fuller's first thesis, assuming that the second is relatively sound. My purpose is to show that understanding a rule does not necessarily require a grasp of its purpose, and if I am right in this, Fuller's second thesis would be rendered harmless anyway.

One of the prominent arguments thought to support Fuller's thesis is, what might be called, the argument from defeasibility.[32] The argument runs as follows: Since it is the case that any legal rule—if construed literally—might, under certain circumstances, have utterly immoral or otherwise absurd results, a judge must always ask himself whether the case before him is one in which the results would be unacceptable if the rule were thus applied. The fact that the answer is often obvious, so the argument continues, does not mean that the question need not always be asked and answered. Thus the application of a legal rule to any set of facts necessitates that the judge consider the purpose of the rule and ask himself whether the purposes at play would not be defeated were the rule to be construed literally. This, in turn, is taken to entail that it never makes sense to speak of a straightforward, or literal, application of a rule, as Hart's thesis entails.[33]

There are several confusions here which ought to be unraveled. On an immediate reflection, the argument is rather puzzling: it seems to hold that since any rule—if construed literally—*can* result in absurd consequences, no rule can be construed literally, which is an obvious fallacy. Thus, if the argument from defeasibility is to make any sense at all, its conclusion must be revised: the argument should be taken to lead to a prescriptive conclusion as to what judges ought to do. This, in fact, is just how Moore understands (and subscribes to) Fuller's argument; Fuller's best argument, he says, "is a normative one urging judges to *disregard* that meaning when it does not fit into their notion of the rule's purpose."[34] Understood in view of such a prescriptive conclusion, the argument would be stated as follows: Since any rule—if construed literally—can lead to absurd consequences, a judge should always ask himself whether this danger is present, and when it is, decide according to standards which would avert the iniquity.

---

31. *Id.*, at 666.
32. The term should not be thought to imply that the argument to be explored here dwells on Hart's own ideas expressed in his inaugural lecture (reprinted in his *Essays in Jurisprudence and Philosophy, supra* n. 4 at 21-48). There he suggested that there is a kind of defeasibility endemic in legal language which renders it *sui generis*, a view which he seems to have abandoned shortly afterwards. See G. Baker, "Defeasibility and Meaning", in Hacker & Raz (eds.) *Law, Morality and Society*, (Oxford: Clarendon Press, 1977) at 26-57. (As opposed to Baker though, I do not find this thesis being restated in H.L.A. Hart, *The Concept of Law*.)
33. See M. Moore, "The Semantics of Judging", *supra* n. 8 at 277-279; see also his "Razian Reasons", at 890-893, where the same objection is raised against Raz's analysis of law.
34. M. Moore, "The Semantics of Judging", *supra* n. 8 at 227.

But if the argument is understood in this way, it cuts no ice in the dispute with Hart (or with any other legal positivist for that matter). Moore's version of the argument confuses the question of what *following a rule consists in* (which interested Hart), with that of *whether a rule should be applied in the circumstances*. Even if we concede that judges should always ask themselves the latter question (which is far from clear), it does not follow that rules cannot be understood, and then applied, without reference to their alleged purposes or any other considerations about what the rule is there to settle.

Let me expound this point, since it is of crucial importance. It should be remembered that our discussion commenced with the positivist doctrine of the separation between law as it is and law as it ought to be. We have seen that for this thesis to be acceptable, it must be accompanied by the assumption that judges can *identify* the law, and apply it, without reference to considerations about what the law ought to be in the circumstances. Clearly, whether this latter assumption is warranted or not, depends on considerations about what understanding and following a rule consist in. In particular, it turns upon the question whether there is a sense in which following or applying a rule does not consist in, or is not mediated by, an interpretation of the rule. Now one can see that the argument from defeasibility, construed as Moore understands it, tackles a different question altogether: Namely, whether the rule *should* be applied (or not) in the circumstances. Needless to say, the answer to this normative question is bound to be affected by the moral contents of the particular law and legal system in question. But this is something which neither Hart nor Raz have any reason to deny.

Perhaps Moore would reply that I have missed an important point in his argument, namely, that from the outset, his objection to the Hartian thesis is based not on conceptual, but rather on moral considerations. But this would put him on safer ground, only on the basis of the assumption that Hart's thesis makes a moral difference in the first place, which is far from clear. Moore's assumption that it does, seems to be drawn from the view which he attributes to Hart, that legal cases *should* be decided "on the basis of linguistic intuition alone".[35] Yet this is just another confusion. Hart's commitment to what follows from linguistic or conceptual analysis alone carries him only so far as to ground a conceptual distinction between easy and hard cases. It does not extend beyond that, to the question of how judges ought to decide various cases i.e. from a moral point of view. In other words, an easy case is not one in which, *ipso facto* a judge should, as a matter of moral duty, apply the rule in question.

Perhaps Moore was misled here by the argument which Fuller attributes to Hart, namely, that the latter's thesis is motivated by considerations about the "ideal of fidelity to law".[36] But this is a rather puzzling point. To begin with, it should be noticed that Hart himself doesn't propound any such argument explicitly, either in the article which is the subject of Fuller's review, or, to the best of my knowledge, in any other place. Nor does such a position fit his

---

35. M. Moore, "The Semantics of Judging", *supra* n. 8 at 277.
36. Fuller, "A Reply to Hart", *supra* n. 12 at 664.

general line of thought: Has Hart ever thought that fidelity to law is an *ideal*? Is it at all reasonable to suppose that one so clearly concerned with the conceptual separation between law as it is and law as it ought to be, would ground his descriptive conception of law on the basis of considerations about 'the ideal of fidelity to law'? Wouldn't that be too obvious a fallacy?[37]

In short, the argument from defeasibility—construed as a moral objection to Hart's thesis—doesn't seem to hit the right target. On the other hand, it is not clear whether Fuller meant his argument to be understood along the lines suggested by Moore. I would suggest that Fuller's most interesting objection to the Hartian thesis is meant to be a conceptual one, based on considerations about what understanding a legal rule consists in. Basically, Fuller seems to maintain that understanding a rule always consists of (*inter alia*) a grasp of its purpose. If this view is conceptually sound, it would amount to a serious objection to the Hartian thesis, one which would repudiate it on its own terms. Furthermore, if we add to this the assumption that typically, determining the purpose of a rule involves interpretive hypothesis about what the rule is there to settle, not only Hart's distinction between easy and hard cases would be repudiated, but also the separation thesis distinguishing the law as it is from the law as it ought to be. Thus, a careful examination of Fuller's suggestion is of great importance.

4. Wittgenstein on following a rule

The question we should consider now is the following: Does it make sense to claim that one can understand a rule only in view of the purposes it is taken to advance? Note that this is not the same question as whether all interpretation is (or should be) purposive, as it were. The reason is straightforward enough: A negative answer to the former question might be based precisely on the point that understanding, and following, a rule does not consist in, and is not mediated by, imposing an interpretation upon it.

I have argued elsewhere[38] that the notions of understanding e.g. an utterance, and interpreting it, should not be used interchangeably, and I cannot repeat the argument here. However, it might be thought that even if this is generally conceded, it still remains an open question whether one can be said to be acting in accord with a rule, without the rule being thus interpreted. The idea that interpretation is always required in order to determine which acts are in accord with a rule (and hence also which acts go against it), seems supported by the idea that rules, as such, are indeterminate. Indeed, no sense can be given to the idea that a rule contains its own application, as it were. Hence, there seems to be a gap between a rule—which constitutes a sign—

---

37. At some point, Fuller seems to be aware of these difficulties, when he suggests the following diagnostic observation: "I believe we can say that the dominant tone of positivism is set by a fear of a purposive interpretation of law and legal institutions, or at least by a fear that such an interpretation may be pushed too far. *id.*, at 669. But since nothing of the sort has been suggested by Hart, one is bewildered about the source of this diagnosis, let alone, its accuracy.

38. *Interpretation in Legal Theory*, D. Phil. Thesis submitted to the University of Oxford, Hilary term 1989/90, ch.2. See also: P.M.S. Hacker, "Language, Rules, and Pseudo-Rules" (1989), 8 *Language and Communication* 159 (hereafter "Rules and Pseudo-Rules").

and its application—which is an action—a gap which can only be bridged by interpretation.

Repudiating this idea (along with the various misconceptions involved in it) was one of Wittgenstein's main concerns in his rather extensive discussion of following rules in the *Philosophical Investigations* sect. 143-242. Needless to say, a full account of Wittgenstein's discussion of following a rule would be far beyond the scope of this essay (or of my competence, for that matter). Instead, I shall try to summarize those of his arguments which have a direct bearing on our present concerns.

Wittgenstein's concern with what following a rule consists in derives from his conception of meaning: Knowing the meaning of an expression is not an inner state of mind, but rather an ability (or an array of abilities) to use the expression in accordance with the rules of the language, and the ability to explain the meaning of the expression (e.g. by an ostensive definition). Hence, the relation of the meaning of an expression to its use(s) is a particular instance of the relation of a rule to its application.[39]

Let us begin with the clarification of two general points. first, as has already been mentioned, one of Wittgenstein's most important observations about language is that the meaning of expressions in language are perspicuous throughout. Using language is a rule governed activity, like a game, hence the rules in question are normative, and like all normative rules, they explicitly guide actions, serve as standards of evaluation, play an explanatory role in making actions intelligible, fulfill a crucial role in instructing learners how to engage in the pertinent activity, etc.. The moral to be drawn from this is, that rules must be perspicuous, i.e. that it doesn't make sense to speak of 'hidden rules', or rules that can be *discovered* only through scientific or quasi-scientific exploration.[40]

Furthermore, the rules constituting a language-game should be clearly distinguished from the background state of affairs in which there is a point of having such rules, and against which they are intelligible.[41] Every rule guided activity presupposes a particular background which is not part of the activity itself but makes it possible and relevant. The game of tennis, for instance, is made possible only against the background of the laws of gravitation, the fact that we are normally capable of telling whether a ball has fallen inside or outside the marked lines, the fact that the desire to win a game fits the human predicament, etc. All this is part of the background against which there is a point to having the game. Yet under normal circumstances none of these points would be cited as being part of the rules constituting the game. Furthermore, as Wittgenstein pointed out, although we can envisage things being otherwise,

39. Cf. G. Backer & P.M.S. Hacker, *Rules, Grammar and Necessity, supra* n. 9 at84.
40. See P.M.S. Hacker, "Rules and Pseudo-Rules", *supra* n. 38 at 162-165; see also C. McGinn, *Wittgenstein On Meaning*, at 119.
41. Cf. G. Baker & P.M.S. Hacker, *Rules, Grammar and Necessity, supra* n. 9, ch. 5; see also: D. Pears, *The False Prison—A Study of the Development of Wittgenstein's Philosophy*, vol. 2 (Oxford: Clarendon Press, 1988), (hereafter *The False Prison*) at 425.

the more abnormal the case, the more doubtful it becomes what we are to say. And if things were quite different from what they actually are .... this would make our normal language-games lose their point.[42]

The distinction is relevant here for the following reason: Had Fuller's thesis been confined to the contention that rules in general, or legal rules in particular, are made intelligible only against the background of *(inter alia)* certain purposes which they can be taken to advance—that is, in the sense of background as outlined above—it would have been a sound observation. But in the present context, it would have been quite innocuous as well. The distinction between easy and hard cases as maintained by legal positivism concerns the question of what following a rule consists in, not the question what makes it possible to follow the rules of this game rather than another.[43]

The second point, which is perhaps the key to the whole discussion, is that Wittgenstein conceived of the relation between a rule and its application as a grammatical one, i.e. one which is internal to language: To understand a rule is to be able to specify which actions are in accord with it (and hence which would go against it), just as to understand a proposition is to be able to specify its truth conditions. In other words, it simply doesn't make sense to say that one has understood a rule and yet he doesn't know the actions which are in accord with it.[44] This should be clarified in more detail.

Wittgenstein begins his discussion of following a rule with putting forward the idea of the indeterminacy of rules. He asks us to consider the following example: A pupil is ordered to continue an arithmetical series, say from 1000 on, according to the rule n + 2; he then writes 1000, 1002, 1004, 1008...; two main questions are exemplified here: first, any rule, it seems, can be misinterpreted, and it is not clear what this misinterpretation consists in.[45]

Second, the actions in accord with a rule seem to be under-determined by the rule's formulation: whatever one does can be brought into accord with the rule on some interpretation of it. Both contentions, however, manifest profound misunderstandings. Thus, consider *Philosophical Investigations,* sect. 198:

"But how can a rule shew me what I have to do at this point? Whatever I do is, on some interpretation, in accord with the rule." This is not what we ought to say, but rather: any interpretation still hangs in the air along with what it interprets, and cannot give it any support. Interpretations by themselves do not determine meaning.

---

42. *Philosophical Investigations,supra* n. 22, s. 142.
43. It is possible that many of Fuller's arguments in his book *The Morality of Law,* (New Haven: Yale University Press, 1969), New Haven) concerning the "inner morality of law" as he calls it, can be accounted for along the lines suggested here; if so, it also suggests that, contrary to appearance, many of his theses are in fact reconcilable with legal positivism. But of course, this is a large topic which exceeds the interests of this essay.
44. G. Baker & P.M.S. Hacker, *Rules, Grammar and Necessity, supra* at 91; see also D. Pears, *The False Prison,* at 468.
45. The following discussion will not dwell on Wittgenstein's alleged rule skepticism as it struck Kripke. (see his *Wittgenstein on Rules and Private Language,* (Oxford: Basil Blackwell, 1982) Kripke's interpretation of Wittgenstein has been repeatedly (and cogently) criticized by numerous writers. See for example G. Baker & P.M.S. Hacker, *Skepticism, Rules and Language,* (Oxford: Basil Blackwell, 1984), (hereafter *Skepticism, Rules and Language*). See also C. McGinn, *Wittgenstein On Meaning.*

And the same point in sect. 201:

> It can be seen that there is a misunderstanding here from the mere fact that in the course of our argument we give one interpretation after another; as if each one contended us for a moment, until we thought of yet another standing behind it. What this shows is that there is a way of grasping a rule which is *not* an *interpretation*, but which is exhibited in what we call "obeying a rule" and "going against it" in actual cases.

This is the crucial point: *If a rule could not determine which actions were in accord with it, then no interpretation could do this either.* Interpretation is just another formulation of the rule, substituting one rule with another, as it were. Hence it cannot bridge the gap between a rule and an action. A rule, in other words, is a sign, and its meaning cannot be determined by another sign; the meanings of rules, like that of all symbols, must be determined by the actions themselves, that is, by the way they are *used*. Hence also, understanding a rule consists in one's ability to specify what actions are in accord with the rule, which is not an interpretation of the rule, but is exhibited by "obeying the rule" and "going against it", i.e., in practice. Consider how sect. 198 continues:

> "Then can whatever I do be brought into accord with the rule?"—Let me ask this: what has the expression of the rule—say a sign-post—got to do with my actions? What sort of connexion is there here?—Well, perhaps this one: I have been trained to react to this sign in a particular way, and now I do so react to it.
> But that is only to give a causal connexion; to tell how it has come about that we now go by the sign-post; not what this going-by-the-sign really consists in. On the contrary; I have further indicated that a person goes by a sign post only in so far as there exists a regular use of sign-posts, a custom.

This completes the previous point. If the meaning of rules and signs is determined by their use, one might surmise that any action can be made to be in accord with the rule. In other words, one still remains puzzled as to how rules can determine the actions in accord with them, if it is the actions which determine the meaning of the rule. But of course, there is a normative connection between rules and actions,[46] which consists in the fact that there is a custom of using the sign or rule thus and so, and not otherwise. Which is to say that learning how to follow a rule is learning to master a technique.[47] Yet Wittgenstein is careful to warn us against a potential misunderstanding: It might be thought that instead of explaining what following a rule consists in, he has provided a kind of causal or psychological explanation of how, for example, one learns to follow a rule. But this, of course, is not the point. Something *is* a sign-post only in so far as there exists a regular use of that sign for particular purposes, and it is this regularity of use which provides the meaning of the sign.

---

46. Contra Kripke, Wittgenstein does not take a skeptical standpoint here: "if everything can be made out to accord with a rule, then it can also made out to conflict with it. And so there would be neither accord nor conflict here." *Philosophical Investigations, supra* s. 201. This is evidently absurd not a skeptical standpoint which has to be taken seriously, *supra* n. 45.
47. *Philosophical Investigations, supra* n. 22 s. 199.

Wittgenstein's contention that the use of rules consists in there being a custom is potentially misleading. One is inclined to think that 'custom' is meant to indicate the necessity of a community of users, a social practice. But, as Baker and Hacker made clear, this is wrong: Wittgenstein's emphasis here is on the multiplicity of the occasions of use, not on the multiplicity of users. As they put it, "The contrast here is not between and aria and a chorus, but between looking at a score and singing."[48]

A further possibility of misunderstanding might arise from the idea that the meaning of rules is determined by their use:

> Hence there is an inclination to say: every action according to the rule is an inter-pretation. But we ought to restrict the term "interpretation" to the substitution of one expression of the rule for another.[49]

Suppose one concedes Wittgenstein's analysis so far, but still wishes to insist that every action according to a rule involves interpretation. Now, one cannot say that the action is *mediated* by interpretation, since, as we have seen, the gap between a rule and its application cannot be bridged by another formulation of the rule. But perhaps one could say that although interpretation does not mediate between rules and actions, still acting according to the rule *is* an interpretation of the rule. But this would be misleading since in one sense it is vacuous, and in another wrong. It is vacuous if by "interpreting" we simply mean "this is how he understood the rule", and thus we can also say that he has misunderstood the rule. However, if "interpretation" is taken to mean something which amounts yet to another formulation of the rule, then of course it would be wrong: Acting according to the rule does not constitute another formulation of it, but rather exhibits that one has understood the rule correctly.

But here one might think of counter examples: Doesn't a performance of a symphony, for instance, amount to an interpretation of it? On the face of it, Wittgenstein's proposal of limiting the term interpretation to the substitu-tion of one expression of the rule with another is too restrictive, as it were. This would be a misunderstanding, however, since Wittgenstein need not deny that there are occasions in which actions manifest a certain interpreta-tion of a rule. It would, however, be wrong to suggest that *every* instance of following a rule is an interpretation of it, which would be irreconcilable with the normative aspect of rules and rule following. To interpret a symphony, whether by its performance in a certain way or otherwise, one must first have a pretty good idea of what the scores mean.

The idea that all rules must be subject to interpretation might still be thought to be essential, if we connect Wittgenstein's discussion of vague-ness, with his own conception of what understanding a rule consists in. The idea here would run as follows. Rules formulated in our language, such as

---

48. G. Baker & P.M.S. Hacker, *Skepticism, Rules and Language, supra* n. 45 at 20; see also D. Pears, *The False Prison, supra* n. 41 at 500.
49. *Philosophical Investigations, supra* n. 22 s. 201.

legal rules[50], are bound to employ general concept-words with various degrees of vagueness; yet if we concede Wittgenstein's point that understanding a rule consists in one's ability to specify which actions are in accord with the rule, we are led to the conclusion that we can never have a complete grasp of a rule. Our understanding of rules will always be deficient, as there will always be instances as to which one cannot tell whether the rule applies or not. Hence to allow for a complete understanding of rules, so the argument continues, we must also admit that every rule is bound to be interpreted.

The answer to this is that the quest for completeness is misguided here. It is one of the most important observations in Wittgenstein's discussion about the concept of explanation that the quest for completeness—if understood as a demand for the removal of every possible doubt—is incoherent:

> an explanation serves to remove or to avert a misunderstanding—one, that is, that would occur but for the explanation; not every one that I can imagine.[51]

The same holds true of a complete understanding of a rule. The assumption that there must be more to understand there derives, in both cases, from the same source of confusion, namely, the presumption that a complete account of the meaning of an expression is only a Merkmal-definition, i.e., providable in terms of necessary and sufficient conditions.[52] Thus, just as it is misguided to presume that unless one can specify necessary and sufficient conditions for the applicability of a concept-word, one's grasp of its sense is in some way incomplete; it is equally misguided to assume that the complete understanding of a rule must remove all possible doubts about its applicability.

This should not be taken to mean that the distinction between complete and incomplete understanding or explanation is out of place. It is only that we should jettison the association of completeness with necessary and sufficient conditions. An explanation would be complete, if it fulfills its particular purpose, i.e., removes the misunderstanding that would have otherwise existed. Equally, "the sign-post is in order—if, under normal circumstances, it fulfills its purpose."[53] And one has a complete grasp of a rule, if under normal circumstances, one is able to specify which acts are in accord with the rule, and hence also, which would go against it.

It should be emphasized that all this is not meant to imply that whenever there is a disagreement about the applicability of a given rule (e.g. due to vagueness), Wittgenstein would maintain that "anything goes", as it were. It very well might be the case that interpretation is required to determine the applicability of a rule in certain circumstances, and interpretation can, of course, be based on *reasons*. But interpretation here should not be confused with the understanding of the meaning of the rule: If the formulation of a particular rule is inadequate for purposes of determining a particular result in certain circumstances, then there is nothing more to explain or understand

---

50. To be sure, there is nothing unique to legal rules here; all rules can be formulated in language, including the rules of langauge itself.
51. *Philosophical Investigations, supra* n. 22 s. 87.
52. See G. Baker & P.M.S. Hacker, *Meaning and Understanding, supra* n. 21 at 29-45.
53. *Philosophical Investigations, supra* n. 22 s. 87.

about *its* meaning; what is required is a new formulation of the rule—one which would remove the doubt—and this is what the term 'interpretation' properly designates.

We can return to Fuller's thesis at this point, as its inadequacies should be clear by now. His assumption that one can understand a rule only in view of the purposes it is taken to advance, violates the distinction between following a rule and interpreting it. To follow a rule, one needs to understand and act according to it, with the intention of doing so. As we have seen, the relation between a rule and its application is a grammatical one, i.e., internal to language. Understanding a rule consists in one's ability to specify which actions are in accord with the rule (and hence also, which actions would go against it). Thus, it doesn't make sense to say that one has understood a rule yet doesn't know which actions would be in accord with it. On the other hand, one's assumptions about the purposes a rule is meant to advance are interpretive assumptions which do not mediate between a rule and its application but rather between one formulation of the rule and another. Hence, the thesis that one always needs to determine the purpose of the rule in order to be able to specify which actions are in accord with it, amounts to contending that the application of a rule always requires its translation into another rule, which is an obvious absurdity.

Thus, unless it can be shown that there is something unique to adjudication which requires this constant translation procedure, as it were, one has no reason to doubt that legal rules *can* often be simply understood, and then applied, without the mediation of interpretive hypotheses about the rules' purposes. Interpretation is required only when the formulation of the rule leaves doubts as to its applicability in a given set of circumstances. In such cases, assumptions about the purposes the rule is meant to advance would take a prominent—perhaps even preeminent—role in solving the particular difficulties encountered.

8

The Application (and Mis-Application) of Wittgenstein's Rule-Following Considerations to Legal Theory

Brian Bix

A

Wittgenstein's writings on "rule-following" remain an important—and sharply contested—part of his later thought. The reference to "rules" in those writings was both broader and more basic than the use of that term in most discussions of practical reasoning or legal theory. Wittgenstein's use of "rule" refers to all normative constraints which apply over an indefinite variety of cases, to practices where our actions might be said to be guided, to situations where characterizing actions as "correct" or "incorrect" makes sense. However, "[h]e aimed not to write a book on rules but to examine specific problems arising out of insights into the normative nature of a language, of logic and of reasoning."[1] He focused in particular on normative practices that on the surface do not seem troubling or difficult to understand: for example, using a word correctly, understanding a signpost, and continuing a simple mathematical series.[2] In such examples, the interesting question is not whether a particular response or continuation is right or wrong; Wittgenstein specifically chose examples where there would be consensus on that issue. Wittgenstein's question is what is it about the rule or about ourselves which makes our responses right or wrong (or which justifies us in reaching that evaluation)?

Wittgenstein's discussions on rule-following have been brought to bear on the issue of legal determinacy primarily by those who argue that law is radically indeterminate. They offer a reading of Kripke's reading of Wittgenstein[3] to support the position that rules do not have determinate applications. The argument runs along the following lines. Wittgenstein (Kripke) has shown that there is no fact of the matter to prove that I mean the same thing by my current use of a word as I did by a former use, and no fact of the matter to prove that I am applying the word (the rule that governs the word's

I wish to thank Joseph Raz, Gordon Baker, Simon Blackburn, David Helman and Alan Thomas for their helpful comments on earlier versions of this article.

1. G.P. Baker & P.M.S. Hacker, *Wittgenstein: Rules, Grammar, and Necessity* at 39 (Oxford: Blackwell, 1985).
2. See L. Wittgenstein, trans. G.E.M. Anscombe *Philosophical Investigations* ss. 143-242 (New York: MacMillan Company 1953).
3. S. Kripke, *Wittgenstein on Rules and Private Language* (Oxford: Blackwell, 1982); see, *e.g.,* C.M. Yablon, "Law and Metaphysics" (Book Review) (1987), 96 *Yale Law Journal* at 613. At one point in his book, Kripke hedges regarding the extent to which the argument he elaborated was actually Wittgenstein's. Kripke, *id.,* at 5. At other places, he is more confident about the ascription. See, *e.g.,id.,* at 70-71. My view is that Kripke's reading does not accurately reflect Wittgenstein's position, and that Wittgenstein's actual position is superior to the one Kripke (more or less) ascribes to him. While I will in passing offer arguments to support both of these assertions, it is not my purpose in this paper to go into these disputes in any depth. See also *infra* n. 10.

usage) correctly.[4] Furthermore, "there is [no] fact about our past use, intention, or attitude towards a word ... that controls or restricts or limits our
future uses of that word."[5] If there is no fact of the matter that tells us how to
use a word, if any way we go on can be characterized as following the rule,
then, it seems, anything goes.[6] The legal indeterminacy theorists then follow Wittgenstein (Kripke) in concluding that judgments of correctness and
incorrectness (in following a rule, in the use of a word)—that is, the whole
concept of meaning—is based on (can only be based on) the consensus of the
community. We are using a word correctly if and only if our use agrees with
that of the vast majority of our peers.[7] This approach fits well with the position of many legal indeterminacy theorists. They need not, and do not, deny
that there are "easy cases" in the law. However, they attribute the easiness of
these cases not to language but to a (temporary) consensus of the society (or
the relevant legal subset of society).[8] This consensus has a political or ideological component, and some might assert that it has been imposed by more
powerful elements of the community upon the rest. If and when the society's
ideology changes, which cases are considered easy will, according to this
approach, also change.[9]

B

Wittgenstein's lessons are different.[10] Kripke is right in reading
Wittgenstein as asserting that there is no fact of the matter (no "superlative
fact"[11]) which justifies the way we understand rules.[12] He is wrong, however,

4. See S. Kripke, *Wittgenstein on Rules and Private Language, supra* n. 3 at 70-71.
5. C.M. Yablon, "Law and Metaphysics", *supra* n. 3 at 628 (footnote omitted).
6. See *Wittgenstein on Rules and Private Language,* 11-13, 77-78, 84-93; see, *e.g.,* C.M. Yablon, "Law
and Metaphysics", 632; *cf.Philosophical Investigationssupra* n. 2, s. 201:

   This was our paradox: no course of action could be determined by a rule, because every course of
   action can be made out to accord with the rule. The answer was: if everything can be made out to
   accord with the rule, then it can also be made out to conflict with it. And so there would be neither
   accord nor conflict here.

   (However, s. 201 continues: "It can be seen that there is a misunderstanding here ....")
7. See *Wittgenstein on Rules and Private Language* at 90-98, 110-112; see, *e.g.,* C.M. Yablon, "Law
and Metaphysics", *supra* n. 3 at 632-636.
8. See, *e.g.,* C.M. Yablon, "Law and Metaphysics", *supra* n. 3 at 632-636; C.M. Yablon, "The
Indeterminacy of the Law: Critical Legal Studies and the Problem of Legal Explanation" (1985), 6
Cardozo Law Review 917, 918-920, 929-945; M. Tushnet, *Red, White, and Blue* (1988) at 54-56, 60-69.
9. See, *e.g.,* C.M. Yablon, "Law and Metaphysics", *supra* n. 3 at 632-636.
10. It is very hard to find a Wittgenstein Scholar who is in substantial agreement with Kripke's reading. For
contrary readings, see, *e.g.,* J. McDowell, "Wittgenstein On Following a Rule" (1984), 58 *Synthese*
325; S. Blackburn, "The Individual Strikes Back" (1984), 58 *Synthese* 281; G.P. Baker & P.M.S.
Hacker, *Scepticism, Rules and Language* (Oxford: Blackwell, 1984); C. McGinn, *Wittgenstein on
Meaning* (Oxford: Blackwell, 1984) 59-92; E. Goldfarb, "Kripke on Wittgenstein on Rules" (1985), 82
Journal of Philosophy 471; N. Malcolm, *Nothing is Hidden* (Oxford: Blackwell, 1986) at 154-181; D.
Pears, *The False Prison, Vol. 2* (Oxford: Clarendon Press, 1988) at 463-501; A. Lewis, "Wittgenstein
and Rule-Scepticism" (1988), 38 *Philosophical Quarterly* 280.

   One note of caution: Wittgenstein's ideas in the *Philosophical Investigations, supra* n. 2, including
the material on rule-following, is presented in short passages which are often aphoristic or cryptic. To
read a particular argument or viewpoint into these comments requires an implicit or explicit filling out
of details and clarification of ambiguities. The interpretation I present is by no means the only tenable
one. However, it does coincide generally with those given by Peter Hacker, Gordon Baker, David
Pears, John McDowell, Colin McGinn, and Simon Blackburn, among others (who, whatever their
disagreements about other aspects of Wittgenstein scholarship, are in consensus or near-consensus
regarding the aspects of rule-following relevant to my discussion).
11. See *Philosophical Investigations, supra* n. 2, s. 192.
12. Simon Blackburn notes that Wittgenstein would not have expressed the point in those terms. See
Blackburn, "The Individual Strikes Back" (1984), 58 *Synthese* 281, 285. As an alternative more con-

in portraying this as a "sceptical problem" which requires a "sceptical solution".[13] If the signs and symbols of the rule were somehow insufficient to allow us to know whether a certain action was or was not in accordance with the rule, how could the addition of further signs and symbols in our minds (or in the Platonic realm of Ideas) remedy this insufficiency? If we "restrict the term 'interpretation' to the substitution of one expression of the rule for another", "[w]hat this shews is that there is a way of grasping a rule which is *not* an *interpretation*, but which is exhibited in what we call 'obeying the rule' and 'going against it' in actual cases."[14] The idea of a "sceptical problem" comes from the philosopher's temptation, the philosopher's anxiety, to find some magical intermediary between rules and actions. As David Pears wrote,

> The point is not just that there is often a need to interpret rules by defining their terms, but also that this process of defining a term and then defining the terms in the definition cannot possibly close all gaps, because sooner or later there will have to be a leap, not guaranteed by any definition, from language to the world.[15]

There is a sense in which even Pears' discussion concedes too much to Wittgenstein's critics: to write of "gaps" and "a leap ... from language to the world" implies that language can be understood separate from its applications to and in the world, a position Wittgenstein would not have endorsed.

In easy cases at least, we all apply the rule in the same way. For example, we would all continue the series "add 2": "1000, 1002, 1004, ...".[16] The "we" of the previous two sentences would include all those who share the same form of life, who have been trained in the same rules in the same way. (I will discuss Wittgenstein's concept of a form of life later in this article.) In these easy cases, it is not fuel for scepticism that nothing more can be offered in justification for how the rule is applied. The sceptic's complaint is unwarranted because there is nothing more that *could* be offered as justification and there is nothing more that is needed as a justification.[17] To the sceptic who keeps asking why, a different form of response is eventually necessary. "If I have exhausted the justifications I have reached bedrock, and my spade is turned. Then I am inclined to say: 'This is simply what I do.'"[18] One might

---

genial to Wittgenstein's approach, Blackburn offers: "taking a term in a certain way is something different from *presenting* anything as an aid to understanding it, or from *accepting* anything as aids to understanding it." *Id.*, at 288.

13. See *Wittgenstein on Rules and Private Language, supra* n. 3 at 61-69. Crispin Wright has pointed out that Kripke's reading of Wittgenstein inverts the focus of Wittgenstein's discussions. Kripke's Sceptic has us wondering how we could know what rule we are or had been following, wondering, in fact, about "the very existence of rules and rule-following". C. Wright, Critical Notice, (reviewing C. McGinn, *Wittgenstein on Meaning, supra* n. 10, (1989)), 98 *Mind* 289, 303. By contrast, Wittgenstein was actually concerned with "the nature and epistemology of rule-following"—that is, how we can know what a rule requires of us in a particular situation. *Id.*

14. *Philosophical Investigations, supra* n. 2, s. 201.

15. D. Pears, *The False Prison*, Vol. 2, *supra* n. 10 at 432.

16. See *Philosophical Investigations, supra* n. 2, ss. 185-187.

17. See L. Wittgenstein, *Tractatus Logico-Philosophicus* (London: Routledge and Kegan Paul, 1951), s. 6.51:

    Scepticism is *not* irrefutable, but obviously nonsensical, when it tries to raise doubts where no question can be asked.

    For doubt can exist only where a question exists, and an answer only where something *can be said*.

18. *Philosophical Investigations, supra* n. 2, s. 217.

also reply: "that is just *what we call* 'adding 2' (or 'the colour red', and so on)."[19] There is no room in the language game for further justification or for further doubt. "If after full training and all the recommended checks I still 'doubt' whether I am using a word correctly, my 'doubt' goes beyond the particular language-game and is automatically transformed into a request for an answer to the conceptual question 'What counts as following a rule?'"[20]

The way we are inclined to go on is *what we call* the "correct response". However, the *fact* that we all go on the same way is not what makes it correct (though, as I will discuss later, it *is* what makes our practices possible). We do not determine whether a flower is red by first asking everyone around what they think the flower's colour is.[21]

Like H.L.A. Hart, Wittgenstein sought a middle position on rules. Wittgenstein "attempt[ed] to point to an alternative account of normativity to the 'rules-as-rails' imagery of platonism, to explain how there can be a stand-able middle ground between the hypostatization of rules and the denial of their existence."[22] On one hand, Wittgenstein did not want to ascribe the application of rule to the rules themselves *qua* metaphysical entities. On the other hand, he did not wish to deny that (it makes sense to say that) a rule determines its correct application or interpretation.[23]

C

Wittgenstein's discussions on rule-following in *Philosophical Investigations* focused on easy cases, like the mathematical series "add 2".[24] In section 240, he wrote:

> Disputes do not break out (among mathematicians, say) over the question whether a rule has been obeyed or not. People don't come to blows over it, for example. That is part of the framework on which the working of our language is based (for example, in giving descriptions).

Wittgenstein focused on "easy cases" because he was interested in dispelling certain misunderstandings and mythologies regarding what makes these instances of applying a word or continuing a series easy. There cannot be a fact which determines how to go on: no mental state, inner voice, or disposition, and no platonic rule-entity that we somehow grasp. For Wittgenstein, there is no mediating entity which can justify or explain why we all go on the same way when continuing the series "add 2" or applying the colour-word

---

19. G.P. Baker & P.M.S. Hacker, *Scepticism, Rules and Language, supra* n. 10 at 85; see also *id.,* at 78:
    If the question is: "What do you mean by 'W'?", then it is fully answered by an explanation of meaning (hence without reference to any community). If the question is "Are you sure that you know what 'W' means?" (or "Are you sure that your explanation of what 'W' means is correct?") then it is typically (though not necessarily) answered by "Yes, of course I know what 'W' means! I speak English. I have used 'W' innumerable times and heard it used innumerable times." [footnote omitted]
20. D. Pears, *The False Prison,* Vol. 2 *supra* n. 10 at 442.
21. See L. Wittgenstein, *Zettel* (Berkeley: Univ. of Calif. Press, 1967), s. 431.
22. Wright, "Critical Notice" (reviewing C. McGinn, *Wittgenstein on Meaning,* (1984)) (1989), 98 *Mind* 289, 297.
23. See G.P. Baker & P.M.S. Hacker, *Wittgenstein: Rules, Grammar and Necessity, supra* n. 1 at 81-106.
24. *Philosophical Investigations, supra* n. 2, ss. 185-187.

"red". It simply is the case that persons who share the same form of life and are trained in the same way go on in the same way in following rules. As John McDowell described Wittgenstein's position: "nothing ... keeps our practices in line except the reactions and responses we learn in learning them."[25] The analysis is complicated somewhat by the recognition that for Wittgenstein concepts like "the same" and "agreement" cannot be understood *a priori,* or otherwise independent of the problem of rule-following:

> The word "agreement" and the word "rule" are *related* to one another, they are cousins. If I teach anyone the use of the one word, he learns the use of the other with it.
>   The use of the word "rule" and the use of the word "same" are interwoven. (As are the use of "proposition" and "true".)[26]

For Wittgenstein, the easiness of easy cases derives from certain background facts regarding agreement in judgments, agreement in social context, and stability of the world. In *Philosophical Investigations* section 242, he stated:

> If language is to be a means of communication there must be agreement not only in definitions but also (queer as this may sound) in judgments. ... It is one thing to describe methods of measurement, and another to obtain and state results of measurement. But what we call "measuring" is partly determined by a certain constancy in results of measurement.

Briefly, "judgments" here includes all the connections we make (through our actions) between language and the world: between a rule and its application, between how we have used a term before and whether we apply it to a particular new instance, between how we have been trained to understand a practice (for example, adding or measuring) and how we perform it ourselves, and so on.[27]

It is a matter of fact that we all go on the same way in the series "add 2" after we have been trained in mathematics; we do not tend to diverge in our answers upon reaching 1000. After learning how to use a ruler, all of our measurements of the same object will be the same. Similarly, after being taught the colour words by ostensive definitions, we will all agree that this particular tomato is red and that patch of grass is green.[28] If differences in individual judgment created divergences in the way persons continued the series "add 2" or if instabilities in the world caused us to get different results every time we measured the same object, then the concepts within those practices—and the practices themselves—would cease to have meaning.[29]

One could say that the fact that we all go on the same way in our practices and in our uses of words after rudimentary training is just a happy coinci-

---

25. J. McDowell, "Non-Cognitivism and Rule-Following", in *Wittgenstein: To Follow a Rule,* S. Holtzman & C. Leich, eds. (London: Rourledge abd Kegan Paul, 1981) at 149.
26. *Philosophical Investigations, supra* n. 2, ss. 224-225.
27. See C. McGinn, *Wittgenstein on Meaning,* (Oxford: Blackwell, 1984) (equating "judgment" with "unreflective and 'blind' application of a sign").
28. See L. Wittgenstein, G.E.M. Anscombe trans. *Remarks on the Foundation of Mathematics* rev'd ed. (Cambridge: MIT Press, 1978).
29. See, *e.g.,Philosophical Investigations, supra* n. 2, s. 142:
   The procedure of putting a lump of cheese on a balance and fixing a price by the turn of the scale would

dence[30], though a coincidence without which communication would be impossible.[31] In section 241, Wittgenstein writes:

> "So you are saying that human agreement decides what is true and what is false?"—
> It is what human beings *say* that is true and false; and they agree in the *language*
> they use. That is not agreement in opinions but in form of life.

The following is from one of Wittgenstein's unpublished manuscripts[32]:

> How is the application of a rule fixed? Do you mean "logically" fixed? Either by
> means of further rules, or not at all!—Or do you mean: how is it that we agree in
> applying it thus and not otherwise? Through training, drill and the forms of our
> life.

> This is a matter not of a consensus but of forms of life.

"Form(s) of life" in part sums up, in part hints at an explanation for, the fact of our general agreement.[33] Rudolf Haller has shown that Wittgenstein uses this phrase in at least two different ways: 1) (in the singular, *Lebensform*) to summarize "the common human way of acting", that which is distinctly and universally human; and 2) (in the plural, *Lebensformen*) to emphasize diversity between societies and even between different communities within a single society.[34] The role the concept "form of life" might play in explaining disagreement will be discussed in a later part of this article. For now, one can get an overview of Wittgenstein's analysis of agreement: we go on the same way because of commonalities in our training and in our nature. It is far from inevitable that all persons will always react in all matters in the same way; where we do not go on the same way there will simply be no stable practice.

In contrasting Wittgenstein with certain Critical Legal Theorists, I do not mean to imply that there is any basis in his thought for denying the Critical Theorists' point that some "easy cases" are easy because of political or ideological consensus rather than because of some more peremptory claim about

---

lose its point if it frequently happened for such lumps to suddenly grow or shrink for no obvious reason.
*Cf.*L. Wittgenstein, *Zettel* s. 351 (1967):
"If humans were not in general agreed about the colours of things, if undetermined cases were not exceptional, then our concept of colour could not exist." No—our concept *would* not exist.

For a more detailed discussion of how Wittgenstein saw agreement in judgments and stability in nature work as presuppositions in our ideas, see G.P. Baker & P.M.S. Hacker, *Wittgenstein: Rules, Grammar and Necessity, supra* n. 4 at 229-251.

30. *Cf.* D. Pears, *Ludwig Wittgenstein* 179 (New York: Viking, 1986): "We could say that this is fortunate, except that this would be like saying that it is fortunate that life on earth tolerates the earth's natural atmosphere. What we ought to say is that there is as much stability as there is."
31. See *Philosophical* Investigations, *supra* n. 2, s. 242, quoted above.
32. It is quoted in G.P. Baker & P.M.S. Hacker, *Wittgenstein: Rules, Grammar and Necessity, supra* n. 1 at 258, and labelled "MS 160, 51".
33. For an overview of how Wittgenstein used the concept of "form(s) of life", see R. Haller, *Questions on Wittgenstein,* (Lincoln: Univ. of Nebraska Press, 1988), at 129-136.
34. R. Haller, *Questions on Wittgenstein,* 130-136. One example of the second usage appeared in L. Wittgenstein, *Lectures and Conversations on Aesthetics, Psychology & Religious Belief,* C. Barrett ed. (Berkeley: Univ. of California, Los Angeles, 1978), at 58: "Why shouldn't one form of life culminate in an utterance of belief in a Last Judgment?"

For an argument that Wittgenstein's phrase "form(s) of life" referred primarily to cultural rather than biological aspects of human nature, see G.P. Baker & P.M.S. Hacker, *Wittgenstein: Rules, Grammar and Necessity, supra* n. 1 at 238-243.

the correct or incorrect use of words. That a certain practice is or is not a violation of "equal protection" may seem clear and obvious to us; but the clearness of the question may disappear if we go either forward or backward one generation in time. Finally, I am not sure that there is a bright line between those "easy cases" that fit under the rubric of Wittgenstein-on-rule-following and those that do not. That is, I am not sure that a theorist can usually (if ever) be confident in determining which interpretation questions are completely beyond the pale of legitimate debate ("outside the language game").

D

If there is a danger—exemplified by Kripke and others—of reading Wittgenstein on rule-following as a sceptic who undermines meaning and certainty, there is also an opposite danger of over-reading Wittgenstein's message of assurance. Wittgenstein wanted to assure us that despite (because of) the absence of some "internal" or platonic facts of the matter, we can speak of "correct" and "incorrect" in our most basic normative behaviour, including the application of words and the answering of mathematical questions in the easiest of cases. The over-reading danger occurs when Wittgenstein's message is interpreted as guaranteeing ascriptions of correctness or the achievement of consensus in more controversial matters. For example, while Brian Langille argued correctly that legal theorists could not use Wittgenstein to ground positions of radical indeterminacy, he went too far in implying that a correct appreciation of Wittgenstein could be used to rebut all sceptical analyses of law.[35]

In his article, Langille focused on "strong claims about the indeterminacy of language and the impact of this alleged indeterminacy upon our ideas about the nature of constitutional discourse."[36] His particular targets were those theorists who claimed that Wittgenstein's writings were the basis of their arguments. For the reasons given earlier, I agree with Langille that Wittgenstein did not believe that language was radically indeterminate, and that Wittgenstein's writings could not be used to support the conclusions of the indeterminacy theorists.[37] However, I must part company with Langille when he tried to take his interpretation of Wittgenstein a step further, writing of "the explication of the grammar of law, and ... the grammar of constitutional jurisprudence."[38]

Wittgenstein used "grammar" in a way somewhat broader than, but clearly connected to, the ordinary usage of that term.[39] "In [Wittgenstein's] sense

---

35. Langille, "Revolution Without Foundation: The Grammar of Scepticism and Law", (1988), 33 *McGill Law Journal* 451; see also Hutchinson, "That's Just the Way It Is: Langille on Law" (1989), 34 *McGill Law Journal* 145.

36. Langille, *id.*, at 452.

37. See *id.*, at 452-475, 486-495.

38. *Id.*, at 498. See also Langille, "The Jurisprudence of Despair, Again" (1989), 23 *University of British Columbia Law Review* 549; *id.* at 558 ("the grammar of judicial review"); *id.* at 560 n.43 ("*law's* grammar", "the grammar of common law adjudication"); and *id.* at 562 ("the grammar of constitutional adjudication"). The point is simple: Wittgenstein used the term "grammar" when talking about words and concepts, and it is at best misleading to move that analytical tool to a different set of topics—social practices.

39. See generally G.P. Baker & P.M.S. Hacker, *Wittgenstein: Rules, Grammar and Necessity, supra* n. 1 at 34-64.

the grammar of a term includes a wide variety of practices connected with its use and the criteria and background conditions that govern its normal application."[40] A phrase's grammar is constituted in part by the rules which determine how that phrase can be used, such that if those rules are violated the resulting sentence will have no sense. For example, it is part of the grammar of numbers that colours cannot be ascribed to them and part of the grammar of pain that one cannot claim to be in doubt about one's being in pain.[41]

Wittgenstein argued that many philosophical problems resulted from violating grammatical rules (for example, by mistakenly applying the grammar of material object statements to first-person psychological statements).[42] If we would only follow strictly to a term's grammar and stay within the language game we are considering, he argued, we would avoid metaphysical muddles and temptations to scepticism.[43]

When Langille used Wittgenstein's arguments about the relevance of human nature and human practices to the meaning of simple terms to ground his own statements about "the grammar of law" and law "being grounded in a bedrock of practice"[44], he was not following Wittgenstein's ideas, he was flouting them. He was doing just what Wittgenstein warned against, taking terms—in this case, Wittgenstein's concepts of "grammar", "practice" and "bedrock"—outside their usual context, outside their language game. These concepts belong to Wittgenstein's analysis of "easy cases" and unreflective applications.

The jump from the grammar of language to "the grammar of law" implies that the definitions of legal terms and the moves within the legal discourse cannot sensibly be challenged and are not in need of further justification. I am not arguing that Wittgenstein's approach, or even his analysis in terms of "grammar", could never be helpful in the analysis of social institutions or social theory.[45] However, Langille makes the significant move to "the grammar of law" without either arguing for the transition or even noting why argument might be needed.

Langille's comments here are brief and cryptic, but they hint at an argument that cannot be sustained. Along with his reference to "the grammar of law" and "the grammar of constitutional jurisprudence", Langille describes Owen Fiss as having created "the 'structural conditions' for a Wittgensteinian view of law—the existence of a set of constraining rules utilized by judges as a social group"[46], and states that "Hart's idea of judges utilizing social rules from the internal point of view is the bringing of Wittgenstein's fundamental point about rule following to the judicial role."[47] Within its context, these comments seem to imply that for Langille the practice of law is like the series "add 2" and the application of the colour-term "red" in needing no further

40. E. Wolgast, *The Grammar of Justice* (Ithaca: Cornell Univ. Press, 1987), at x.
41. See *Philosophical Investigations, supra* n. 2, s. 246.
42. See *Zettel, supra* n. 21, s. 434.
43. See, *e.g.,Philosophical Investigations, supra* n. 2, ss. 90, 520.
44. Langille, "Revolution Without Foundation", *supra* n. 35 at 497-498.
45. *Cf.* E. Wolgast, *The Grammar of Justice, supra* n. 40.
46. Langille, "Revolution Without Foundation", *supra* n. 35 at 498.
47. *Id.,* at 499.

justification (and that any present consensus in law can be explained in much the same way as Wittgenstein explained our all going on the same way in the series "add 2").

If Langille in fact held this position—and perhaps he did not—then I must disagree with him. The analogy does not hold. Unlike the matters with which Wittgenstein was concerned, law is a reflective activity: the participants consider, discuss and argue over how they should go on. Contrary to Wittgenstein's descriptions of mathematicians and mathematical series[48], disputes *do* break out in law over the question of whether a rule has been obeyed or not. Legal practice, locally and generally, *is* subject to criticism and *is* in need of further justification.

An initial and basic point in understanding the limitations of applying Wittgenstein's rule-following considerations to legal theory (at least the limitations of any *direct* application) is seeing how those considerations were meant to leave language and life just the way they are. Though Wittgenstein (and some commentators on Wittgenstein) may at first or on a superficial level seem to be proposing a sceptical position on meaning, the only role scepticism plays in his rule-following considerations is as the absurd consequence of mistaken premises he sought to correct: "*if* this conception of the facts were the right one, *then* we wouldn't know such and such, but we do, so we need this other conception of the facts."[49] Words *do* have meaning, and there *are* unique correct answers to simple arithmetic questions. These are the starting points both for us in our daily use of language and for Wittgenstein in his rule-following considerations. Wittgenstein's aim is "to alter our conception of the facts we take ourselves to know"[50]; but whether he succeeds or fails in persuading us, we have no reason to create or apply rules differently from the way we do now. Most, if not all, of the problems in law and legal theory occur at a different level of abstraction (or in a different area of philosophy altogether) from Wittgenstein's rule-following considerations.[51]

E

Wittgenstein's discussions of rule-following centre on what explanations can and cannot be given in understanding the consensus that pervades most of our uses of language (and mathematics). My interest in this paper has been in whether those remarks, though aimed specifically at "easy cases"—in particular, at explaining (causally and conceptually) our agreement in such cases— can also help us understand what explanations can and cannot be given for our failure to reach consensus in other ("hard") cases. There are ample reasons to believe that we cannot directly apply Wittgenstein's ideas, meant for easy cases, to hard cases. As Simon Blackburn has pointed out, it is the "automatic and compelling nature of rule-following" in easy cases that made

---

48. *Philosophical Investigations, supra* n. 2 s. 240, quoted above; see *supra* text accompanying note 24.
49. S. Blackburn, *Spreading the Word* (Oxford: Clarendon, 1984), at 99 n. 17.
50. *Ibid.*
51. See F. Schauer, *Playing By The Rules: A Philosophical Examination of Rule-Based Decisionmaking in Law and in Life* (forthcoming) (Oxford: Clarendon Press, 1991), s. 4.3.

them interesting to Wittgenstein.[52] The way we think about easy cases—and about "correct" and "incorrect" in easy cases—differs sharply from our thinking in hard cases. As Blackburn wrote, "we [may] have some title to regard ourselves as thinking the truth when (as when we accept a proof) we can form no conception of what it would be to think differently. But it would not follow at all that we have the same title when we are all too aware of the possibility of thinking differently."[53]

John McDowell offered some suggestions on how Wittgenstein's ideas about easy cases might be extended to hard cases (though he admitted that these thoughts may be *extensions* of Wittgenstein's ideas[54]). First, in cases where there is no consensus on how to extend some word or concept (particularly common with evaluative concepts), it might still be the case that, to one person, how to go on seems obvious. Though that person knows that other people disagree, he may not be able to understand how they could. His reaction to them might be: "'But surely you can see...?'"[55] That quote from *Philosophical Investigations* continued: "That is just the characteristic expression of someone who is under the compulsion of a rule."[56] In other words, McDowell is suggesting that in many hard cases, some persons have the same feelings that they have in easy cases, in cases of consensus. In an analysis that parallels the work of Stanley Fish, he hints that the difference between easy cases and hard cases might reflect the difference between people who share the same "whirl of organism"[57] and those who have (belong to) different ones. Thus, there could be seen to be a variety of intermediate situations between the easiest of easy cases and the hardest of hard cases. There are two parameters: the extent of agreement amongst persons and how many believe that their chosen result is obvious (and they could not imagine a contrary conclusion). For example, there could be consensus about the result without any participant having the same (type of or level of) certainty he or she would have in (e.g.) continuing the series "add 2".

McDowell's second suggestion was that in the background of hard cases there might be an underlying agreement about what constitutes reasonable or acceptable arguments.[58] This reflects a viewpoint that seems to have strong intuitive appeal within the legal community.[59] Lawyers and legal theorists often argue that though there may be little agreement about results, legal practice is kept relatively stable and orderly by some rough consensus regarding what kind of arguments lawyers and judges can use. I will not consider the validity of that position at this point.

If we cautiously move forward from Wittgenstein's comments—knowing

---

52. S. Blackburn, "Rule-Following and Moral Realism", *supra* n. 25 at 170.
53. *Id.*, 170-171.
54. McDowell, "Non-Cognitivism and Rule-Following", *supra* n. 25 at 160 n.14.
55. *Philosophical Investigations, supra* n. 2 s. 231; McDowell, "Non-Cognitivism and Rule-Following", *supra* n. 25 at 151-152.
56. *Philosophical Investigations, supra* n. 2 s. 231.
57. McDowell, "Non-Cognitivism and Rule-Following", *supra* n. 25 at 151-153; Fish's analogous concept is "interpretive communities", Wittgenstein's is "forms of life".
58. *Id.*, 160 n.14.
59. See, *e.g.*, Bell, "The Acceptability of Legal Arguments", in *The Legal Mind* N. MacCormick & P. Birks, eds. (Oxford: Clarendon, 1986) at 45-65; O.M. Fiss, "Objectivity and Interpretation" (1982), 34 *Stanford Law Review* 739.

that generally what we say cannot be ascribed to him, but at best can only be said to follow from his ideas or to be in his spirit—there are a number of ways in which we might begin to analyze or explain the disagreement in hard cases. In hard cases, everyone involved does not react the same way; there is no broad "agreement in judgments". We can follow McDowell and Fish—and even have some warrant in ascribing the position to Wittgenstein— to say that in some cases persons react differently because they have (or "participate in") different forms of life.[60] The social contexts, cultures, practices, and training are different. Within the subgroups of persons who share the same form of life, there would (by definition) be no divergence in reaction, and these same cases would seem to be "easy cases".[61]

1.

There would also be hard cases where the divergent reactions could not be ascribed to the fact that the people had (came from) divergent forms of life. In some cases, different individuals might simply tend to go on differently even when given the same initial training. Along this line, W.B. Gallie suggested that the controversy over the use of terms like "democracy" and "work of art" might be explained by the fact that different persons interpret differently (in Wittgenstein's terminology, "go on in different ways from") paradigm examples to which all agree the terms should apply (analogous to the initial ostensive definition).[62]

To see whether Gallie's discussion has added anything to our understanding, his analysis must be considered more closely. What would it mean for two people to disagree about the application of a concept but to agree that the touchstone for understanding the concept is a particular example? There seem to be two possibilities, which I will describe as a strong paradigm and an absolute paradigm.

In a strong paradigm case, a person would say, for example, "if anything is law, a traffic statute is law"[63] or "if any place ever had a democratic form of government, ancient Athens did". Here the paradigm coincides well with one's pre-reflective intuition about the concept ("law" or "democracy"), but it is not used to set the terms of the concept. It is possible, if unlikely, that one may someday conclude that this particular example does not, in fact, instan-

---

60. *Cf. Philosophical Investigations, supra* n. 2 s. 185:
   Now we get the pupil to continue a series (say +2) beyond 1000—and he writes 1000, 1004, 1008, 1012.

   We say to him: "Look what you've done!"—He doesn't understand. We say: "You were meant to add *two*: look how you began the series!"—He answers: "Yes, isn't it right? I thought that was how I was *meant* to do it."—Or suppose he pointed to the series and said: "But I went on in the same way."—It would now be no use to say: "But can't you see ....?"—and repeat the old examples and explanations.—In such a case we might say, perhaps: It comes natural to this person to understand our order with our explanations as *we* should understand the order: "Add 2 up to 1000, 4 up to 2000, 6 up to 3000 and so on."

   Such a case would present similarities with one in which a person naturally reacted to the gesture of pointing with the hand by looking in the direction of the line from finger-tip to wrist, not from wrist to finger-tip.

61. S. Fish, in his analysis of "interpretive communities", is particularly good in describing these scenarios in which issues seem obvious within a subgroup but highly controversial across subgroups.

62. W. Gallie, "Essentially Contested Concepts", *Proceedings of the Aristotelian Society*, Vol. 56 (London: Harrison, 1955-56), at 167.

63. See R. Dworkin, *Law's Empire* (Cambridge, Mass: Harvard Univ. Press, 1986) at 87-91.

tiate the concept.[64] For example, upon deeper reflection, one might conclude that ancient Athens excluded too many of its residents from the *polis* to be considered a democracy, or one might learn that new archaeological discoveries rebut the picture of ancient Athens one had accepted.

In the absolute paradigm case, the paradigm *defines* the concept, such that the paradigm could never be understood as *not* exemplifying the concept and any change in belief about the paradigm would result in a change in belief about the concept. An instance of this approach appears in religious thinking: for example, for those who believe that living a good life consists in living as much as possible like Jesus lived.[65]

This approach is always vulnerable to some version of Socrates' challenge: is something holy because it is dear to the gods or is something dear to the gods because it is holy?[66] If the good can be separated from what God commanded (or from how a divine figure had lived), then, at least in principle, the concept of the good could be defined and delimited independent of the paradigm and the paradigm might even be found to have diverged from goodness at some point. In other words, we are back at the strong paradigm case. Only if the respondent insists that something is good because and only because God ordered it are we still in an absolute paradigm case.

The absolute paradigm case is nothing more than an elaborate form of guidance by ostensive definition—"do as I do" or "follow me"—with all of the confusions and uncertainties that come with that process.[67] Gallie's analysis seems to offer nothing new in understanding the source or the nature of disagreement in such cases. The strong paradigm case is, if anything, even less helpful to our analysis. It describes a convergence—the reference to a particular example as a paradigm—that may be due merely to custom or practice[68], but explains neither that convergence nor the divergence in how different persons' apply the concept in question.

2.

When there is substantial disagreement about the definition or application of some term, and there seems to be no hope that further discussion will bring the various sides closer to consensus, there is always the suspicion that the disputants are not actually talking about the same thing.[69] At the level of concepts—as contrasted with words which refer to particular material objects—some theorists wonder if it is even *possible* for people who ascribe different meanings to concepts to be talking about the same concept. For example, Colin McGinn wrote:

> we have not, in the case of concepts, the idea of a single meaning-bearing item (word) about which we can press the question what establishes constancy in its meaning; there isn't the gap between a concept and its content that there is between a word and its meaning—a concept *is* (so to speak) its content.[70]

64. See *id.*, at 87-90.
65. Cf. Gallie, "Essentially Contested Concepts", *supra* n. 62 at 168, 180-181.
66. Plato, *Euthyphro* 10c-11b, in *The Dialogues of Plato,* Vol. I, (New York: Liveright, 1953) at 319-320.
67. See, *e.g.*, H.L.A. Hart, *The Concept of Law* (Oxford: Clarendon Press, 1961), at 122-123.
68. See R. Dworkin, *Law's Empire, supra* n. 63 at 65-66, 87-91.
69. See, *e.g.*, Gallie, *supra* n. 62, at 175-176.
70. C. McGinn, *Wittgenstein on Meaning, supra* n. 10 at 146; see also *id.*, at 147 ("we cannot ... make

Perhaps in part to get around this argument, Ronald Dworkin wrote of having "different conceptions of [the same] concept".[71] He is not always clear, however, about what it is that makes these different "conceptions" different conceptions of the *same concept* rather than simply being different concepts.

Gallie had suggested that in many of the "inevitably endless conflicts"[72] over religious, political, and artistic concepts, the disputants are in fact arguing about the same thing: the various versions of each concept in dispute having derived from an exemplar (either a single example or a particular tradition).[73] In *Law's Empire*, Dworkin explained the difference between concept and conception for the purpose of that book as being "a contrast between levels of abstraction at which the interpretation of the practice can be studied."[74] In that discussion, the concepts are concepts *of a practice;* what ties different conceptions together is that (echoing Gallie's work) they purport to describe the same practice.[75] In Dworkin's discussion of creative interpretation of social practices, the disputants are by definition talking about the same thing: a particular practice (defined tentatively at a "'pre-interpretive'" stage[76]) in a particular community. The interpretations are kept convergent by a requirement of substantial fit with the pre-interpretive content and by a shared world-view.[77]

I note in passing that Dworkin may have too quickly dismissed the possibility that lawyers and legal theorists talking about law could be talking about different things. At most, Dworkin's discussion[78] showed that "the law" has a relatively stable single reference in that a number of inter-related institutional processes go on every day under that name. However, the fact that lawyers (and social scientists) are not talking past each other about "the law"—the rules and procedures that operate within a particular community at a particular time—does not show conclusively that they are not talking past one another when they talk about "Law"—a particular form of social institution common to many communities.[79]

Dworkin's fleeting discussions of concepts and conceptions may conflate two different types of analytical moves. When he wrote of different conceptions of the same concept, John Rawls' earlier use of that distinction is implicitly invoked. Rawls spoke of people having a shared concept of justice in the sense that "they understand the need for, and they are prepared to

sense of employing a concept with a different content from that originally intended—it would just be a *different concept*.").

71. R. Dworkin, *Taking Rights Seriously* (Cambridge, Mass: Harvard Univ. Press, 1978), at 128.
72. Gallie, "Essentially Contested Concepts", *supra* n. 62 at 196.
73. *Id.,* 176.
74. R. Dworkin, *Law's Empire, supra* n. 63 at 71.
75. *Id.* at 43-49, 68-76; see also *id.,* 424-425 n.20 (discussing why this analysis would not work as well with "justice and other higher-order moral concepts" which have a global claim and no strong connection with any particular community's practices).
76. *Id.,* at 65-66.
77. *Id.,* at 87-89.
78. *Id.,* at 44.
79. Some might argue that Dworkin's conflation here of "Law" with "the law" reflects a similar conflation that permeates and defines his approach to legal theory. See H.L.A. Hart, "Comment on Dworkin", in *Issues in Contemporary Legal Philosophy,* R. Gavison, ed., (Oxford: Clarendon 1986) at 36; J. Finnis, "On Reason and Authority in *Law's Empire"* (1987), 6 *Law and Philosophy* 357, at 367-370.

affirm, a characteristic set of principles for assigning basic rights and duties and for determining what they take to be a proper distribution of the benefits and burdens of social cooperation."[80] For Rawls, there is an agreed concept (of which there are varying conceptions) because "justice" is used merely as the name of a particular subsection of moral thought. To the extent that the shared concept has substantive content, it is only whatever (if anything) is presupposed ("*a priori*" or "grammatically") by a moral approach to social ordering.[81]

On the other hand, when Dworkin writes in *Law's Empire* about different conceptions of the same concept of courtesy, he is closer to Gallie's analysis of "essentially contested concepts", discussed above. For Gallie, divergent theories are sometimes related by being different interpretations of the same practice. The Rawls approach is not suited for interpretation of practices, and the Gallie approach is not suited for purely abstract concepts, and imprecise analysis might result if the two approaches are confused.

F

In Paul Johnston's book *Wittgenstein and Moral Philosophy*, he explained how in at least some cases the divergence of opinions in hard cases can be understood within Wittgenstein's approach to language and to morality. The analysis was based on "the grammatical differences between ethical and non-ethical language games",[82] between the application of descriptive and evaluative terms. Whether a particular descriptive term ("red", "banana", "table", and so on) should be used turns on applying the rules which constitute the term's meaning and certain agreed procedures for verification (for example, comparison of an object with an authoritative colour sample to determine whether the object is indeed red).[83] The language game for descriptive terms both assumes and depends upon substantial agreement in the application of rules and verification procedures.[84]

In contrast, evaluative terms serve a different function and are grounded differently. Terms like "good" and "noble", according to this analysis, reflect the speaker's approval of the object or activity described, the object's congruence with the speaker's ethical system—the speaker's way of looking at the world and living in the world. "Here agreement in reactions is presupposed [only] in the sense that our being able to use words such as 'good' involves our reacting in ways mutually recognizable as reactions of approval, etc."[85] There are no set criteria for applying evaluative terms; since the appli-

---

80. J. Rawls, *A Theory of Justice* (Cambridge, Mass: Belknap Press, 1972) at 5.
81. See *id.*: "no arbitrary distinctions are made between persons ... and ... the rules determine a proper balance between competing claims"; though, of course, what distinctions are considered legitimate and what is considered a proper balance of claims is left to the various conceptions of the concept of justice.
It would be left open, I believe, for other theorists to argue that there is no necessary or *a priori* content (or structure) to theories of justice.
82. P. Johnston, *Wittgenstein and Moral Philosophy* (London: Routledge and Kegan Paul, 1989) at 93.
83. See *id.*, at 95-96.
84. *Id.*, at 96.
85. *Id*

cation of such terms will reflect different persons' different ethical systems, divergence in use is to be expected and does not undermine the language game.[86] Johnston's reading of Wittgenstein would give us one way to explain the existence of hard cases where moral or evaluative phrases (e.g., "reasonable rates", "bad faith", "due process") were involved, and would counsel us why we should not expect to reach consensus in such cases.

Conclusion

Both proponents and opponents of radical legal indeterminacy have tried to use Wittgenstein's discussions on rule-following to ground their positions. In my opinion, both sides find more in Wittgenstein than is actually there. The discussions on rule-following do, however, have some limited use in understanding the problem of easy cases and hard cases.

Some easy cases are easy because of the (short-term) determinacy of descriptive terms. Our consensus in applying such terms is due to some combination of our common human nature, our common training, and our common way of life. Wittgenstein did not discuss extensively cases the situation where consensus was absent, though some potential explanations for hard cases can be derived from his writing: e.g., that the people involved have different forms of life or that the key terms are evaluative rather than descriptive.

---

86. *Id.*, at 99-101.

9

Rules and the Rule-Following Argument

Frederick Schauer

Sparked by books by Saul Kripke and Crispin Wright, the last several years have seen a renewal of interest in Wittgenstein's remarks on rules. A large part of the contemporary discussion centers on what it is to follow a rule, how it is that human beings come to follow them, and what facts, mental or otherwise, determine or explain why some but not other logically equivalent extensions of a rule are deemed to constitute a *following* of the rule.

I have no reason to believe I have anything to contribute to the debate that has engaged not only Kripke and Wright, but also many others, including G.E.M. Anscombe, G.P. Baker & P.M.S. Hacker, Paul Boghossian, Robert Fogelin, Colin McGinn, and Guy Stock. Yet regardless of who has the better of the debate, it remains the case that the debate itself has an obvious relevance to those of us who think about regulative rules, the rules governing our moral conduct, our manners, our religious practices, and, perhaps most obviously, our conduct as citizens in a nation of laws. Moreover, the debate about rule-following has even more relevance in thinking about regulative rules as influencing the behavior and decisions of various officials, including judges, administrative officials, and the cop on the beat.

As is unfortunately all too often the case, legal scholars who have perceived the relevance of Wittgenstein and the debate about rule-following to legal theory have proceeded to apply misunderstood or simply erroneous readings of the lessons of the issue in the service of their own pre-philosophical jurisprudential inclinations. Two varieties are particularly egregious.[1] The first sees Wittgenstein's interlocutor as the chief player in the drama, rather than as Thrasymachus-like philosophical foil. Consequently, the challenges posed by the interlocutor are taken to be unanswerable and thus sound. The result of reading Wittgenstein in this way, of course, is the generation of a profoundly skeptical conclusion about the possibility of following any rule, including a legal rule. If it is the case, according to this reading of the lessons of the interlocutor, that a rule can be anything the so-called rule-follower wants it to be, then judges, for example, cannot be expected to and thus should not do anything other than follow their own rule-independent personal, psychological, moral, or political preferences. If the lesson of the rule-following argument is that constraint by rule is illusory, then the accompanying lesson is that constraint by legal rule is equally illusory.[2]

The second variety of spectacular misreading of the rule-following argu-

Earlier versions of this article have been presented at the Dartmouth College Department of Philosophy, Washington University Department of Philosophy, and University of Alberta Faculty of Philisophy.

1. References are omitted to protect the guilty.
2. This is not to say that there are not interesting and important issues surrounding the legal-rule-skepticism commonly referred to as Legal Realism. Indeed, if the rule-skepticism of Legal Realism is a claim that legal decisionmakers are not in fact constrained by rules in the way in which they purport to be in their articulated justifications (such as judicial opinions), or a claim that legal decisionmakers are constrained by rules other than the rules they claim constrain them, then it is in many domains true. But if Legal Realism is true, it is because some decisionmakers do not in fact follow the rules they claim to follow, and not because it is impossible to follow a rule.

ment consists of the conclusion that meaning, including the meaning of a rule and its constituent terms, is solely a function of the particular context in which the language of a rule is applied. Starting from the "meaning is use" slogan, this argument moves from this slogan to the conclusion that meaning is therefore coextensive with how language is used on a particular occasion—that the particular context of utterance is the sole determinant of meaning. This approach, rejecting semantics in favor of pragmatics as the exclusive determinant of meaning, and collapsing sentence meaning into utterance meaning, has the effect of rejecting the idea that the language of a legal or other regulative rule can have a meaning independent of the meaning it has when applied to a particular event or a particular dispute. As should be obvious, the result is to collapse rule-based constraint into a determination of what, all things considered, should be done on this occasion. And as with the argument described in the previous paragraph, the upshot is to embed an entirely plausible theory of judicial empowerment in an entirely implausible theory of meaning.[3]

Take as an example the standard jurisprudential chestnut, a "No vehicles in the park" rule. Now suppose the question arises whether a police car is to be excluded pursuant to that rule.[4] A number of responses are possible. One is to say that the enforcer or interpreter of the rule ought not to follow it when it would produce an absurd or otherwise undesirable result, just as we would not expect the authorities to enforce a speed limit against someone rushing a critically injured person to the hospital. A related response would say that it is a desirable or even a necessary characteristic of law that it authorize or even require its officials to refuse to follow the literal indications of the rule in such cases, and still another would recognize that other rules in the system might explicitly authorize such refusal to follow this rule. But none of these responses denies that a police car is still literally a vehicle, that this rule is still literally violated by the police car, and that it is conceptually possible to imagine a system in which even desirable violations of the rule would be treated as violations. Such a system may or may not be worth having, but it is not impossible. The question of whether the police car should be excluded is thus distinct from the question whether it is a vehicle, and it does not become less of a vehicle just because it would be undesirable to exclude it from the park.

* * *

Now that we have disposed of some of the less plausible applications of the rule-following argument to questions about regulative rules, let us make a new start. In doing so I will retrace some quite familiar terrain, but doing so

---

3. "The meaning of an expression cannot be identified with the object it is used, on a particular occasion, to refer to. The meaning of a sentence cannot be identified with the assertion it is used, on a particular occasion, to make. For to talk about the meaning of an expression or sentence is not to talk about its use on a particular occasion, but about the rules, habits, conventions governing its correct use, on all occasions, to refer or to assert." P.F. Strawson, "On Referring", (1950), 59 *Mind* 327. See also William Alston, "Meaning and Use", (1963), 13 *Philosophical Quarterly*, 107-24.

4. See David Brink, "Legal Theory, Legal Interpretation, and Judicial Review", (1988), 17 *Philosophy and Public Affairs*, 105-48.

will expose the foundations and therefore the potential weaknesses in the argument.

Let us start with the example of the numerical series 1000, 1002, 1004, 1006, and put it in the form of the question, "What number comes next in the series 1000, 1002, 1004, 1006, ____?" It is central to the Wittgensteinian point, as well as part of what has passed into the commonplace of mathematical theory, that there is no uniquely correct logical answer to that question. A rule could be constructed to make any answer to the question correct.[5] For example, the rule, "If *n* is less than 1006, add 2, but if *n* is equal to or greater than 1006, add 13," would explain all members of the existing series, but would generate and justify the answer 1019, rather than the answer 1008. The point of this, of course, is that something other than the prior numbers in the series makes 1008 correct and 1019 incorrect, with the debate being about just what that "something other" is, with Kripke and Wright talking about community practices, McGinn suggesting some natural inclination, and Baker and Hacker urging that faithfulness to Wittgenstein's conception of Wittgenstein's project would lead us to understand why we ought not even to be asking the question.[6]

But now suppose that the same question—"What number comes next in the series 1000, 1002, 1004, 1006, ____?"—were accompanied by the linguistically and canonically formulated instruction, "always add 2." If "always add 2" were an *instruction* incorporated within the question, then 1008 would become the right answer, and 1019 would be simply wrong. "If *n* is less than 1006, add 2, but if *n* is equal to or greater than 1006, add 13" is a permissible rule extracted from the series standing by itself, but it is not a permissible interpretation of "always add 2," and it is thus not a permissible rule if "always add 2" is one of the parameters determining which results are permissible.

Before you, the reader, tear up this paper in disgust, I know that at first it appears that what I have said just misses the point entirely. Why is it, Wittgenstein's skeptical interlocutor asks, that "always add 2" is inconsistent with "if *n* is less than 1006, add 2, but if *n* is equal to or greater than 1006, add 13?" Why can't we ask the same skeptical questions about each component term that we did about the question in its entirety? Why, therefore, couldn't the word "always" mean "in every case except those in which a series ending in a number equal to or greater than 1006 is involved, in which case all instructions inconsistent with 'add 13' are void"?[7]

To ask these questions, however, is to conflate two quite different inquiries.

---

5. It was in fact Leibniz who first made this point. "[I]f someone draws an uninterrupted curve which is now straight, now circular, and now of some other nature, it is possible to find a concept, a rule, or an equation common to all the points of the line, in accordance with which the very changes must take place. . . . Thus we may say that no matter how God might have created the world, it would have always been regular and in a certain general order." *Discourse on Metaphysics,* trans. R.H.D. Martin and S. Brown, (Manchester: Manchester Univ. Press, 1988) at 304.

6. No one but the skeptic claims that there is nothing that serves this purpose, for "if it were *always* possible ... to give a rule to justify any answer, a rule to make any answer *correct,* then there is no sense of the idea of 'incorrect,' and thus no sense of operating according to a rule at all." Guy Stock, "Leibniz and Kripke's Sceptical Paradox", (1988), 38 *Philosophical Quarterly,* 326-29.

7. "And besides, what about quaddition?" "And what about '2'?"

The reason that "always" does not mean something other than always is the very topic of the debate about what it is that supplies the benchmark for following or breaking a rule *of language*, where the very characterization of that bedrock question makes it circular and question-begging to answer the question in terms of the existence of rules of language. Community practices, to refer (without endorsement) to just one possible answer to the skeptic, is what and only what makes "always" mean always. Yet once something, whatever it is, *has* determined that "always" means always, the word "always" can *then* be used to refer to always. That is, skeptical questions about the foundations of language and the foundations of mathematics do not suggest that the techniques of language or of mathematics are non-existent, nor even that those techniques cannot themselves provide the foundation for practices other than those of language and mathematics. Thus, a practice of following rules articulated *in* language is not rendered problematic by the difficulty in explaining why it is that language operates in the way in which it plainly does operate. Our difficulty, to use Kripke's example, in explaining *why* 68 + 57 equals 125 and not 5 does not mean that the right answer to the question, 68 + 57 = ?, today and in this linguistic and mathematical community, is not 125. And if 68 + 57 does in fact, today in this world, equal 125, then *that* fact can provide the basis, today in this world, for some number of other practices, such as building bridges, calculating bank balances, and making change at the supermarket.

The question about rules other than the rules of language, therefore, is not why the rules of language work, but whether the rules of language, which *do* work (whether we can explain why or not), enable *other* rules to work. If we presuppose the ability of the rules (or conventions, or whatever) of language to generate meaning, then "1000, 1002, 1004, 1006, ____?," supplemented by the formulated instruction "always add 2" is crucially different from the question "1000, 1002, 1004, 1006, ____?," without that linguistically formulated direction. Adding the specific instruction makes all the difference. Thus, the question whether a sign reading "No dogs allowed" excludes seeing eye dogs is not a question whose answer requires direct reference, even according to Kripke and Wright, to community practices. Instead, the rule builds on and refers the rule-follower to the phrase "No dogs allowed," a phrase whose meaning exists apart from the question whether the community believes that seeing eye dogs should be allowed in restaurants.

* * *

That an account of prescriptive or regulative rules *builds on* the existence of language, and therefore does not itself engender the same kind of skepticism as do theories that seek to explain the operation of language, does not mean that this form of Wittgensteinian inquiry has little relevance for those interested in regulative rules. Two groups of issues are most important.

First, Wittgenstein's skeptical interlocutor compels us to wonder what it takes to constrain or at least to guide future behavior, and the message is now clear: The ability to explain the constraints *of an unformulated or unformulatable rule* is highly problematic. All agree that if *any* answer is correct to the question, "1000, 1002, 1004, 1006, ____?," then there is no rule. Suppose the restaurant I referred to above had no sign on its door, but had in the past excluded a Scottish terrier, a bulldog, and a cocker spaniel. When the question now arises whether an Irish wolfhound is to be excluded, the past instances themselves do not logically compel the first rather than the second and third of the following three rules, any of which would explain all of the previous decisions: "No dogs allowed"; "No short dogs allowed"; "No animals weighing less than 60 pounds allowed." Rule construction in cases such as this is like the process of theory construction in science, and burdened with the same problems of underdetermination. As a result, only an authoritative formulation of a rule will privilege the first over the others, and thus it appears to be precisely the authoritative formulation of a rule that makes it possible to say that some acts conform to the rule and others do not. The "No dogs allowed" rule, when formulated, acts just as "always add 2," when formulated, acts, building on the workability of language to exclude some otherwise eligible candidates as successors in the series. Without the formulation, it appears as if any rule could be constructed consistent with the previous decisions, and thus without the formulation there appears to be no rule at all.

This appears highly relevant to thinking about the common law, characterized, in theory, precisely by its absence of canonical formulations, and by the way in which a given common law decision is an extension of a previous series of decisions. What we now see, however, is not that there is no basis for preferring one extension over another, but that the basis is not something contained *in* the previous decisions in the series. Just as the existing categorial and conceptual apparatus of the human mind is likely to extract "No dogs allowed" rather than "No short dogs" or "No animals under 60 pounds" from the series of previous exclusions of specific dogs, so too might an array of community practices, subcommunity practices, and categorial presuppositions lead a legal decisionmaker to extend a series of previous decisions in one direction rather than another. But once we recognize that any number of extensions are logically compatible with the previous decisions in the series, we are led to examine those undisclosed assumptions and practices that make some extensions permissible and others not, and we are led as well to question the extent to which claims of compulsion with respect to some extensions are claims that mask the degree of choice actually available to the extender.

Second, examining regulatory rules through a Wittgensteinian lens enables us to see that even linguistically formulated regulatory rules owe their ruleness to a process by which those rules are internalized as reasons for action by some putative rule-follower. I have shown above that the logically prior rules of language make the internalization of formulated rules possible, but thinking in this way leads us to look at the rules that themselves influence and facilitate the internalization of formulated rules. A formulated rule may be internalized according to the rule, "Treat the indications of the ordinary language meaning of the formulated rule as a reason for acting (or deciding) in accordance with those indications," but other rules *of* internalization are possible as well. Another might substitute technical meaning within a linguistic subcommunity for ordinary meaning, another might incorporate an "except where doing so would be absurd" qualification, and still another might mandate that the rules should be viewed only as rules of thumb transparent to their background justifications.[8] All of these are possible, and thus the ruleness of a regulative rule can be seen to be a function not only of the fact of its internalization by some decisionmaker, but also of the *conditions* of its internalization. By recognizing that rules do not determine their own application, we are thus led not to reject the possibility of rule-based constraint, and not to reject the importance of rule-formulations in supplying the meaning that is at the heart of ruleness, but to acknowledge that the tools of language as embodied in a rule-formulation are necessary but not sufficient conditions for treating a rule as a reason for action. And when we look for the other conditions that contribute to the existence of a regulative rule, we see both the importance and the incompleteness of focusing on the formulation of that rule.

---

8. On the distinction between "real" rules and rules of thumb, and on the relation between rules and both their formulations and their background justifications, see my forthcoming *Playing By the Rules: A Philosophical Examination of Rule-Based Decisionmaking in Law and in Life* (Oxford: Clarendon Press, 1991).

PART THREE

Politics

10

Political World

Brian Langille

INTRODUCTION

It is not transparently obvious why legal theorists are increasingly attracted to the ideas and methods of Ludwig Wittgenstein.[1] After all, Wittgenstein's
writings are notoriously difficult and he said almost nothing, and certainly
nothing sustained, about law.[2] And why would self-proclaimed legal theorists
be attracted to someone who was quite explicitly hostile to "theory", who
viewed philosophy as a sort of therapy, and who said, famously, "philosophy
leaves everything as it is"?[3] But a still more interesting question is, why has
Wittgenstein received such curious and conflicting treatment at the hands of
the critical legal theorists? On the one hand critical legal theory celebrates
Wittgenstein's work as a key to the dismantling of traditional jurisprudence,[4]
but on the other hand critical scholars bemoan his alleged debilitating
endorsement of the status quo.[5] It is this last question upon which this essay is
focussed.

   While much may be said in response to this question Stanley Fish has
recently offered an account of the fascination which Wittgensteinian style

---

1. In addition to the essays in this volume, the attraction of Wittgensteinian ideas is evident in: Joan
   Williams,"Critical Legal Studies: The Death of Transcendence and the Rise of the New Langdells"
   (1987), 62 *New York University Law Rev.* 429; Stephen Brainerd, "The Groundless Assault: A
   Wittgensteinian look at Language, Structuralism, and Critical Legal Theory" (1985), 34 *American
   University Law Rev.* 1231; Dennis Patterson, "Interpretation in Law—Toward a Reconstruction of
   the Current Debate" (1983-84), 29 *Villanova Law Rev.* 671; Dennis Patterson, "Wittgenstein and the
   Code: A Theory of Good Faith Performance and Enforcement under Article Nine" (1988), 137
   University of Pennsylvania Law Rev. 335; Margaret Jane Radin, "Reconsidering the Rule of Law"
   (1989), 69 *Boston University L.R.* Towards a Non-Reductive Account Law" (1989), 47 *University of Toronto Faculty of Law Rev.* 939;
   James Penner, "The Rules of Law: Wittgenstein, Davidson and Weinrib's Formalism" (1988), 46
   University of Toronto Faculty of Law Rev. 488; Daniel Stroud, "Law and Language: Cardozo's
   Jurisprudence and Wittgenstein's Philosophy" (1984), 18 *Valpariso University Law Rev.* 331; C.M.
   Yablon, "Law and Metaphysics" (1987), 96 *Yale L.J.* 613.
2. Although when Wittgenstein did briefly discuss the law he had interesting things to say, such as:
       "A law is given for human beings, and a jurisprudent may well be capable of drawing consequences
   for any case that ordinarily comes his way; thus the law evidently has its use, makes sense. Nevertheless
   its validity presupposes all sorts of things, and if the being that he is to judge is quite deviant from ordinary human beings, then e.g. the decision whether he has done a deed with evil intent will become not
   difficult but (simply) impossible." (Wittgenstein, *Zettel* G.E.M. Anscombe and G.H. von Wright, eds.,
   Anscombe, trans. (Berkeley: University of California Press, 1967) para. 350)
   See also para. 48 where Wittgenstein makes an interesting remark about governmental intention.
   In *On Certainty* (G.H. von Wright and G.E.M. Anscombe, eds., B. Paul and G.E.M. Anscombe, trans.
   (New York: Harper Torch Books, 1969)) Wittgenstein occasionally makes references to procedures in
   courts of law—see, for example, paras. 335, 441, 485, 604.
3. The famous quotation actually comes from the *Philosophical Investigations* (G.E.M. Anscombe trans.
   Oxford: Basil Blackwell, 1968) para. 124. On the nature of Wittgenstein's philosophy see the sources
   cited *infra* at n. 49 and text.
4. See the sources discussed in B. Langille "Revolution Without Foundation: The Grammar of Scepticism
   and Law" (1988), 33 *McGill L.J.* 451, especially Mark Tushnet, "Following the Rules Laid Down"
   (1982), 96 *Harvard Law Rev.* 781. For a similar assessment of Tushnet's views see Don Herzog, "As
   Many as Six Impossible Things Before Breakfast" (1987), 75 *California Law Rev.* 609 at 628-360.
5. Allan Hutchinson, "That's Just the Way It Is: Langille on Law" (1989), 34 *McGill L.J.* 145; Rosemary
   Coombe, "Same as it Ever Was: Rethinking the Politics of Legal Interpretation" (1989), 34 *McGill L.J.*
   603.

philosophy holds for legal theorists which is particularly telling in relation to critical legal theory.[6]

In discussing foundationalist and anti-foundationalist theory in general, Fish discusses what he calls "theory hope" and "theory fear". By foundationalism Fish means "theory that promises to put our calculations and determinations on a firmer footing than can be provided by mere belief or unjustified practice".[7] Anti-foundationalism on the other hand "demonstrates that the norms and standards and rules that foundationalist theory would oppose to history, convention, and local practice are in every instance a function or extension of history, convention, and local practice".[8] Foundationalism is naturally associated with "theory hope" because it offers the comfort of putting our knowledge on a firm footing, a foundation. And in general anti-foundationalism breeds "theory fear" precisely because it seems to remove the foundations of our knowledge. This "natural" association of anti-foundationalism with theory fear is a phenomenon, in Fish's view, of the political Right. Their fear is that anti-foundationalist theory stands for a loss of objectivity and of standards. But on the political Left there is an optimistic view of anti-foundationalist theory which gives rise to "anti-foundationalist theory hope". The view here is that anti-foundationalist theory is a good thing because it will "[free] us from the hold of unwarranted absolutes so that we may more flexibly pursue the goals of human flourishing ...."[9] Fish's own argument is that anti-foundationalist theory is a basis for neither theory fear nor theory hope. Theory does nothing for us; "theory has no consequences."[10] Leaving aside Fish's own conclusions, his map of foundationalist theory hope, anti-foundationalist theory fear, and anti-foundationalist theory hope is useful in tracking the reaction of legal theorists to the philosophy of Ludwig Wittgenstein. Until recently Fish's map accurately described the attitude of both the Left and the Right to Wittgensteinian ideas as they played within legal theory. But now we need to take Fish's typology one step farther. For Fish anti-foundationalist theory fear is a phenomenon of the Right and anti-foundationalist theory hope is a phenomenon of the Left. But Wittgenstein's reception by legal theorists of the Left is now in fact characterized by both fear and hope. Initially, Wittgenstein was celebrated as the proponent of an exceptionally strong anti-foundationalist theory which critical legal scholars of the Left believed was deeply corrosive of "formalism", "liberal legal theory" and "mainstream legal thought".[11] Wittgenstein was seen to offer liberation from what they viewed as the foundationalist and essentialist basis of the dominant legal theory they criticized. But Wittgenstein is *now* loathed and feared as an apologist for the status quo and as providing a recipe for at best complacency, or at worst reaction.[12]

---

6. Stanley Fish, "Consequences" in his book *Doing What Comes Naturally* (Durham, N.C.: Duke University Press, 1989).
7. *Id.* at 321.
8. *Id.*
9. *Id.* at 323.
10. *Id.* at 325.
11. See sources *supra* n. 4.
12. Hutchinson, *supra* n. 5; Coombe, *supra* n. 5.

In "Revolution Without Foundation: The Grammar of Scepticism and Law"[13] I examined the anti-foundationalist hope approach to Wittgenstein's later philosophy of certain critical legal scholars. In the critical legal literature I there discussed, Wittgenstein was invoked as an ally in the critics' assault upon orthodox legal reasoning as the critics understood or at least depicted it. Wittgenstein was a source of inspiration and hope for the critics—a supplier of theoretical arms in a war of liberation upon dominant modes of thought. Their basic argument was that Wittgenstein destabilized language and was a sceptic about the possibility of language and all rule following, even in the simplest cases. Thus law (common law, statutes, constitutions) is inherently unstable and indeterminate. Although the Emperor had no clothes we saw the Emperor other than naked because of our arbitrary social conventions. This view continues to be put forward as a good reading of Wittgenstein with important lessons for legal scholars.[14] My argument[15] against this use of Wittgenstein's ideas was that a scepticism of the broad theoretical sort advocated by these critics was a mistake, resting upon a mistaken reading of Wittgenstein's ideas about rule following. I also said that it was a very self-destructive mistake. If we took this scepticism seriously it undermined the critics' own arguments.

The reaction to my arguments in "Revolution Without Foundation" has been of two sorts. First, some readers,[16] including some non-sceptical readers of Wittgenstein, view the argument as a very un-Wittgensteinian attempt to "ground" the legal enterprise in a Wittgensteinian "theory". They claim I offer a particularly bad version of foundationalist theory hope. I will return to this point later.[17] But the second and more immediate response has been from critics on the Left who now argue that Wittgensteinian theory is a cause for fear, that the ideas promoted ("philosophy leaves everything as it is") are dangerously conservative and engender an attitude of compliance and complacency about our law and politics. This is anti-foundationalist fear from the Left.

My view is that Left anti-foundationalist theory fear based upon Wittgenstein's writing is as bad a piece of misreading of Wittgenstein as Left anti-foundationalist theory hope was. In the end it is an interesting question why certain legal theorists continue to manipulate or seek to understand Wittgenstein in certain ways, for certain purposes, and at certain times. Wittgenstein's philosophy, and indeed "theory" in general, involves more than mere opportunistic political posing. I shall return to this issue at the end of this essay.[18] But I would like first to turn to the arguments of Allan

---

13. *Supra* n. 4.
14. See Yablon, "Law and Metaphysics" *supra* n. 1; and Radin, "Rethinking the Rule of Law" *supra* n. 1.
15. Following, among others, the arguments made by G. Baker and P.M.S. Hacker in *Scepticism, Rules and Language* (Oxford: Basil Blackwell, 1984).
16. Peter Lin, "Wittgenstein, Language and Legal Theorizing: Towards a Non-Reductive Account of Law" *supra* n. 1; Hutchinson, "That's Just the Way it Is: Langille on Law" *supra* n. 5; Coombe "'Same as It Ever Was': Rethinking the Politics of Legal Interpretation" *supra* n. 5; Joel Bakan, "Constitutional Arguments: Interpretation and Legitimacy in Canadian Constitutional Thought" (1989), 27 *Osgoode Hall L.J.* 123; Hutchinson, "The Three 'Rs': Reading/Rorty/Radically (1989), 103 *Harvard Law Rev.* 555 at 577.
17. See *infra* S. II.
18. See *infra* S. IV.

Hutchinson[19] and Rosemary Coombe[20] and the shift from hope to fear.

II.WITTGENSTEIN AND LEGAL CONSERVATISM

Both Hutchinson and Coombe have taken issue with the arguments in "Revolution Without Foundation" and both, in the end, have reached the conclusion that my non-sceptical reading of Wittgenstein is severely debilitating. They say that a philosophy advancing such arguments is given to "profound resignation and obeisance"[21] which engenders "passivity".[22] Both Hutchinson and Coombe, who are both my colleagues and friends, use even stronger words from time to time.[23] But the essence of their view is that they see as dangerous a philosophy which says "philosophy leaves everything as it is". Thus they entitle their essays "That's Just the Way It Is" and "Same as it Ever Was".

Hutchinson begins his essay with a mistake. He claims that "the point of Langille's exercise is to salvage the legal enterprise from the storm whipped up by strong sceptics."[24] This is misleading. My essay "Revolution Without Foundation" is not devoted to salvaging the legal enterprise from strong sceptics, but rather salvaging critics, such as Hutchinson, from their own strong scepticism. I wrote to point out their own theoretical excesses (strong scepticism, etc.) and to invite them to return from the resulting self-imposed critical exile. My view is that their own strong scepticism undermines their criticisms of our law, trivializes it, and renders it meaningless. Thus "Revolution Without Foundation" is largely a ground clearing one: It says "Here is a mistake you can avoid."

Hutchinson also mistakenly says that I invoked Wittgenstein in a conversation-stopping sort-of-way, that I simply appealed to Wittgenstein's authority in the manner of "some fundamentalist Christian or dogmatic Marxist".[25] But my argument was more complex than that. I turned to Wittgenstein because certain strong sceptics did so. They invoked Wittgenstein in support of their strong scepticism relying upon an interpretation of Wittgenstein staked out in the philosophical literature by Kripke.[26] My point was that this is a shallow reading of Wittgenstein. Hutchinson also makes a series of other errors which are not central to the arguments which interest me most.[27] What

19. Hutchinson *supra* n. 5.
20. Coombe *supra* n. 5.
21. Hutchinson, *supra* n. 5 at 154.
22. Coombe, *supra* n. 5 at 638.
23. Readers can review these texts and find a rich diet of similar terms.
24. Hutchinson, *supra* n. 5 at 146.
25. *Ibid.* at 419.
26. Saul Kripke, *Wittgenstein on "Rules and Private Language"* (Cambridge: Harvard University Press, 1982).
27. First, Hutchinson misunderstands Wittgenstein's philosophy. He states, for example,
    "A major lesson of Wittgenstein was that while meaning is not perennially illusive a text (including his own) it is more a site for the struggle between competing interpretations and not an occasion for the resolution of them; [and,] Wittgenstein ... shares the same profound ideological commitments and assumptions as those who seek to rest meaning on textual objectivity; they are mirror images ...".
    This is completely wrong. Furthermore, Hutchinson equates Wittgenstein's use of grammar with the ordinary use of that word. Wittgenstein sees that the word grammar has to do with what it makes sense to say, not with what rules we must use in putting together correct sentences. This is a distinction between "depth" grammar and "surface" grammar—see John Canfield, *Wittgenstein, Language and*

interests me most is that Hutchinson says that my view of Wittgenstein leaves me with nothing to say and that it drives me to a conservative acceptance of our law and legal practices as they are. This is wrong. This error results, in the end, from Hutchinson's failure to understand the basic point of the rather simple argument in "Revolution Without Foundation".

First, we should note just how curious Hutchinson's view is. His view is that a Wittgensteinian philosophical view is a view which results in a slavish adherence to the status quo. But this is a complete misreading which amounts to "philosophy does *not* leave everything as it is"; that is, "philosophy changes everything": it freezes our forms of life, ends debate, makes criticism impossible. But our forms of life are not frozen, debates continue, criticism abounds. What a wild idea that philosophy could revolutionize our existence so. And wilder still to suggest it to be a Wittgensteinian idea.

The point is that Wittgenstein's philosophy is not a recipe for radicalism or conservatism. It is not a recipe *for* anything. In Wittgenstein's philosophy achieving conceptual clarity and eliminating confusion and metaphysical nonsense is the name of the game. So, in "Revolution Without Foundation" the lesson is two-fold. First, here is an instance of conceptual confusion (the sort of strong scepticism advocated by many critics) and second, it is a severe mis-reading of Wittgenstein to read him as maintaining such a position.

To put this in concrete terms we can note that Hutchinson claims that there is an inconsistency between the "labour law Langille" and the "legal theory Langille". He believes that my views about theory contradict my substantive work in labour law criticising certain labour law doctrines.[28] Hutchinson says that the "theory" cannot be correct (philosophy leaves everything as it is) because I do something else in practice (argue for reconceptualization or change). This is Hutchinson at his most outrageous. Here he reverses our true positions, but with a heavy rather than a sleight of hand. To see this we can begin by noting that, as I said in "Revolution Without Foundation", I agree with some of Hutchinson's critiques of the Supreme Court of Canada's constitutional decisions and I have reason to believe that Hutchinson shares some of my view about that Court's labour law decisions. My view, far from undermining my activity as a labour law critic helps me understand what I am doing when I undertake that sort of exercise. It shows that such activity is not meaningless or, more accurately, is not threatened by the fundamental and strong sort of scepticism advocated by Hutchinson and others. The debilitating philosophy here is the strong scepticism of Hutchinson. My view is that this debilitating view is a mistake. Philosophy removes that mistake. It per-

---

World (Amherst: University of Massachusetts Press, 1981). Finally when Hutchinson draws *concrete* conclusions, he just gets it wrong. He writes, "Doctrinal consistency and regularity are not contributable to law, but to the politics of lawyers." I am not entirely certain what this means, but insofar as it says that "consistency" and "regularity" are not attributes of law, I think it is simply *wrong*. And this does not depend upon the politics of lawyers, but upon the concept of law. Maybe Hutchinson has an argument for a different concept of "law" (or whatever it might be called), but this argument is not made and I doubt whether Hutchinson would wish to make it.

28. See, for example, Langille, "'Equal Partnership' in Canadian Labour Law" (1983), 21 *Osgoode Hall L.J.* 496 (criticizing the received wisdom in Canadian and American labour law that there are "reserved management rights"); Langille and Macklem, "Beyond Belief: Labour Law's Duty to Bargain" (1988), 13 *Queen's L.J.* 62 (criticizing the dominant understanding of the duty to bargain in good faith contained in Canadian labour law legislation).

mits us to get on with the job of criticizing. It is Hutchinson's views which are debilitating. And in the end he obviously knows this and undertakes exactly the same sort of substantive criticism as I do. Theory just gets Hutchinson in trouble. It gets in his way. He should stick to arguing the political and moral merits of his self-declared political claims.

But behind Hutchinson's hyperinflated language and political posturing lies a common mistake. Whether he knows it or not he is associating himself with one side in the longstanding debate about Wittgenstein's relationship to conservative thought.[29] In his essay, "Was Wittgenstein a Conservative Thinker?"[30] Andrew Lugg helpfully identifies a number of different strands in the arguments associating Wittgenstein with conservatism and I think rightly disposes of them all. Although it is difficult to tell I believe that Hutchinson makes the simplest error in suggesting Wittgenstein's ideas result in abject adherence to the status quo and political conservatism. This view argues that Wittgenstein's insistence that we focus upon actual practices and his idea that practices are "bedrock" disables us from criticizing our current practices and thus makes us apologists for the status quo. Even if this was a good argument, and it is not,[31] it is difficult to see how someone so self-declaredly wedded to an hermeneutic approach as Hutchinson could make it.[32] The error is moving from the observation that "what has to be accepted, the given, is— so one could say—*forms of life*"[33] to the reading that "what has to be accepted, the given, is—our particular forms of life that we already have". As Lugg puts it, "Wittgenstein is not saying that we must dutifully submit ourselves to the established order, but only that we always start out from practices already in place".[34]

The error in Hutchinson's argument has even been pointed out by others who believe that Wittgenstein is reactionary, such as Terry Eagleton. As Eagleton puts it:

> The relationship between discourse and forms of life is necessary, not contingent; for Wittgenstein the language of sensation in particular would be incomprehensible if it were not closely bound up with actual behaviour.

> It follows that "what has to be accepted, the given, is—so one could say—*forms of life*". This is not an expression of political conservatism: there is no reason why what has to be accepted are *these particular* forms of life, and indeed little reason to

---

29. See J.C.Nyiri, "Wittgenstein's Later Work in Relation to Conservatism" in B. McGuinness ed. *Wittgenstein and His Times"* (Oxford: Basil Blackwell, 1982) at 44; Andrew Lugg, "Was Wittgenstein a Conservative Thinker?" (1985), 23 *Southern Journal of Philosophy* 465; Terry Eagleton, "Wittgenstein's Friends" in Terry Eagleton ed. *Against the Grain* (London: Verso Books, 1986) at 99; Paul Johnston, *Wittgenstein and Moral Philosophy* (London: Rutledge, 1989) c. 1; Sabina Lovibond, *Realism and Imagination in Ethics* ed. in Clark and Simpson *Anti-Theory in Ethics and Moral Conservatism* (Albany: State University of New York Press, 1989); David Bloor, *Wittgenstein: A Social Theory of Knowledge* (New York: Columbia University Press, 1983) chapters 8 & 9; J. Shulte, "Wittgeinstein and Conservatism" (1983), 25 *Ratio* 69.
30. *Supra* n. 29.
31. Among the useful contributions making this point see Drucilla Cornell, "Convention and Critique" (1986), 7 *Cardozo Law Rev.* 679 ("a form of life is not a straightjacket that binds our thoughts ..." (at 690)).
32. See Hutchinson's collected writings in his book *Dwelling on the Threshold: Critical Essays on Modern Legal Thought* (Toronto: The Carswell Co. Ltd., 1988).
33. *Philosophical Investigations, supra* n. 3, Part II p. 226.
34. Lugg, *supra* n. 29 at 468.

believe that Wittgenstein himself was in the least content with his own society. It is just that even if existing forms of life were to be revolutionized, those transformed practices and institutions would still in the end provide the only justification for why people spoke and thought as they did.[35]

Andrew Lugg has expanded upon this point by noting,

> Radicals, no less than conservatives, must "rest content with assumption". Like everybody else, they must accept a wide range of considerations, conjectures and techniques without question; they too must proceed on the basis of some practice or tradition. Without some assumptions, no criticism is possible .... Where radicals and conservatives differ is with regard to what they accept and what they chose to put into question, not with regard to whether they start from scratch and submit everything they believe to scrutiny.[36]

Wittgenstein does *not* "privilege" the status quo. Our concepts, practices and abilities are all that we have and thus give us the only possible method of getting a grip or the necessary traction[37] for critical thought.

Another way of coming at this point is to consider our relationship and interactions with others we encounter from different cultures or ways of life. In Sabina Lovibond's *Realism and Imagination in Ethics*[38] this phenomenon is usefully explored. The parallel between this question of encounters with others and our ability to challenge our own practices is evident when we consider our reaction to cultural divergence. Does the Wittgensteinian view of philosophy encourage either the "conservative" or "liberal" approach to those who differ? The liberal here "commends a policy of toleration" while the conservative "calls for a strict policing of *Sittlichkeit*". Lovibond writes:

> Essential to the Wittgensteinian picture is the idea that people whose behaviour is psychologically alien to us will to that extent fail to qualify as candidates for participation, along with ourselves, in a shared language—game: i.e. that in order to communicate with other people we need to be able to "find our feet" with them (P.I. II p. 233). Now these alleged truths of reflection supply no information whatsoever as to the possibility of finding our feet with specific individuals or groups. They do not tell us at what point a cultural divergence becomes so wide as to make any attempt at understanding pointless; neither do they tell us what to do in any actual situation where we may find ourselves unable to achieve understanding. *In such a situation, we cannot turn to the above-mentioned parts of Wittgenstein's philosophy either for authority to lynch anybody, or for authority to insist upon toleration.*[39] (emphasis added)

Just as Wittgenstein's view leaves the radical and the conservative in exactly the same position concerning which of our own practices to call into doubt, so too Wittgenstein's philosophy leaves the question of whether to adopt the "liberal" or "conservative" attitude to "alien" language games, untouched. Lovibond adds perceptively in relation to the strong position taken by Allan

---

35. Eagleton, *supra* n. 29. See also Coombe *supra* n. 5 at n. 138.
36. Lugg, *supra* n. 29 at 468-469.
37. *Philosophical Investigations, supra* n. 3, Part II, 223.
38. *Supra* n. 29 at 263.
39. *Id.*

Hutchinson (that on the Wittgensteinian view one becomes a promoter of existing language games and forms of life) that this is a form of "opportunistic abuse".[40] As Lovibond notes:

> *It is, in fact, a matter of experiment* how much we have to "accept"—how far our "agreement in judgments" with other members of our community can be dismantled by critical thinking before it begins to be in danger of losing a sense of our own identity, or of ceasing to be able to occupy the position of a subjective judgment.[41]

The basic point, which is crucial to understanding Hutchinson's error, is that on Wittgenstein's view theory predetermines nothing in terms of the possibility of critique. It is "a matter of experiment"—of "looking and seeing".

Coombe[42] seems to take a similar tack but goes one step farther in her essay on legal interpretation. While she has much sympathy with the contributions Wittgenstein's philosophy has made to our modern understanding of human life and culture, Coombe believes that (at least on my interpretation) Wittgenstein's significance for legal theory is limited or stunted in that it "assumes that politics .... ceases to be an issue".[43] She adds, *"the recognition that our interpretations are inscribed in the practical forms of our lives should force us to acknowledge just how pervasive and ubiquitous the 'politics of interpretation' really is, rather than give us licence to ignore or deny it."*[44]

For Coombe the action starts right where Wittgenstein stops. She quotes approvingly Eagleton's observation that "Wittgenstein's philosophy is reactionary not in its referring of beliefs and discourses of social activity but in its assumption that such referring constitutes a liberation from the metaphysical. ... And where ... could metaphysics be more at home than in the everyday?"[45] Coombe goes on to state

> While I agree with Langille that the "conventionalism" to which Wittgenstein points in his reference to the "normality conditions" that underlie "forms of life," does not require conscious (by which I believe he means intentional or volunteristic) agreement or consensus, it is nonetheless the case that "normality conditions" are socially based, culturally and historically differential, and thus *contingent,* in the sense that things could be, and have been, otherwise .... In other words, complacent, pacificatory declarations that .... "It is not reasonable or unreasonable. It is there, like our life" and the passivity that these declarations engender (It's the same as it ever was; it just is), *can and should be resisted.*[46]

> We may accept that there are no foundations for ethics, knowledge, or language, and that, as Langille approvingly cites John Searle, no such foundations are necessary, because the lack of such foundations "doesn't threaten science, language, or common sense in the least." As Wittgenstein says, "it leaves everything exactly as it is."

---

40. *Id.* at 278.
41. *Id.*
42. *Supra* n. 5.
43. *Id.* at 620, footnote 63.
44. *Id.* at 626.
45. *Id.* at 638, n. 138, quoting Eagleton *supra* n. 29 at 107.
46. *Supra* n. 29 at 638-39.

...

For some of us, however, leaving things exactly as they are, is quite problematic.

...

To the extent that "law as a set of social rules" embodies a "language game" ... we should attempt to understand *if* and *how* "the use, the context, the activity, purpose, the game which is being played" ... exacerbate rather than alleviate hunger, pain, grief, and the rage of disempowerment. We can only do so from a position which attempts to understand the experiences of those who suffer such hunger, pain, grieve and rage, and in a manner which conveys and amplifies the voices of those whose experiences these are.[47]

This reaction to Wittgenstein's views, at least as I presented them in "Revolution Without Foundation" seems compelling, but it is in the end confused. It reveals many distinct strands in the "Wittgenstein as conservative" movement identified by Lugg. But more importantly it rests upon a misreading of Wittgenstein's understanding of *philosophy* and the limits of philosophy.

Coombe reads Wittgenstein who said "philosophy leaves everything as it is", as advocating leaving everything as it is. So too she believes that Wittgenstein is a conservative but because he does not go the next step and discuss or evaluate our current practices or suggest how this ought to be done. In this she associates herself with the view that Wittgenstein is a conservative because of his singular failure to indicate how our practices ought to be changed. "To be a radical critic of society is to provide what Wittgenstein scrupulously refrained from providing, namely a sense of how things can be changed for the better."[48]

Wittgenstein's conception of philosophy is the problem here. A failure to come to grips with this lies at the heart of this particular confusion of Wittgensteinian ideas with conservatism.[49]

To understand the sort of criticisms levelled by Hutchinson and Coombe, it is not necessary to give a full account of Wittgenstein's understanding of philosophy. It is sufficient to draw attention to the distinction between the conceptual and the empirical. As Johnston puts it: "the proper aim of philosophy was not truth but clarity—what was needed was not a system of definitive answers but a method which would allow the philosopher to achieve a clarity in the face of which the questions which troubled him would themselves disappear".[50] Further, "the philosopher is not called upon to discover profound truths nor to offer explanations; rather, his task is to eliminate conceptual confusion by carefully depicting relationships between con-

---

47. *Id.* at 640-641.
48. Lugg, *supra* n. 29 at 472.
49. On Wittgenstein's conception of philosophy see P.M.S. Hacker *Insight and Illusion: Themes in the Philosophy of Wittgenstein* (Oxford: Clarendon Press, 1986) revised ed., ch. 6 "Wittgenstein's Later Conception of Philosophy"; Anthony Kenny, "Wittgenstein and the Nature of Philosophy" in Anthony Kenny ed. *The Legacy of Wittgenstein* (Oxford: Basil Blackwell, 1984); Johnston, *Wittgenstein and Moral Philosophy, supra* n. 29; David Pears, *The False Prison, The Study of the Development of Wittgenstein's Philosophy Vol. 1* (Oxford: Clarendon Press, 1987) c. 1.
50. *Supra* n. 29 at 2.

cepts".[51] Philosophical problems arise when we take language out of its everyday context, when "language goes on holiday"[52] i.e. when it is not at work doing its job in our lives. The aim of the philosopher is to eliminate confusion by bringing "words back to their everyday use"[53] and to draw attention carefully to the grammar which actually governs the use of our concepts. It is in this sense that Wittgenstein focuses relentlessly upon describing our actual linguistic practices. In this way the metaphysical confusions which have occupied philosophers of mind, mathematics, rule following, language, etc. are dispelled. Now the important point for Hutchinson, Coombe and others is made by Paul Johnston in his recent book *Wittgenstein and Moral Philosophy*. As Johnston points out: "Our concepts provide rules for the use of words to describe the world" and "thus it would be wrong, for example, to argue that our colour concepts do (or do not) accurately capture the real nature of colour".[54] For Wittgenstein it makes "no sense to ask if grammar is correct" because "grammar is autonomous (i.e. not answerable to reality)".[55] Wittgenstein is interested in what it makes sense to say, not what is true, etc. So, to return to the example of the colour concept: "The concept of red is not answerable to what red 'really is', for what red really is is only given by the linguistic rules which specify our concept red. People who used different rules would not be wrong, but would simply not mean what we mean by red ...".[56] Johnston goes on to say,

> Grammatical rules do not themselves represent the world but provide a framework for representation, and like the rules laying down a system of measurement, if they can be used there is no further scope for questioning their legitimacy. Thus a grammatical remark does not capture a deep truth about reality; rather it is part of a network of purely linguistic connections and what gives that network life is the fact that we use it.[57]

The charge of conservatism, as Johnston notes, based upon the non-substantive nature of Wittgenstein's philosophy, is confused. Wittgenstein's aim is not to defend the status quo, but rather to reject *confused* criticism of it. And on Wittgenstein's view "where language-games clash (and issue in different practices) it makes no sense to seek to adjudicate between them in purely conceptual terms".[58] This is because an "independent assessment of grammar ... makes no sense".[59]

Johnston's book is of particular relevance to the issues raised by Hutchinson and Coombe in that it focuses upon *moral* philosophy. But even here the point is the same. In discussing real ethical dilemmas in which one is torn between conflicting ideas about what paths to follow Johnston writes,

51. *Id.*
52. Wittgenstein, *supra* n. 3, para. 39.
53. *Id.* para. 116.
54. *Supra* n. 29 at 8.
55. *Id.* at 7.
56. *Id.* at 8.
57. *Id.*
58. *Id.* at 10.
59. *Id.*

"Although each moral standpoint claims for itself a unique status, Wittgenstein's point is that there is no independent way of adjudicating between them. This, however, does not imply that all moral standpoints are wrong to claim a unique status, for that too would be a particular kind of substantive position, viz. extreme relativism. Rather than making any substantive claims of this sort, Wittgenstein simply underlines two grammatical points: first, that the appeal to independent assessment—be it in terms of logic or reality—makes no sense; and second, that for this reason assessing a moral standpoint itself always involves advancing substantive (and hence contestable) claims."[60]

The idea here, as with the idea of different colour concepts, is "conceptual". As Johnston says, "it makes no sense to claim that one can stand *outside* the various ways of looking at the problem and adjudicate between them."[61] Wittgenstein's non-substantive notion of philosophy which aims at clarifying these separate concepts does not presume to decide the question that Hutchinson and Coombe insist be answered. But the value in Wittgenstein's philosophy is evident in the way that it shows us the error of Hutchinson's own scepticism. Hutchinson's metaphysics render his claim for political progress meaningless on his own terms. That is the point of "Revolution Without Foundation". That article urges writers like Hutchinson to avoid such philosophical mistakes.

When we have clarified the various language games available, it is then a question of our attitude towards them "and as such will have a moral dimension; which means that philosophy, from the present view of that activity, cannot pronounce upon it".[62] And as Lovibond goes on to explain:

... Wittgenstein should not be taken to suggest that ordinary language (and the life in which it is grounded) is "alright" as it happens historically, to be, in that it would be a mistake to try and change anything. Wittgenstein in his capacity as a philosopher of language should not presume to offer an answer to that question."[63]

As Lugg puts it, Wittgenstein's claim "is not that we should stick with what we have, but that changing the world involves more than understanding and explanation".[64]

Finally it should be noted[65] by philosophers of the Left, such as Hutchinson and Coombe, that such a position is far from obviously a conservative one. More than one author has drawn attention to the striking similarity between Wittgenstein's position and Marx's Eleventh Thesis on Feuerbach:

The philosophers have only *interpreted* the world in various ways; the point is, to *change it*.[66]

---

60. *Id*. at 143.
61. *Id*. at 141.
62. Lovibond *supra* n. 29 at 282.
63. *Id*.
64. Lugg, *supra* n. 29 at 472.
65. As it has been by others such as Eagleton, *supra* n. 29, at 100 and Lugg *supra* n. 29 at 472.
66. Karl Marx, *Theses on Feuerbach* as edited in L.D. Easton and K.H. Guddat (eds.) *Writings of the Young Marx on Philosophy and Society* (Garden City, New York: Doubleday, 1967) 400 at 402.

Wittgenstein wrote: "The sickness of a time is cured by an alteration in the mode of life of human beings ...".[67] *Philosophy* in Wittgenstein's sense, must leave everything as it is for its aims are description and conceptual clarity. But *people* (including lawyers) should take no instruction from this to leave everything as it is. As Lugg put it, "The answers we require must be forged in practice; they cannot be generated by philosophers out of their own meager experience".[68]

III   WITTGENSTEIN AND THE LEGITIMACY OF LAW

The other sorts of negative reaction to "Revolution Without Foundation", sometimes mixed with the first,[69] has been to argue that I abuse Wittgenstein's ideas by actually advocating a version of anti-foundationalist theory hope.[70] For example Hutchinson has lately referred to our exchanges as being about "the possibility of using Wittgenstein to ground the jurisprudential enterprise."[71] And Peter Lin accuses me of missing the whole point of Wittgenstein's philosophy as therapy and of using that philosophy "to establish substantive conclusions" and to "justify judicial legitimacy".[72] In fact I made a much more limited claim in "Revolution Without Foundation". I wrote:

> In this essay I trace the reliance of ... strong sceptics (labelled in this essay "strong internal sceptics") upon the philosophy of Ludwig Wittgenstein. My claim is that strong internal sceptics misuse this potent source of inspiration, reading in sceptical conclusions which Wittgenstein would regard as nonsense. But my claim also goes beyond mere exegetical detail. It is my view that strong sceptics are quite correct in turning to Wittgenstein in their efforts to understand law, and that an alternative and non-sceptical reading of Wittgensteinian philosophy is available. This non-sceptical reading, far from corroding our ideas of law, permits insight into the fundamental nature of legal and constitutional discourse. The word "fundamental" carries a lot of freight here. Reading Wittgenstein will not solve concrete constitutional cases. As Wittgenstein repeatedly emphasized "philosophy leaves everything as it is". But, and this is the critical claim, the lessons of Wittgensteinian philosophy let us see what we do when we argue and decide constitutional cases.[73]

I did not and do not argue that Wittgenstein "justifies" or "grounds" or reveals "as determinate" judicial decision-making, constitutional jurisprudence, or law. The key to the essay is that the better reading of Wittgenstein leads us to reject what I labelled as strong internal and external scepticism and lets us "see what we do when we argue and decide." The essay actually says very little about what we see when we take off the metaphysical blinkers of strong scepticism. My view *is* that when we reject strong scepticism we

---

67. Wittgenstein, *Remarks on the Foundation of Mathematics* (Oxford: Basil Blackwell, 3rd ed. 1978) at 132.
68. Lugg, *supra* n. 29 at 472.
69. Hutchinson and Coombe, *supra* n. 5.
70. Lin, *supra* n. 1; Hutchinson, *supra* n. 16; Coombe, *supra* n. 5; Bakan, *supra* n. 16.
71. Hutchinson, "The Three Rs: Reading/Rorty/Racially" *supra* n. 16 at 577.
72. He argues that "I claim that our underlying agreement in judgment makes legal interpretations determinate and therefore judicial interpretation legitimate." Lin, *supra* n. 1 at 968 n. 62.
73. Langille, "Revolution Without Foundation" *supra* n. 4 at 453.

learn lessons about how not to think about rule following and language. This permits insight into the "fundamental" nature of legal and constitutional discourse. Whether constitutional discourse is "justified" or "determinative" is not a matter I would presume to decide as a matter of theory. My view is that we must *look and see* how legal concepts and practices actually work. Whether our law in general, or our constitutional law in particular, lives up to the ideals of the rule of law (that is, for example, whether it is sufficiently determinate to achieve that ideal) is a matter of investigation, not of theory. In the essay I do voice the view that those who in a general way take this tack, and use this approach, of "looking and seeing" are "surely correct".[74]

But endorsing the general anti-foundational hermeneutic approach actually says nothing about whether adjudication is determinate etc. I was merely most anxious to point out that it is not indeterminate in the way argued for by strong internal sceptics, nor is it made determinate by the methods of those I called strong external sceptics.

In a subsequent essay "The Jurisprudence of Despair" I wrote, after reviewing the basic sceptical arguments advanced by Hutchinson and others, as follows:

What is the importance of philosophy, particularly this language philosophy of Ludwig Wittgenstein for the law? Recall that Wittgenstein viewed philosophy as a method for avoiding misunderstanding—"Philosophy leaves everything as it is". But philosophy may, by clearing away confusion in the form of across-the-board scepticism, enable us to see what it is we do when we do constitutional law. It may permit some self-understanding.

What Wittgenstein suggests for those interested in constitutional adjudication is that our practices here are public and social, and that our practices here constitute a language game, or a set of language games, which have a point. Thus, the first task of constitutional theories to explicate the grammar of that practice that is constitutional adjudication (and not some other practice, of a hockey, chess, tort law, statutory interpretation, let alone religious celebration or, even, academic commentary on constitutional theory.) This is not a guarantee of quiet, peaceful times. It may only provide an avenue for understanding our torment.

It also leaves us with a final objection with which we must come to grips. It is an objection which is not based upon an across-the-board scepticism, but which accepts the idea of practices and the basic legitimacy of our constitutional practices. Instead, it is an objection which says that when we look at our constitutional practices, we do not see sufficient certainty, predictability, and coherence to enable us to call that practice constitutional *law*. It denies that practice lives out its ideals. This is the best objection. It is not an objection from *theory*. It is an objection which must play out in the nitty gritty examination of what actually is going on in our early constitutional jurisprudence. In the end, I think, it is an objection which fails, but it is an objection which is meaningful because it appeals to a basic (grammatical) point about law, that is, that the requirement that it be sufficiently certain and predictable as to be capable of guiding behaviour in the world. It is an objection we pursue not by thinking, but by looking.[75]

---

74. Langille, *supra* n. 4 at 499.
75. Langille, "The Jurisprudence of Despair" (1989), 23 *University of British Columbia Law Rev.* 549 at 560-561.

There are risks here. In particular, there is the risk that readers will conclude that the use of the word "grammar" implies the view that there is an obvious transition from Wittgenstein's easy cases of rule following and language use ("+2", "red", etc.) to hard cases such as the meaning of "freedom of association" in a particular constitutional context.[76] This would be to take Wittgenstein as standing for the proposition that all cases are easy cases. Nothing could be farther from the truth in my view. Exactly how agreement and disagreement are possible in our substantive law, and the search for the best explication of the concept of law, are matters involving much "looking and seeing". But the idea that Wittgenstein's *method* is obviously inapplicable to institutions and concepts such as law—and the idea that the notion of the grammar of law is a confusion—seem to me to be equally wrong. Elizabeth Wolgast's *The Grammar of Justice*[77] and Paul Johnston's *Wittgenstein and Moral Theory*[78] are recent concrete examples which strongly suggest the vitality of the very project of exploring these ideas.[79]

IV.   THE USES AND ABUSES OF "THEORY"

The reaction to Wittgenstein's ideas on the part of critical legal scholars is problematic and worrying. Ideas are here treated in an extremely curious way. Rather than assessing the ideas themselves the ideas are assessed against a pre-established order of ends, usually self-declared principles of radical politics. A reading is then adopted which gets the writer where he or she wishes to go. This nagging thought has pursued me for some time, but now I find that Hutchinson has expressed it with such clarity that it is fruitless to resist commenting upon it. In his recent review of Richard Rorty's book, *Contingency, Irony and Solidarity*[80] Hutchinson writes:

> The contending positions in contemporary jurisprudence track and often derive from those in the larger political scene. Legal scholars take the hermeneutical stance as they do because of their prior and more fundamental political commitments: their point of entry (and exit) in the debate over the nature of legal reasoning is largely ideological in character and motivation.[81]

In character *and motivation!* This is an extraordinary charge to lay against legal scholars in general. I believe it to be largely wrong. But leaving aside much which could be said let us focus our concern upon Hutchinson's own position. Where does he think this pronouncement leaves his *own* "hermeneu-

76. Cf. Brian Bix, "The Application (and Mis-Application) of Wittgenstein's discussions on Rule-Following to Legal Theory". This volume.
77. E. Wolgast, *The Grammar of Justice* (Ithaca, N.Y.: Cornell University Press, 1987).
78. *Supra* n. 29.
79. And it must not be forgotten that H.L.A. Hart's *The Concept of Law* (Oxford: Clarendon Press, 1961) owes a great deal to Wittgensteinian theory—see Hacker "Hart's Philosophy of Law" in P.M.S. Hacker and J. Raz eds., *Law and Morality in Society: Essays in Honour of H.L.A. Hart* (Oxford: Clarendon Press, 1977) at 1. Readers should also refer to the articles by Lin and Penner, *supra* n. 1 and Postema, "'Protestant' Interpretation and Social Practices" (1987), 6 *Law and Philosophy* 281. Indeed all of the sources cited in this article, as well as many not cited, reflect the view that at the very least Wittgenstein is important to those who worry about law.
80. Hutchinson, *supra* n. 16.
81. *Id.* at 573.

tical stance", now that he has revealed it to be mere political posing and opportunism? He seeks not "the truth" (even on his own understanding of it) nor even to "make sense", nor "the best or most illuminating account", but the view which he can best manipulate to achieve his pre-established substantive political goals. Yet on Hutchinson's own view it is extremely difficult to know where the substantive goals could come from, how they could be generated. The theory required to do *that* would also require some pre-established ends, etc. But even ignoring that point we are left with a declaration that he does not write what he believes about legal reasoning. It may, I suppose, be the case that Hutchinson believes that legal reasoning actually is determinate, legitimate, but that this view of legal reasoning is not politically convenient because it tends, in his view, to reinforce existing power relations, etc. Therefore it is not adopted. Or it may be that Hutchinson does not care whether legal reasoning is determinate or not and simply adopted the view he has because it is obviously, in his view, a politically productive one. There are of course other possibilities. Interestingly, the one possibility which does not exist is that Hutchinson really believes that there are *good reasons* for saying legal reasoning has the character he says it has. Because if he really believed there to be good reasons for saying what he says, then he would not have written that scholars say what they say simply and largely because of prior political commitments.

In his essay I have spent much of my time taking on the view that Wittgenstein, as I read him, leads one to be complacent about the status quo. In his connection it is good to remember that Wittgenstein wrote:

Resting on your laurels is as dangerous as resting when you are walking in the snow. You doze off and die in your sleep.[82]

But an equally important Wittgensteinian insight is that "ambition is the death of thought".[83] Those who are more concerned not with the power of ideas but with their current political cash value reveal the truth of this remark.

In the end Wittgenstein's ideas are too radical for writers such as Hutchinson. He guarantees nothing by way of either conservative or radical politics. Wittgenstein asks that we give up our own political ambitions for, and the security blanket of, theory. He asks us to *look and see* whether the Emperor has clothes. *In the end* there is no *theoretical* answer to that question.

---

82. Wittgenstein, *Culture and Value*, (Peter Winch trans.) (University of Chicago Press, 1980).
83. *Id.* at 77.

11

Are Judges Liars?
A Wittgensteinian Critique of *Law's Empire*

Charles M. Yablon

When Legal Realism first appeared in American jurisprudential thought in the 1920's and early 1930's[1], it was frequently misunderstood as an attack on the integrity and truthfulness of the American judiciary. After all, wasn't it a central tenet of Legal Realism that judges did not decide cases by applying preexisting and authoritative legal rules, but merely decided cases in whichever way they thought was best? Such considerations led to the derogatory restatement of the Realist position as holding that the law is determined by "whatever the judge ate for breakfast".[2]

But this rather unflattering picture of the American judiciary was far from the view actually held by most Realists. Quite the contrary, most Realists admired, perhaps even idealized, the great common law judges. They extolled jurists like Marshall, Story and Holmes who, reacting to the "felt necessities of the times"[3], molded and shaped the law into a vehicle for meeting the political and economic challenges of their day.[4] To be sure, to accomplish this molding and shaping, the judges often had to bend, stretch, or even abandon some preexisting doctrinal rules, but this was precisely the Realists' point. The process of adjudication, in their view, always involved more than the mere application of a determinate and authoritative rule to a specific factual situation. Rather, cases always presented judges with a choice, with numerous potentially applicable facts and doctrinal formulations, which

---

1. The literature on Legal Realism is voluminous. Some important recent works include: L. Kalman, *Legal Realism at Yale, 1927-1960* (Chapel Hill: Univ. of N.C. Press, 1986); J.H. Schlegel, "The Ten Thousand Dollar Question" (1988), 76 *Calif. L. Rev.* 467; B. Altman, "Legal Realism, Critical Legal Studies, and Dworkin" (1986), 15 *Phil. & Pub. Aff.* 205; Z.B. Wiseman, "The Limits of Vision: Karl Llewellyn and the Merchant Rule" (1986), 100 *Harv. L. Rev.* 465; J.H. Schlegel, "American Legal Realism and Empirical Social Science: From the Yale Experience" (1979), 28 *Buffalo L. Rev.* 459. See generally, W. Rumble, *American Legal Realism* (Ithaca: Cornell Univ. Press 1968). See also, C. Yablon, "Justifying the Judge's Hunch: An Essay on Discretion" (1990), 41 *Hastings L.J.* 231.
2. This popular formulation of the sceptical position is cited by Dworkin. R. Dworkin, *Law's Empire* (Harvard: Harvard Univ. Press, 1986) at 36. Neither Dworkin nor any other source I have consulted is able to locate the precise origins of the phrase. I suspect, however, that it derives from a statement by Pound in which he contrasts a system of law to the arbitrariness of "Cadi" justice. Pound refers to "the oriental Cadi administering justice at the city gate by the light of nature tempered by the state of his digestion." Pound, "The Decadence of Equity" (1905), 5 *Col. L. Rev.* 20, 21. Twenty five years later, in seeking to refute the notion that non-rule based decisionmaking necessarily involved arbitrariness, Jerome Frank made reference to Pound's comment and answered "no more than in France, Germany, England or the United States, is the judge in Mohammedan countries supposed to decide cases according to his passing whim or the temporary state of his digestion". Jerome Frank, "Are Judges Human?" (1931), 80 *U. of Pa. L. Rev.* 17, 24.
3. O.W. Holmes, *The Common Law* (Boston: Little, Brown, 1881). This work, and particularly its first chapter, became an almost sacred text to the Realists, its thesis adumbrated in numerous other articles. See e.g. Max Radin, "Law as Logic and Experience", *Yale L.J.* (1940); F.S. Cohen, "Transcendental Nonsense and the Functional Approach" (1935), 35 *Col. L. Rev.* 809, 825-829; John C.W. Wu, "Realistic Analysis of Legal Concepts: A Study in the Legal Method of Mr. Justice Holmes" (1932), 5 *China L. Rev.* 1,2.
4. *See generally,* discussions of the "Grand Style" of judging in K. Llewellyn, *The Common Law Tradition: Deciding Appeals* (Boston: Little, Brown, 1960); G. Gilmore, *The Ages of American Law* (New Haven: Yale Univ. Press, 1977) 23-40.

enabled, indeed required, that judicial decisions be based on something other than mere application of the "correct" legal rule.

Yet, while such a view of the judical branch, or at least its most creative members, was highly complimentary, it could not entirely clear judges of the charge of prevarication. After all, the judges still wrote their opinions, as they do to this day, in a manner which presented their rulings primarily, often exclusively, as the determinate result of the application of preexisting legal rules. If the Realists were right, if the legal rules applicable to most cases are indeed indeterminate, and such decisions therefore almost always the result of factors other than mere application of doctrinal categories, then aren't judges lying when they seek to present their decisions as the determinate result of the application of preexisting rules?[5]

The question of judicial meretriciousness has acquired new currency with the publication of *Law's Empire* by Ronald Dworkin[6]. In that work, which has attracted wide attention, Dworkin resuscitates the charge that Legal Realism requires one to view many judicial opinions as prevarications. He then compares Legal Realism with his own jurisprudential theory (which he calls, in a phrase which emphasizes the contrast, "Law as Integrity"). Dworkin believes that both jurisprudential theories provide plausible explanations of judicial decisionmaking, and appear to fit the facts of judicial activity reasonably well. Dworkin argues, however, that his theory is preferable to the pragmatic scepticism of Legal Realism (and its unruly offshoot, Critical Legal Studies), primarily because it does not require one to treat many judicial opinions as falsehoods and judges as liars.

Dworkin's attempted refutation of Legal Realism and, by extension, his defense of his own jurisprudential theory, rests strongly therefore on Dworkin's claim, echoing that of earlier critics of the Legal Realists, that accepting the Realist view of doctrinal indeterminacy also commits one to the view that judges who present their decisions as determinate applications of doctrinal rules are simply lying—lying perhaps in the service of a noble end, but lying nonetheless.

But is Dworkin's critique of Legal Realism valid? I do not think so, and, in the pages that follow, I hope to demonstrate why. Dworkin's argument is based on a rather simple view of the role language plays in the judicial decision. For Dworkin, language is a sort of mirror, providing a reflection of the judicial reasoning process that resulted in the judicial decision. That reflection may be an accurate reflection of the reasoning process which gave rise to

---

5. The Legal Realists were not unmindful of this problem, and many seemed to accept the idea that judges are often less than candid in the way they presented their opinions. For example, Gilmore called Justice Story's opinion in *Swift v. Tyson* (1848), 41 U.S.(Pet.) 1 a "masterpiece of disingenuousness", G. Gilmore, *Ages of American Law* at 33, while writing appreciatively of that opinion. Jerome Frank's famous book, *Law and the Modern Mind* (New York: Coward-McCann, 1930) was in part an attempt to explain, in psychological terms, the apparent need of judges and lawyers to portray legal decisions in (to Frank's mind) misleadingly rigid and determinate formulations. Of course, since the Realists envisioned a new form of legal discourse in which the policy grounds and social science evidence for judicial action would be clearly and honestly stated, they cannot really be charged with advocating judicial prevarication, merely tolerating it as a transitional step to the open and honest development of law as a social science.

6. R. Dworkin, *Law's Empire* (Harvard: Harvard Univ. Press, 1986) (hereafter *Law's Empire*).

the decision, in which case it is true, or it may have little correspondence to the mental process which gave rise to the decision, thereby rendering it false.

But we need not accept Dworkin's view of the role of language in the judicial decision. We have available to us a far richer and more sophisticated understanding of the relationship between language and practice—that contained in the later work of Ludwig Wittgenstein. If we view the judicial opinion, not as the true or false description of a decisionmaking procedure taking place in the mind of the judge, but as part of a Wittgensteinian language game, not only does Dworkin's critique of Legal Realism lose its force, but a whole new range of questions is opened. We can begin to inquire into the roles of argument and explanation in the practice of writing opinions, of the institutional "form of life" that gives it coherence. We may discover that the judicial opinion does not correspond to any particular person's mental processes. It may not be a depiction or description of a judge's thoughts at all. But, at the same time, a judicial opinion may *do* any number of things, particularly when viewed in its institutional context.

The following essay seeks to examine judicial decisionmaking and opinion writing from such a Wittgensteinian perspective. Using Dworkin's argument as a starting point, it seeks to understand the judicial opinion as a set of moves in a Wittgensteinian language game. Such an approach eschews any attempt to make the language of judicial opinions correspond with some other thing, like the judge's mental processes of decision. Rather, it seeks to examine the language of judicial opinions within the institutional and social context in which such judicial opinions are made, and to look at the role they play in the practice of adjudication.

The essay is divided into two parts. The first examines Dworkin's arguments against Legal Realism contained in *Law's Empire* in some detail. The second part attempts a refutation of those arguments from a Wittgensteinian perspective, by exploring the difference between statements of causes and statements of explanations, the institutional context in which judges make moves in the language game called opinion writing, and the role of argument in language games generally and in judicial opinion writing in particular.

A. Dworkin's Refutation of Legal Pragmatism

In *Law's Empire*, Dworkin considers views that may loosely be ascribed to Legal Realism at a number of different points in his argument. First, it appears as "internal scepticism",[7] a claim not about law, but about interpretive strategies generally. The internal sceptic, according to Dworkin, utilizes a set of standards internal to the practice being interpreted to deny that any coherent, demonstrably "best" interpretation of the practice is possible. Such internal scepticism may be asserted with respect to a single text, (i.e., "Hamlet is too confused and jumbled to be about anything at all: it is an incoherent hotch-potch of a play."[8]), or it may be asserted about an entire practice, in

---

7. *Law's Empire, supra* at 79.
8. *Id.* at 78.

which case Dworkin calls it "global" internal scepticism[9].

Dworkin's example of global internal scepticism is a citizen who surveys the practices of courtesy viewed as valuable by his neighbors and concludes that they "serve no useful purpose or, even worse, that they serve a malign one. So he condemns as perverse all the different interpretations of courtesy his colleagues construct and defend against one another."[10]

Dworkin recognizes the possibility that one might take a position of global internal scepticism with regard to the practice of law, and recognizes that such a position would "threaten our own enterprise"[11]. Yet he defers consideration of such a position until later in the book.

Dworkin moves from a discussion of interpretation and interpretative strategies generally to a discussion of possible interpretations of a particular practice, namely law. Dworkin devotes three chapters of his book to consideration of the strengths and weaknesses of three interpretative approaches to the practice of law, that is, to three jurisprudential theories. The first, which Dworkin calls conventionalism, corresponds roughly to Austinian positivism, and will not concern us here. The second, which Dworkin calls legal pragmatism, corresponds roughly to Legal Realism. The third is Dworkin's own theory, "Law as Integrity". While the outcome of this battle between the three jurisprudential theories is never in much doubt, (Law as Integrity, of course, turns out to be the champ), legal pragmatism is by far the stronger of the two contenders.

Dworkin presents legal pragmatism as the "internal sceptical" position applied to law, and ascribes to it the potentially "shocking"[12] position that "denies that a community secures any genuine benefit by requiring that a judges' adjudicative decisions be checked by any supposed right of litigants to consistency with other political decisions made in the past"[13]. Note that this is almost exactly the position that Dworkin's global internal sceptic took toward the practice of courtesy, only in this case it is the practice of attempting to conform decisions to past precedent that is asserted to serve no useful purpose. Accordingly, Dworkin's legal pragmatist, "strictly speaking, reject[s] the idea of law and legal right deployed in [Dworkin's] account of the concept of law"[14].

Dworkin's legal pragmatists do not, however, assert that judicial decisions have no appropriate justification and are simply manifestations of the state of the judge's digestion. Rather, legal pragmatism has a clear and strong normative position as to the proper basis for judicial decisionmaking, that "judges do and should make whatever decisions seem to them best for the community's future, not counting any form of consistency with the past as valuable for its own sake"[15].

Dworkin recognizes that, stated in this way, the position of the legal prag-

---

9. *Id.* at 79.
10. *Id.*
11. *Id.*
12. *Id.* at 151.
13. *Id.* at 95.
14. *Id.*
15. *Id.*

matists does not appear to conform very well to the actual statements of judges and lawyers. Judges and lawyers talk about past decisions all the time. Lawyer's arguments almost invariably cite prior cases as a ground, a reason, often the only compelling reason for deciding the case in a particular way. Judges, in writing the opinions which set forth the reasons for their decision, also rely very heavily on prior precedent. It seems unlikely, therefore, that the pragmatists can be right when they assert, as a factual matter, that judges decide cases without "counting consistency with the past as valuable for its own sake".

But Dworkin recognizes that legal pragmatism cannot be defeated so easily. In Chapter 5 of *Law's Empire* he provides a more "complex"[16] version of legal pragmatism which enables it to account for the extensive discussion of precedent in actual legal discourse and the judiciary's apparent efforts to conform their decisions to past decisions. The key to this revised defense of legal pragmatism is the recognition that a form of consistency with the past can be justified under pragmatist theory on the ground that "judges must sometimes act *as if* people had legal rights, because acting that way will serve society better in the long run."[17]

Utilizing this "as-if strategy", Dworkin shows that pragmatism can be accommodated with, and even used to justify, much of the rule centeredness and concern for consistency that is found in legal discourse. As he puts the pragmatist position:

> [C]ivilization is impossible unless the decisions of some well-defined person or group are accepted by everyone as setting public standards that will be enforced if necessary through the police power. Only legislation can establish tax rates, structure markets, fix traffic codes and systems, stipulate permissable interest rates, or decide which Georgian squares should be protected from modernization. If judges were seen to pick and choose among legislation, enforcing only those statutes they approved, this would defeat the pragmatist's goal because it would make things not better but much worse. So pragmatism may be an eligible interpretation of our legal system after all, if it turns out that our judges declare people to have legal rights only, or mainly, when a self-consciously pragmatist judge would pretend that they did."[18]

The word "pretend" in the last sentence of the above quotation obviously foreshadows Dworkin's conclusion that the need to defend pragmatism by assumptions of judicial pretense make it a less attractive legal theory than Law as Integrity. Yet the word "pretend" in that sentence also raises an epistemological problem that is of interest from a Wittgensteinian perspective.

Dworkin has just finished telling us that a pragmatist judge might well conclude 1) that she should decide cases in the way that will best serve society and 2) that society will be best served if she consistently enforces statutes and other authoritative rules that give rise to beneficial social regularities. If so, then such a judge might well feel herself normatively compelled to rule in favor of litigants who seek enforcement of such statutes. Similarly, a compe-

---

16. *Id.* at 151.
17. *Id.* at 152 (emphasis in original).
18. *Id.* at 153.

tent lawyer, who was aware of the judge's legal philosophy, and was repre-
senting a client who sought enforcement of such a statute, might well argue to
the judge that she was obligated or required to rule in favor of his client. If
judges and lawyers, therefore, operating under the assumptions of legal pragmatism, can coherently view a litigant as having the power to compel a ruling
in favor of that litigant, in what sense are they merely "pretending" that the
litigant has rights?

Certainly, from a Wittgensteinian perspective, the statement appears a little odd. Is "pretending" that the litigant has rights similar to pretending that
someone has a million dollars? In the latter case, the difference between pretending to have a million dollars and actually having it is revealed when the
pretended millionaire fails to meet the expectations of some creditor, or even
in the refusal to extend credit (since everyone is merely "pretending" that the
person is a millionaire). Suppose, however, that a banker has agreed to pretend, for the indefinite future, that the person in question is a millionaire.
Accordingly, that person is permitted to spend as much as he wants on whatever he wants, with no fear that his banker will stop the pretense (perhaps
because he knows the banker believes it is in the bank's interest to maintain
the pretense). If the banker's pretense results in him having a million dollars
worth of capital to spend, in what sense is it false to describe him as a millionaire?[19]

Obviously, a similar argument can be made with respect to Dworkin's
legal pragmatist judge. If she is not only willing consistently to rule in favor
of litigants who invoke certain statutory rules, but feels compelled to do so, in
what sense is it false to describe her as recognizing legal rights? Dworkin recognizes this problem to some degree, since he notes that, in practice, pragmatism might be less radical than it appears in theory[20] Yet he still seems to
feel there is some important ontological difference between the rights granted by a legal pragmatist judge (the best he can do is call them "as-if rights")
and the rights that would be recognized by a judge who really believed in
rights, yet he never quite comes to grips with what that distinction might be.

Dworkin is quite clear, however, that since the criteria a legal pragmatist
judge would use for determining when to enforce such rights would be different from that used by a non-pragmatist judge, the scope, or type of cases in
which rights would be recognized by legal pragmatist judges will be different
from the scope of the rights enforced by judges who "really" believe in conforming their rulings to prior decisions. This then provides Dworkin with a
way of empirically testing the validity of the claims of legal pragmatism, by
seeing whether the rights enforced by actual judges occur only in circumstances where such enforcement can also be justifed on legal pragmatist
grounds.

Dworkin concludes that legal pragmatism fits the actual practice of judges
fairly well. He illustrates this by considering a case in which society would

---

19. *Compare* Wittgenstein's discussion of the difference between reading and pretending to read in L.
Wittgenstein, *The Blue and Brown Books* 2d. Ed. (Oxford: Basil Blackwell, 1960) 120-121 (hereafter *The Brown Book*).
20. *Law's Empire, supra* n. 6 at 153.

immediately benefit from a ruling for one party (perhaps because he will donate the entire recovery to charity) but such a ruling can only be achieved if the judge refuses to apply to that case a socially beneficial rule (e.g. failing to hold that, as a murderer, he may not inherit from his victim). Dworkin states that "at first look", an imaginative pragmatist judge might be tempted to give the rule that murderers may not inherit prospective application only, thereby obtaining both the benefit of the socially desirable rule and the recovery for charity. But Dworkin argues that, as she "thinks the matter through" the pragmatist judge will reject such prospective rulings in most circumstances, primarily because she will recognize that retrospective application of judicial rules will induce most people to conform their behavior to socially desirable rules without judicial intervention.[21]

Although he still cannot quite view this as enforcing rights, Dworkin recognizes that a judge who has determined to apply legal rules retrospectively and consistently with prior practice, even if her underlying justification for doing so is a pragmatist one, is going to talk and act very much as actual judges do. She will discuss prior cases and present her ruling as a conscientious attempt to conform her decision to prior practice. Is she lying when she does this? Obviously not. Dworkin has just told us that such a judge will conscientiously attempt to apply retrospectively the rule that is most consistent with prior practice because she believes that is the most socially beneficial thing to do. Accordingly, Dworkin recognizes that, in many, perhaps most instances, a pragmatist judge has "other reasons, quite apart from any strategy of the noble lie"[22] to appear to act in conformity with precedent. Indeed, in such cases, it is hard to see any distinction between "appearing" to act in conformity with precedent, and actually doing so.

But Dworkin does believe that, in at least some circumstances, the practice of actual judges cannot be explained on pragmatist grounds except by reference to a "noble lie". He cites two such phenomena: 1) the concern judges express about discerning legislative intent in order to interpret and apply unclear statutes and 2) the concern judges express about discerning the appropriate scope of unclear or controversial past decisions.

Both these illustrations reflect the same underlying point, which is that while Dworkin can understand why a pragmatist judge would consistently apply clear statutory enactments and prior precedents, in order to promote beneficial habits of order and social regularity, this justification only exists when the potentially authoritative rule is reasonably clear and well understood by the people being regulated. When the issue is unclear, and the potentially authoritative rule provides no such guidance, Dworkin can think of no reason why a pragmatist judge would seek to discern an intent or meaning in such a rule. Rather, the pragmatist judge would simply determine the most socially beneficial rule as best she could, and apply that rule.

Dworkin rejects the notion that beneficial social regularities would be enhanced by attempting to apply even unclear precedents. As he says, "The

---

21. *Id.* at 156-57.
22. *Id.* at 155.

general power of precedents to guide behavior will not be much jeopardized if judges refuse to follow them when the advice they give is garbled and murky".[23] Similarly, Dworkin argues that it will do no harm to legislative functions if judges "decline to speculate about how to read cloudy rules from the dead past or what the intentions of people very different from contemporary legislators would have been."[24] Accordingly, he concludes that a pragmatist judge will only behave in the way we observe actual judges behaving in these hard cases (i.e. express concern over discerning legislative intent) if she "has an indirect, noble-lie reason for pretending that legislative intentions are relevant".[25]

Dworkin never explains what such a "noble-lie reason" might be, but it is not hard to imagine such reasons. For example, a judge might decide that it is important for society's welfare to establish the rule that the state may not use electronic eavesdropping or wiretapping devices unreasonably to invade the privacy of its citizens. Because such a rule, to be effective, must restrain executive and legislative action, she claims to have derived it, not from her own views of social welfare, but from the vague "penumbras" emanating from certain two hundred year old provisions in the basic law of the land, which, despite its antiquity, the citizens hold in very high esteem. Such a statement is a lie, in that she did not, in fact, derive the rule in that manner, nor does she believe that the founding fathers had any intention of prohibiting electronic eavesdropping when they wrote those provisions. Nonetheless, it is a "noble lie", like Socrates' myth of gold, silver and bronze men at the end of *The Republic*,[26] because it is taken with a sincere belief that such dishonesty will strengthen the rule and inure to the benefit of the people in the long run.

Dworkin apparently believes that similar considerations are the only way legal pragmatists can explain and justify judicial attempts to present their decisions as applications or elucidations of vague and uncertain precedents. While not absolutely disqualifying legal pragmatism as an eligible conception of law, Dworkin does think that the unattractiveness of embracing this form of judicial hypocrisy is a strong count against it. As he states (in what I take to be his key argument against Legal Realism):

> So pragmatism can be rescued as a good explanation for our cross-section picture of adjudication only by procrustean machinery that seems wildly inappropriate. It can be rescued only if we do not take judicial opinions at face value at all; we must treat all the judges who worry about problematical statutes and precedents as practicing some unmotivated form of deception. They must be seen as inventing new rules for the future in accordance with their convictions about what is best for society as a whole, freed from any supposed rights flowing from consistency, but presenting these for unknown reasons in the false uniform of rules dug out of the past. Pragmatism requires epicycles to survive as an eligible interpretation of our own practice, and these epicycles can be tolerated only if pragmatism is so powerful along the second dimension of legal interpretation, so attractive as a political justification for state coercion, that it merits heroic life support. Does it?[27]

23. *Id.* at 159.
24. *Id.* at 158.
25. *Id.*
26. Plato, *The Republic*, Book VIII.
27. *Law's Empire* at 159-60.

The answer of *Law's Empire*, of course, is no. The next two chapters are devoted to showing that a better theory, "Law as Integrity", presents an equally coherent justification of law, without requiring us to accept the view that our legal system is based on pervasive judicial prevarication. Note, however, that this argument only counts as a definitive defeat for legal pragmatism because Dworkin believes he has already established, in the argument we have just analyzed, that legal pragmatism is unattractive as a legal theory because it requires us to accept the view that judges systematically engage in lying and deceit.

B. A Wittgensteinian Critique of Dworkin's Argument

"Is lying a particular experience? Well, can I tell someone 'I am going to tell you a lie' and straightway do it?"[28]

I would be quite possible, I believe, to counter Dworkin's attack on Legal Realism while agreeing with its epistemological and psychological assumptions, agreeing, in short, that judges are often lying when they purport to base their decisions on an application of vague precedents or obscure statutory intent. Indeed, much of current legal scholarship, such as that which seeks to explain and justify judicial decisions as "really" based on considerations of microeconomic policy, seem to embody some such assumption. Plato himself was an exponent of the "noble lie" as a basis for justifying state coercion, and it is easy to imagine political theories which argue that difficult political choices can and should be made more acceptable to the populace by being falsely presented as the ineluctable application of sacred texts rather than as the fallible and tentative conclusions of living judges.

I do not intend to undertake such an argument in this paper, however. Rather, I want to challenge Dworkin's premise that accepting the tenets of Legal Realism requires us to conclude that judges are indeed lying when they say their decision is based on vague precedents or legislative intent. Such an argument requires us to reexamine the assumptions Dworkin makes about the relationship between judicial language, thought and action, and to examine those relationships from a new perspective, that of the later Wittgenstein.

For Dworkin, the judge's statement that she has reached her decision by applying a vague precedent is an empirical statement of some sort, which is true if and only if it corresponds to some actual event. So, the statement "My decision is based on penumbral rights emanating from the Fourth Amendment" would be true if and only if the decision in question was actually generated by consideration of the penumbral rights emanating from the Fourth Amendment. On this view, the judge's statement describes some internal event or mental process she experienced in the course of reaching her decision.

Alternatively, Dworkin might claim that he does not need to indulge in any

---

28. L. Wittgenstein, *Zettel* (Berkeley: Univ. of Calif. Press, 1967) Para. 189. (hereafter *Zettel*).

such psychologizing. Rather, it is enough to argue on logical grounds that 1) Legal Realist judges, by definition, do not believe consistency with prior decisions is a reason for deciding cases a certain way; 2) in their opinions, however, such judges offer prior decisions as reasons for their decisions; 3) accordingly, such opinions constitute untrue statements by judges concerning the reasons for their decisions, i.e. lies.

Both these versions of Dworkin's argument, however, contain assumptions that are highly questionable from a Wittgensteinian point of view. The first assumes an individual's statement of the reasons for her actions is true only insofar as it accurately describes some internal psychological state the speaker experienced while deciding upon the action. Yet it is quite easy, in reflecting on common usage, to find many perfectly coherent statements of reasons that seem hardly plausible as statements about contemporaneous psychological states. "I married him because I was naive and fooled by his superficial charm" certainly is not what the speaker was thinking at the time of her marriage, nor does the statement "I took Corporate Tax because I didn't know it would be so hard" reflect the speaker's thinking at the time of registration. Yet both are perfectly sensible statements of reasons for decisions and might very well be considered true even though they do not correspond to what the speaker was thinking at the time of the decision. Rather, they constitute a reflective analysis and *explanation* of the decision previously made. We shall return to the distinction between statements of causes and explanations a little later in this essay.

Equally questionable, from a Wittgensteinian point of view, is the assumption that these statements are identified with and refer to various internal states that the judge experienced while making her decision. Wittgenstein was very sceptical of a too-easily assumed correspondence between language and mental states. Consider the following excerpt from the *Brown Book:*

> 12. If I had said "When I told him that the train was leaving at 3.30, believing that it did, nothing happened than that I just uttered the sentence", and if someone contradicted me, saying "Surely this couldn't have been all, as you might 'just say a sentence' without believing it",-my answer should be "I didn't wish to say there was no difference between speaking, believing what you say, and speaking, not believing what you say; but the pair 'believing'/'not believing' refers to various differences in various cases (differences forming a family), not to one difference, that between the presence and the absence of a certain state.[29]

The problem with Dworkin's argument, therefore, is that he assumes that a judge either "believes" the reasons set forth in her opinions, or does not believe them, in the same unproblematic way one believes or does not believe that the train is leaving at 3:30. Wittgenstein does not deny the existence of such internal mental states or feelings, but he cautions against the assumption that a certain word (e.g. "belief) easily corresponds to a particular mental state. Rather, the judge may "believe" the reasons set forth in her opinion are valid in a way quite different than the way in which she "believes" they are

---

29. *The Brown Book, supra* n. 19 at 152.

the reasons that caused her to decide the case a particular way. The two forms of "belief" may have a family resemblance, but be part of different language games.

With respect to the other, "logical" formulation of Dworkin's argument, the defect here seems to be identification of all untrue statements as lies. As the quotation from Wittgenstein which began this section reminds us, lying is not simply a matter of the truth value of a statement, but of the context in which the statement is made. If I say I am going to tell you a lie, I may then be able to utter an untruth, but I will not be lying. Untrue statements of the sort "I have a frog in my throat", "I am dying, Egypt, dying" (when spoken by an actor in *Antony and Cleopatra*) or "Sorry, but I'm busy that night" (when spoken by someone you have just asked for a date) are not generally judged to be lies, (Although someone unaware of the conventions of playacting, seeing Antony taking his bows at the end of the play, might well accuse him of lying.)

This is not because the speakers in question did not *intend* to lie. As Wittgenstein points out, once I tell you I am going to lie, I cannot do so, whatever my intent may be. Describing a statement as a lie is not a description of the truth value of the sentence, nor of the psychological state which accompanied its utterance, but the description of an event taking place within a specific social context. I believe that is what Wittgenstein was alluding to when he wrote:

> To what extent am I aware of lying while I'm telling a lie? Just insofar as I don't 'only realize it later on', and all the same I do know later that I was lying. The awareness that one is lying is a knowing-how. It is no contradiction of this that there are characteristic feelings of lying. [marginal note: Intention][30]

I may well be aware of lying when I'm telling a lie, but sometimes I may not realize it until later. Sometimes I am aware that I am humming a tune, other times I am humming, but without realizing it, or become aware only as I stop. Yet it would be foolish to confuse my awareness of my humming with the humming itself, just as it would be foolish to confuse the characteristic feelings of lying with lying itself. Rather, my awareness of my lying, like my awareness of my humming, is an awareness that I *know how* to do the thing I perceive myself doing.

With these insights in mind, let's reexamine those judicial opinions Dworkin characterizes as lies. The first thing we must do, from a Wittgensteinian perspective, is understand the social context in which such statements make sense. To whom are they being made, and what is the understanding of the people hearing or reading those statements?

For whom do judges write opinions? A moment's reflection yields many likely candidates, none mutually exclusive of the others. Judges write opinions for other judges, for lawyers, for litigants and for the general public. All are interested, in various ways, in the judge's decision, yet it is also worth

---

30. *Zettel, supra* n. 28 at para.190.

noting that the people most likely to read many judicial decisions, to spend time carefully analyzing their arguments and reasoning, are others engaged in the practice of legal discourse, that is, other judges and lawyers. This immediately calls into question the "noble lie" hypothesis, because it would seem these are just the people least likely to be taken in by the noble lie.

Appellate judges, reading the decisions of the lower court judge, are unlikely to be fooled if a Realist judge, seeking to disguise the fact that the rule she announces is one she has formulated on her own, announces it as the rule she has "derived" from some vague and ancient higher court precedents. The appellate judges, equally familiar with the practice of judging, know that under the conventions of legal reasoning, equally plausible arguments could be made to support a number of different readings of those vague and ancient precedents. Moreover, if they had any doubt on that score, they probably have before them a brief, submitted by the losing party below, which contains just such an argument demonstrating that a judgment for the losing party could also have been justified on the basis of vague and ancient precedents.

Now it is possible, of course, that the judge below really could not see any plausible reading of the precedents other than the one she adopted (much as some people, presented with an optical illusion drawing that can be seen as two entirely different images, are unable to see one or the other). But would not we tend to view this as a defect in the judge, a problem for someone whose job is to weigh and evaluate the arguments of both sides?

Notice the interesting dilemma which this institutional perspective on judicial opinions has placed us. On the one hand, it seems unlikely that a "noble lie" justification of the judical decision would convince the other judges and lawyers reading it, who are aware of the vagueness of the precedents on which the trial judge's opinion is based. For that same reason, however, an "honest" judge, who "really believes" that the vague precedent compels her to reach a particular result, seems at best naive and at worst, kind of dumb.

Dworkin offers one response to this dilemma. It is the opinion his Herculean judge writes when faced with the question of whether to provide liability for emotional injury caused by an accident to family members in cases where the emotional injury was not suffered at the scene of the accident. The opinion weighs two competing general rules, testing each for their "fit" with respect to prior decisions, finds that each fits fairly well but not perfectly, and finally declares that:

> [I]ntegrity demands some resolution of the [two general rules'] competing impact on accident cases when unlimited liability would be disastrous, a choice that our practice has not made but that must flow, as a postinterpretive judgment, from my analysis. Integrity demands this because it demands that I continue the overall story, in which the two principles have a definite place, in the best way, all things considered. In my view this is done best by ranking the second principle [liability for all reasonably foreseeable injury on the basis of fault] prior to the first [the state should prevent people being financially ruined as a result of accidents even if it was their own fault], at least in automobile accident cases when liability insurance is available

privately on sensible terms. I settle on this choice because I believe that though
the impulse behind each of the two principles is attractive, the second is more powerful in these circumstances.[31]

The first thing that strikes one about this "opinion" is how unhelpful it is as
a solution to our previously posed dilemma. While real judges may not write
like Realists, they certainly do not write like Hercules. Indeed, I would ven-
ture to guess there are far more unabashedly Realist opinions in the law
books, where judges confess they can find no guidance in the precedents and
are deciding the case on "policy" grounds, than there are cases in which the
judge wrestles with two potentially applicable rules, both of which fit prior
practice imperfectly, and resolves it by establishing a priority between then
for an individual circumstance. Dworkin may be right that that is what they
should do, but it is certainly not what they *say* they are doing.

We seem then to be back where we started. The law is often vague and
indeterminate, yet judges mostly write about it as if prior practice gave clear
and definitive guidance in most cases. But what are judges doing when they
write about law in their opinions? They are not describing the state of the law,
nor are they describing their own internal thought processes. Rather, they
are making arguments.

The fact that judges are making arguments is most immediately recognizable from the point of view of the institutional relationship between the trial
judge and the appellate court. From that perspective, the trial court opinion
may be thought of as an argument, a brief of sorts to the court to which the
case will be appealed, which is designed to persuade them that the trial court's
decision should be affirmed. The appellate court's opinion, of course, can
be viewed as making similar arguments to persuade yet a higher court to
affirm or refuse to hear the appeal. But other judges are not the only ones to
whom arguments are being made. The lawyers, litigants and public at large
are also the recipients of the judge's argument, although here the objective is
not to induce them to take a particular action with respect to the case (i.e.
affirm), but to *explain* and *justify* the judge's decision.

An explanation is quite different from a statement of causes. From a scientific point of view, the cause of an event includes all the necessary and
sufficient conditions for its occurrence. (E.g. the cause of the water boiling is
that it is being heated, at normal pressure, to over 212 degrees F.) When we
speak of causes in ordinary usage, we are likely to be speaking only of direct
or immediate causes. (E.g. I fell because I slipped on the ice, not because I
was going to class or because it was winter, although these were also necessary conditions for the occurrence of my fall.) When we give an explanation of an event, however, we may refer to only one of many necessary
conditions for its occurrence, and not the one that immediately preceded it in
time (E.g. I married him because I was naive and fooled by his superficial
charm). Statements of other necessary conditions for the same event, however, may fail miserably as explanations (E.g. I married him because I said "I
do" at the appropriate point in the ceremony).

---

31. *Law's Empire, supra* n. 6 at 270-71.

What makes a good explanation good, and an inadequate one inadequate? The short answer is that the expectations of the one receiving the explanation have a great deal to do with judgments of its adequacy.[32] For example, if I ask "why was George Bush elected President" I would probably not find the statement "because he got the most votes in the 1988 election" an adequate explanation, despite the fact that it is a true causal statement. I would be expecting a different kind of statement, perhaps one that speaks about the mood of the electorate, or the nature of his campaign, or perhaps broader socio-economic trends. Accordingly, we may view these expectations regarding the adequacy of the explanation as part of the grammar of the particular language game in which the explanation is made.

With respect to law, there is little doubt that the expectations of the language game are that the judge's opinion will contain a legal argument, and that such an argument will seek to explain and justify the decision in terms of prior authority. But as we have seen, such an explanation need not correspond, need not be a "true" reflection of the immediate or direct cause of the judge's ruling.

Indeed, the whole question of "truth" and "belief" in connection with legal argument is rather complex and vexing. When I think about myself as a lawyer making arguments to a court, I find that I can easily make statements like "The law requires a judgment in favor of my client" or "the precedent on which my opponent relies is clearly distinguishable from the case at bar". In short, I find myself phrasing my arguments in the same language of determinacy and clear meaning that seems so problematic when expressed in judicial opinions.

Do I believe it? Do I really believe that the law requires a judgment in favor of my client? Well, yes, but not in quite the same way I believe that the train will arrive at 3:30. I believe that I have made a good argument, that a ruling for my client would be sensible and just and supportable on the basis of prior precedent, but I am perfectly aware that nothing actually *requires* the judge to rule my way, that other arguments have been made by my opponent, and that it is possible that the judge will rule against my client.

Then why do I speak in the language of requirement, compulsion and determinacy? In part, because those are simply the conventions of my language game. No one expects me to say, indeed would be somewhat surprised if I said, "Truthfully, the precedents could support a ruling either way in this case, but I believe it would be desirable and appropriate to rule for my client." The judge knows very well that when I say the law "requires" or "compels" a given result, I am not denying that she has a choice in the matter. The judge, and everyone else in the process, knows that those words are part of the conventions of making a forceful argument. This in turn makes it impossible for me to express my argument in more ordinary language, closer to my actual belief, that a ruling for my client would be "desirable" or "appropriate",

---

32. For further discussion of the relationship between cause, causal explanation and explanation in law, *see* H.L.A. Hart & A.M. Honore, *Causation in Law* 17-20 (Oxford: Clarendon, 1959); R. Collingwood, *Essay on Metaphysics,* 285-327 (Oxford: Clarendon, 1972); C. Yablon, "The Indeterminacy of the Law: Critical Legal Studies and the Problem of Legal Explanation" (1985), 6 *Cardozo L. Rev.* 917.

because the conventions of legal argument make those terms seem exceedingly weak.

The extensive use of precedents and authorities can also often be part of the convention of legal discourse. There may be little difference between telling an American judge "This speech is protected by the First Amendment" and "This speech should not be censored or suppressed by the U.S. government". Although one is phrased as a declarative statement, and the other as a normative statement, they are both understood by the judge as part of the language game of legal argument. Statutes and precedents are, to a considerable extent, the way lawyers and judges categorize and refer to the practices in which they are engaged. We speak of "*Miranda* warnings", "Rule 11 motions", "501(b) corporations" as simply parts of the legal world, not as applications of the particular authorities to which they refer.

It is very possible then, that much of the use and discussion of precedent in legal argument is also an attempt to define and express legal results, rather than state the causes or reasons for them. When a judge rules that "the Statute of Frauds renders this contract unenforceable" is she saying that her application of the Statute of Frauds caused or required her to rule this way, or is she merely stating her conclusion in a form understandable to other lawyers and in a way which explains its relationship to prior practice? I suspect it is the latter, that she is using precedent to express the result, and to explain and justify it as consistent with prior practice. Accordingly, it is not a lie to express that result in terms of prior precedent, but neither is it a true causal statement of the way in which she reached that result.

In the *Brown Book*, Wittgenstein has an extended discussion of a hypothetical language in which physical states are described in terms of possibilities of action. As he says:

> A tribe has in its language commands for the execution of certain actions of men in warfare, something like "Shoot","Run!"."Crawl!", etc. They also have a way of describing a man's build. Such a description has the form "He can run fast", "He can throw the spear far". What justifies me in saying that these sentences are descriptions of the man's build is the use they make of sentences of this form. Thus if they see a man with bulging leg muscles but who as we should say has not the use of his legs for some reason or other, they say he is a man who can run fast. The drawn image of a man which shows large biceps they describe as representing a man "who can throw a spear far".[33]

What I am suggesting is that, in the language game of legal argument, statements about the possibility of action are often described in terms of legal states or legal status. Thus, if we want to say that the contract should not be given effect, we say that the contract is void under the Statute of Frauds. If we want to say that the complaint should be dismissed because it has no evidentiary basis and is brought for harassment purposes, we say that the complaint violates Rule 11. Thus, while these statements appear to be descriptions of actual legal states, a lawyer would not know how to answer if asked, prior

---

33. *The Brown Book, supra* n. 28 at 102.

to adjudication of the motion, "Does the complaint really violate Rule 11". He might conclude that the person asking the question does not understand the nature of legal discourse and legal argument.

We have seen, therefore, that Dworkin's attempted refutation of Legal Realism on the grounds that it requires us to view judges as prevaricators rests on an oversimplified and questionable view of legal language. It is possible to view judicial language as expressing something quite different from the reasons which floated to the top of the judge's mind as she rendered her decision. Rather, the conventions of legal argument may well lead judges to express their decisions in terms of determinate results of legal rules, although the participants in the process understand these statements as expanations and justifications of the judge's choice in ruling for one side or the other, not as a description of the way in which the judge discovered the "right answer" to the legal problem presented by the case before her.

These descriptions of the language game of legal discourse are, of course, still tentative and incomplete. As Wittgenstein also showed, the forms of ordinary speech, with which we are most comfortable and familiar, often contain hidden mysteries and surprises. Most lawyers know how to speak our legal language fairly well, but we have barely scratched the surface of its mysteries.

About the Book and Editor

Despite the strong and continuing influence of Wittgenstein's thought on many disciplines, very little has been written about the implications of his work for the study of law. This is especially odd because many of Wittgenstein's later themes bear directly on controversial legal and jurisprudential issues.

In this valuable collection, prominent philosophers and legal scholars address the law in the context of Wittgenstein's philosophy. Of special interest are several papers on Wittgenstein's profound discussion of the nature of rules and rule-following behavior. Another important theme is his anti-reductive doctrine that philosophical inquiry should "leave everything as it is," which has clear implications for many recent attempts to explain law in terms of some other field or set of ideas.

This is an important book not just for philosophers and lawyers, but also for other scholars and advanced students of law, society, culture, and political theory.

Dennis M. Patterson is professor of law at Rutgers University, School of Law–Camden. He is the author of three books in commercial law and many articles in legal and philosophical journals.